WET MOON

DROWNED IN EVIL

4

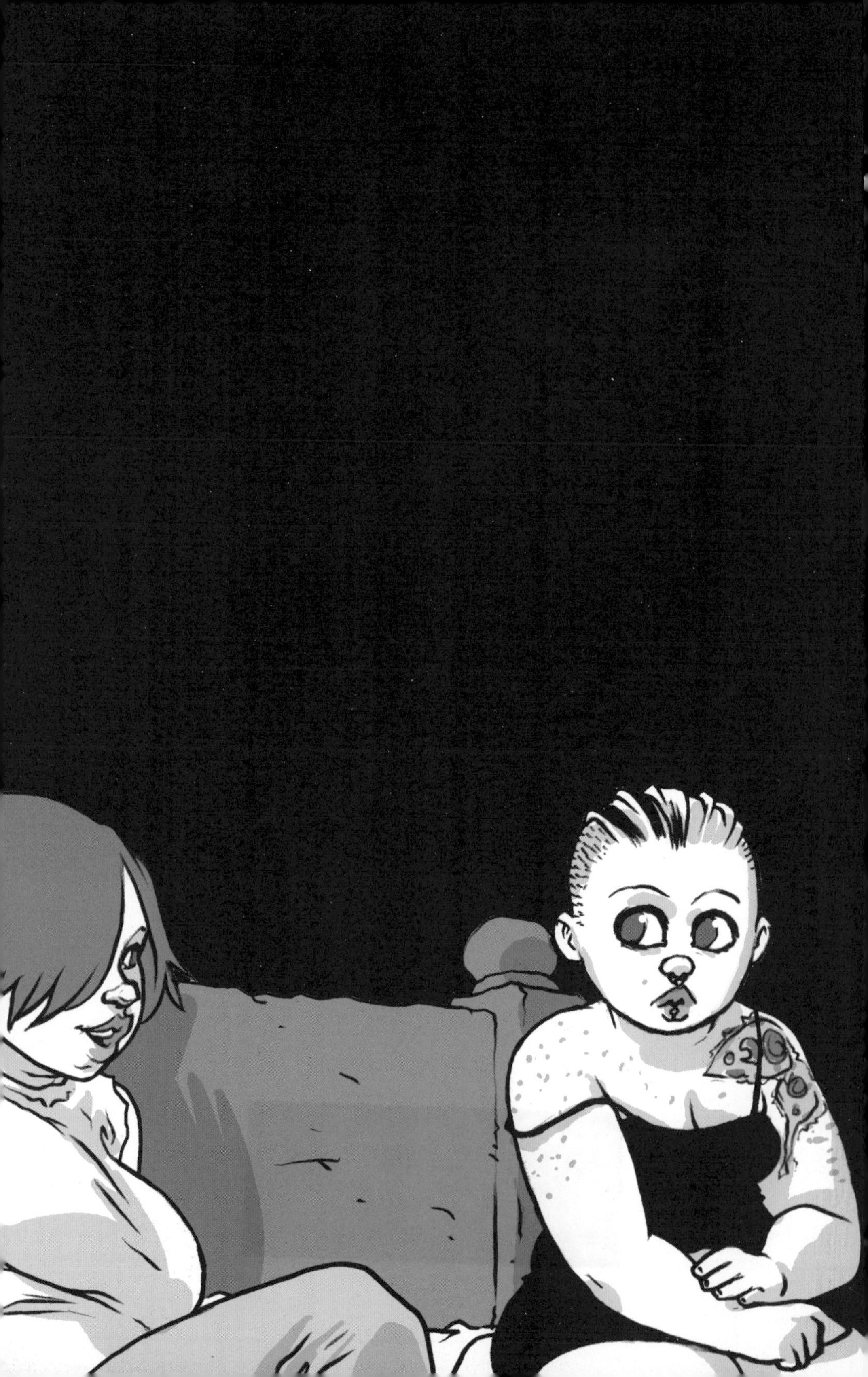

WET MOON

DROWNED IN EVIL

4

written and illustrated by **sophie campbell**
cleo's diary pages by **jessica calderwood**

cover design by **annie mok**
book design by **hilary thompson**
first edition edited by **douglas sherwood & james lucas jones**
new edition edited by **robin herrera**

PUBLISHED BY ONI PRESS, INC.

Joe Nozemack, *publisher*

James Lucas Jones, *editor in chief*

David Dissanayake, *director of sales*

Rachel Reed, *publicity coordinator*

Troy Look, *director of design & production*

Hilary Thompson, *graphic designer*

Angie Dobson, *digital prepress technician*

Ari Yarwood, *managing editor*

Charlie Chu, *senior editor*

Robin Herrera, *editor*

Alissa Sallah, *administrative assistant*

Brad Rooks, *director of logistics*

Jung Lee, *logistics associate*

ONIPRESS.COM
FACEBOOK.COM/ONIPRESS
TWITTER.COM/ONIPRESS
ONIPRESS.TUMBLR.COM
INSTAGRAM.COM/ONIPRESS

First Edition: August 2017

ISBN 978-1-62010-330-2
eISBN 978-1-62010-366-1

Library of Congress Control Number: 2017932347

1 2 3 4 5 6 7 8 9 10

1. Bowden House
2. Vance House
3. Smith House
4. Westmiller House
5. Weitz Hall
6. Polsky Hall
7. Yardley Hall
8. Joseph Hall
9. Simmons Hall
10. Page Hall
11. Meyer Hall
12. Steve Hall
13. Burial Grounds
14. Head-Butt Video
15. House of Usher
16. Denny's
17. Marco's Diner
18. Trilby's Apartment
19. Swamp Things
20. Flower Power
21. Sundae Best
22. Audrey's apartment
23. Penny's apartment
24. Glen's apartment
25. Lorelei Cemetery
26. Polly Poster
27. Zurah Cemetery
28. softball field

wet moon

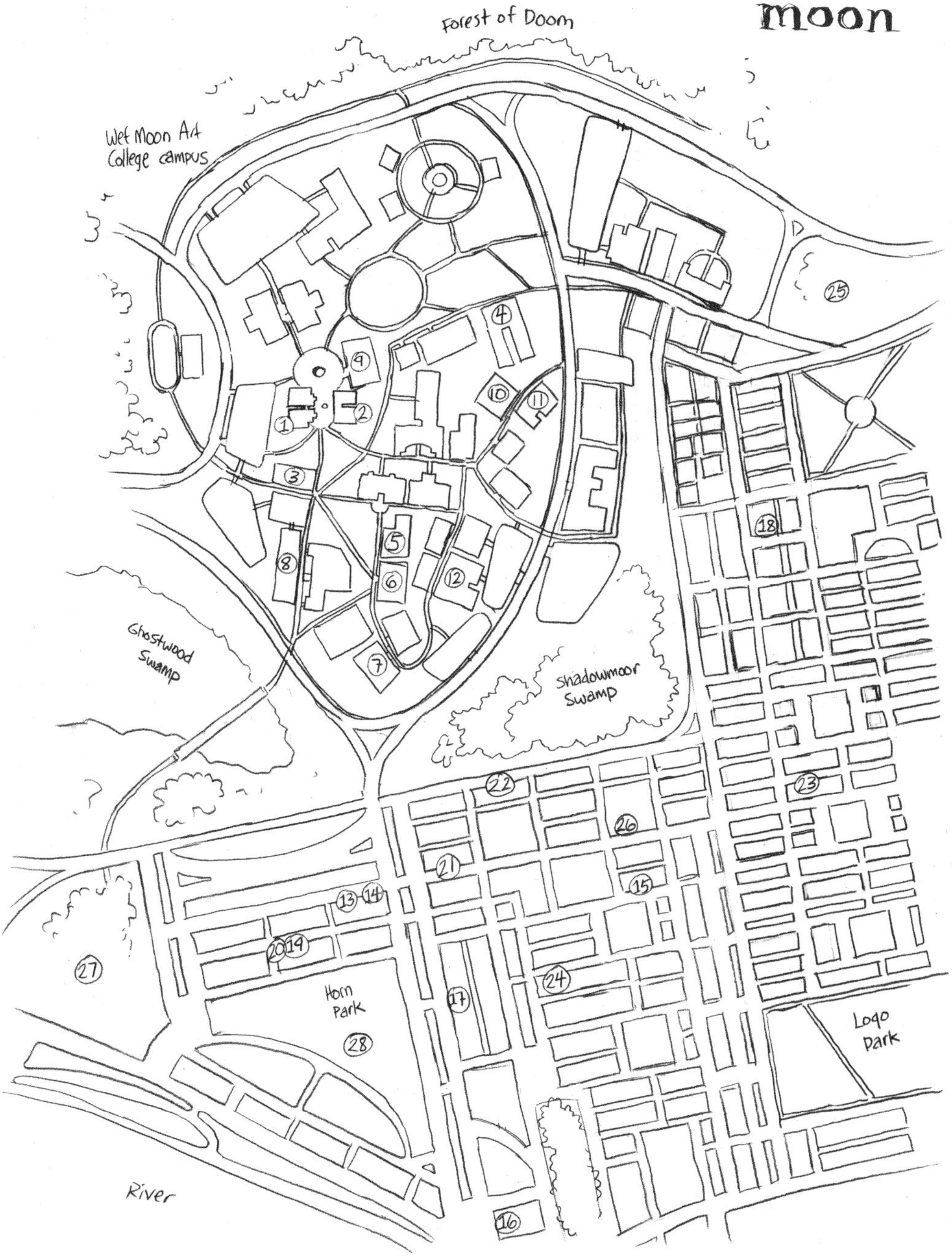

Forest of Doom
Wet Moon Art
College campus
Ghostwood
Swamp
Shadowmoor
Swamp
Horn
Park
Logo
Park
River

28. The Lovedrop Residence
29. The Swanhilde Residence
30. Wet Moon High School
31. The Shoe Tree
32. The Bernarde Residence
33. The Zuzanny Residence

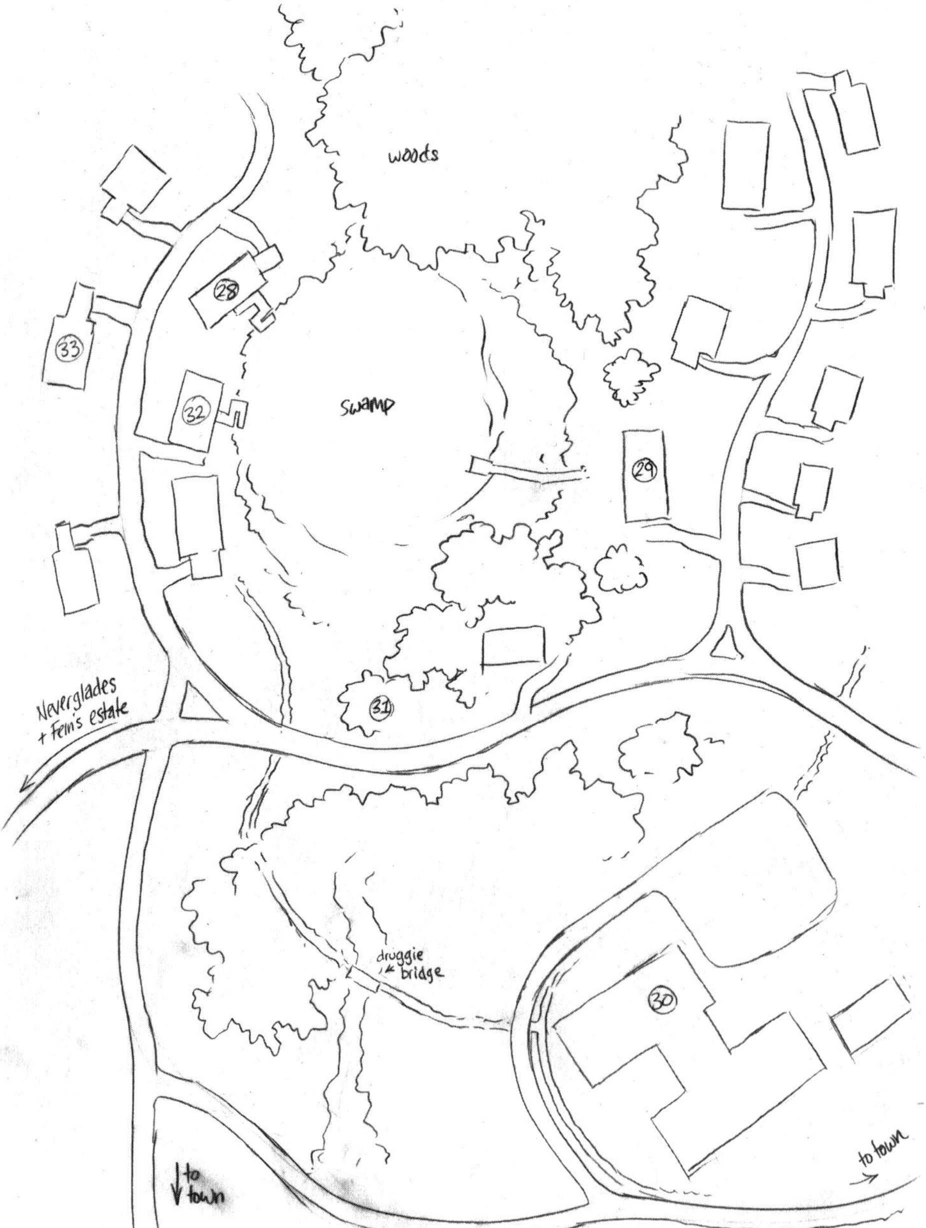
woods
swamp
28
29
30
31
32
33
Neverglades + Fern's estate
druggie bridge
to town
to town

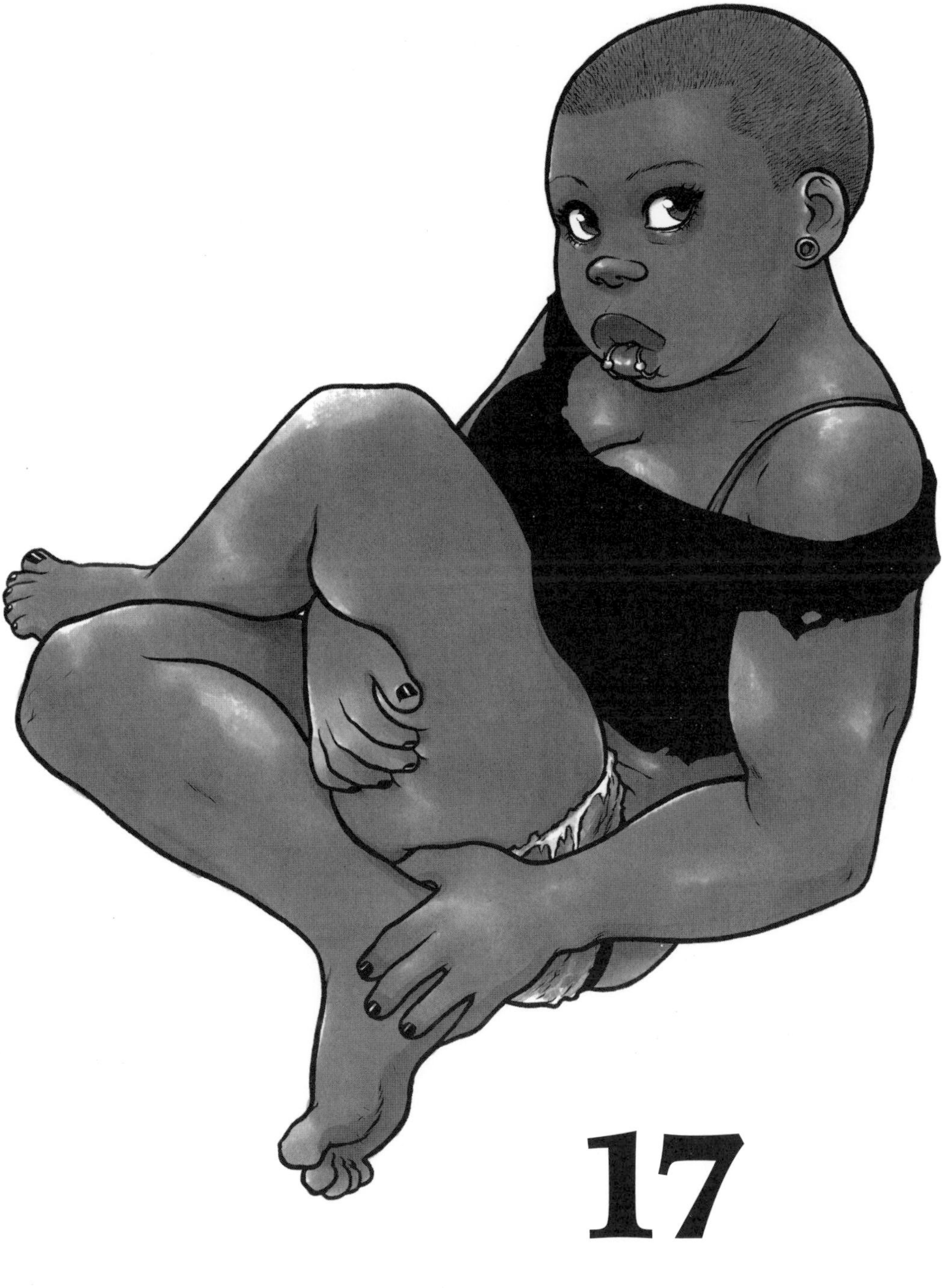

17

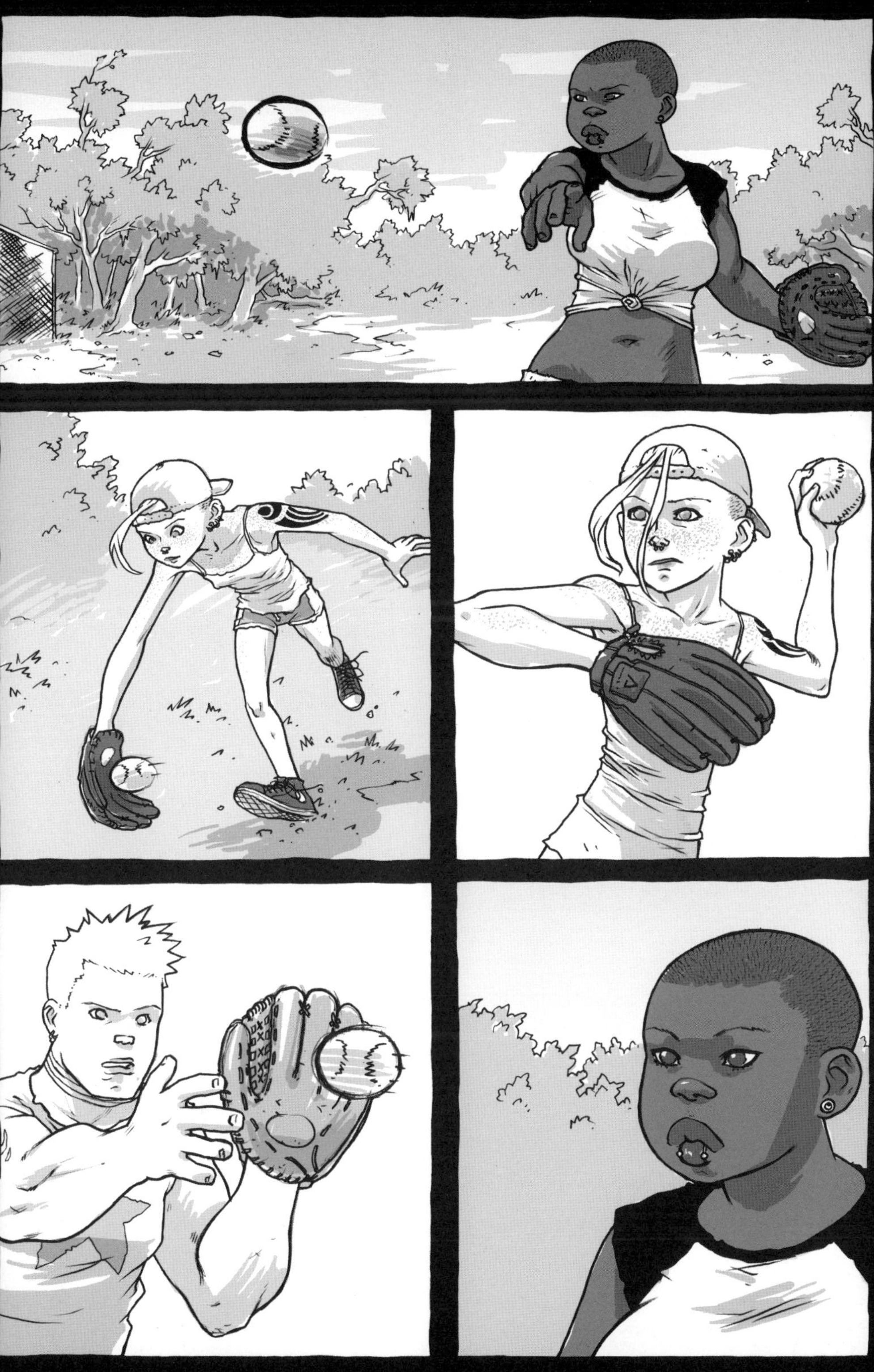

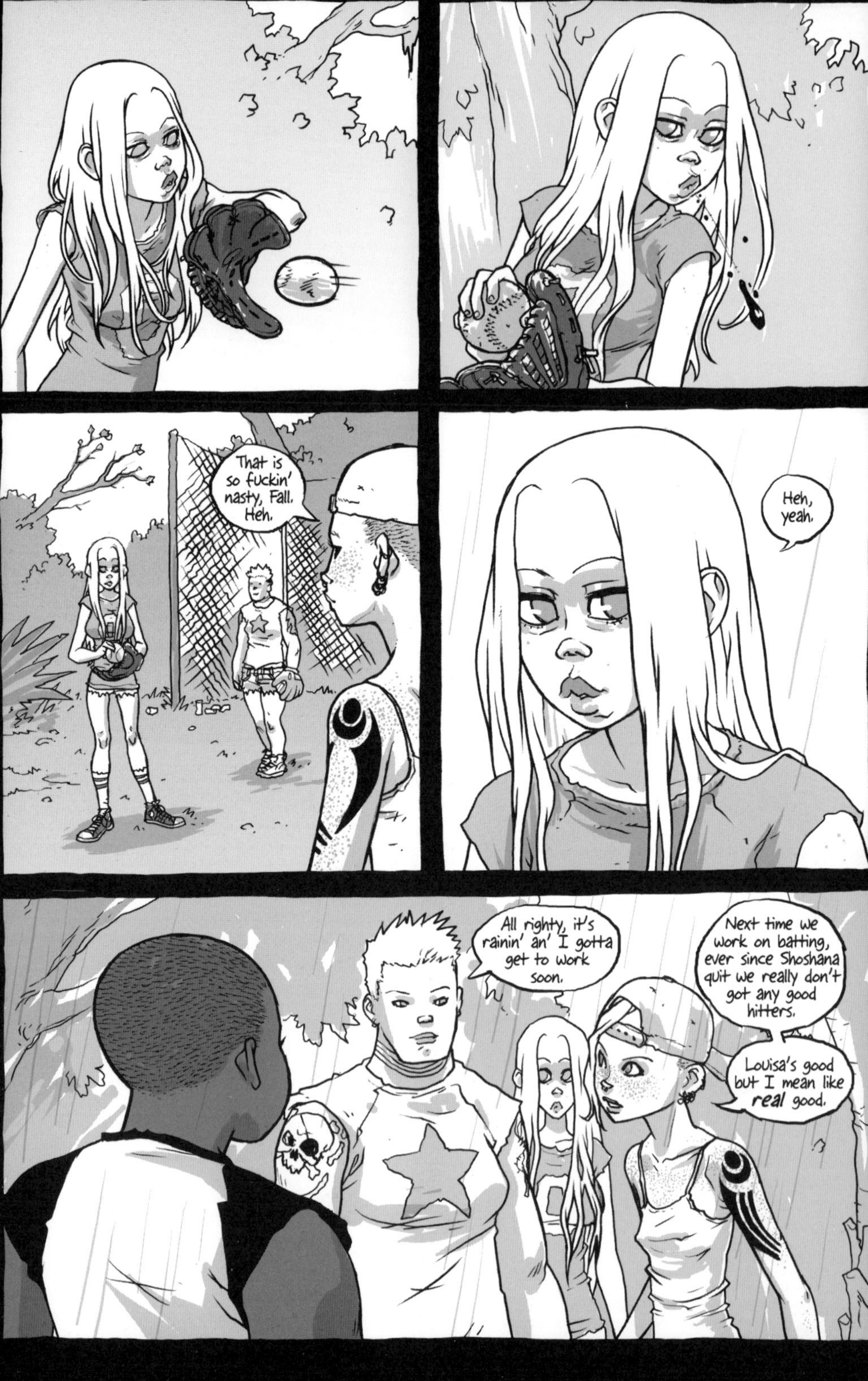
That is so fuckin' nasty, Fall. Heh.
Heh, yeah.
All righty, it's rainin' an' I gotta get to work soon.
Next time we work on batting, ever since Shoshana quit we really don't got any good hitters.
Louisa's good but I mean like **real** good.

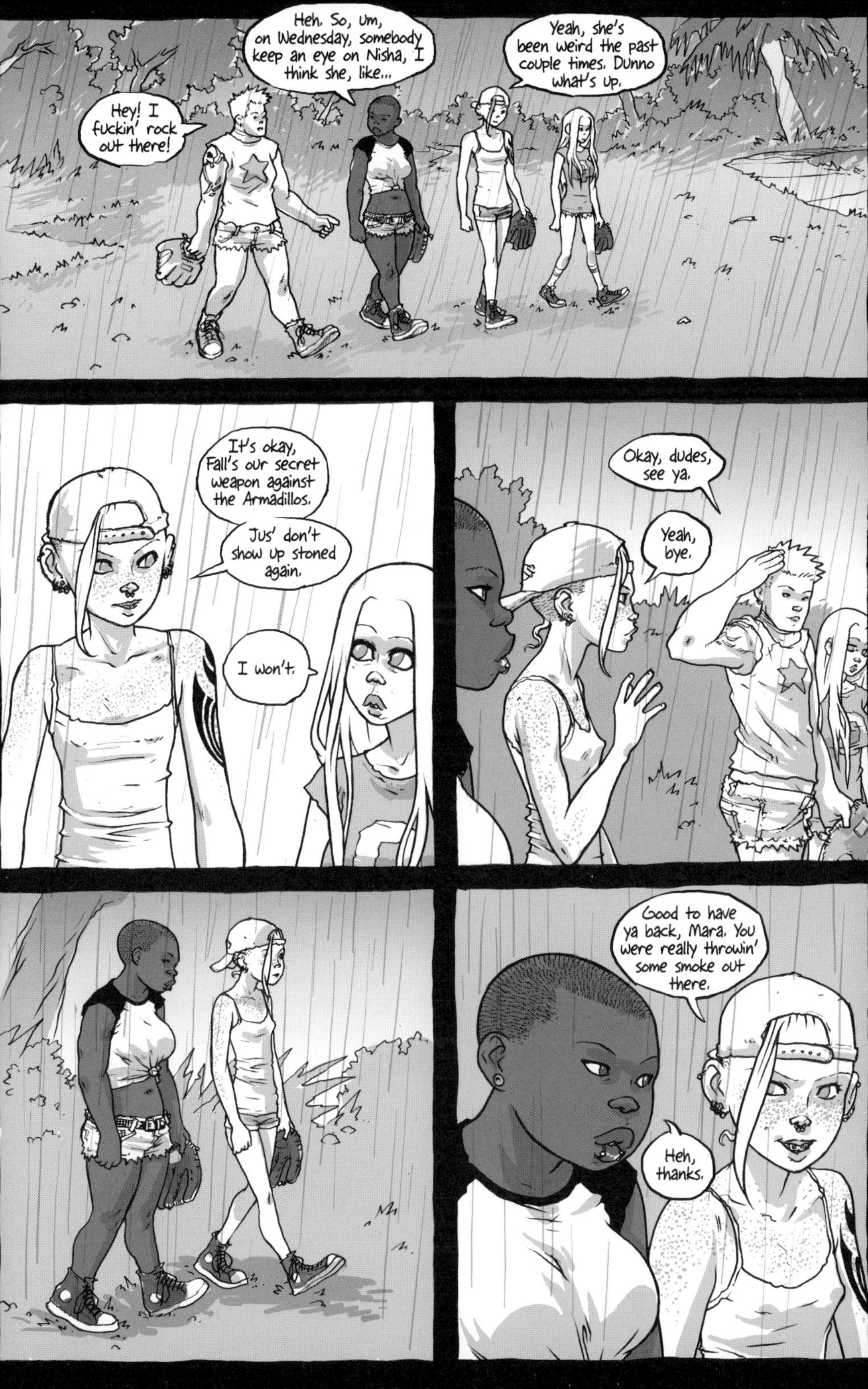
Hey! I fuckin' rock out there!
Heh. So, um, on Wednesday, somebody keep an eye on Nisha, I think she, like...
Yeah, she's been weird the past couple times. Dunno what's up.
It's okay, Fall's our secret weapon against the Armadillos.
Jus' don't show up stoned again.
I won't.
Okay, dudes, see ya.
Yeah, bye.
Good to have ya back, Mara. You were really throwin' some smoke out there.
Heh, thanks.

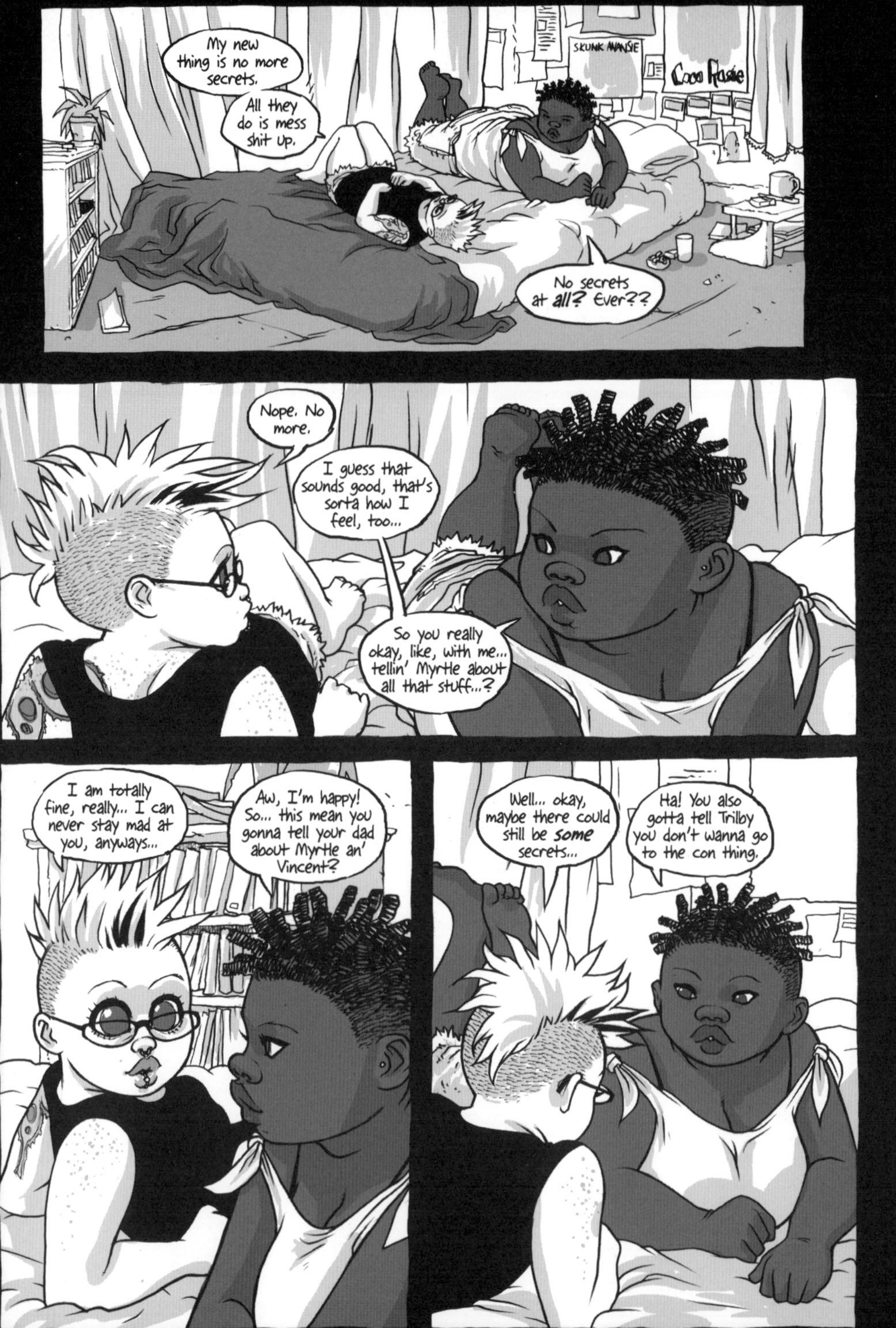
SKUNK ANANSIE
Coco Rosie
My new thing is no more secrets.
All they do is mess shit up.
No secrets at all? Ever??
Nope. No more.
I guess that sounds good, that's sorta how I feel, too...
So you really okay, like, with me... tellin' Myrtle about all that stuff...?
I am totally fine, really... I can never stay mad at you, anyways...
Aw, I'm happy! So... this mean you gonna tell your dad about Myrtle an' Vincent?
Well... okay, maybe there could still be some secrets...
Ha! You also gotta tell Trilby you don't wanna go to the con thing.

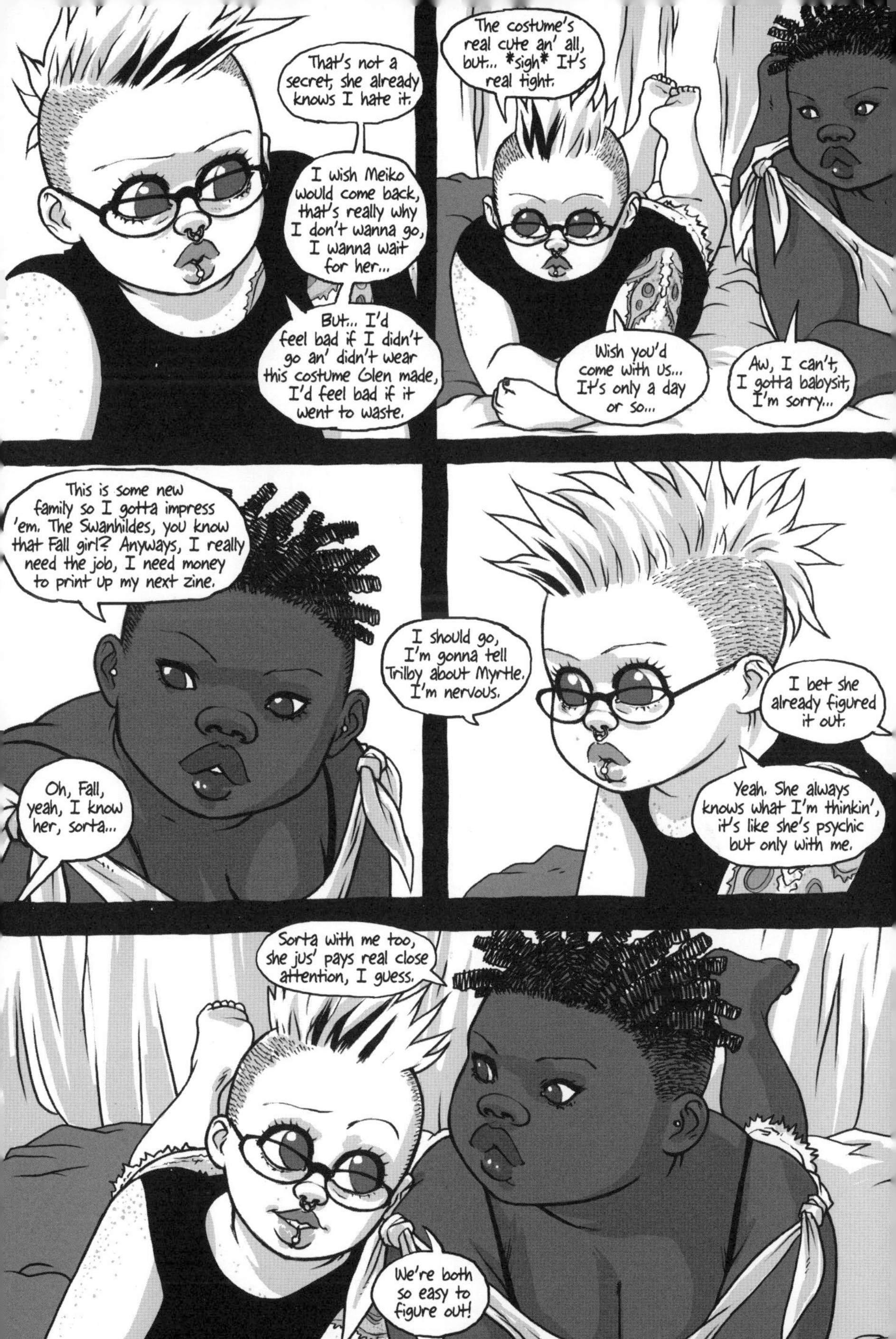
That's not a secret, she already knows I hate it.
I wish Meiko would come back, that's really why I don't wanna go, I wanna wait for her...
But... I'd feel bad if I didn't go an' didn't wear this costume Glen made, I'd feel bad if it went to waste.
The costume's real cute an' all, but... *sigh* It's real tight.
Wish you'd come with us... It's only a day or so...
Aw, I can't, I gotta babysit, I'm sorry...
This is some new family so I gotta impress 'em. The Swanhildes, you know that Fall girl? Anyways, I really need the job, I need money to print up my next zine.
Oh, Fall, yeah, I know her, sorta...
I should go, I'm gonna tell Trilby about Myrtle. I'm nervous.
I bet she already figured it out.
Yeah. She always knows what I'm thinkin', it's like she's psychic but only with me.
Sorta with me too, she jus' pays real close attention, I guess.
We're both so easy to figure out!

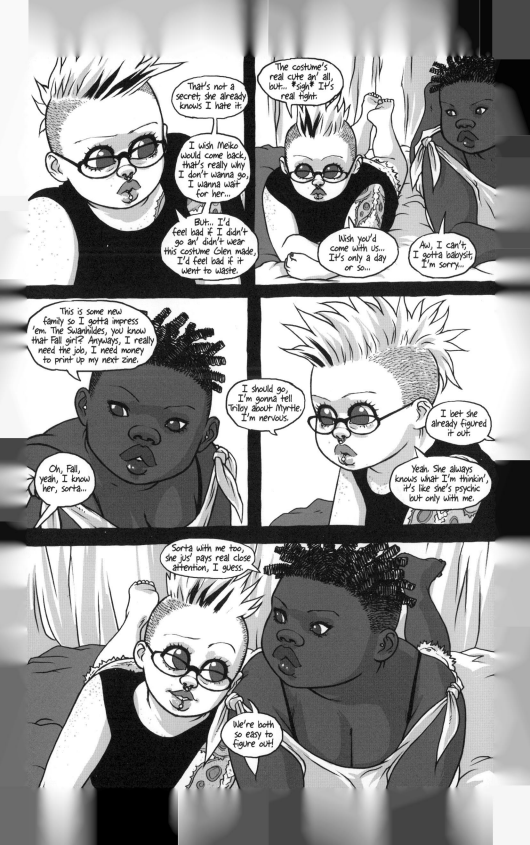

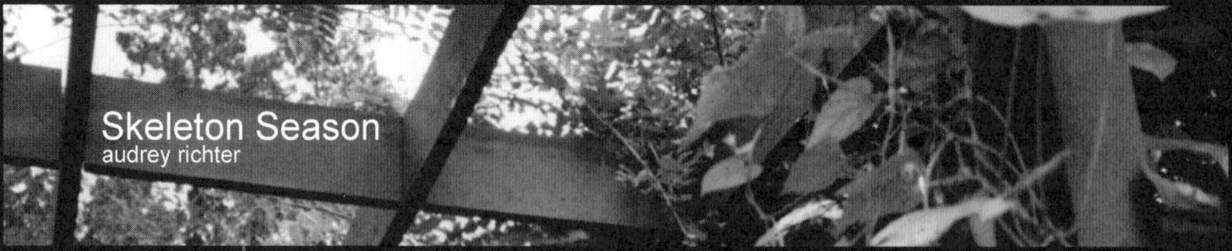
Skeleton Season
audrey richter

Profile

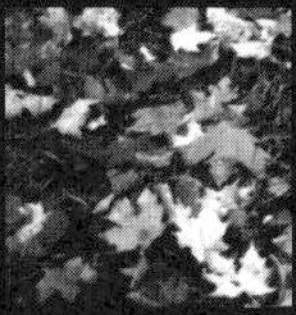

kittyhawk1

Latest Month

October

S	M	T	W	T	F	S
				1	2	3
4	5	6	7	8	9	10
11	12	13	14	15	16	17
18	19	20	21	22	23	24
25	26	27	28	29	30	31

View All Archives

Links

trilbyhatescomics

friendtoroaches

drop-dead

Backyard Birds

Vegans of Color

iamtheshadows.com

kenosha's tomb

230,000 Years Hence

Sisters of Battle

secretcrystal

Evil Galaxy

wetflame

hollow oasis

Twinfold Halfnot

Previous 20

97%!

October 24th, 5:25pm

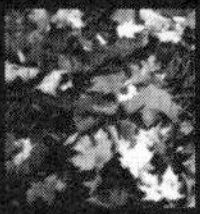

Big babysitting gig this weekend! Actually it's not any different than any others, but I always feel more apprehensive when I get started with a new family who doesn't know me and I don't know how the kids will end up being. But the woman I'm working for, the kids' aunt, said they can be a handful, but I guess every parent/guardian says that.

Anyway, it'll net me a good chunk of cash I can use to put together the next Social Abattoir issue, from which I'll post some pages soon as a teaser! It's like twice the size of the last issue, and I have some interviews with local bands like the Slutty Angels, Nephele, and Gorgon. a friend of mine is dating the vocalist of the Slutty Angels, so I'm getting special treatment! :) I thought about having an advice column, either by me or somebody else, in the zine, but I haven't had time to figure it out yet.

Slicer and I are going to visit his parents at some point, probably for Thanksgiving. How terrible. This will be the first time I've gone anywhere for Thanksgiving in about six years, and it's always so awkward explaining to people that you don't eat meat or dairy anymore, and do I say something beforehand so I don't arrive and they only have turkey and I starve? Maybe I could convince them to come HERE, but I guess our apartment isn't big enough... maybe they could stay in my room or whatever and I could stay... ugh, in Slicer's room...? Still, something to think about, so then I could make the Thanksgiving meal! Thanksgiving is kind of a dumb holiday anyway, it doesn't even mean anything anymore, it's been so distorted into just a day where you get together and eat. That's fine, though, but they should have a different day for it, like... Feast Day or some new thing they could make up that doesn't have any historical or sensitive background. I'd be into Feast Day. Dinner Day? Maybe I'll start my own withmy friends. My friend Cleo is big into baking, she'd be into it.

I got a new pair of binoculars the other day, they can see so far and clear! There are some weird swamp birds here in Wet Moon that I want to go take a look at. I hear all these strange bird calls at night and I always think that maybe since the marshes here are so expansive and mysterious, that I'll someday discover a new species of bird nobody knew about. Maybe a bird that lives underwater and comes up to breathe like a whale? Oh wait I guess that's a penguin. But this one would live in swamps. Or just a bird with gills? haha. I think a lot about new species, how so many species become extinct every day but we also find new ones to replace them (maybe not at the same rate, but maybe it will be when we can fully explore the ocean!), and there is still so much of Earth left unexplored. I went to a lecture last week and the speaker said that we've only explored 3% of our oceans!! What is in that other 97%?? Who knows what's out there! Waterbreathing swampbirds? maybe...

Mood: inquisitive
Current Music: Fugees- temple
Tags: **social abattoir**, **babysitting**, **slicer**, **birds**

3 comments | Leave a comment

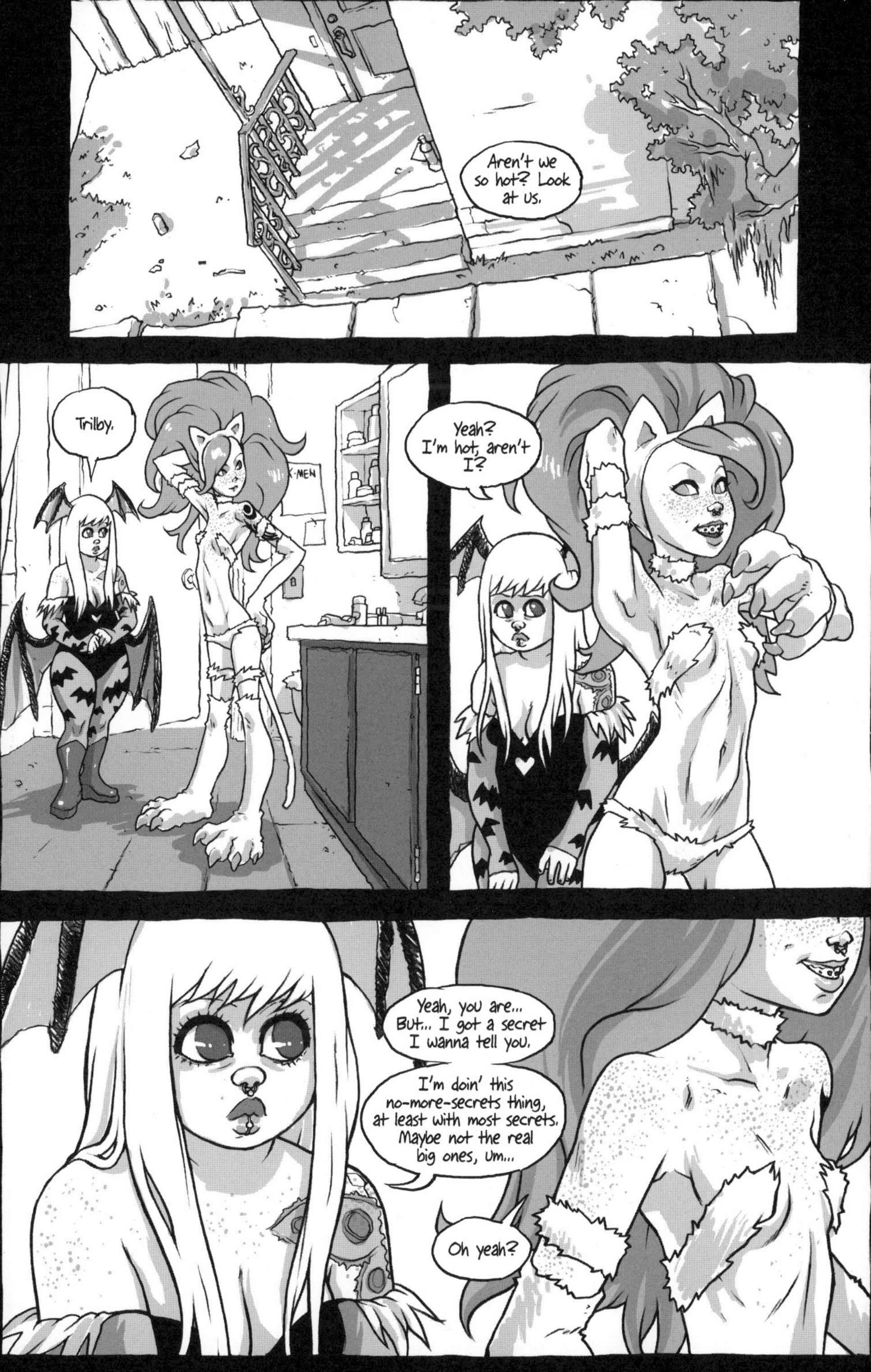

Aren't we so hot? Look at us.
Trilby.
Yeah? I'm hot, aren't I?
Yeah, you are... But... I got a secret I wanna tell you.
I'm doin' this no-more-secrets thing, at least with most secrets. Maybe not the real big ones, um...
Oh yeah?

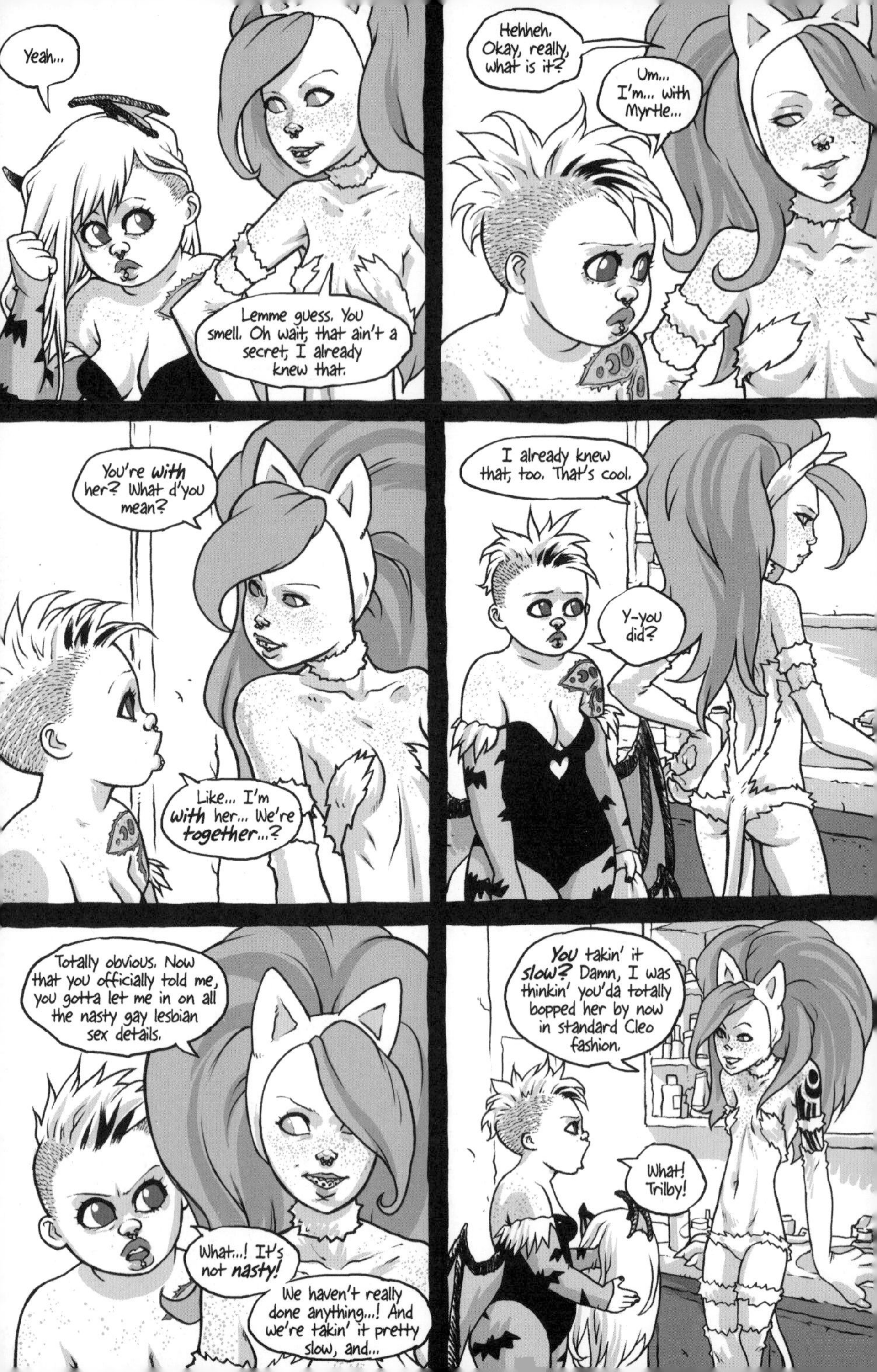
Yeah...
Lemme guess. You smell. Oh wait, that ain't a secret, I already knew that.
Hehheh. Okay, really, what is it?
Um... I'm... with Myrtle...
You're **with** her? What d'you mean?
Like... I'm **with** her... We're **together**...?
I already knew that, too. That's cool.
Y-you did?
Totally obvious. Now that you officially told me, you gotta let me in on all the nasty gay lesbian sex details.
What...! It's not **nasty!**
We haven't really done anything...! And we're takin' it pretty slow, and...
You takin' it **slow?** Damn, I was thinkin' you'da totally bopped her by now in standard Cleo fashion.
What! Trilby!

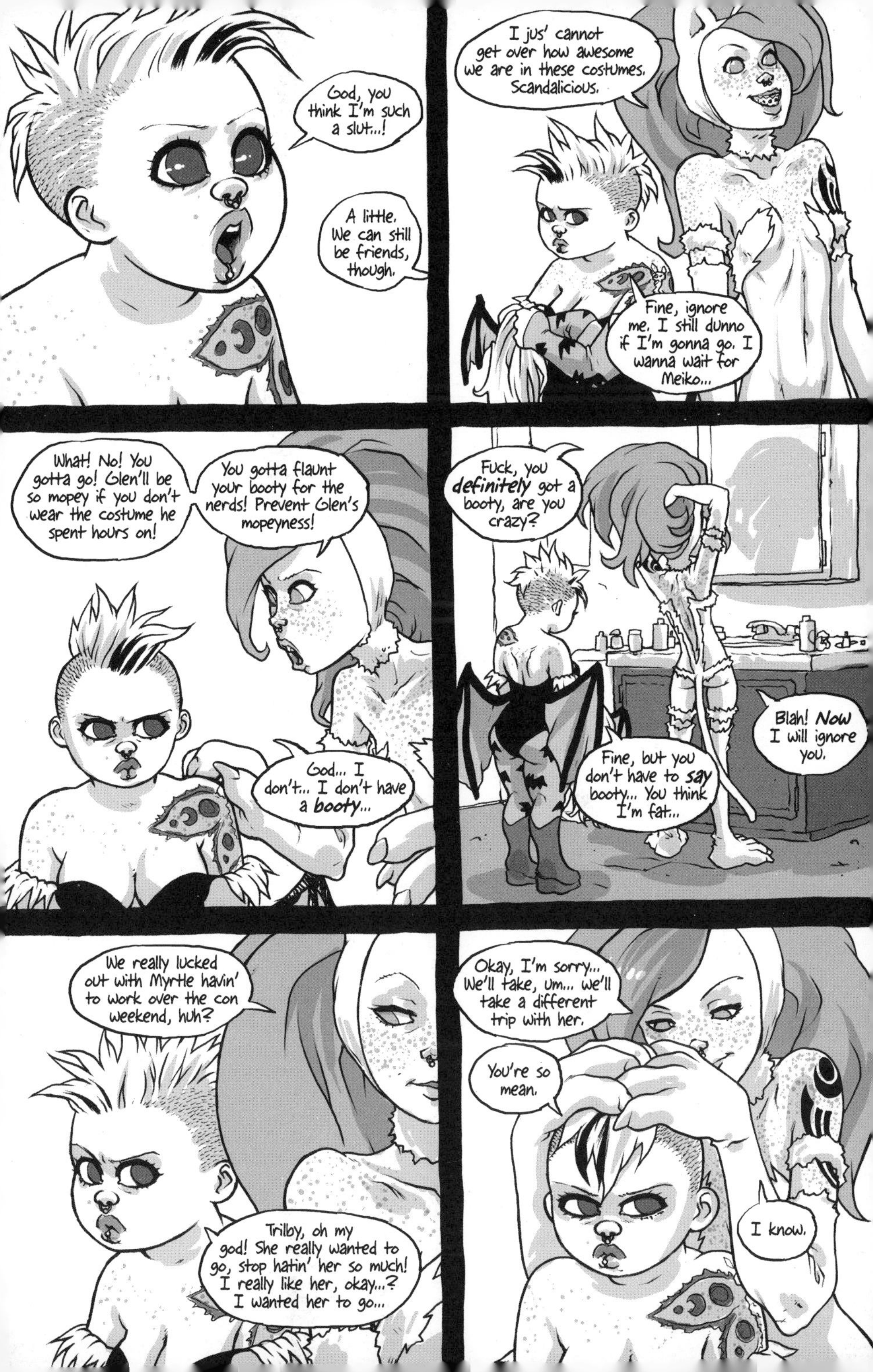
God, you think I'm such a slut...!
A little. We can still be friends, though.
I jus' cannot get over how awesome we are in these costumes. Scandalicious.
Fine, ignore me. I still dunno if I'm gonna go. I wanna wait for Meiko...
What! No! You gotta go! Glen'll be so mopey if you don't wear the costume he spent hours on!
You gotta flaunt your booty for the nerds! Prevent Glen's mopeyness!
God... I don't... I don't have a booty...
Fuck, you definitely got a booty, are you crazy?
Fine, but you don't have to say booty... You think I'm fat...
Blah! Now I will ignore you.
We really lucked out with Myrtle havin' to work over the con weekend, huh?
Trilby, oh my god! She really wanted to go, stop hatin' her so much! I really like her, okay...? I wanted her to go...
Okay, I'm sorry... We'll take, um... we'll take a different trip with her.
You're so mean.
I know.

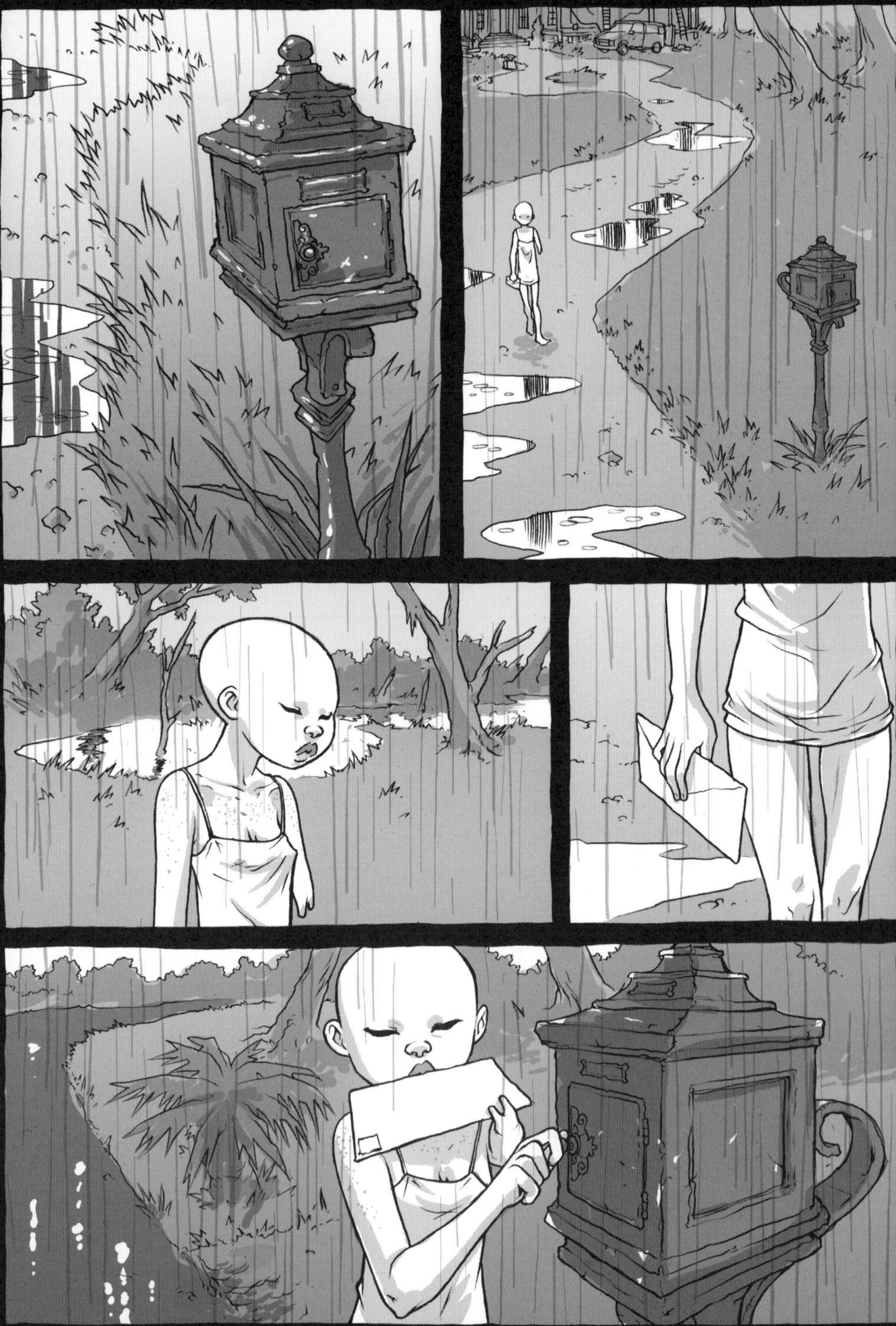

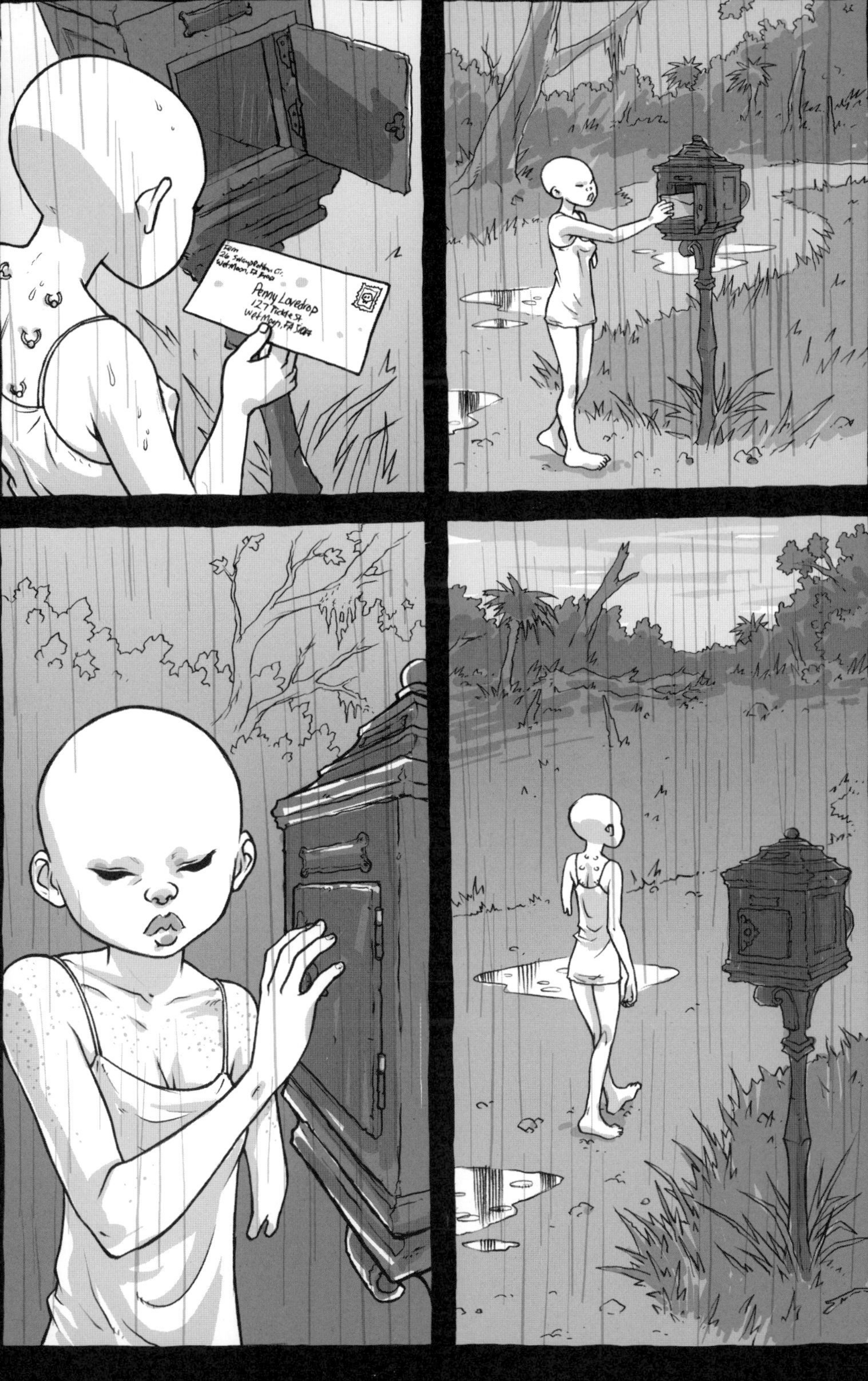
Fern
Penny Lovedrop
127 Tickle St

October 25

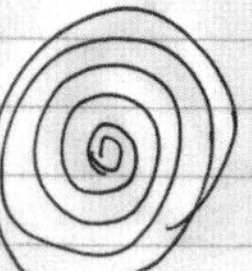

I've been keeping an eye on Malady like Trilby said to. I'm supposed to look for suspicious behavior but I haven't been able to tell if there's been any... Malady's just all around weird all the time, so if she WAS acting suspicious I'd never be able to tell. It could be that she knows I'm onto her, and that's why she isn't putting up any new fliers. I don't even care anymore.

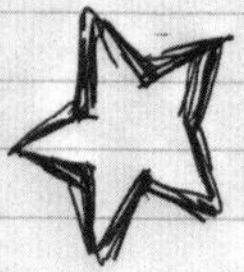

I told Trilby about me and Myrtle. I should have known it wouldn't be a big deal, Trilby said she didn't even care. Or at least she acted like she didn't care. Or tried to. I know she does, like she's weirded out by me liking other girls. Even though she always championed me getting together with Myrtle before. I think maybe I should just go ahead and tell other people, maybe even my dad and Penny, because everyone else seems to be taking it so casually, but I still can't work up the courage. I don't know what'll happen. I don't know where this came from, this me liking girls thing, I don't know if it

means I'm a real lesbian
or what... Is it okay for me
to be with a girl? I still like
guys, though... Even though I
haven't been with a guy since
Vincent... But I've had sex with
a bunch of other ~~----~~ guys
since I was 13, what does that
mean? I could be bi, but Trilby
always makes fun of bisexual
people and stuff, so she'd probably
tell me to knock it off, pick a
gender and stick with it. I don't
know. I think that's kind of
sad.

i'm jealous of everyone's looks.
Penny especially, i think, I wish
i had her body so much. Trilby,
Mara... and Audrey has these
extraordinary curves and boobs...
I could never get like that. i'd
love to have Trilby's body, too.
she works out a lot but even
if I did too I could never get
like that; she's always been
naturally svelte. she says it's
genetics. she can scarf down
so much food and not gain a
pound, she burns it off so
fast! i'm jealous of the whole
world!

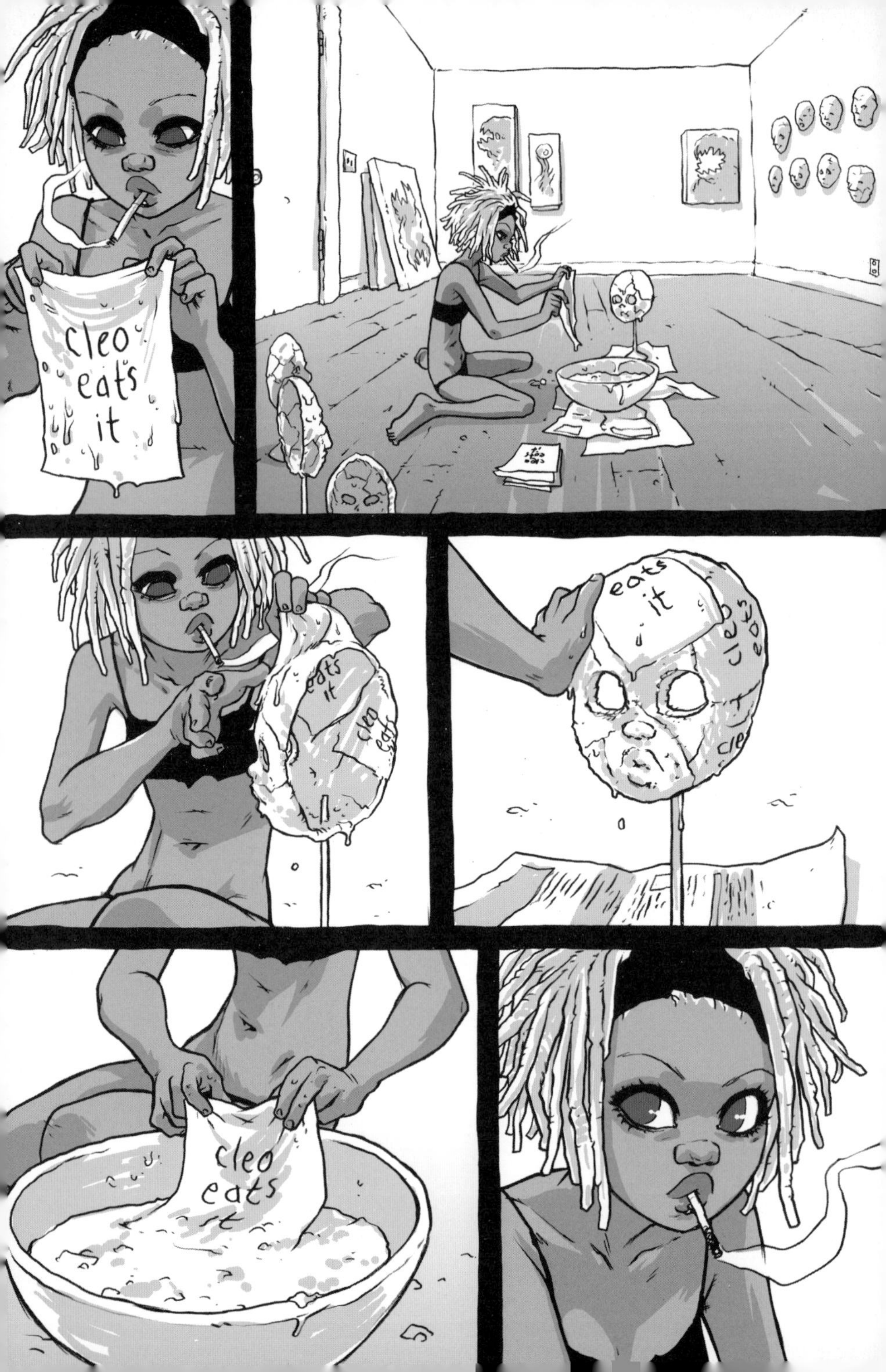

cleo eats it
eats it
cleo eats
eats it
cleo eats
cleo eats

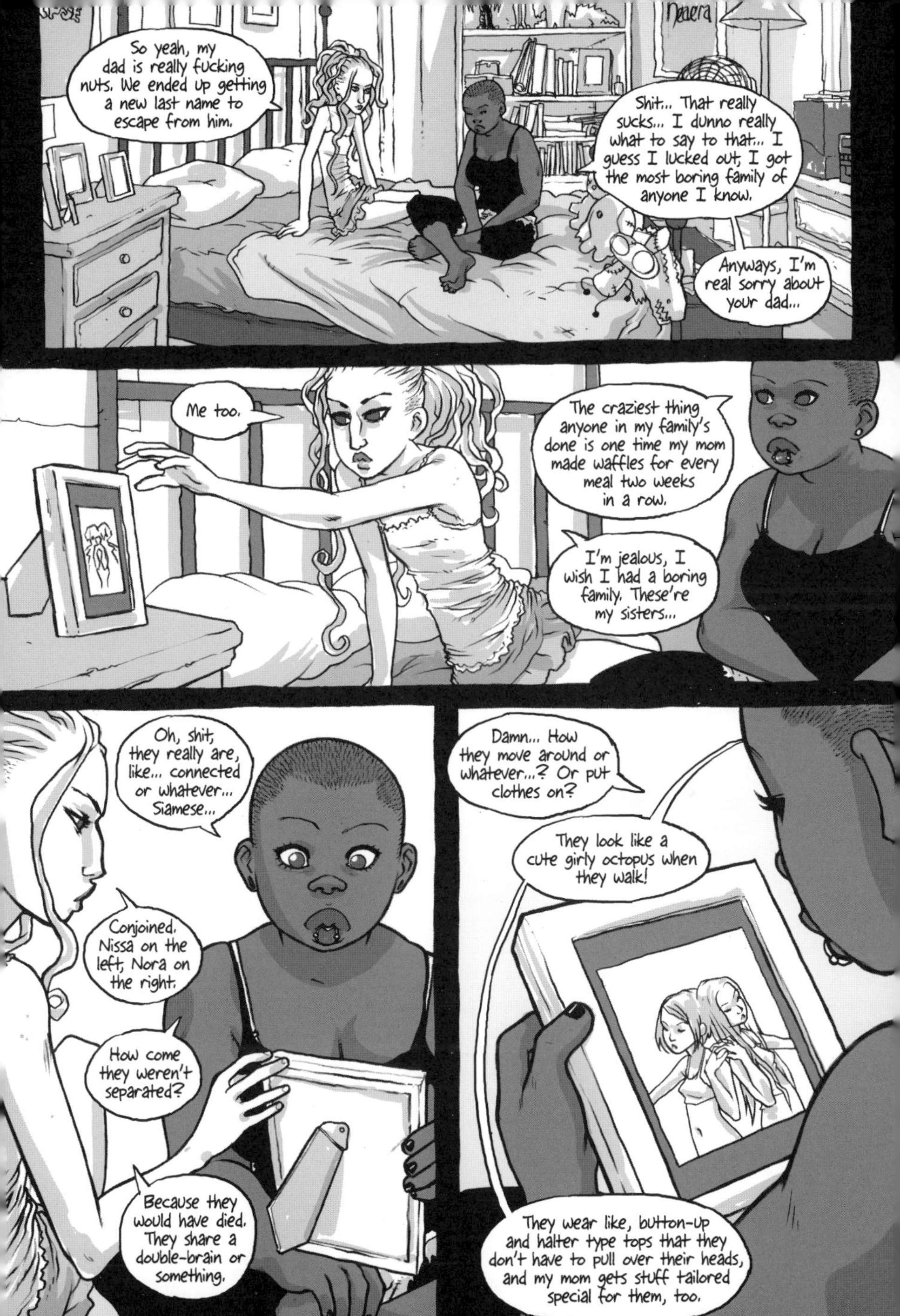
So yeah, my dad is really fucking nuts. We ended up getting a new last name to escape from him.
Shit... That really sucks... I dunno really what to say to that... I guess I lucked out, I got the most boring family of anyone I know.
Anyways, I'm real sorry about your dad...
Me too.
The craziest thing anyone in my family's done is one time my mom made waffles for every meal two weeks in a row.
I'm jealous, I wish I had a boring family. These're my sisters...
Oh, shit, they really are, like... connected or whatever... Siamese...
Conjoined. Nissa on the left, Nora on the right.
How come they weren't separated?
Because they would have died. They share a double-brain or something.
Damn... How they move around or whatever...? Or put clothes on?
They look like a cute girly octopus when they walk!
They wear like, button-up and halter type tops that they don't have to pull over their heads, and my mom gets stuff tailored special for them, too.

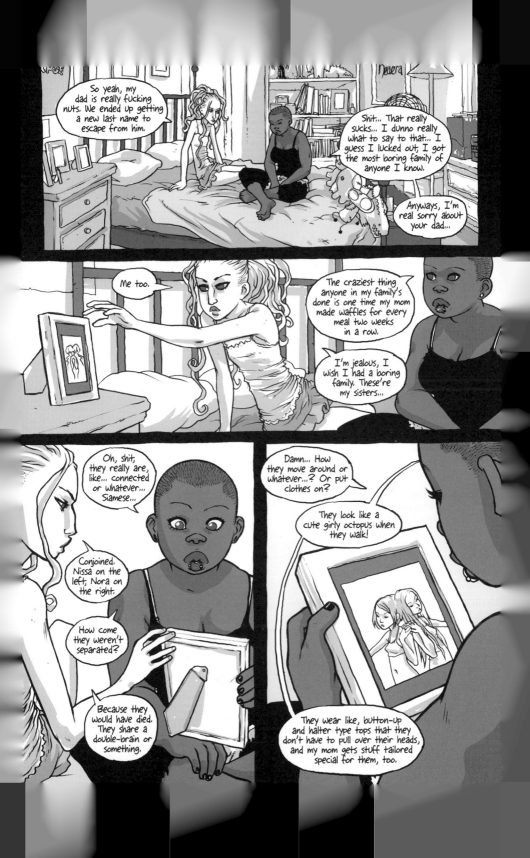

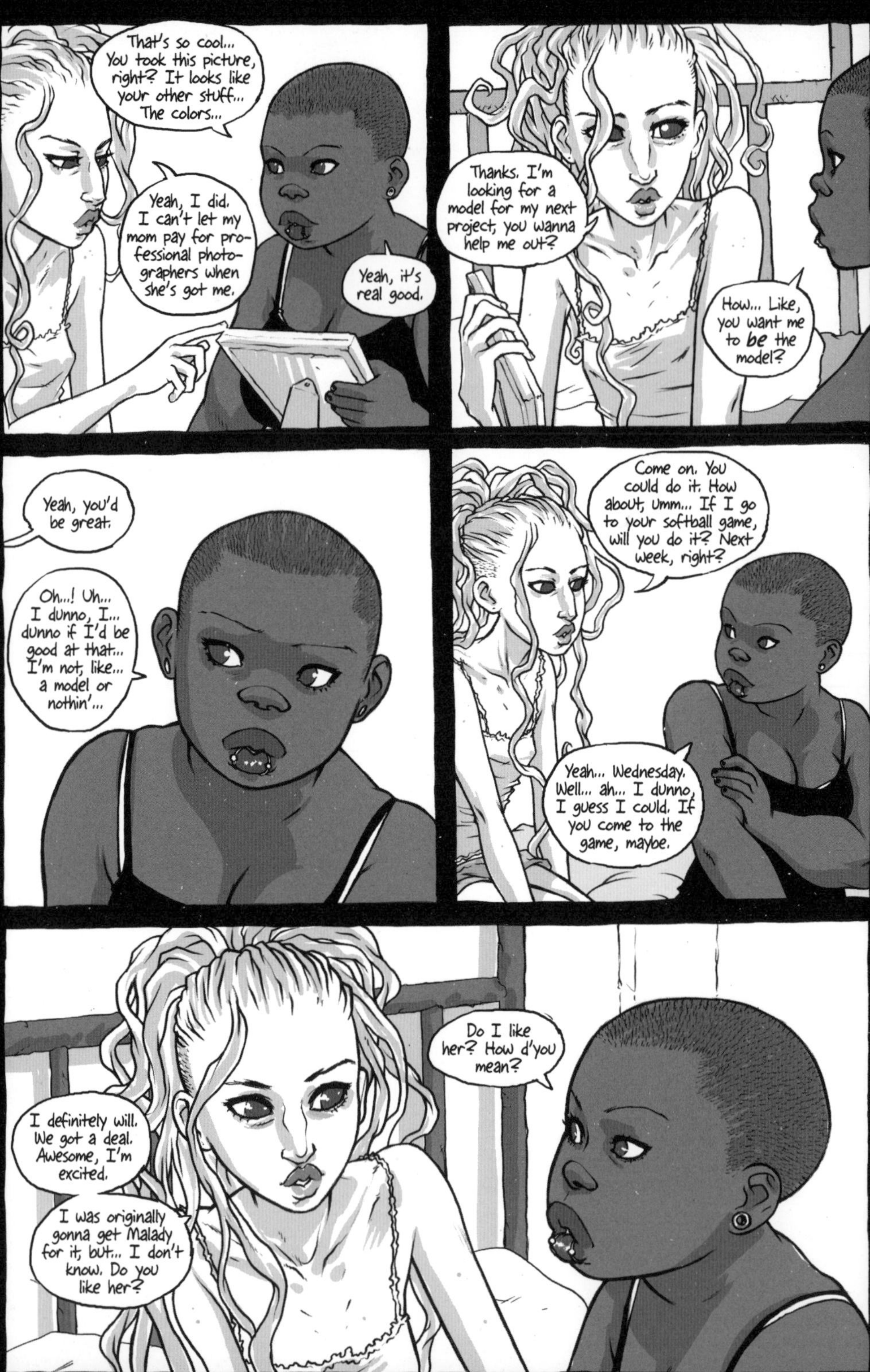
That's so cool... You took this picture, right? It looks like your other stuff... The colors...
Yeah, I did. I can't let my mom pay for professional photographers when she's got me.
Yeah, it's real good.
Thanks. I'm looking for a model for my next project, you wanna help me out?
How... Like, you want me to **be** the model?
Yeah, you'd be great.
Oh...! Uh... I dunno, I... dunno if I'd be good at that... I'm not, like... a model or nothin'...
Come on. You could do it. How about, umm... If I go to your softball game, will you do it? Next week, right?
Yeah... Wednesday. Well... ah... I dunno, I guess I could. If you come to the game, maybe.
I definitely will. We got a deal. Awesome, I'm excited.
I was originally gonna get Malady for it, but... I don't know. Do you like her?
Do I like her? How d'you mean?

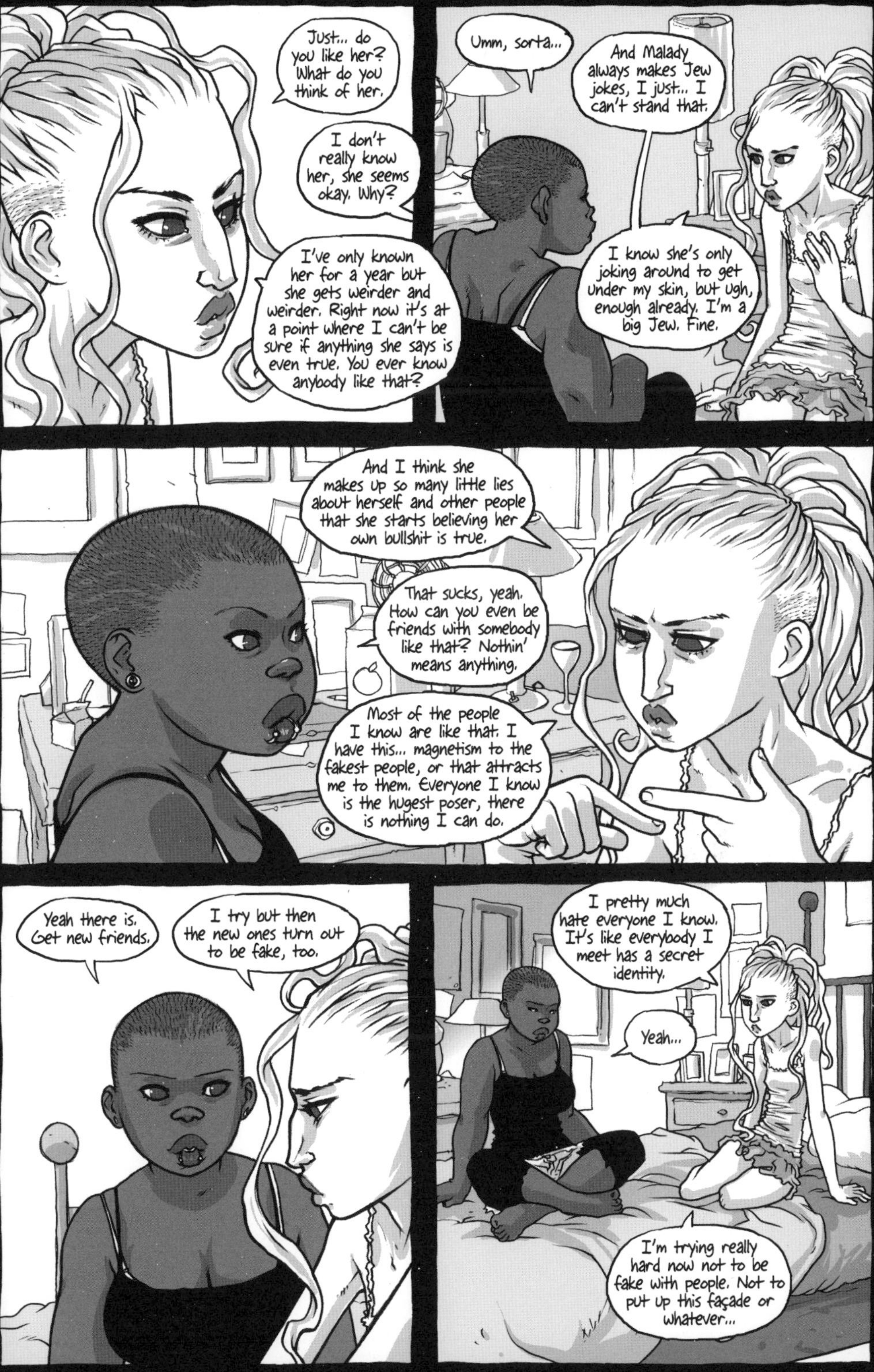
Just... do you like her? What do you think of her.
I don't really know her, she seems okay. Why?
I've only known her for a year but she gets weirder and weirder. Right now it's at a point where I can't be sure if anything she says is even true. You ever know anybody like that?
Umm, sorta...
And Malady always makes Jew jokes, I just... I can't stand that.
I know she's only joking around to get under my skin, but ugh, enough already. I'm a big Jew. Fine.
And I think she makes up so many little lies about herself and other people that she starts believing her own bullshit is true.
That sucks, yeah. How can you even be friends with somebody like that? Nothin' means anything.
Most of the people I know are like that. I have this... magnetism to the fakest people, or that attracts me to them. Everyone I know is the hugest poser, there is nothing I can do.
Yeah there is. Get new friends.
I try but then the new ones turn out to be fake, too.
I pretty much hate everyone I know. It's like everybody I meet has a secret identity.
Yeah...
I'm trying really hard now not to be fake with people. Not to put up this façade or whatever...

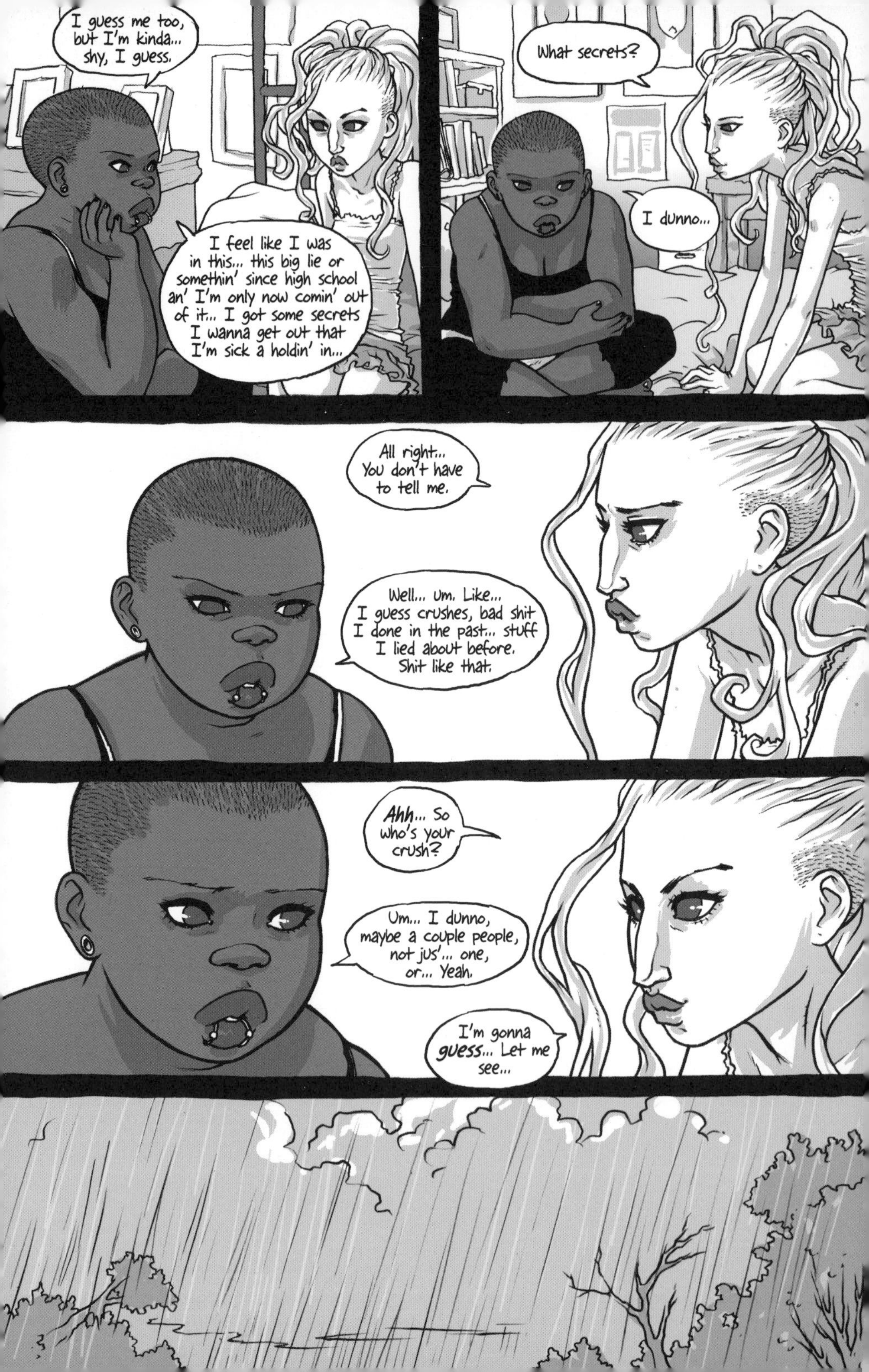
I guess me too, but I'm kinda... shy, I guess.
I feel like I was in this... this big lie or somethin' since high school an' I'm only now comin' out of it... I got some secrets I wanna get out that I'm sick a holdin' in...
What secrets?
I dunno...
All right... You don't have to tell me.
Well... um. Like... I guess crushes, bad shit I done in the past... stuff I lied about before. Shit like that.
Ahh... So who's your crush?
Um... I dunno, maybe a couple people, not jus'... one, or... Yeah.
I'm gonna guess... Let me see...

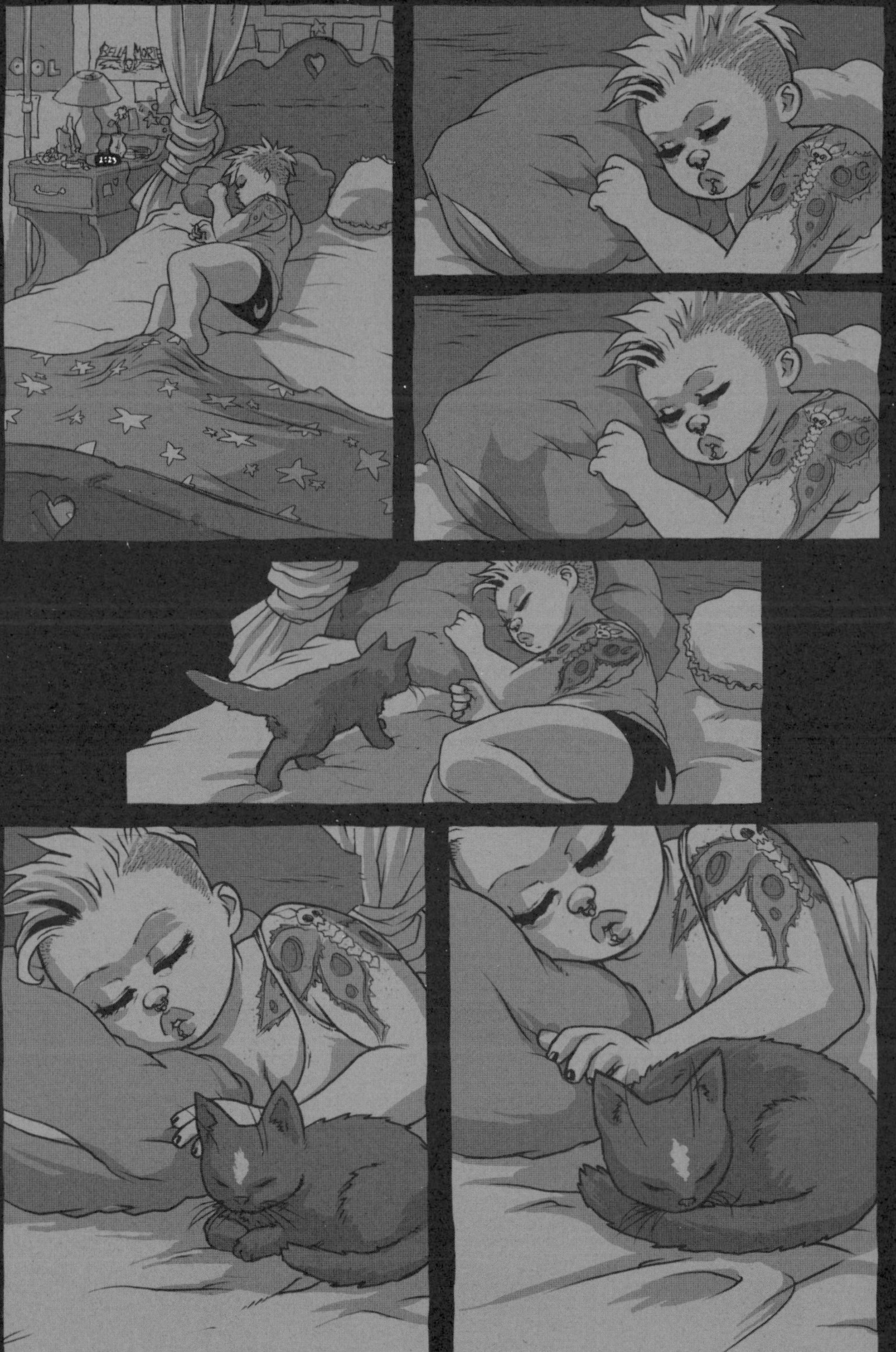
OOL
BELLA MORTE
2:23

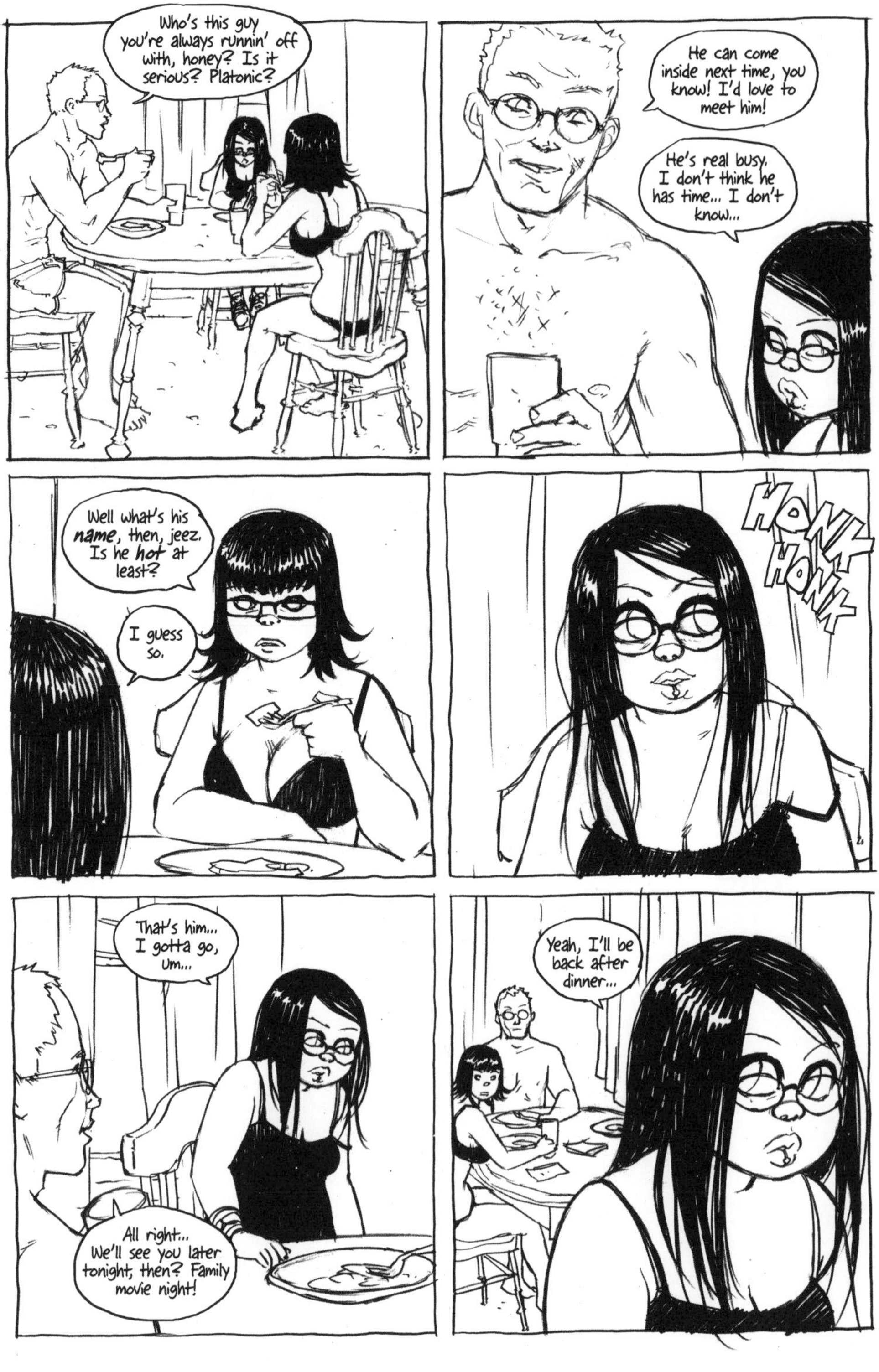
Who's this guy you're always runnin' off with, honey? Is it serious? Platonic?
He can come inside next time, you know! I'd love to meet him!
He's real busy. I don't think he has time... I don't know...
Well what's his ***name***, then, jeez. Is he ***hot*** at least?
I guess so.
HONK HONK
That's him... I gotta go, um...
All right... We'll see you later tonight, then? Family movie night!
Yeah, I'll be back after dinner...

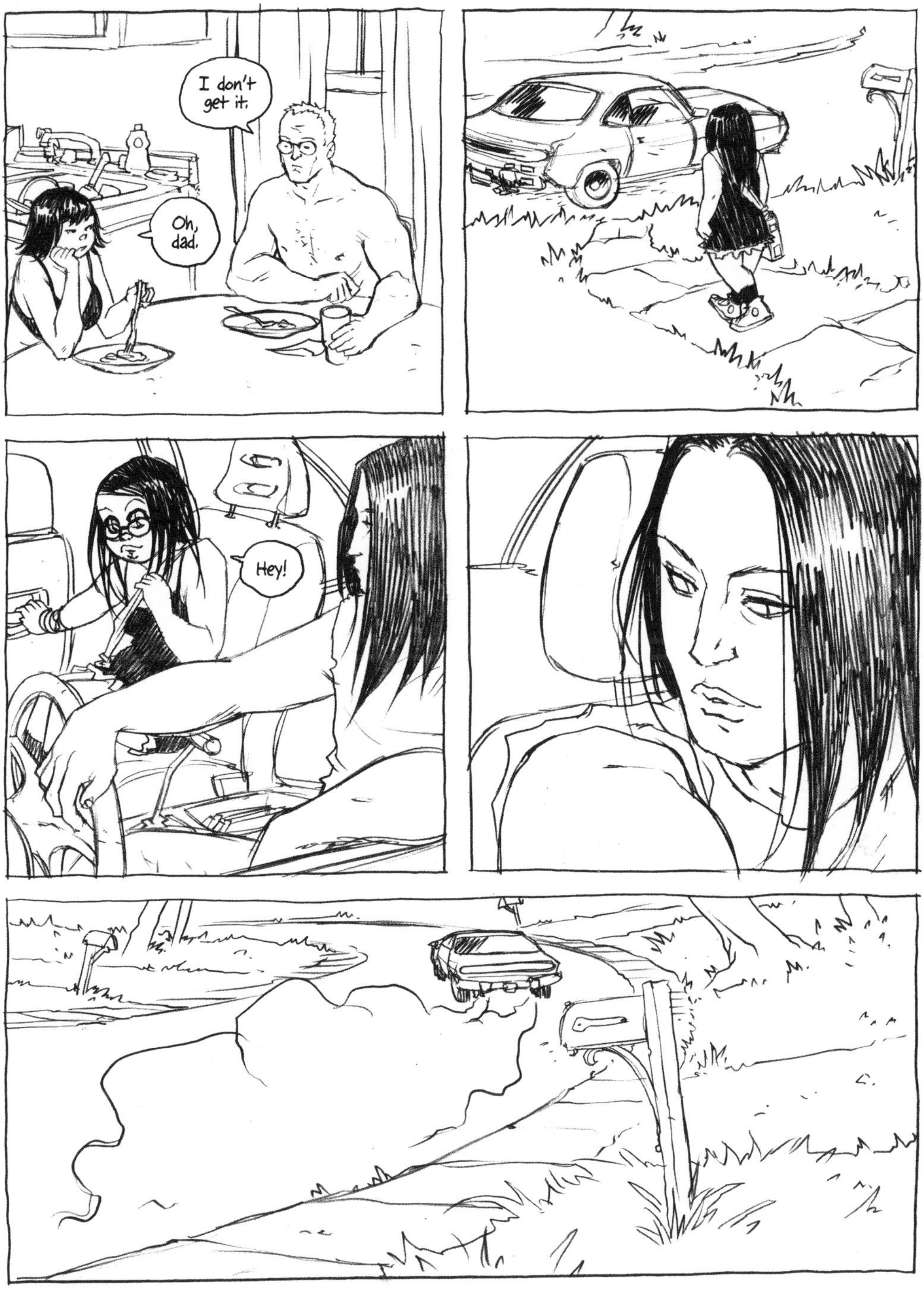
I don't get it.
Oh, dad.
Hey!

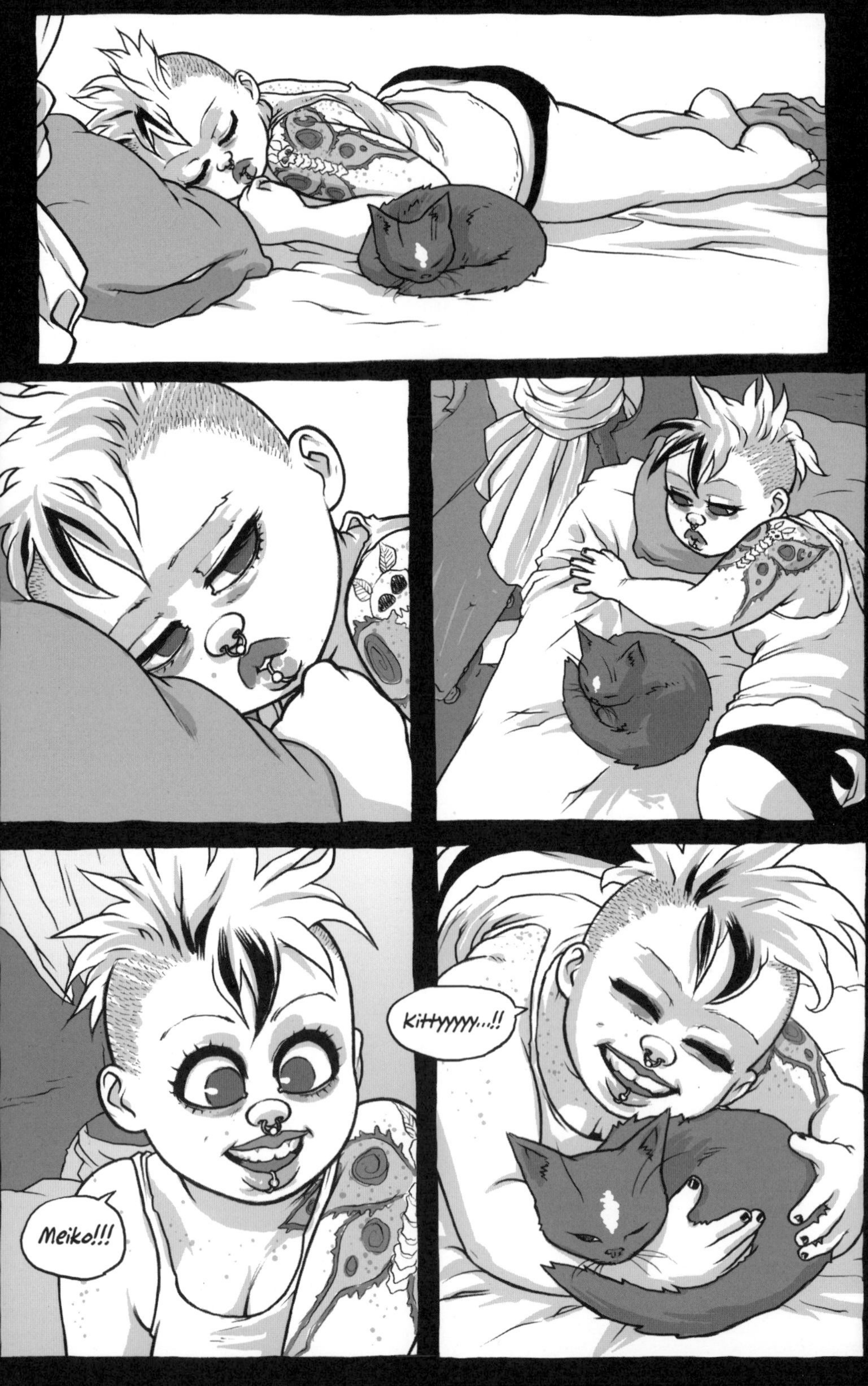
Meiko!!!
Kittyyyyy...!!

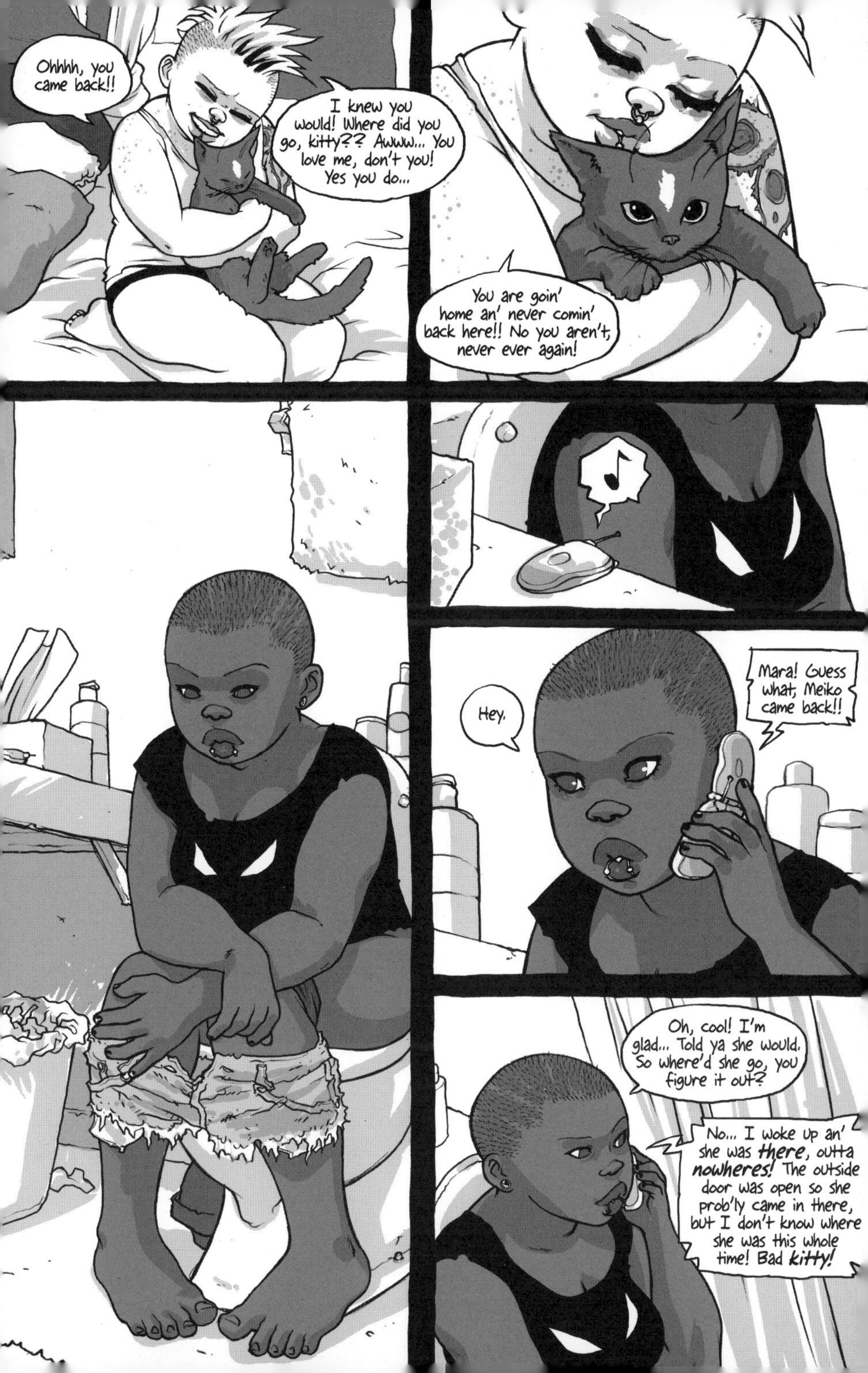

Ohhhh, you came back!!
I knew you would! Where did you go, kitty?? Awww... You love me, don't you! Yes you do...
You are goin' home an' never comin' back here!! No you aren't, never ever again!
Hey.
Mara! Guess what, Meiko came back!!
Oh, cool! I'm glad... Told ya she would. So where'd she go, you figure it out?
No... I woke up an' she was *there*, outta *nowheres!* The outside door was open so she prob'ly came in there, but I don't know where she was this whole time! Bad *kitty!*

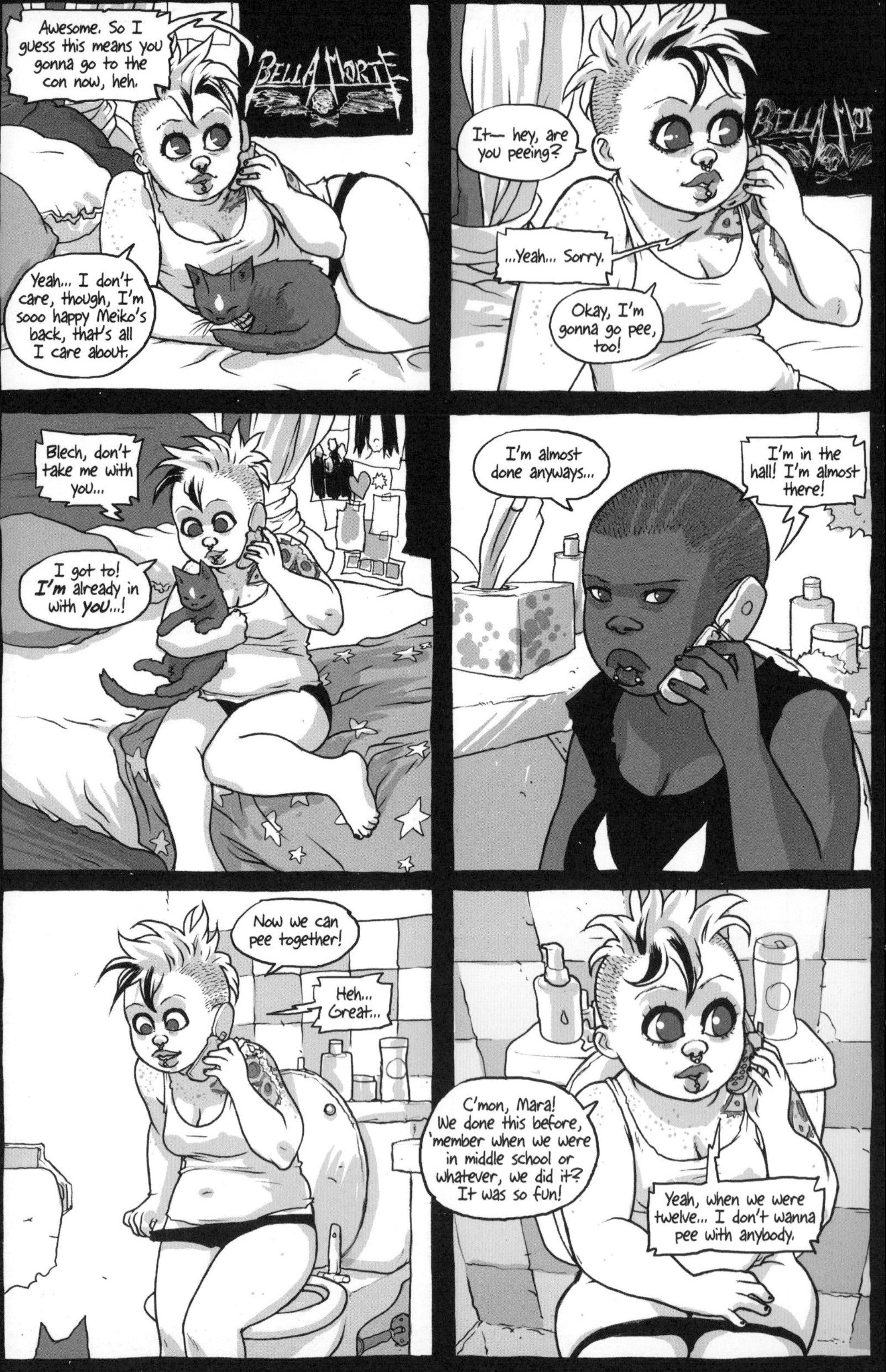

Awesome. So I guess this means you gonna go to the con now, heh.
BELLA MORTE
Yeah... I don't care, though, I'm sooo happy Meiko's back, that's all I care about.
It— hey, are you peeing?
...Yeah... Sorry.
Okay, I'm gonna go pee, too!
Blech, don't take me with you...
I got to! **I'm** already in with **YOU**...!
I'm almost done anyways...
I'm in the hall! I'm almost there!
Now we can pee together!
Heh... Great...
C'mon, Mara! We done this before, 'member when we were in middle school or whatever, we did it? It was so fun!
Yeah, when we were twelve... I don't wanna pee with anybody.

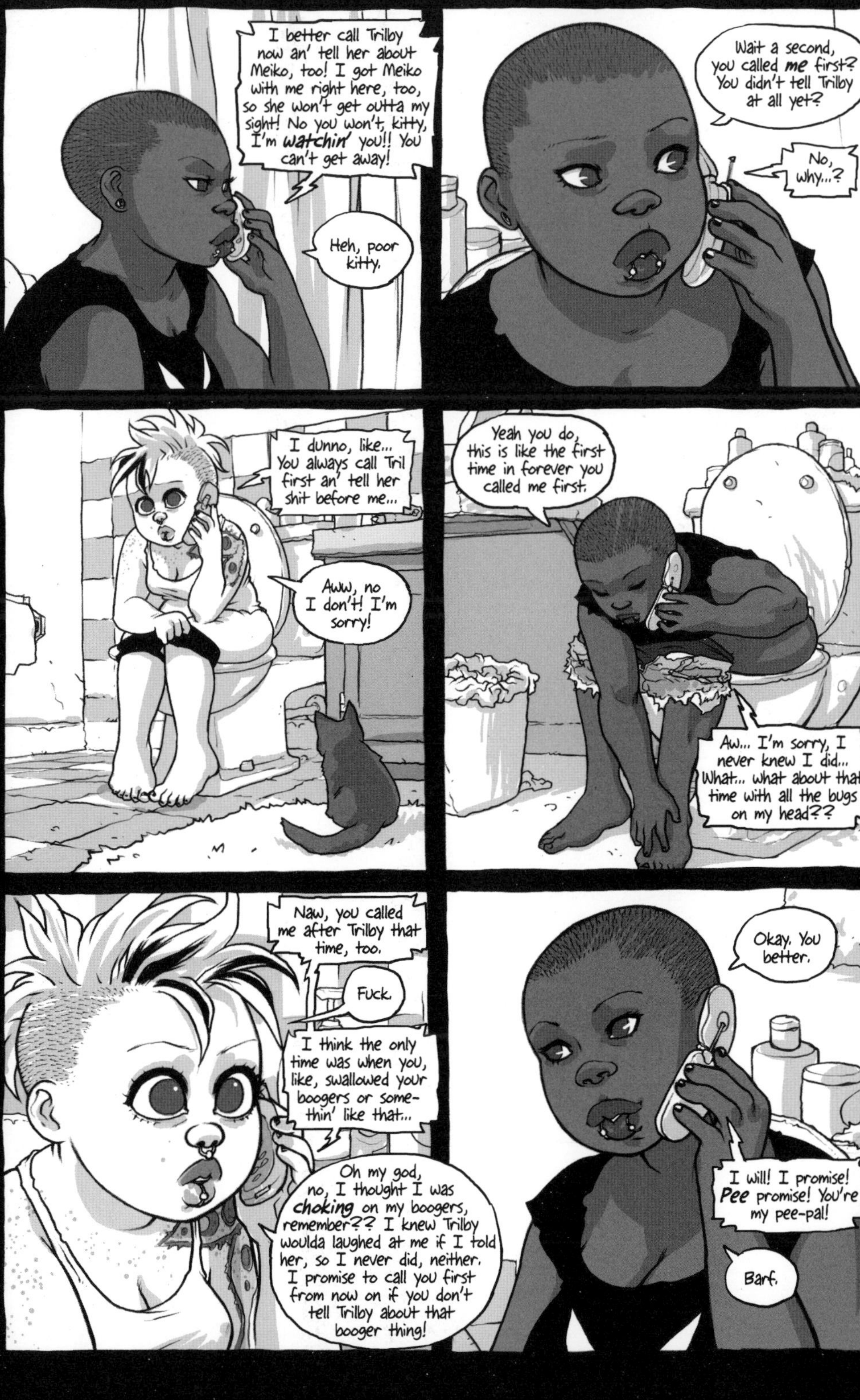
I better call Trilby now an' tell her about Meiko, too! I got Meiko with me right here, too, so she won't get outta my sight! No you won't, kitty, I'm *watchin'* you!! You can't get away!
Heh, poor kitty.
Wait a second, you called *me* first? You didn't tell Trilby at all yet?
No, why...?
I dunno, like... You always call Tril first an' tell her shit before me...
Aww, no I don't! I'm sorry!
Yeah you do, this is like the first time in forever you called me first.
Aw... I'm sorry, I never knew I did... What... what about that time with all the bugs on my head??
Naw, you called me after Trilby that time, too.
Fuck.
I think the only time was when you, like, swallowed your boogers or somethin' like that...
Oh my god, no, I thought I was *choking* on my boogers, remember?? I knew Trilby woulda laughed at me if I told her, so I never did, neither. I promise to call you first from now on if you don't tell Trilby about that booger thing!
Okay. You better.
I will! I promise! *Pee* promise! You're my pee-pal!
Barf.

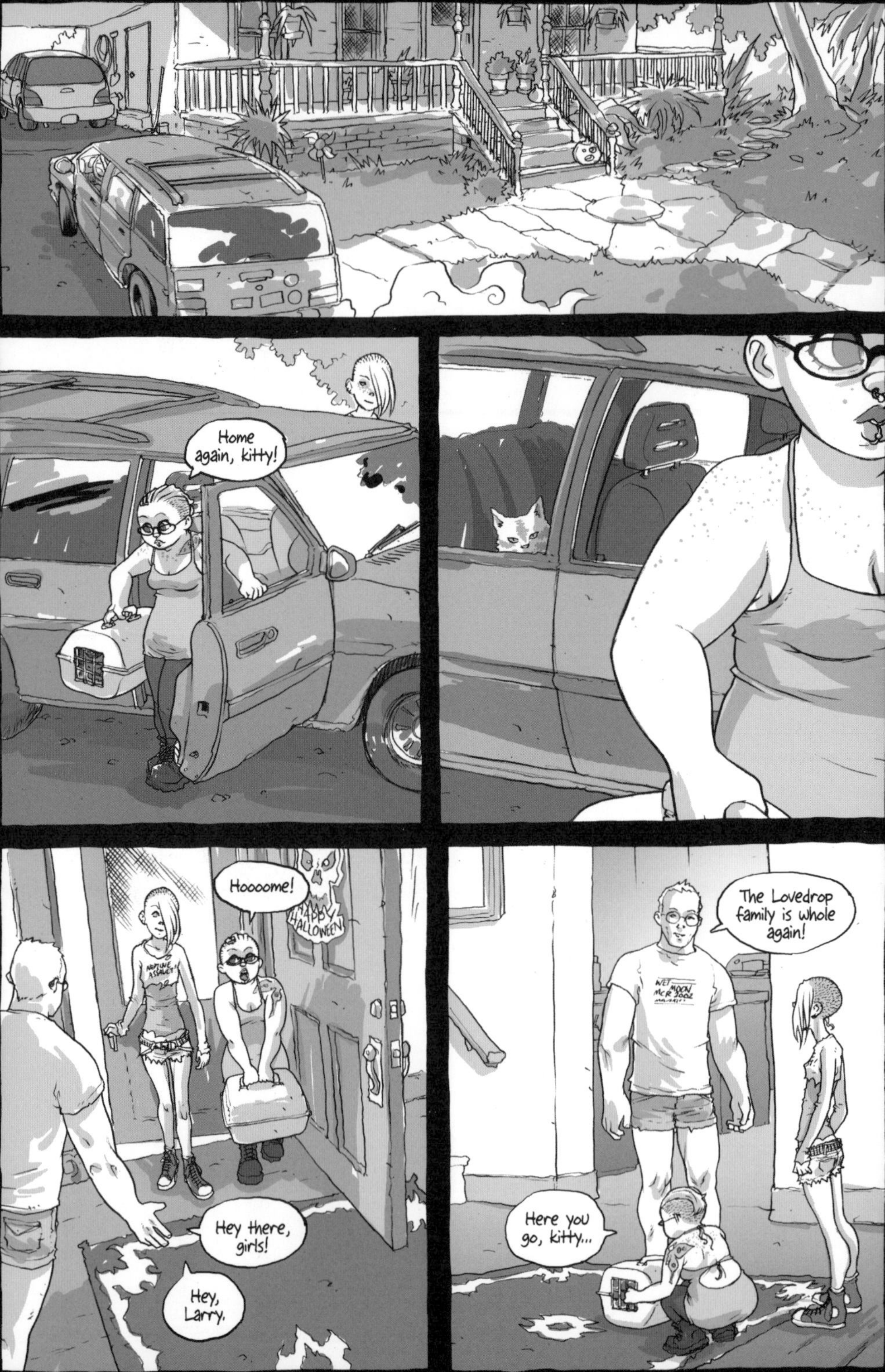

Home again, kitty!
Hoooome!
HAPPY HALLOWEEN!
The Lovedrop family is whole again!
Hey there, girls!
Hey, Larry.
Here you go, kitty...

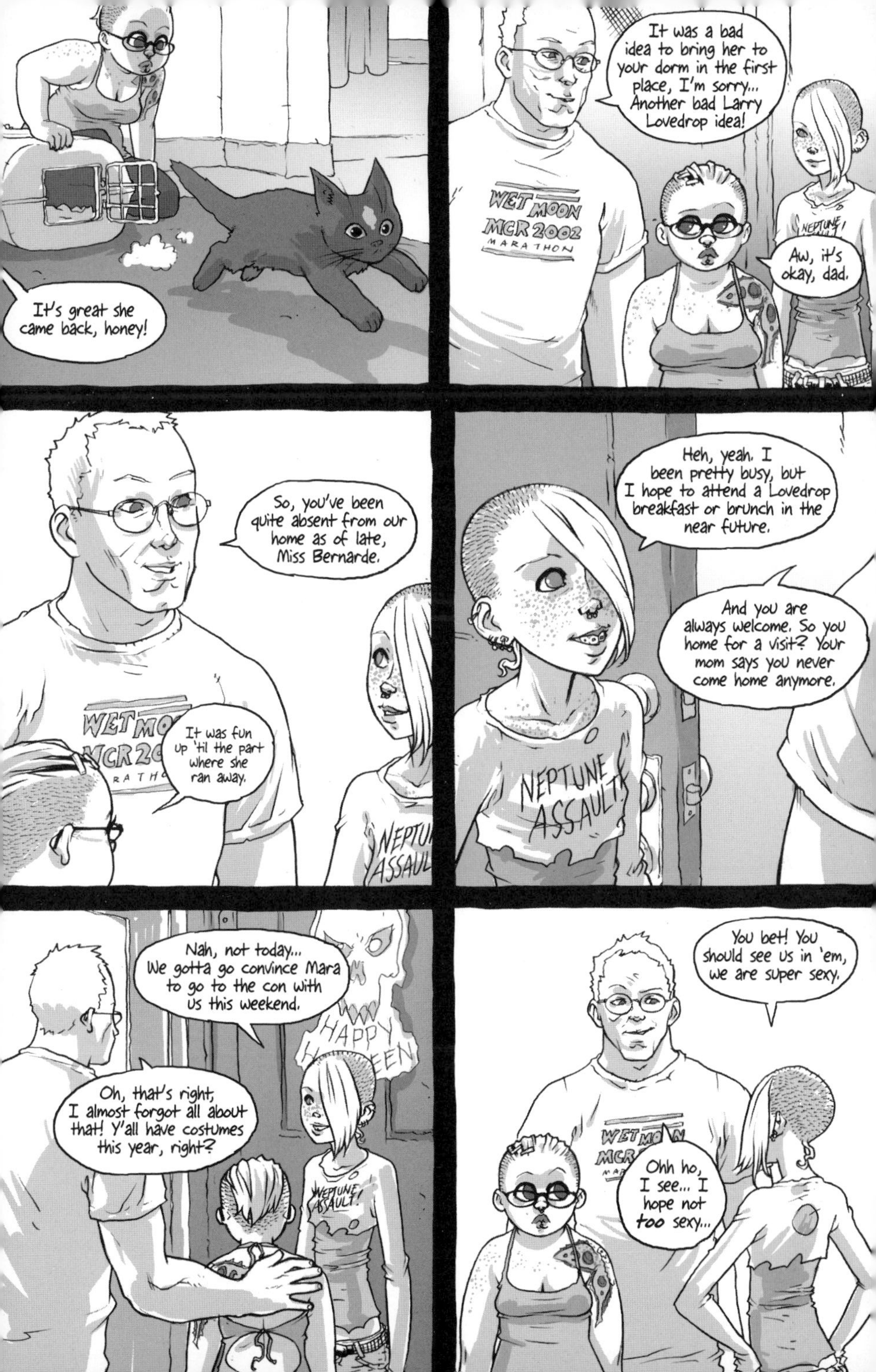
It's great she came back, honey!
It was a bad idea to bring her to your dorm in the first place, I'm sorry... Another bad Larry Lovedrop idea!
Aw, it's okay, dad.
WET MOON MCR 2002 MARATHON
So, you've been quite absent from our home as of late, Miss Bernarde.
It was fun up 'til the part where she ran away.
Heh, yeah. I been pretty busy, but I hope to attend a Lovedrop breakfast or brunch in the near future.
And you are always welcome. So you home for a visit? Your mom says you never come home anymore.
NEPTUNE ASSAULT
Nah, not today... We gotta go convince Mara to go to the con with us this weekend.
Oh, that's right, I almost forgot all about that! Y'all have costumes this year, right?
HAPPY
You bet! You should see us in 'em, we are super sexy.
Ohh ho, I see... I hope not *too* sexy...

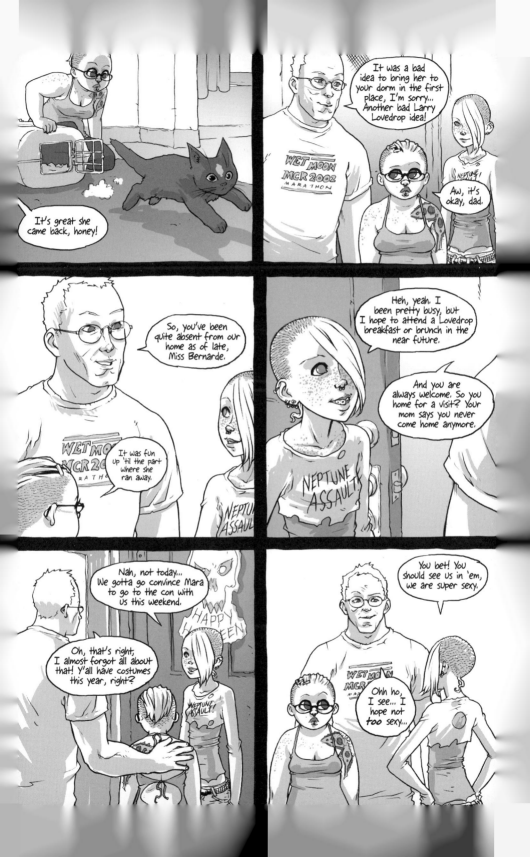

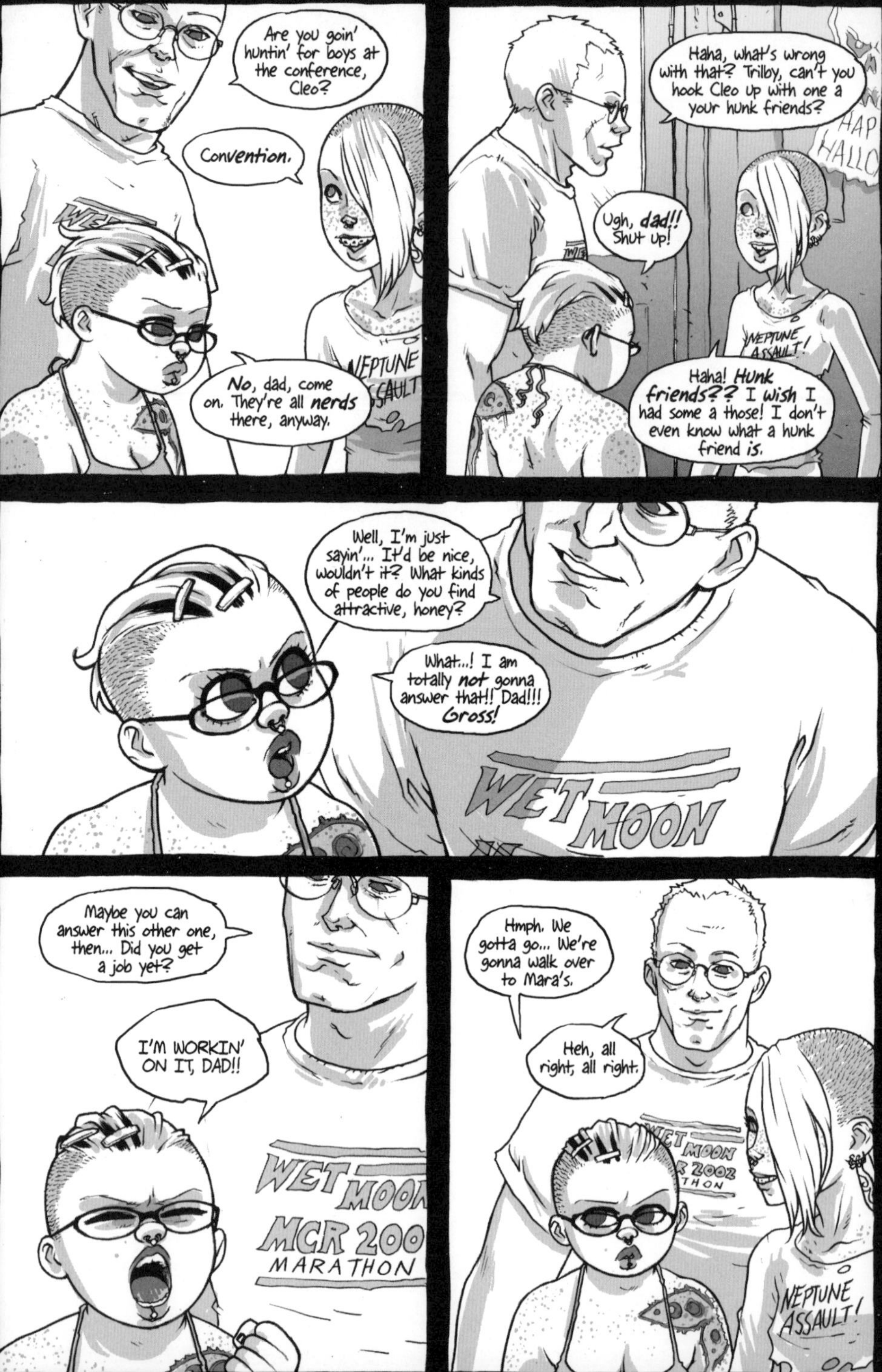

Are you goin' huntin' for boys at the conference, Cleo?
Convention.
No, dad, come on. They're all nerds there, anyway.
NEPTUNE ASSAULT
Haha, what's wrong with that? Trilby, can't you hook Cleo up with one a your hunk friends?
Ugh, dad!! Shut up!
Haha! Hunk friends?? I wish I had some a those! I don't even know what a hunk friend is.
NEPTUNE ASSAULT!
Well, I'm just sayin'... It'd be nice, wouldn't it? What kinds of people do you find attractive, honey?
What...! I am totally not gonna answer that!! Dad!!! Gross!
WET MOON
Maybe you can answer this other one, then... Did you get a job yet?
I'M WORKIN' ON IT, DAD!!
WET MOON
MARATHON
Hmph. We gotta go... We're gonna walk over to Mara's.
Heh, all right, all right.
NEPTUNE ASSAULT!

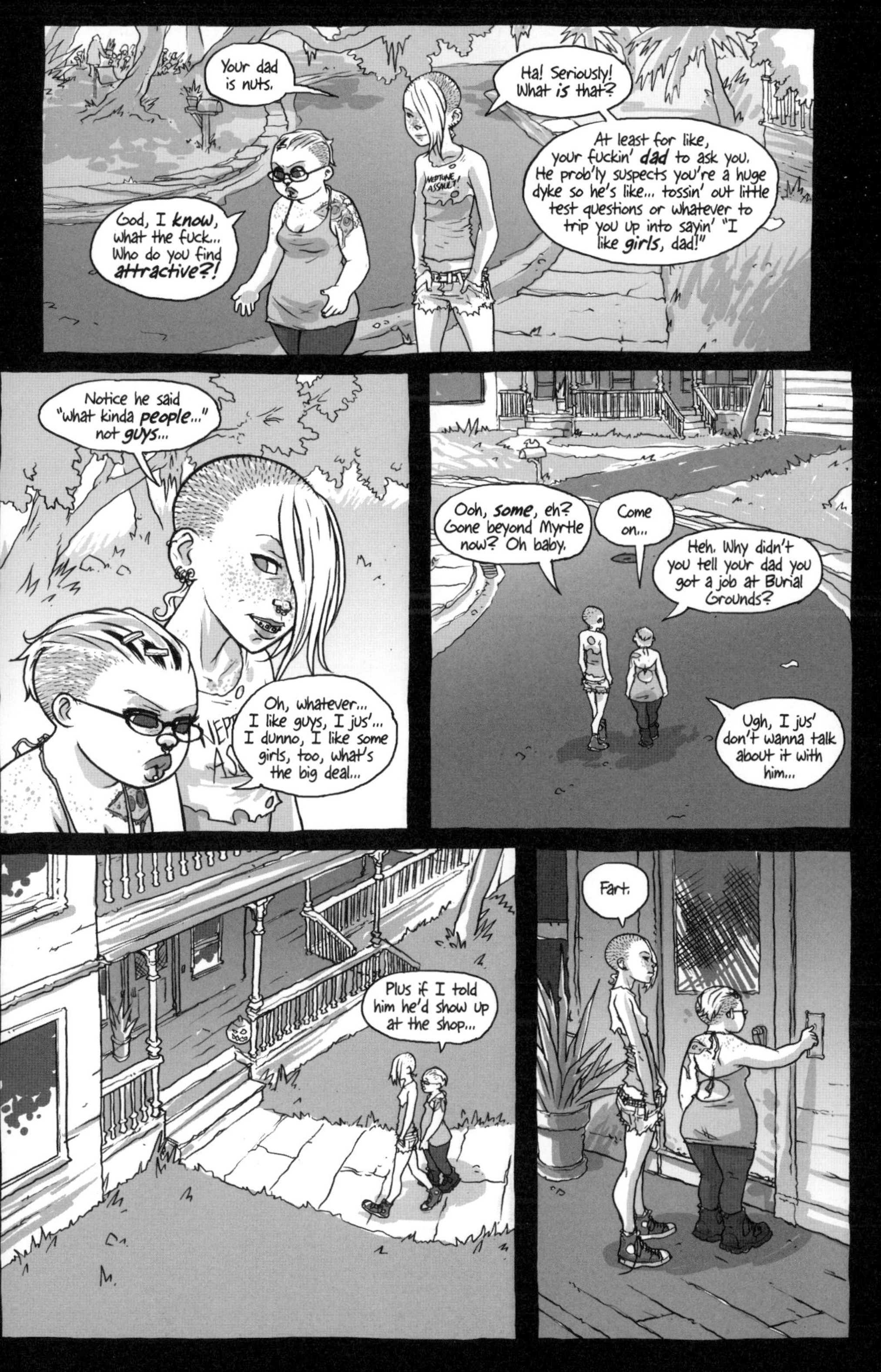
Your dad is nuts.
Ha! Seriously! What is that?
At least for like, your fuckin' dad to ask you. He prob'ly suspects you're a huge dyke so he's like... tossin' out little test questions or whatever to trip you up into sayin' "I like girls, dad!"
God, I know, what the fuck... Who do you find attractive?!
NEPTUNE ASSAULT!
Notice he said "what kinda people..." not guys...
Oh, whatever... I like guys, I jus'... I dunno, I like some girls, too, what's the big deal...
Ooh, some, eh? Gone beyond Myrtle now? Oh baby.
Come on...
Heh. Why didn't you tell your dad you got a job at Burial Grounds?
Ugh, I jus' don't wanna talk about it with him...
Plus if I told him he'd show up at the shop...
Fart.

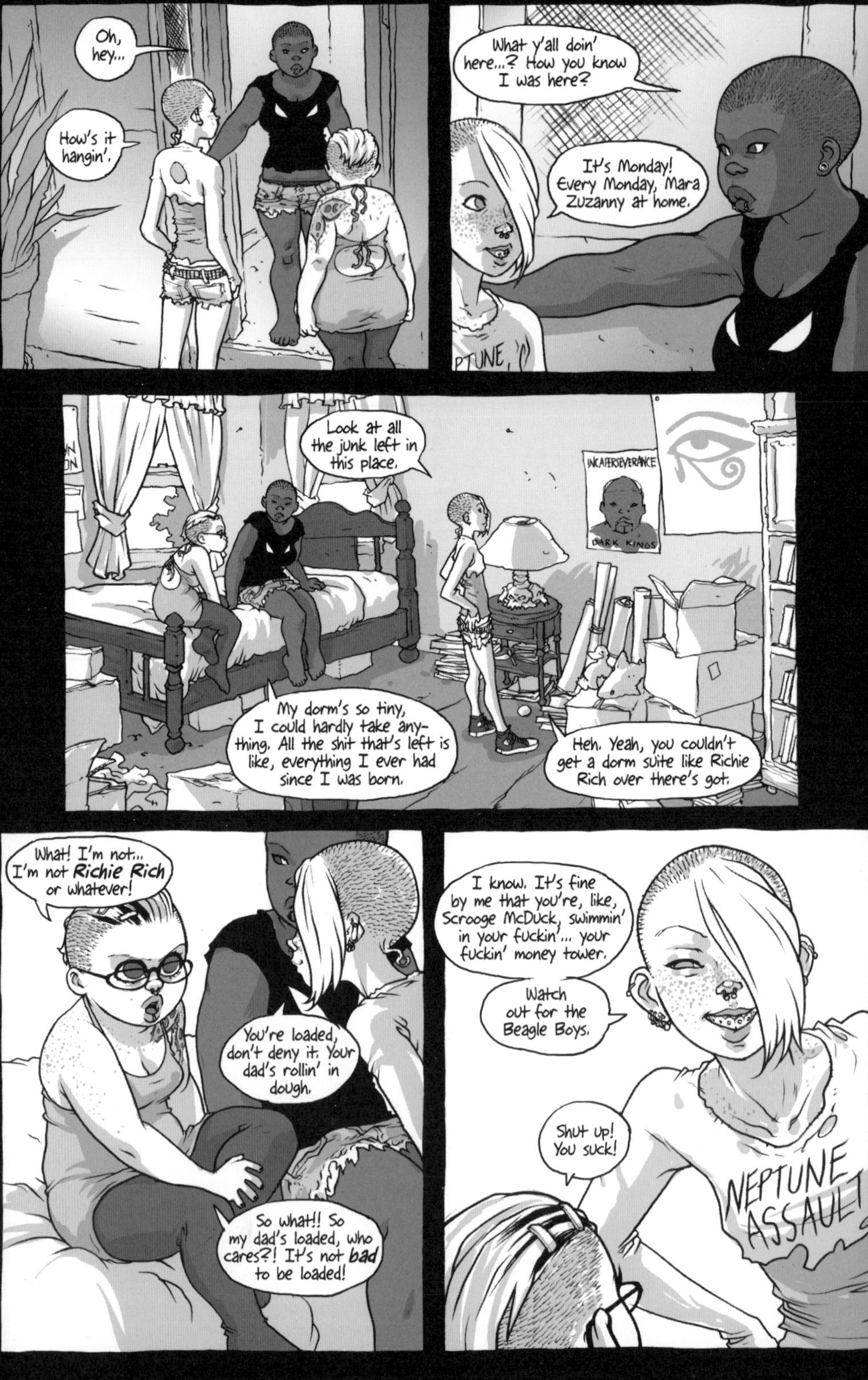

Oh, hey...
How's it hangin'.
What y'all doin' here...? How you know I was here?
It's Monday! Every Monday, Mara Zuzanny at home.
PTUNE
Look at all the junk left in this place.
INKAPERSEVERANCE
DARK KINGS
My dorm's so tiny, I could hardly take anything. All the shit that's left is like, everything I ever had since I was born.
Heh. Yeah, you couldn't get a dorm suite like Richie Rich over there's got.
What! I'm not... I'm not **Richie Rich** or whatever!
You're loaded, don't deny it. Your dad's rollin' in dough.
So what!! So my dad's loaded, who cares?! It's not **bad** to be loaded!
I know. It's fine by me that you're, like, Scrooge McDuck, swimmin' in your fuckin'... your fuckin' money tower.
Watch out for the Beagle Boys.
Shut up! You suck!
NEPTUNE ASSAULT

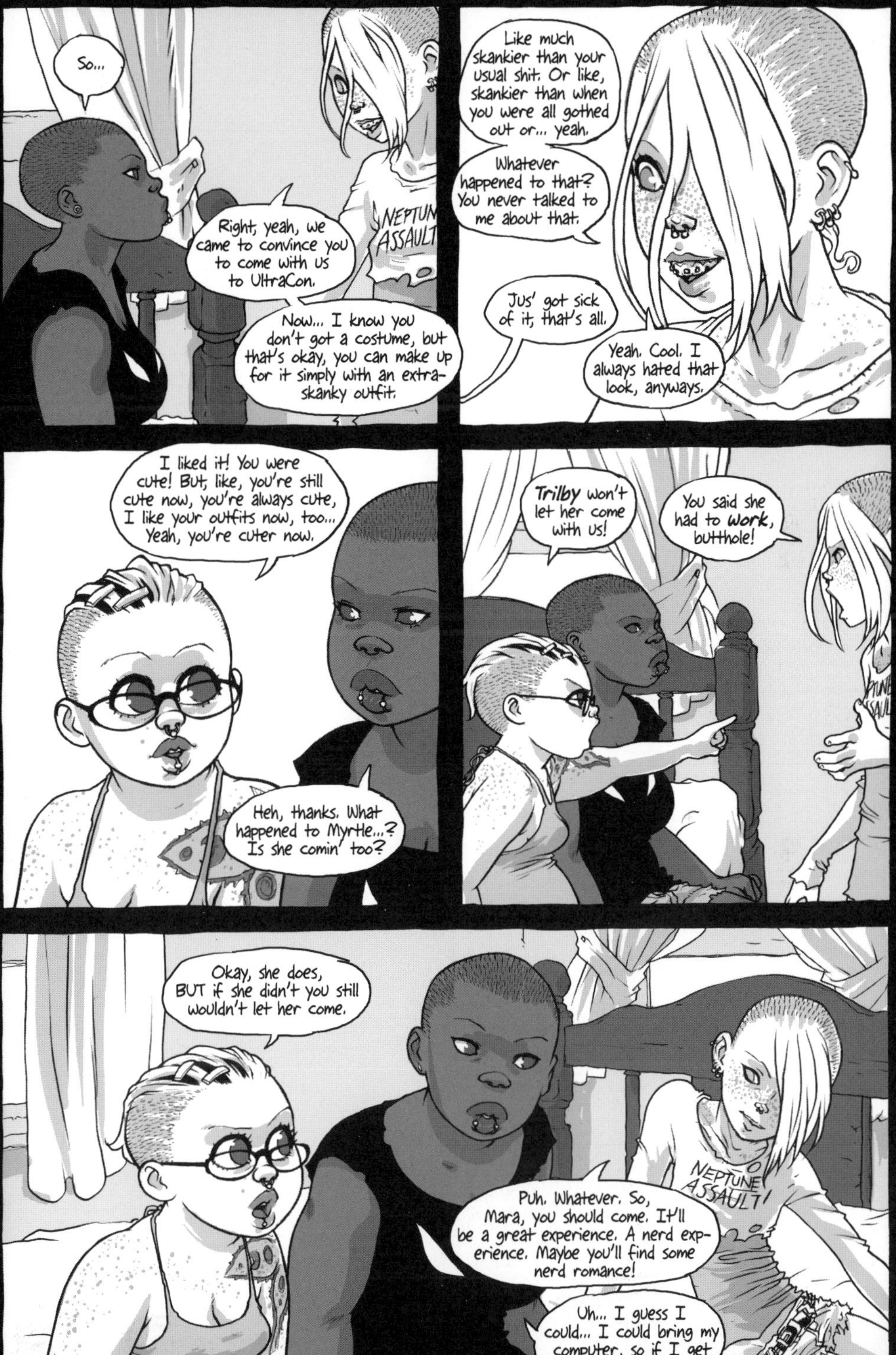

So...
Right, yeah, we came to convince you to come with us to UltraCon.
Now... I know you don't got a costume, but that's okay, you can make up for it simply with an extra-skanky outfit.
Like much skankier than your usual shit. Or like, skankier than when you were all gothed out or... yeah.
Whatever happened to that? You never talked to me about that.
Jus' got sick of it, that's all.
Yeah. Cool. I always hated that look, anyways.
NEPTUNE ASSAULT
I liked it! You were cute! But, like, you're still cute now, you're always cute, I like your outfits now, too... Yeah, you're cuter now.
Heh, thanks. What happened to Myrtle...? Is she comin' too?
Trilby won't let her come with us!
You said she had to work, butthole!
Okay, she does, BUT if she didn't you still wouldn't let her come.
NEPTUNE ASSAULT
Puh. Whatever. So, Mara, you should come. It'll be a great experience. A nerd experience. Maybe you'll find some nerd romance!
Uh... I guess I could... I could bring my computer, so if I get real bored...

October 26

MEiKO is HOME!!!

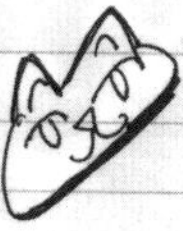

oh my god she just APPEARED!!!!! i woke up and she was there on my bed, i don't know where she came from!!! oh wow, I am so happy now. everything seems perfect now, i feel so relieved! i'm so excited i can hardly even write this! where could she have been? was she hiding out in Bowden House the whole time? is there a secret cat community she went to?? i wish she could talk or that I could understand cat language so i could know. or maybe she could write, she could use her paw in some [illegible] dirt and write what happened. i guess maybe she would only write in cat language, though. meow meow mew meow mewmew mew.

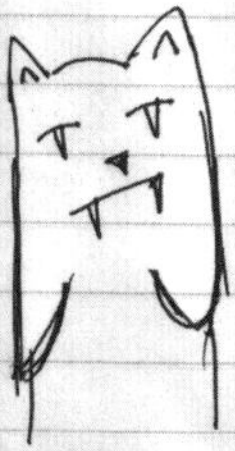

SO HAPPY!!

18

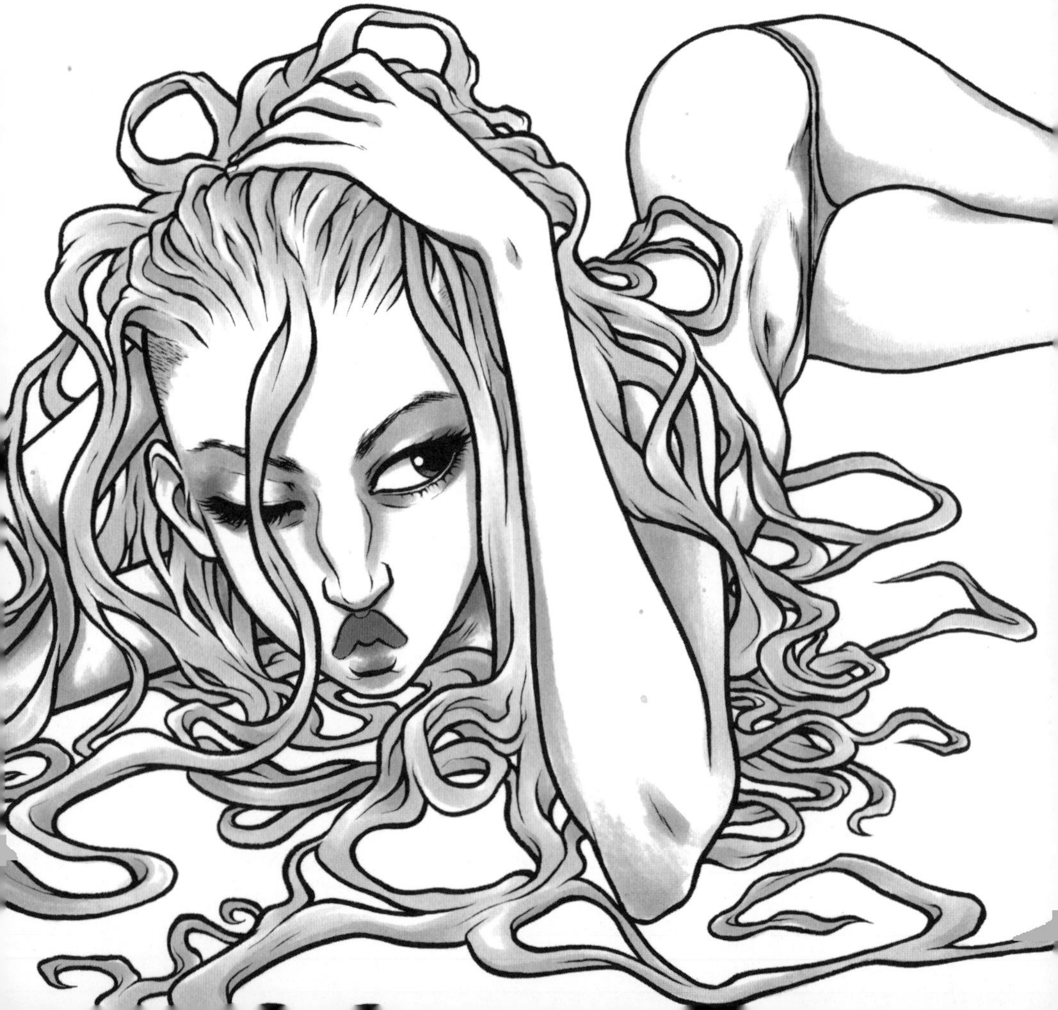

The Wonders At Your Feet

[friendtoroaches@gmail.com]

Recent Entries   Archive   Friends   User Info

mara's journal

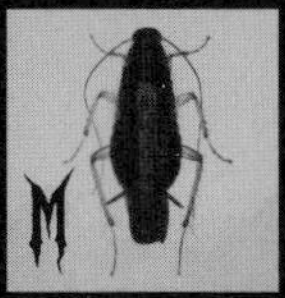
M

profile

October 28th, 1:31am

CATHODE RAYS BLAST LIKE METEOR RAIN TO MY BRAIN.

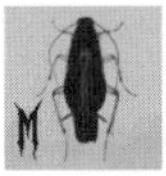
M

i think everythings good with Natalie now. we hung out today for a little while it was cool. but also weird because she lives in the same dorm as Cleo so i felt like i was sneaking around or something. i don't think Cleo was home like usual. Natalie is so skinny. she is so skinny it's painful. i wonder if she's anorexic or something. she wants me to be her model for her photo project, i don't know what i think about that. i'm real flattered on one hand, but totally nervous and weird on the other. why does she want me for the project? she could find a billion other girls who are prettier or hotter or whatever. i don't know. i hope it's not a nude photo shoot. i don't know what the fuck i'd do then. actually i guess it wouldn't be so bad. i'd probably get over it quick. at least i got a little bit of muscle now. anyway i'm glad it looks like we're friends now. i'll probably fuck it up later on though. maybe i should make this post friends-only.

softball is going great. i am excited for the Armadillo game but also scared, i don't know if we can win. i think pretty much everyone on our team smokes, me included, we won't be able to breathe out there. except Trilby. she used to smoke a little but one day she went "i'm quitting" and the next day she really did and she never smoked again. how did she do that. i haven't had any luck quitting so far but i'm really trying. i really want to be able to run really far.

i've been reseraching a lot about ancient Egypt recently. partly because it's cool and partly because i think i want my first film for class to have something to do with Egypt. i wish i could set it IN Egypt, but obviously i cant get over there. i thought at first something with a mummy, but not a super magic world domination wizard mummy like in those Mummy movies. like a fucking badass serious intense elder evil shambling mummy who comes out of a fucking tomb.

mood: nervous
current music: sonic syndicate - only inhuman

[0 comments | leave a comment]

October 23rd, 11:12pm

PEOPLE ARE BEING MURDERED RIGHT NOW.

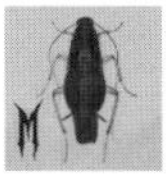
M

my serial killer screenplay is halfway finished. i thought about changing things a little and having TWO killers instead of one, since pretty much every killer story always seems to have only one. but i think i'll probably stick with that and keep the one like i have. i'm really excited to shoot this but i don't know when or if it will ever happen. i think the money part would be easy because there aren't any special effects except blood and no sets have to be built, it's all basic guerilla type filmmaking. i'm just worried about finding actors and a good camera and people willing to put effort in when they're not being paid much or at all. when it's not a job it's easy for people to blow it off.

i hate people who stomp insects and spiders. i read an article the other day about animals, insects too, having personalities. i think i've always thought that way but i guess it's a more scientific idea now with evidence and everything. i hate how people separate animals into the ones they like and they don't, like if an animal is cute they like it but if an animal is gross or loathsome they don't give two shits about it and will kill them without hesitation. but what is the difference? how is a "nice" bug like a ladybug that everyone likes any more threatening than a moth or housefly? or when somebody eats a cow it's okay, but if they eat a dog people flip out about it because dogs are "cute" and used as pets. i think part of it has to do with people projecting human traits onto animals and seeing themselves in a dog or cat, but it's hard for people to do that with more "alien" creatures like insects. but not

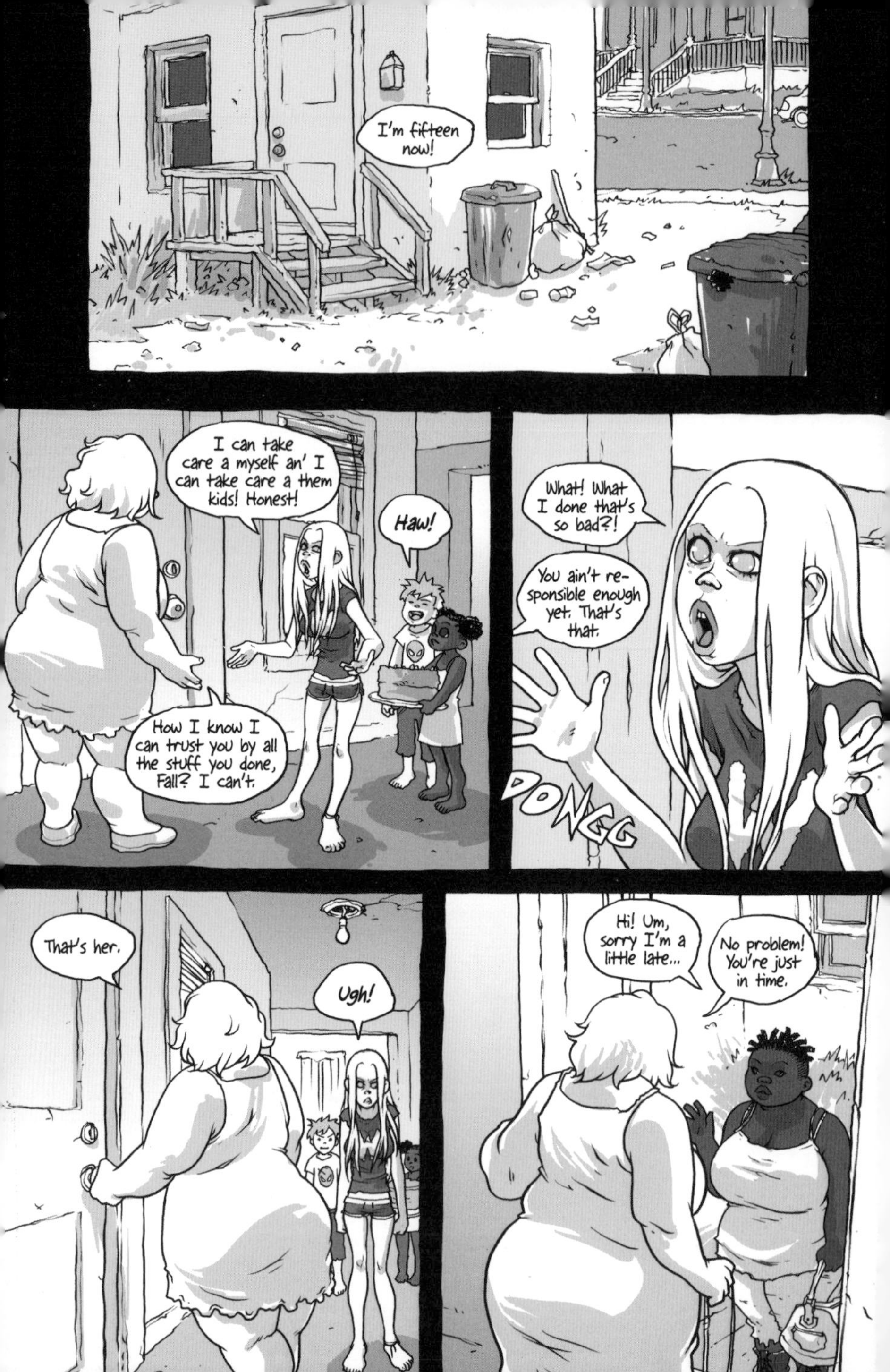
I'm fifteen now!
I can take care a myself an' I can take care a them kids! Honest!
Haw!
How I know I can trust you by all the stuff you done, Fall? I can't.
What! What I done that's so bad?!
You ain't responsible enough yet. That's that.
DONGG
That's her.
Ugh!
Hi! Um, sorry I'm a little late...
No problem! You're just in time.

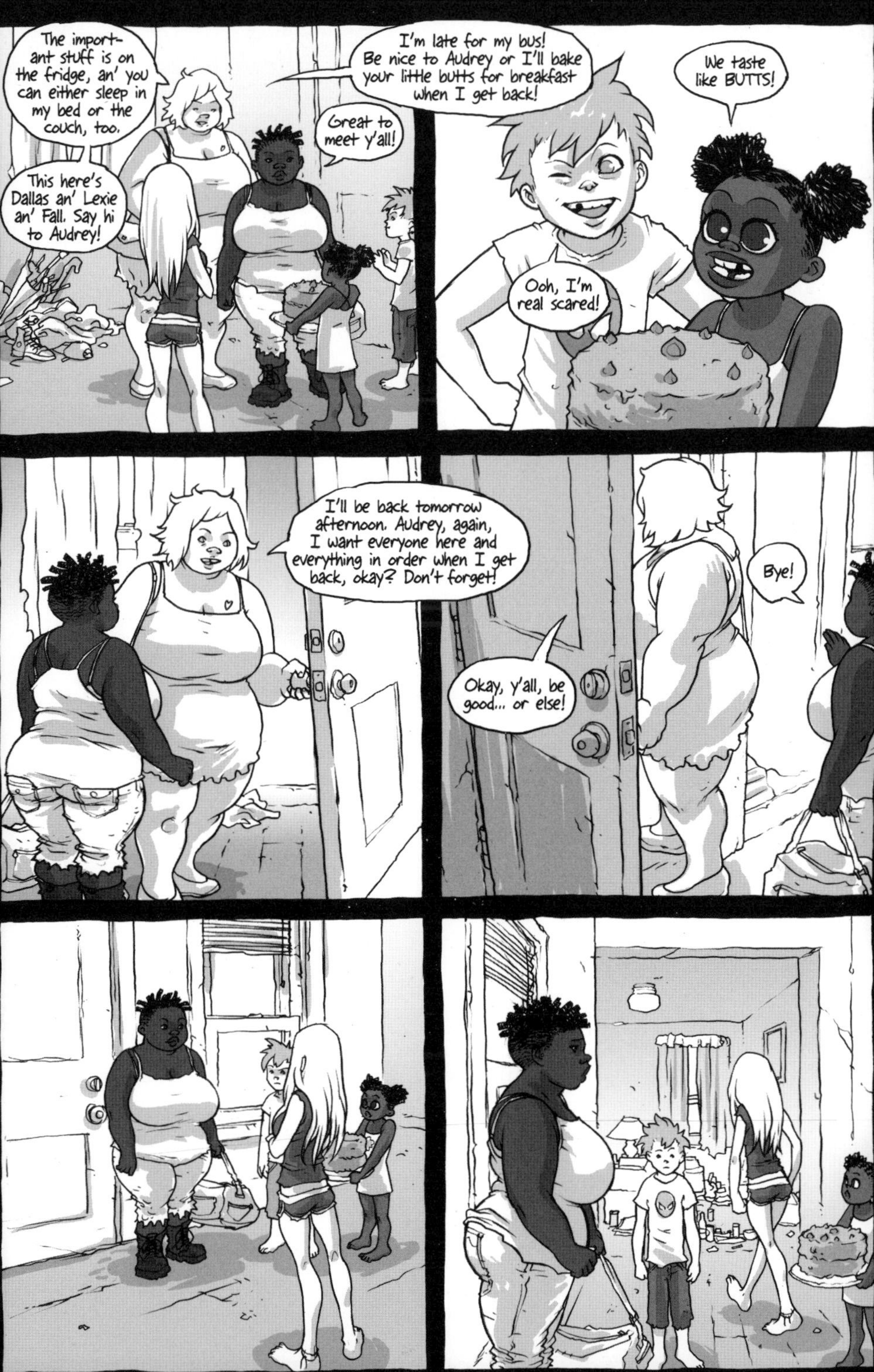

The import-ant stuff is on the fridge, an' you can either sleep in my bed or the couch, too.
This here's Dallas an' Lexie an' Fall. Say hi to Audrey!
Great to meet y'all!
I'm late for my bus! Be nice to Audrey or I'll bake your little butts for breakfast when I get back!
We taste like BUTTS!
Ooh, I'm real scared!
I'll be back tomorrow afternoon. Audrey, again, I want everyone here and everything in order when I get back, okay? Don't forget!
Bye!
Okay, y'all, be good... or else!

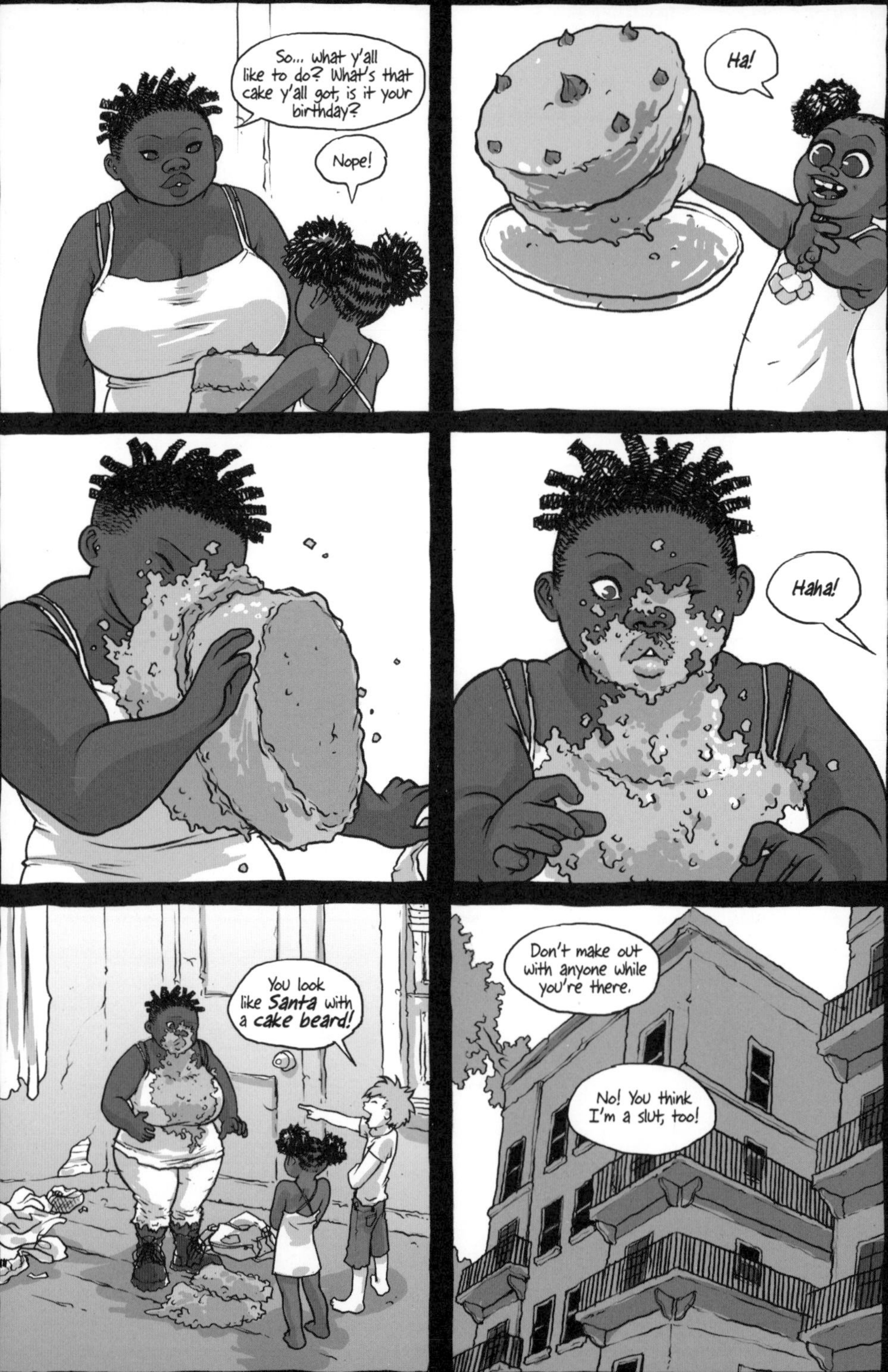
So... what y'all like to do? What's that cake y'all got, is it your birthday?
Nope!
Ha!
Haha!
You look like Santa with a cake beard!
Don't make out with anyone while you're there.
No! You think I'm a slut, too!

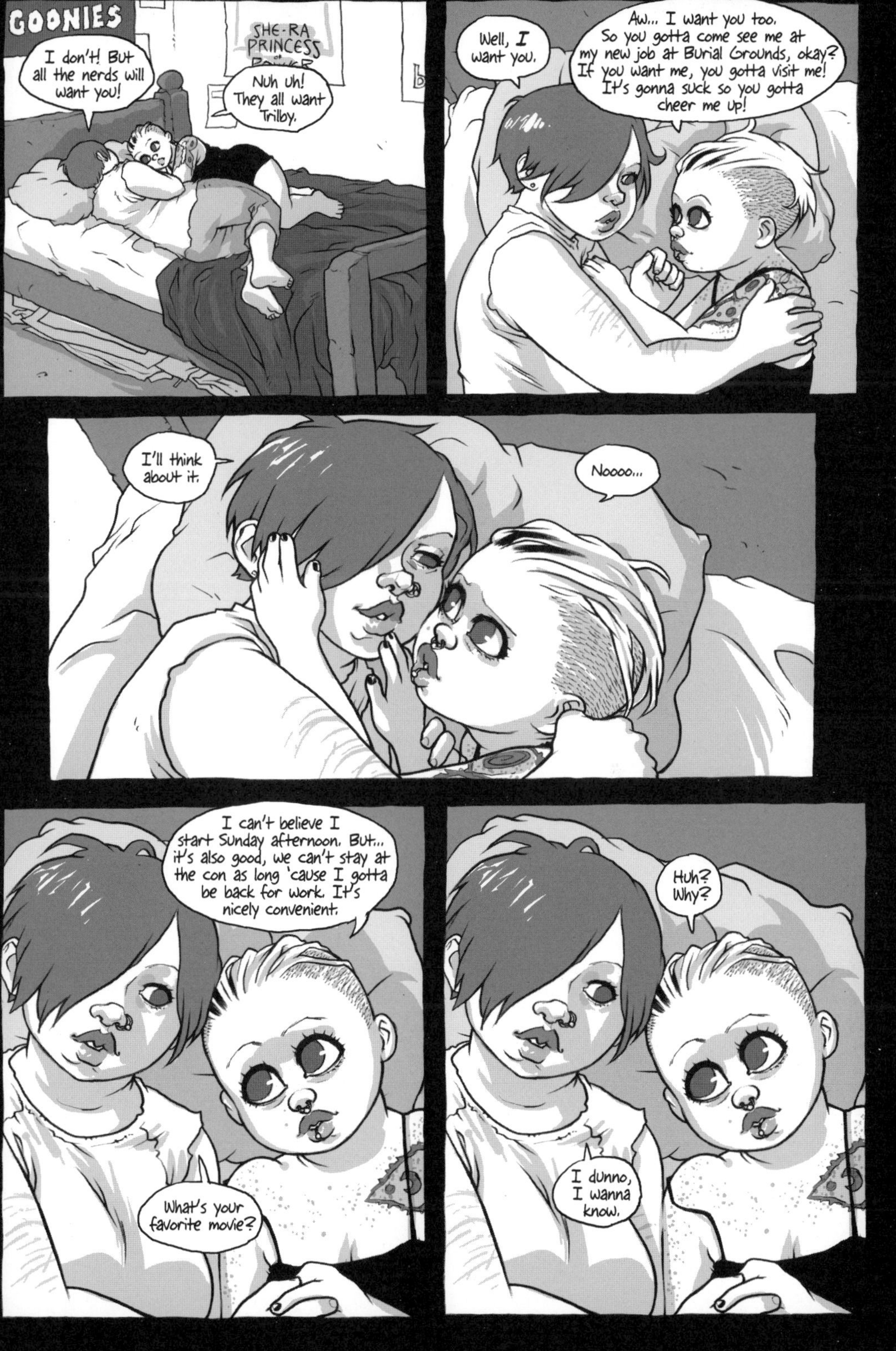
GOONIES
SHE-RA PRINCESS
I don't! But all the nerds will want you!
Nuh uh! They all want Trilby.
Well, I want you.
Aw... I want you too. So you gotta come see me at my new job at Burial Grounds, okay? If you want me, you gotta visit me! It's gonna suck so you gotta cheer me up!
I'll think about it.
Noooo...
I can't believe I start Sunday afternoon. But... it's also good, we can't stay at the con as long 'cause I gotta be back for work. It's nicely convenient.
What's your favorite movie?
Huh? Why?
I dunno, I wanna know.

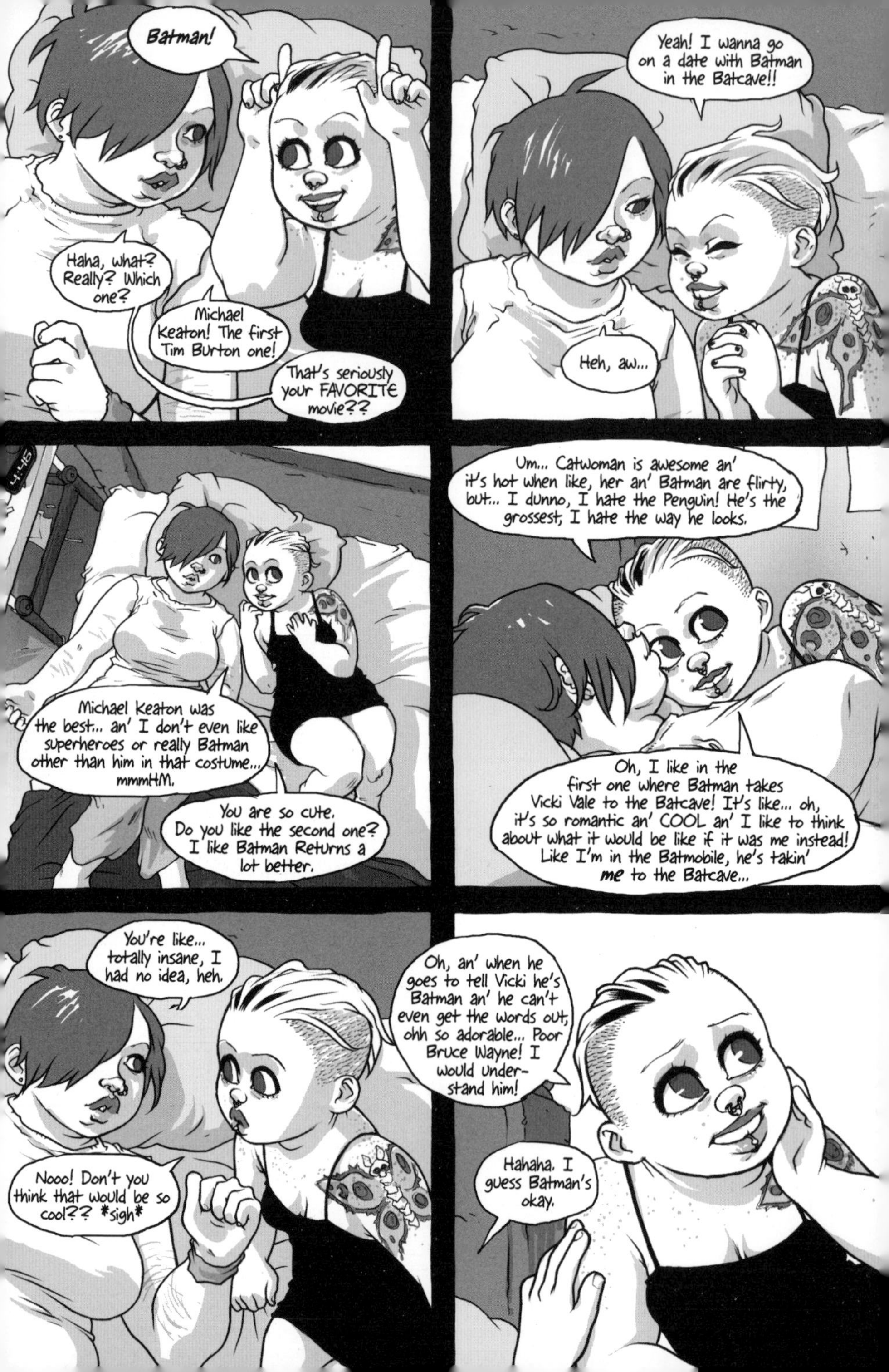
Batman!
Haha, what? Really? Which one?
Michael Keaton! The first Tim Burton one!
That's seriously your FAVORITE movie??
Yeah! I wanna go on a date with Batman in the Batcave!!
Heh, aw...
Michael Keaton was the best... an' I don't even like superheroes or really Batman other than him in that costume... mmmHM.
You are so cute. Do you like the second one? I like Batman Returns a lot better.
Um... Catwoman is awesome an' it's hot when like, her an' Batman are flirty, but... I dunno, I hate the Penguin! He's the grossest, I hate the way he looks.
Oh, I like in the first one where Batman takes Vicki Vale to the Batcave! It's like... oh, it's so romantic an' COOL an' I like to think about what it would be like if it was me instead! Like I'm in the Batmobile, he's takin' *me* to the Batcave...
You're like... totally insane, I had no idea, heh.
Nooo! Don't you think that would be so cool?? *sigh*
Oh, an' when he goes to tell Vicki he's Batman an' he can't even get the words out, ohh so adorable... Poor Bruce Wayne! I would under-stand him!
Hahaha. I guess Batman's okay.

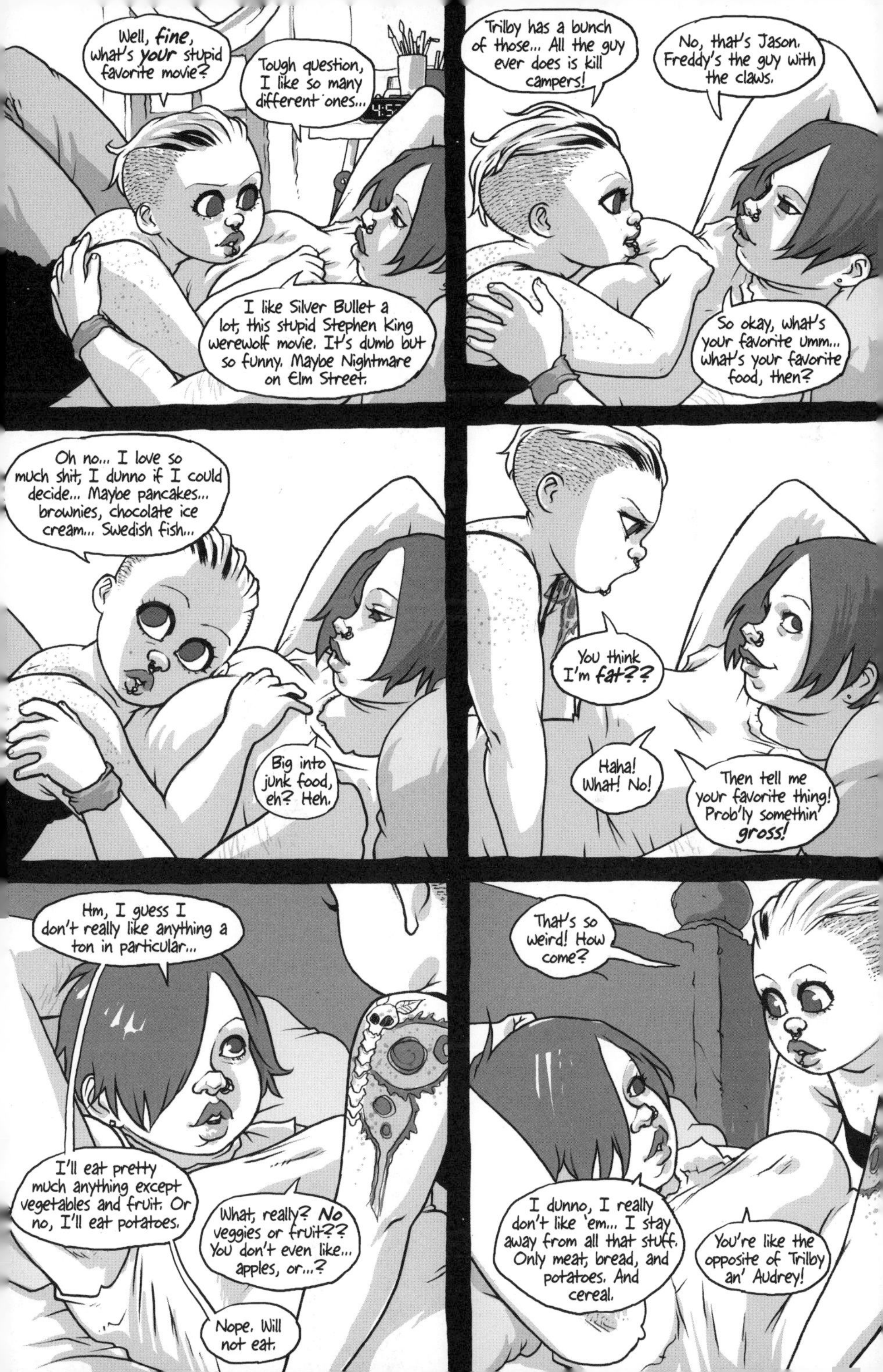
Well, *fine*, what's *your* stupid favorite movie?
Tough question, I like so many different ones...
I like Silver Bullet a lot, this stupid Stephen King werewolf movie. It's dumb but so funny. Maybe Nightmare on Elm Street.
Trilby has a bunch of those... All the guy ever does is kill campers!
No, that's Jason. Freddy's the guy with the claws.
So okay, what's your favorite umm... what's your favorite food, then?
Oh no... I love so much shit, I dunno if I could decide... Maybe pancakes... brownies, chocolate ice cream... Swedish fish...
Big into junk food, eh? Heh.
You think I'm *fat??*
Haha! What! No!
Then tell me your favorite thing! Prob'ly somethin' *gross!*
Hm, I guess I don't really like anything a ton in particular...
I'll eat pretty much anything except vegetables and fruit. Or no, I'll eat potatoes.
What, really? *No* veggies or fruit?? You don't even like... apples, or...?
Nope. Will not eat.
That's so weird! How come?
I dunno, I really don't like 'em... I stay away from all that stuff. Only meat, bread, and potatoes. And cereal.
You're like the opposite of Trilby an' Audrey!

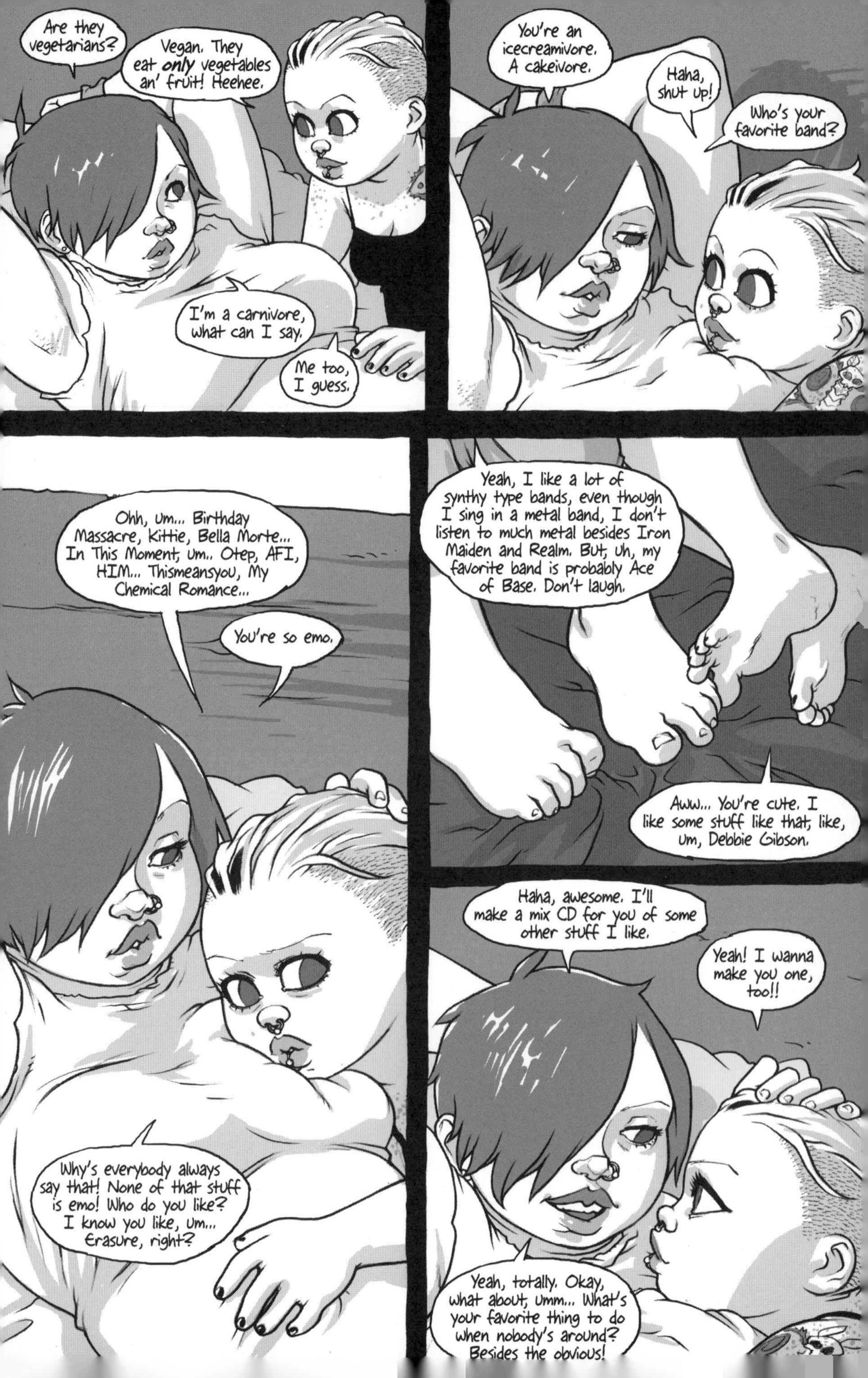
Are they vegetarians?
Vegan. They eat only vegetables an' fruit! Heehee.
I'm a carnivore, what can I say.
Me too, I guess.
You're an icecreamivore. A cakeivore.
Haha, shut up!
Who's your favorite band?
Ohh, um... Birthday Massacre, Kittie, Bella Morte... In This Moment, um.. Otep, AFI, HIM... Thismeansyou, My Chemical Romance...
You're so emo.
Why's everybody always say that! None of that stuff is emo! Who do you like? I know you like, um... Erasure, right?
Yeah, I like a lot of synthy type bands, even though I sing in a metal band, I don't listen to much metal besides Iron Maiden and Realm. But, uh, my favorite band is probably Ace of Base. Don't laugh.
Aww... You're cute. I like some stuff like that, like, um, Debbie Gibson.
Haha, awesome. I'll make a mix CD for you of some other stuff I like.
Yeah! I wanna make you one, too!!
Yeah, totally. Okay, what about, umm... What's your favorite thing to do when nobody's around? Besides the obvious!

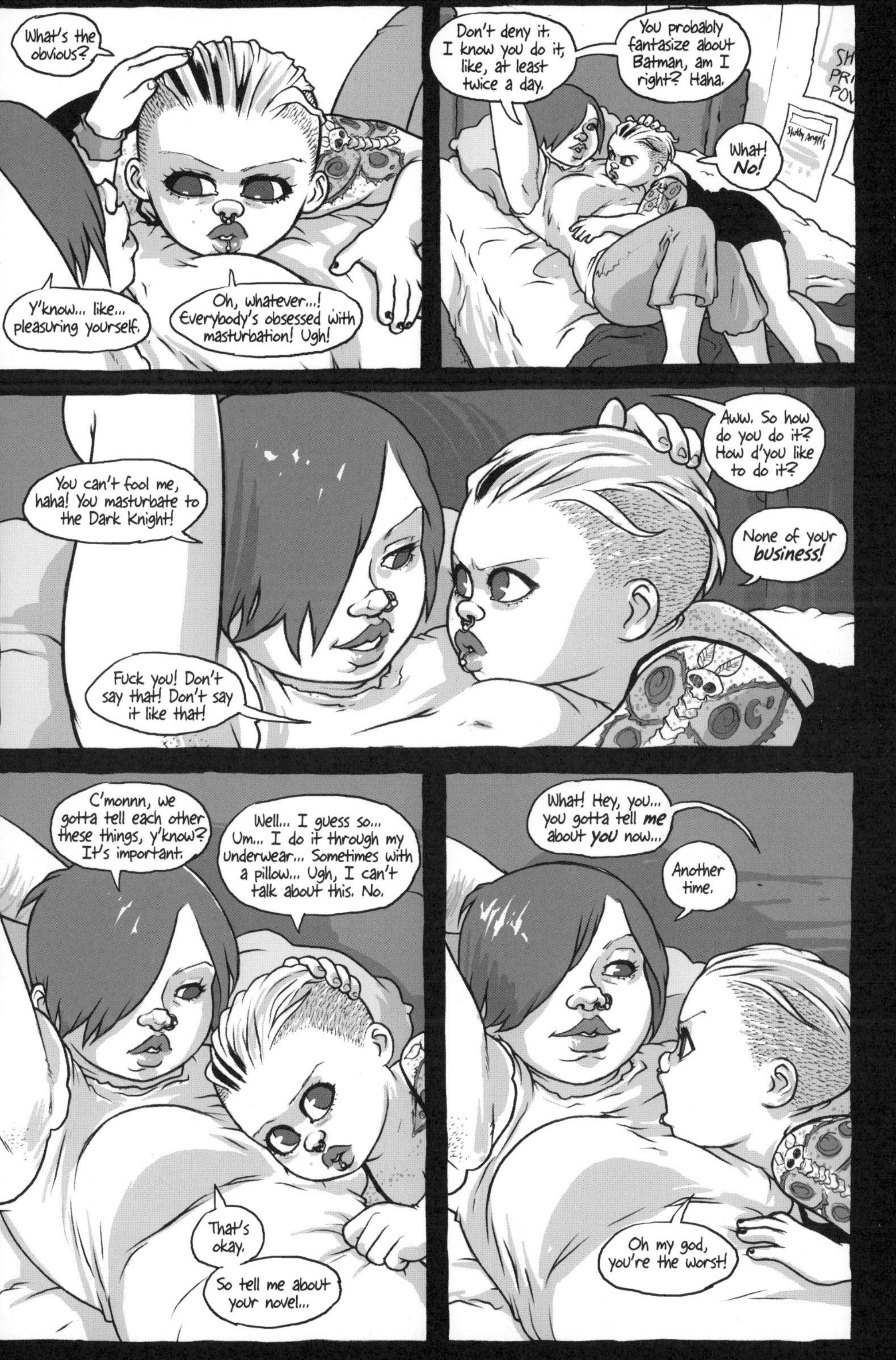
What's the obvious?
Y'know... like... pleasuring yourself.
Oh, whatever...! Everybody's obsessed with masturbation! Ugh!
Don't deny it. I know you do it, like, at least twice a day.
You probably fantasize about Batman, am I right? Haha.
What! No!
You can't fool me, haha! You masturbate to the Dark Knight!
Fuck you! Don't say that! Don't say it like that!
Aww. So how do you do it? How d'you like to do it?
None of your business!
C'monnn, we gotta tell each other these things, y'know? It's important.
Well... I guess so... Um... I do it through my underwear... Sometimes with a pillow... Ugh, I can't talk about this. No.
That's okay.
So tell me about your novel...
What! Hey, you... you gotta tell me about you now...
Another time.
Oh my god, you're the worst!

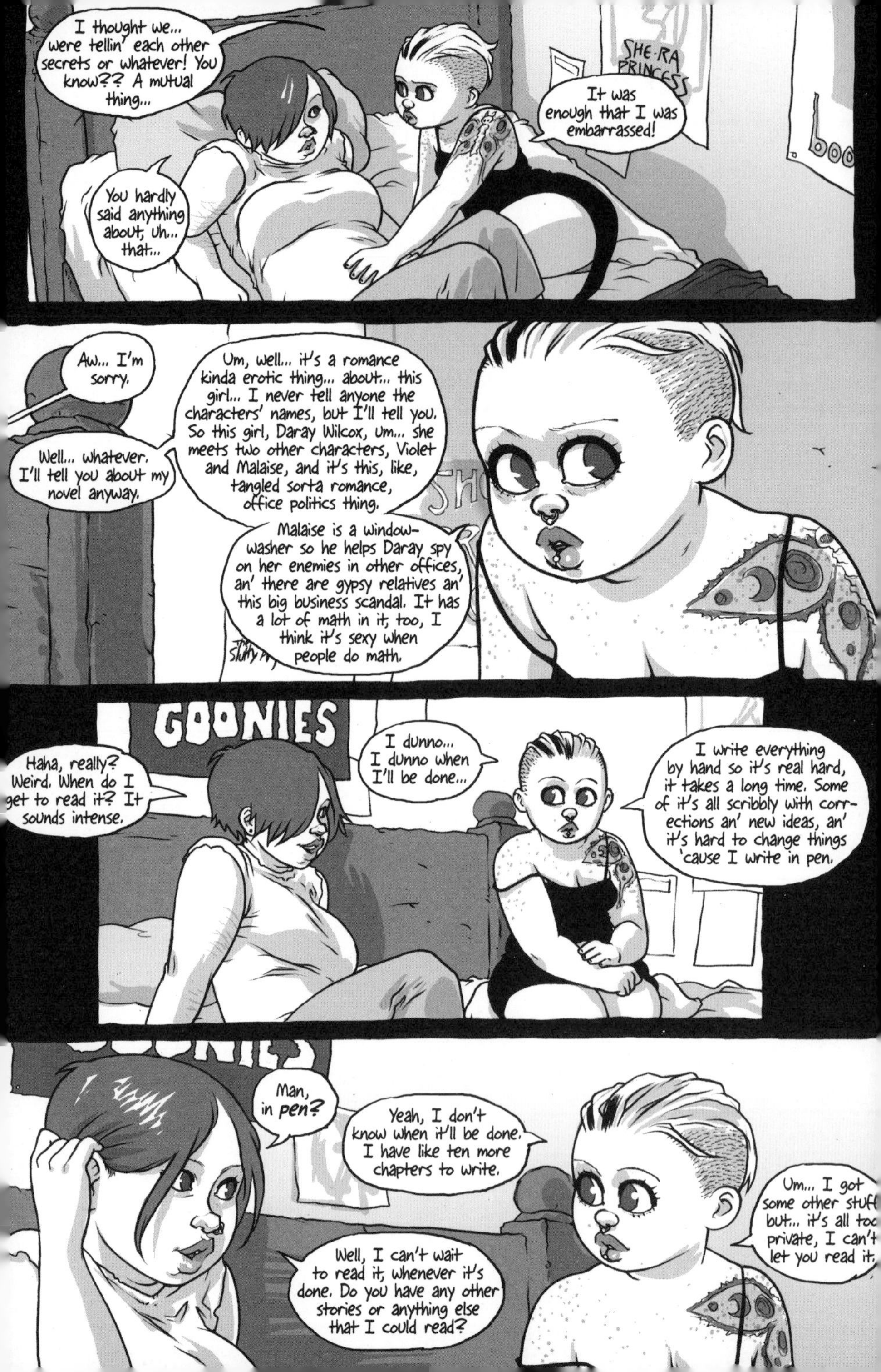

I thought we... were tellin' each other secrets or whatever! You know?? A mutual thing...
SHE-RA PRINCESS
It was enough that I was embarrassed!
You hardly said anything about, uh... that...
Aw... I'm sorry.
Well... whatever. I'll tell you about my novel anyway.
Um, well... it's a romance kinda erotic thing... about... this girl... I never tell anyone the characters' names, but I'll tell you. So this girl, Daray Wilcox, um... she meets two other characters, Violet and Malaise, and it's this, like, tangled sorta romance, office politics thing.
Malaise is a window-washer so he helps Daray spy on her enemies in other offices, an' there are gypsy relatives an' this big business scandal. It has a lot of math in it, too, I think it's sexy when people do math.
GOONIES
Haha, really? Weird. When do I get to read it? It sounds intense.
I dunno... I dunno when I'll be done...
I write everything by hand so it's real hard, it takes a long time. Some of it's all scribbly with corrections an' new ideas, an' it's hard to change things 'cause I write in pen.
Man, in *pen*?
Yeah, I don't know when it'll be done. I have like ten more chapters to write.
Um... I got some other stuff but... it's all too private, I can't let you read it.
Well, I can't wait to read it, whenever it's done. Do you have any other stories or anything else that I could read?

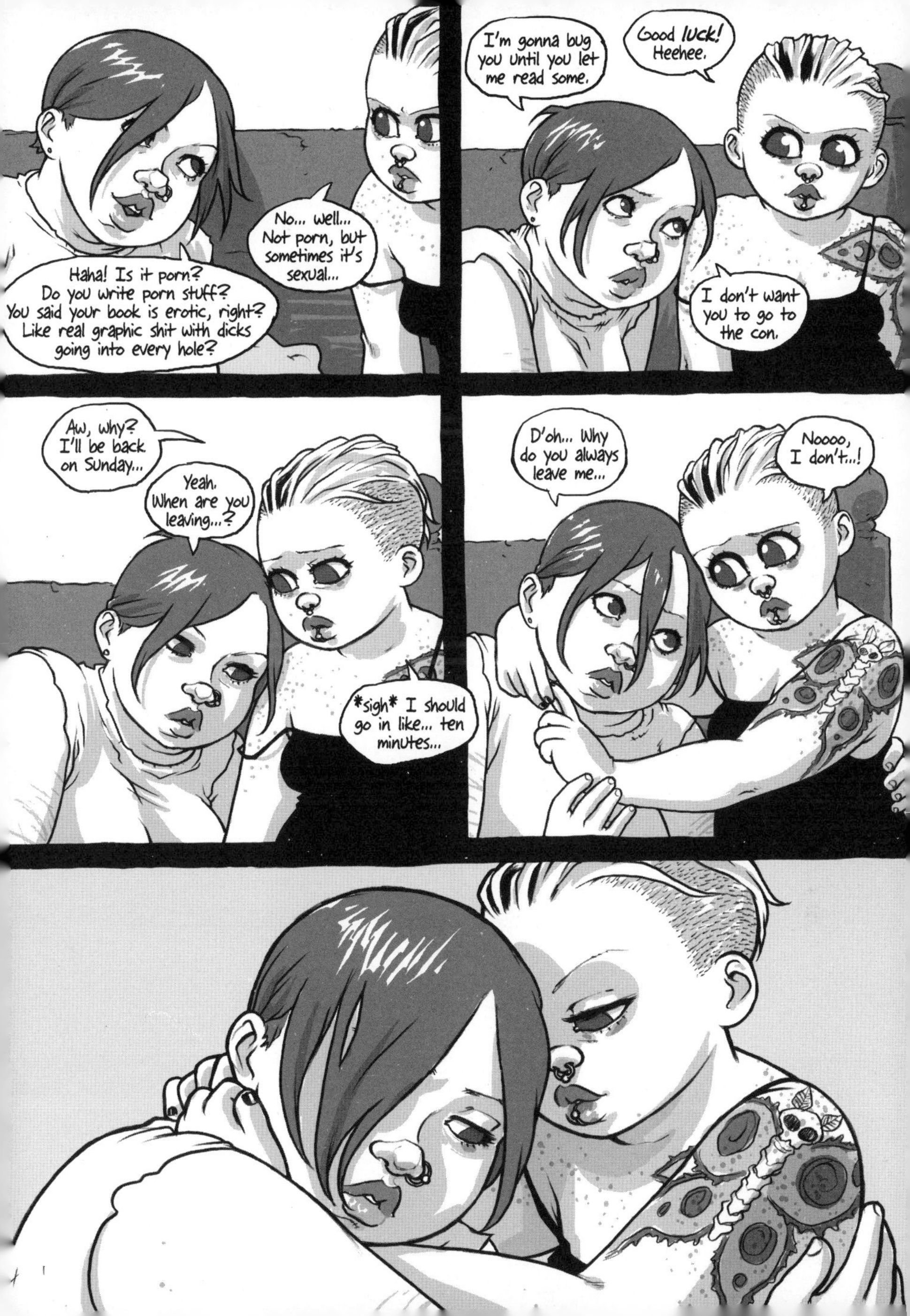
Haha! Is it porn?
Do you write porn stuff?
You said your book is erotic, right?
Like real graphic shit with dicks
going into every hole?
No... well...
Not porn, but
sometimes it's
sexual...
I'm gonna bug
you until you let
me read some.
Good luck!
Heehee.
I don't want
you to go to
the con.
Aw, why?
I'll be back
on Sunday...
Yeah.
When are you
leaving...?
sigh I should
go in like... ten
minutes...
D'oh... Why
do you always
leave me...
Noooo,
I don't...!

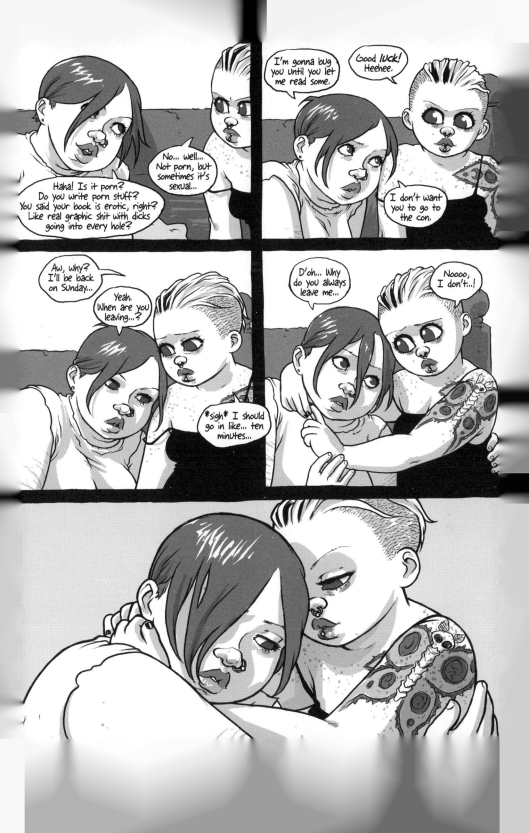

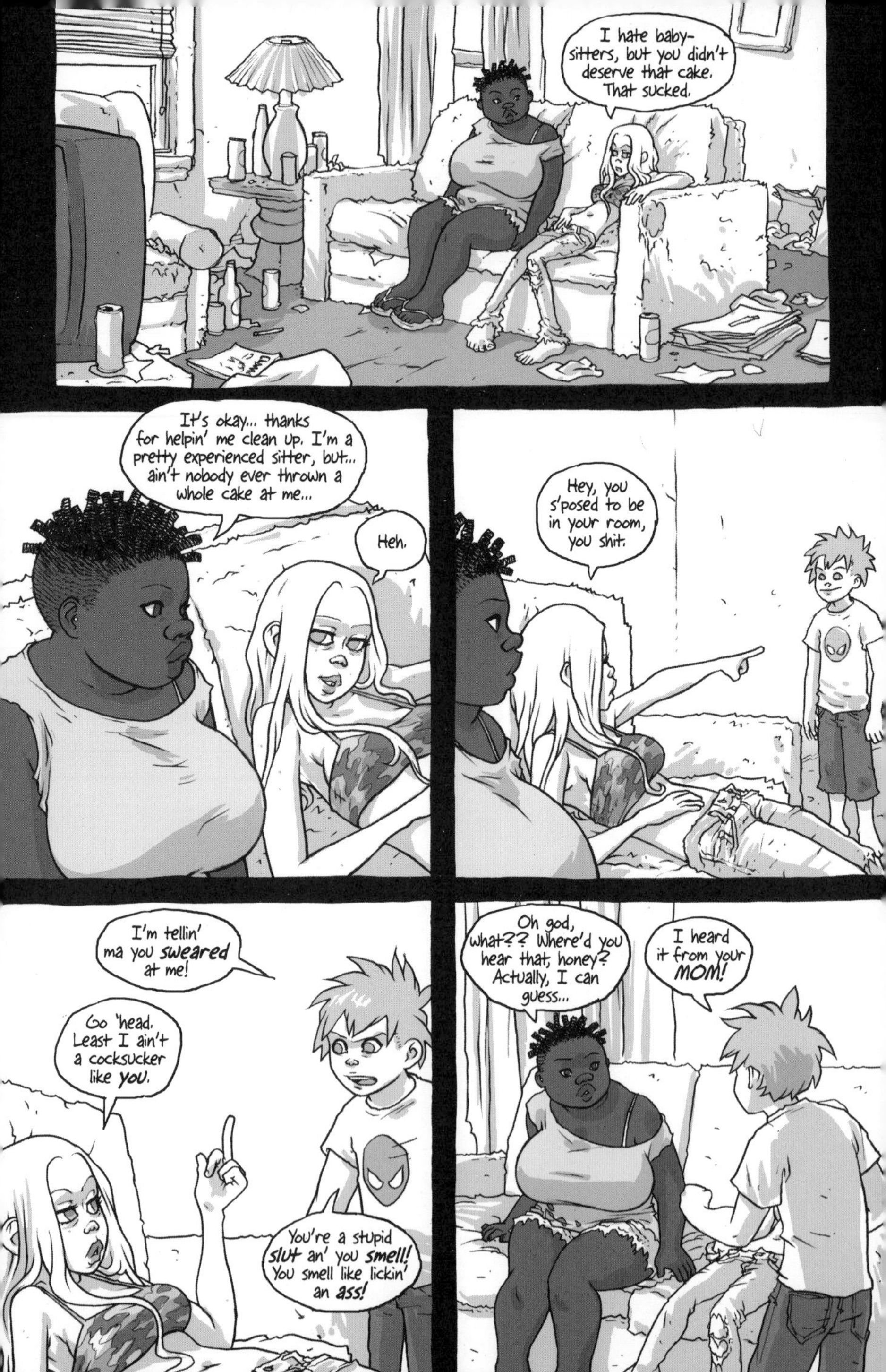
I hate baby-sitters, but you didn't deserve that cake. That sucked.
It's okay... thanks for helpin' me clean up. I'm a pretty experienced sitter, but... ain't nobody ever thrown a whole cake at me...
Heh.
Hey, you s'posed to be in your room, you shit.
I'm tellin' ma you **swearED** at me!
Go 'head. Least I ain't a cocksucker like **you**.
You're a stupid **slut** an' you **smell!** You smell like lickin' an **ass!**
Oh god, what?? Where'd you hear that, honey? Actually, I can guess...
I heard it from your **MOM!**

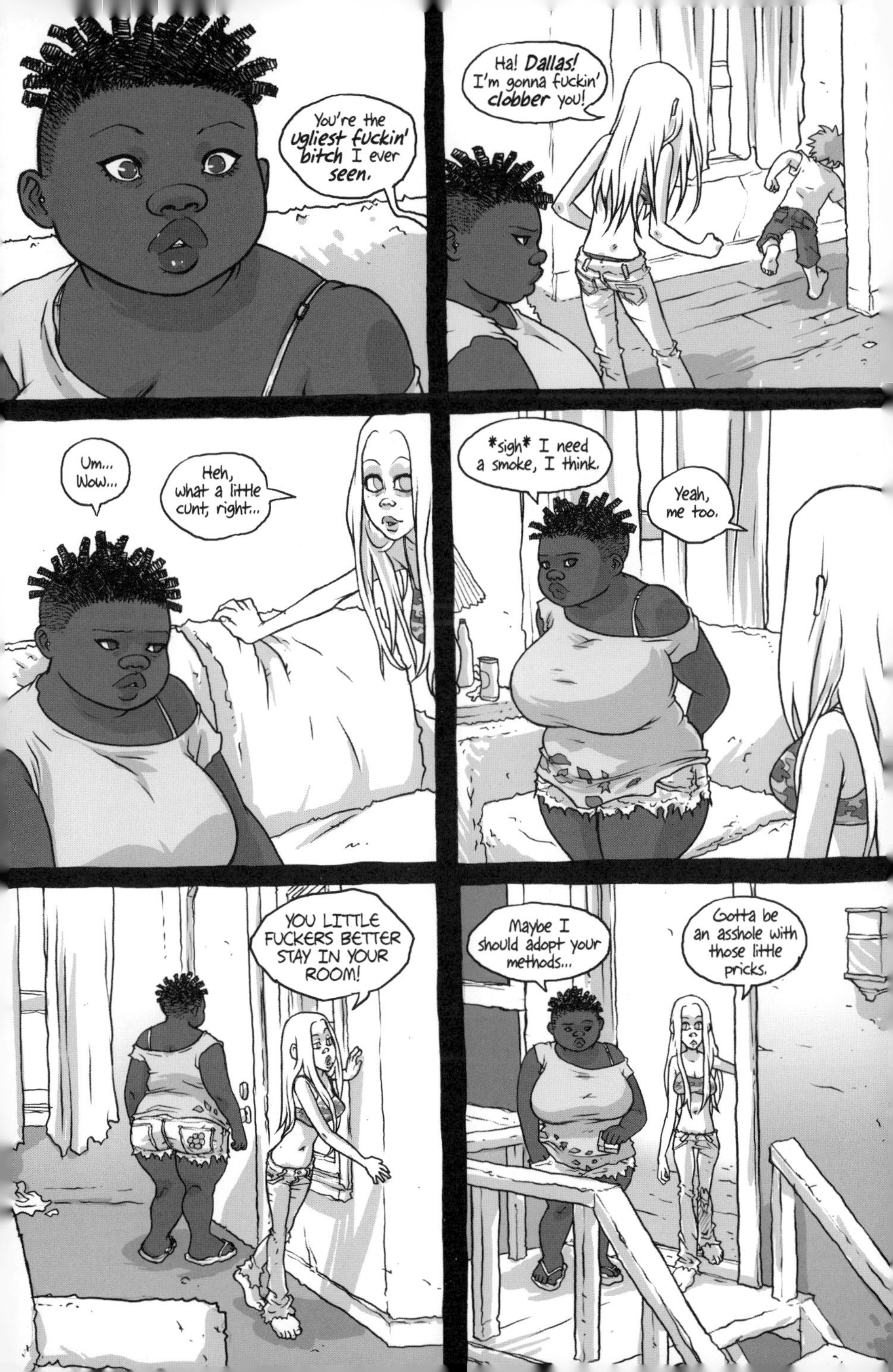
You're the ugliest fuckin' bitch I ever seen.
Ha! Dallas! I'm gonna fuckin' clobber you!
Um... Wow...
Heh, what a little cunt, right...
sigh I need a smoke, I think.
Yeah, me too.
YOU LITTLE FUCKERS BETTER STAY IN YOUR ROOM!
Maybe I should adopt your methods...
Gotta be an asshole with those little pricks.

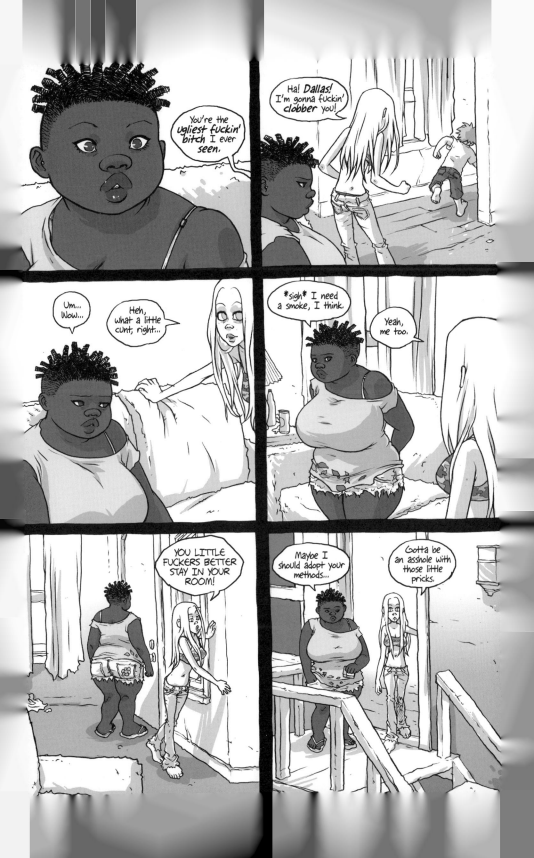

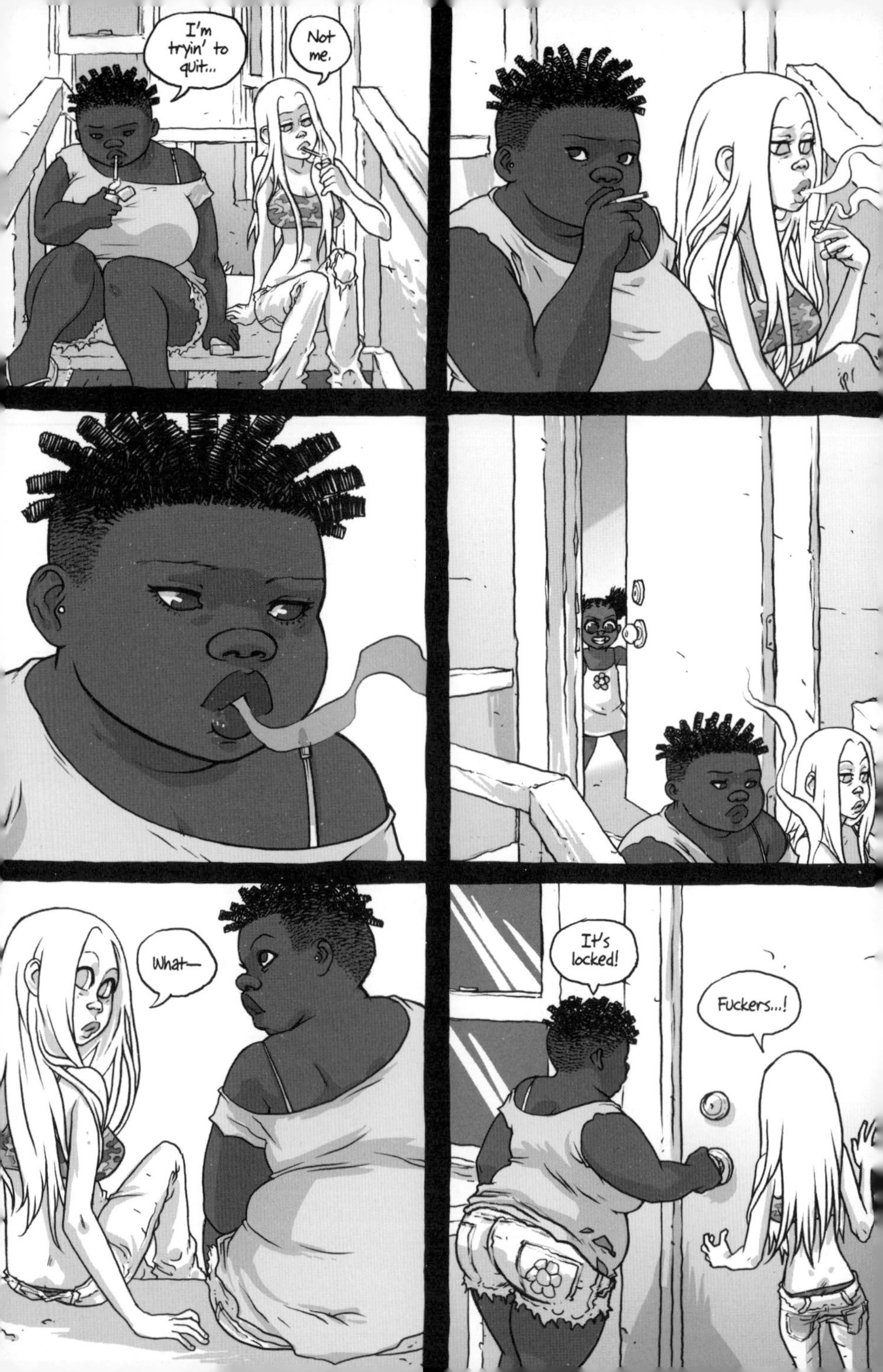
I'm tryin' to quit...
Not me.
What—
It's locked!
Fuckers...!

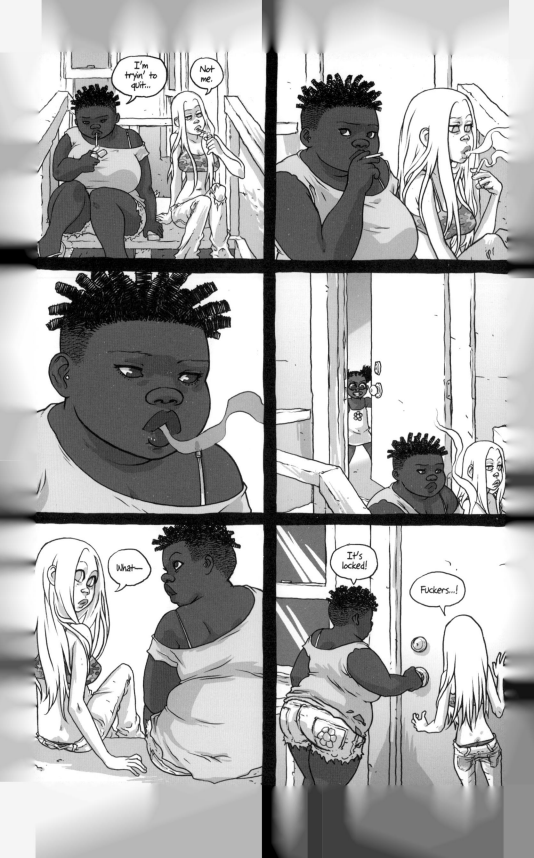

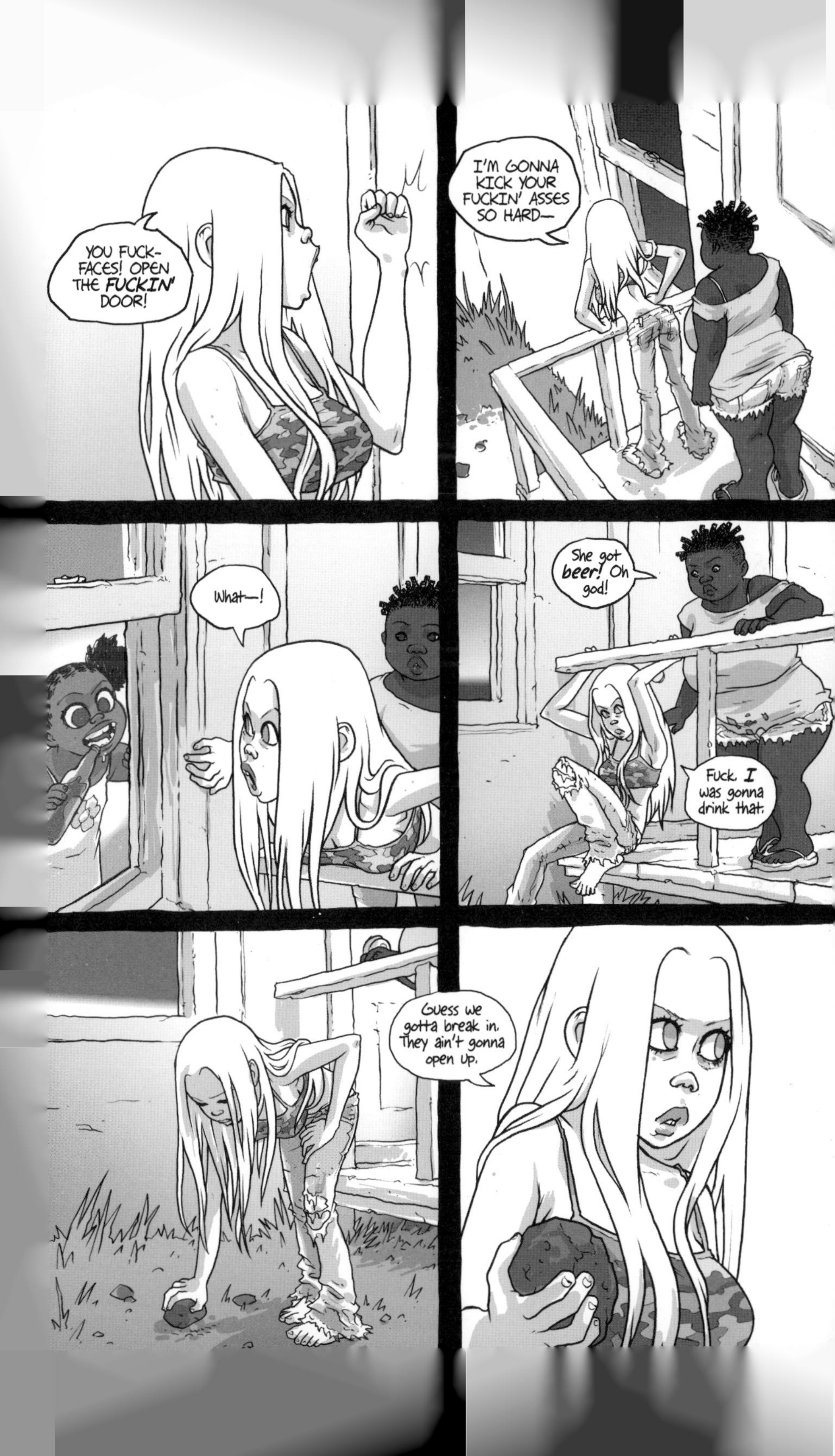
YOU FUCK-FACES! OPEN THE FUCKIN' DOOR!
I'M GONNA KICK YOUR FUCKIN' ASSES SO HARD—
What—!
She got beer! Oh god!
Fuck. I was gonna drink that.
Guess we gotta break in. They ain't gonna open up.

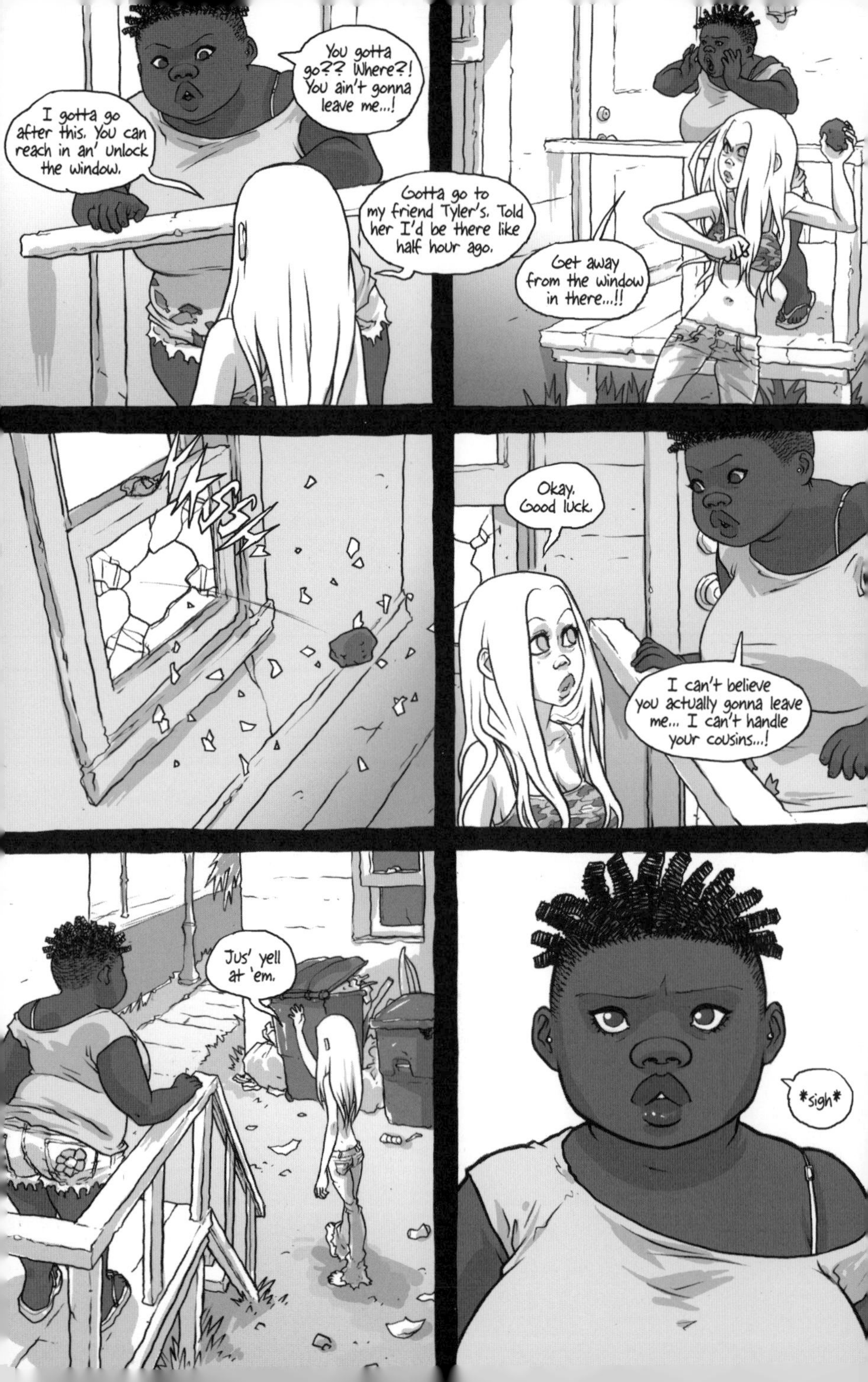
I gotta go after this. You can reach in an' unlock the window.
You gotta go?? Where?! You ain't gonna leave me...!
Gotta go to my friend Tyler's. Told her I'd be there like half hour ago.
Get away from the window in there...!!
WHUSSH
Okay. Good luck.
I can't believe you actually gonna leave me... I can't handle your cousins...!
Jus' yell at 'em.
sigh

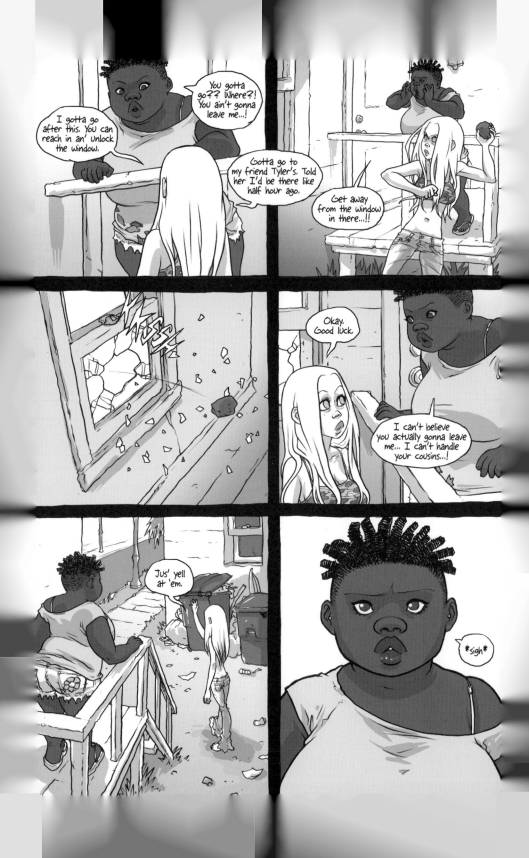

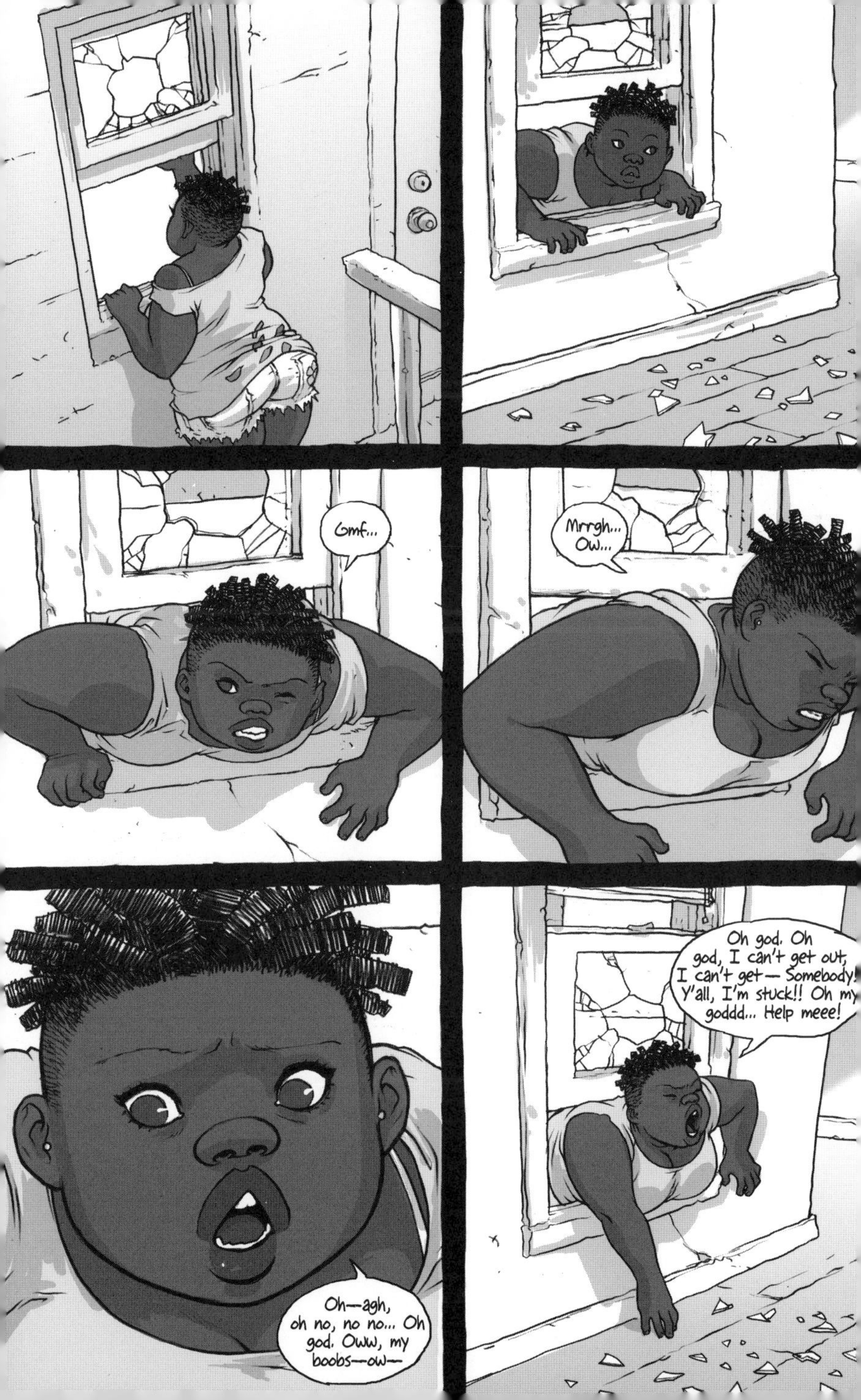
Gmf...
Mrrgh... Ow...
Oh—agh, oh no, no no... Oh god. Oww, my boobs—ow—
Oh god. Oh god, I can't get out, I can't get— Somebody! Y'all, I'm stuck!! Oh my goddd... Help meee!

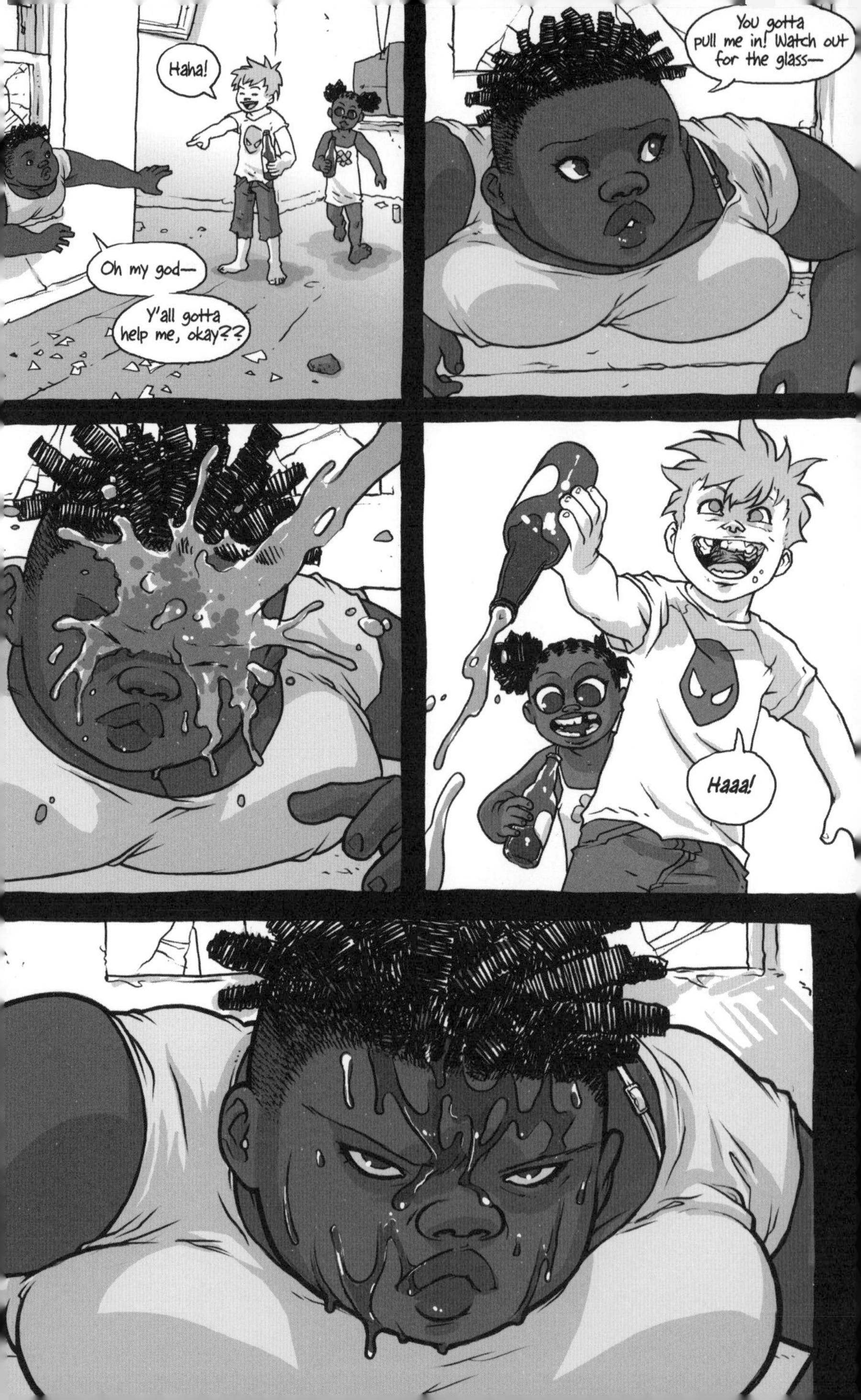
Haha!
Oh my god—
Y'all gotta help me, okay??
You gotta pull me in! Watch out for the glass—
Haaa!

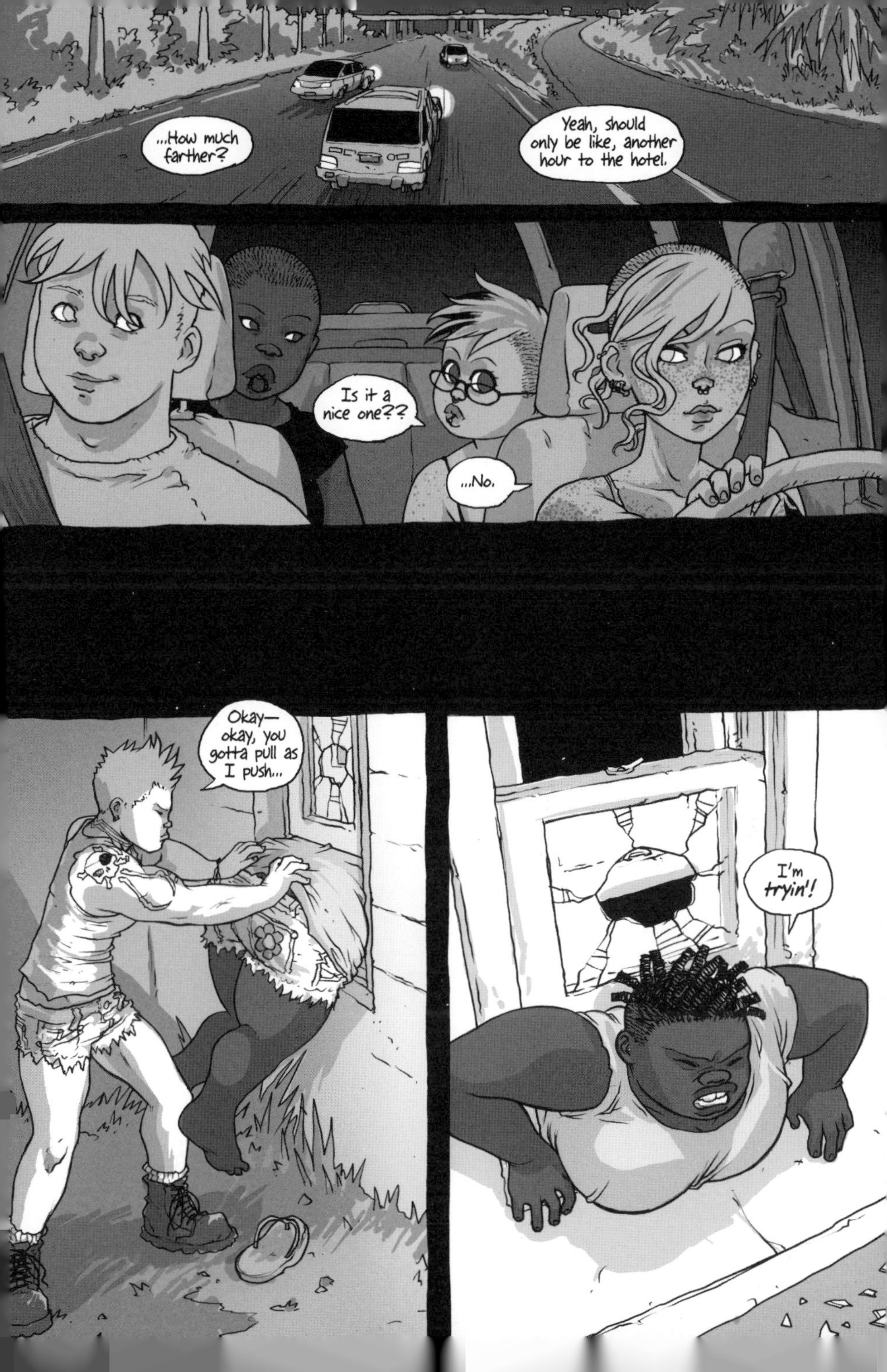
...How much farther?
Yeah, should only be like, another hour to the hotel.
Is it a nice one??
...No.
Okay— okay, you gotta pull as I push...
I'm *tryin'*!

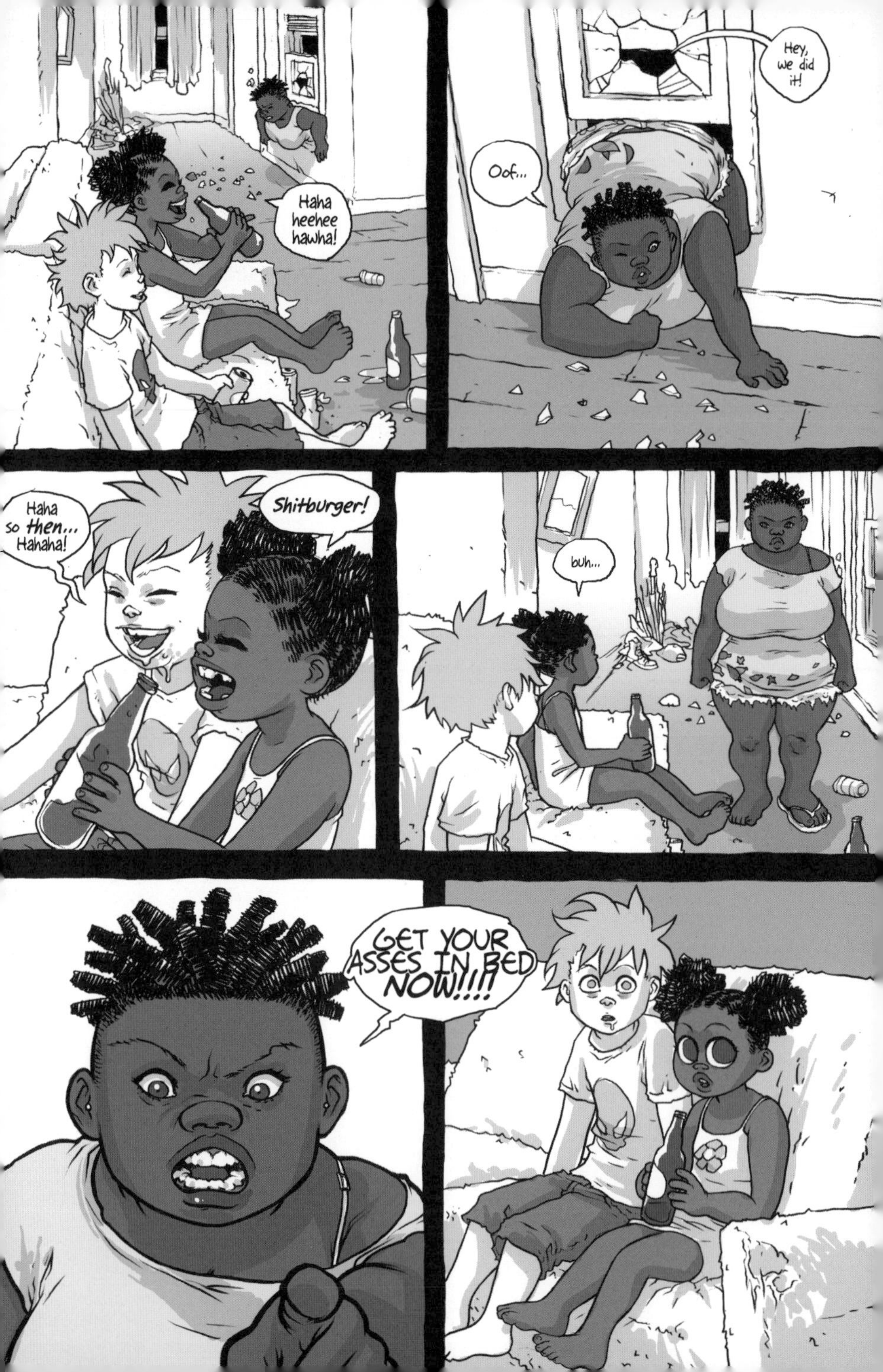
Haha heehee hawha!
Hey, we did it!
Oof...
Haha so then... Hahaha!
Shitburger!
buh...
GET YOUR ASSES IN BED NOW!!!!

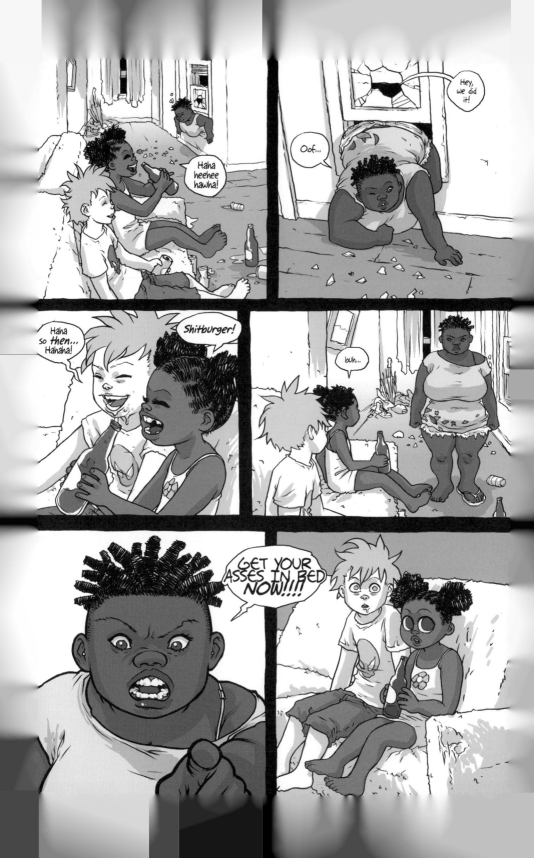

19

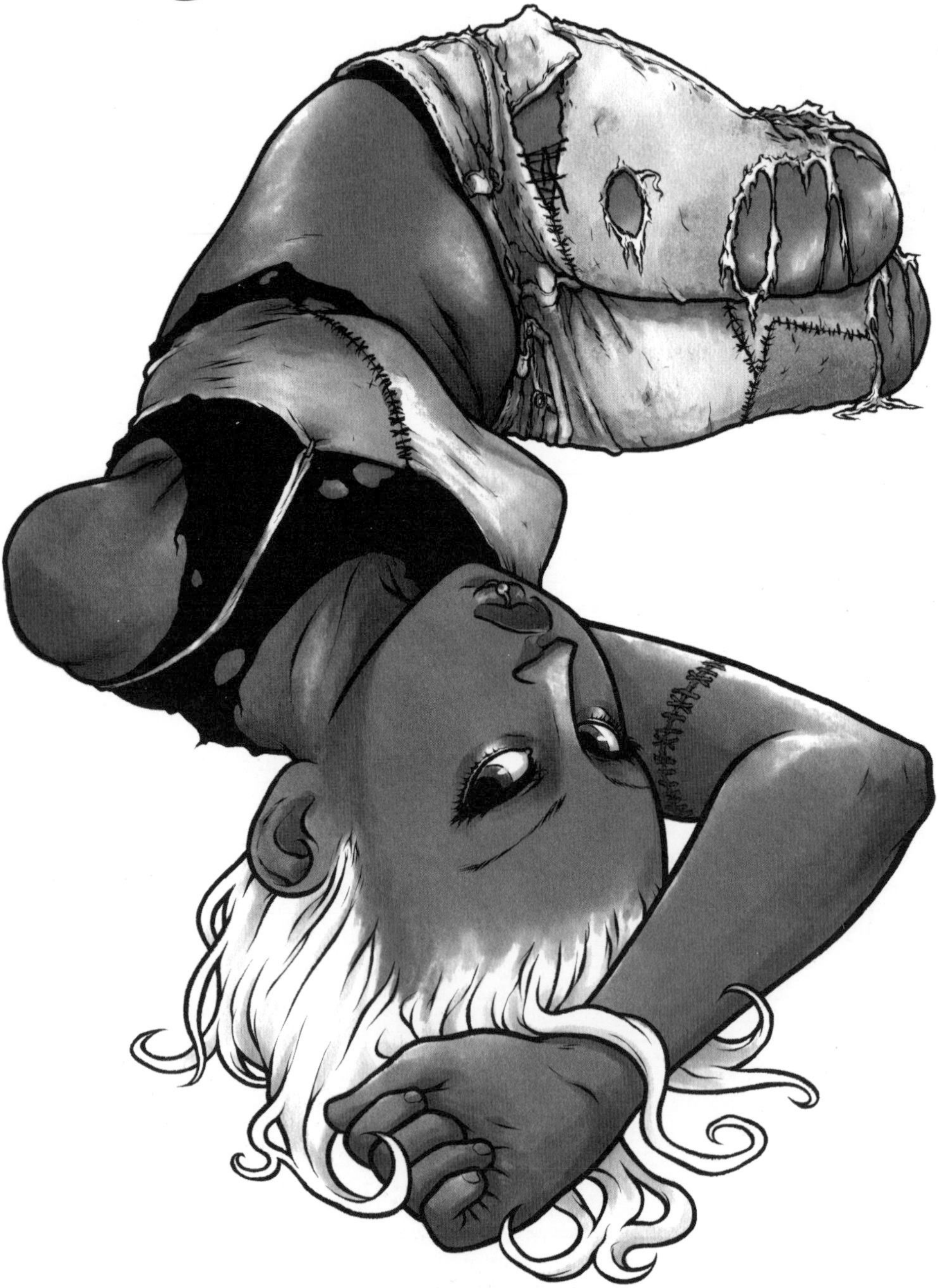

The Wonders At Your Feet

[friendtoroaches@gmail.com]

Recent Entries   Archive   Friends   User Info

mara's journal

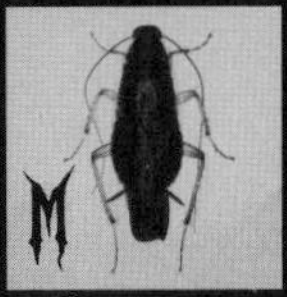

profile

October 31st, 2:22am

OFFERING OF RED RAGE.

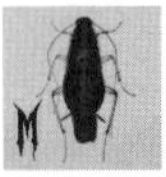

it's officially Halloween, and i have no costume. i'm very pleased about that, i think Halloween is overrated and i hate how people don't dress up in spooky or scary costumes anymore. i thought Halloween was supposed to be about monsters and ghosts and zombies, not nurses or video game characters or pirates. i guess nurses can be scary. but i'm rebelling against that and not dressing up at all. i'm scarier as my regular self than anything i could dress up as.

we finally made it to the hotel which is okay. it's kind of small and a little smelly and there's only one bed, but they actually have wireless internet. the drive down was okay. not too bad. we drove past a big car accident, though, and i saw a bloody guy laying on the road all twisted up like a red, wet pretzel. that's the first time i've ever seen a corpse and i have to say it wasn't that bad. maybe it would be worse if we werent driving by at 50 miles an hour. Cleo seems really upset by it though. she's very sensitive. right now Trilby is watching some alien show on the sci-fi channel, and Martin is taking a shower for some reason.

i can't believe i came to this con thing. it's going to be so stupid. we already saw a ton of nerds (Trilby says to call them con-goers, but i know they're just nerds) all around the hotel. every room must be filled up with con people and we're just four more. one girl was wearing stickers on her boobs and pants and nothing else. i don't get what this con is supposed to be about and it hasn't even started yet.

mood: nervous
current music: sonic syndicate - only inhuman

[0 comments | leave a comment]

October 28th, 1:31am

CATHODE RAYS BLAST LIKE METEOR RAIN TO MY BRAIN.

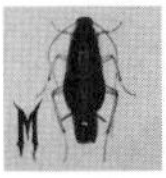

i think everythings good with Natalie now. we hung out today for a little while it was cool. but also weird because she lives in the same dorm as Cleo so i felt like i was sneaking around or something. i don't think Cleo was home like usual. Natalie is so skinny. she is so skinny it's painful. i wonder if she's anorexic or something. she wants me to be her model for her photo project, i don't know what i think about that. i'm real flattered on one hand, but totally nervous and weird on the other. why does she want me for the project? she could find a billion other girls who are prettier or hotter or whatever. i don't know. i hope it's not a nude photo shoot. i don't know what the fuck i'd do then. actually i guess it wouldn't be so bad. i'd probably get over it quick. at least i got a little bit of muscle now. anyway i'm glad it looks like we're friends now. i'll probably fuck it up later on though. maybe i should make this post friends-only.

softball is going great. i am excited for the Armadillo game but also scared, i don't know if we can win. i think pretty much everyone on our team smokes, me included, we won't be able to breathe out there. except Trilby. she used to smoke a little but one day she went "i'm quitting" and the next day she really did and she never smoked again. how did she do that. i haven't had any luck quitting so far but i'm really trying. i really want to be able to run really far.

i've been reseraching a lot about ancient Egypt recently. partly because it's cool and partly because i think i want my first film for class to have something to do with Egypt. i wish i could set it IN Egypt, but obviously i cant get over there. i thought at first something with a mummy, but not a super magic world domination wizard mummy like in those Mummy movies. like a fucking badass serious intense elder evil shambling mummy who comes

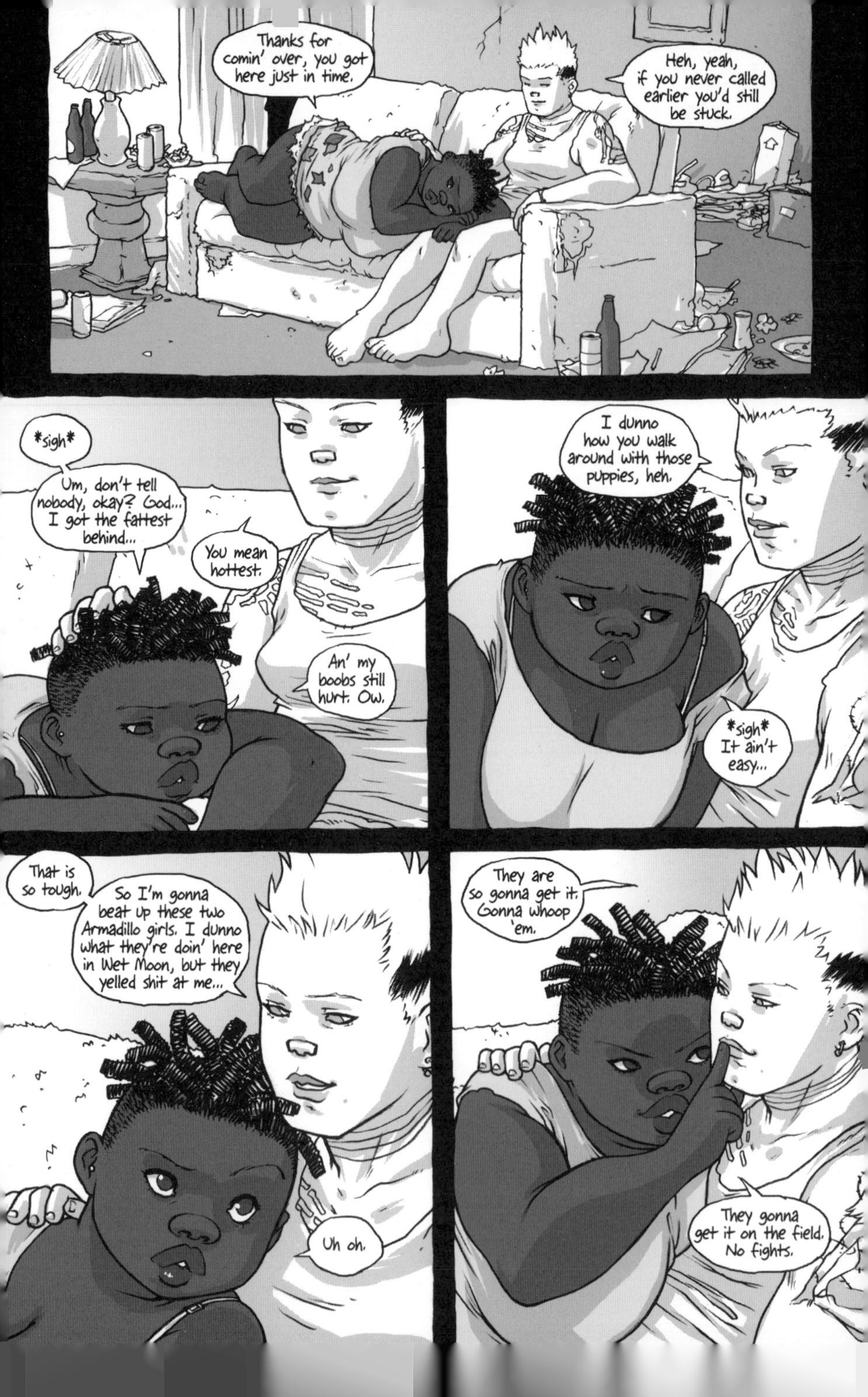
Thanks for comin' over, you got here just in time.
Heh, yeah, if you never called earlier you'd still be stuck.
sigh
Um, don't tell nobody, okay? God... I got the fattest behind...
You mean hottest.
An' my boobs still hurt. Ow.
I dunno how you walk around with those puppies, heh.
sigh It ain't easy...
That is so tough.
So I'm gonna beat up these two Armadillo girls. I dunno what they're doin' here in Wet Moon, but they yelled shit at me...
Uh oh.
They are so gonna get it. Gonna whoop 'em.
They gonna get it on the field. No fights.

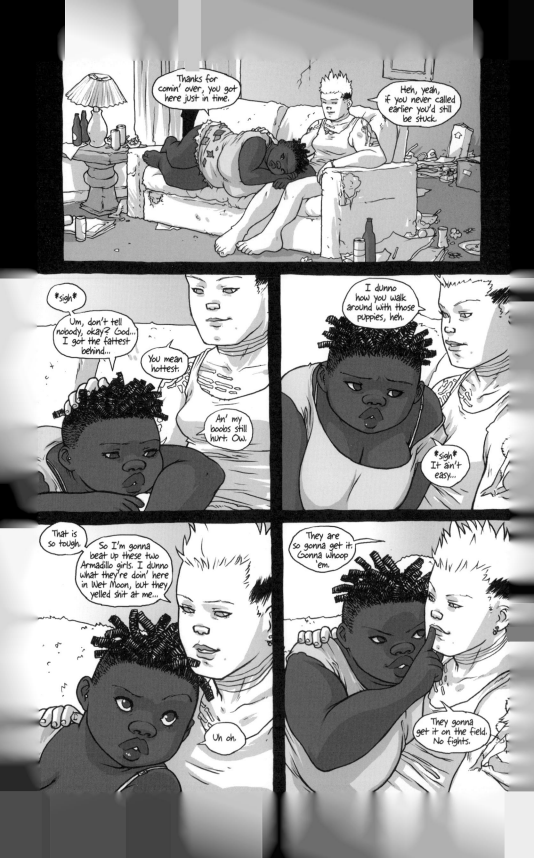

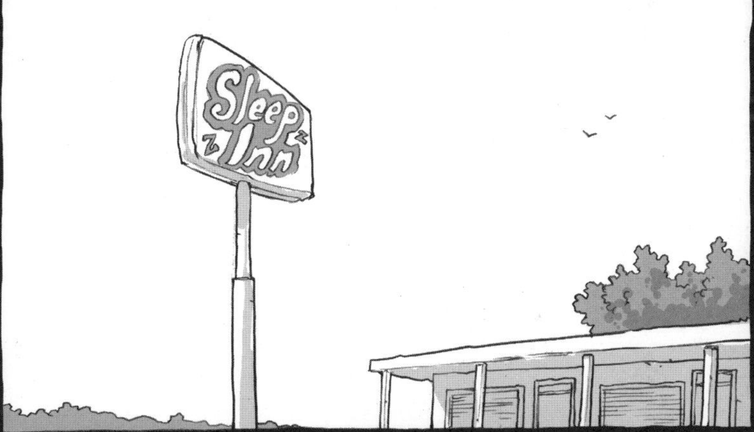
Sleep Inn
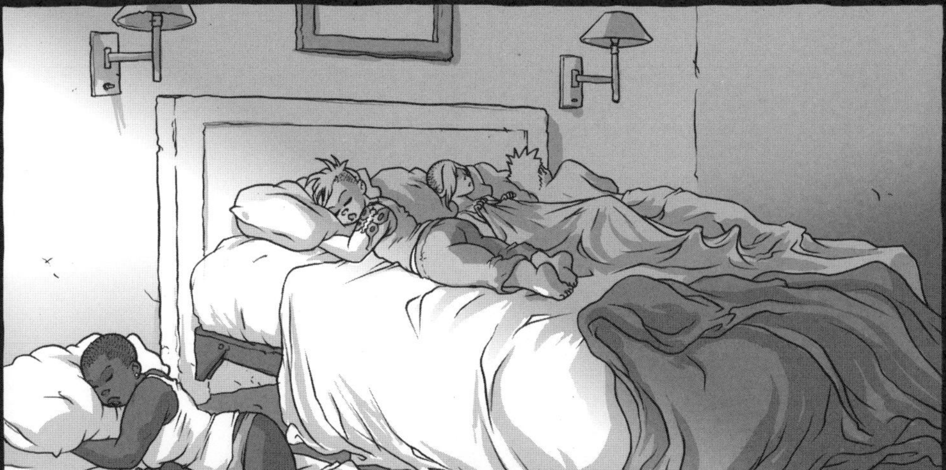

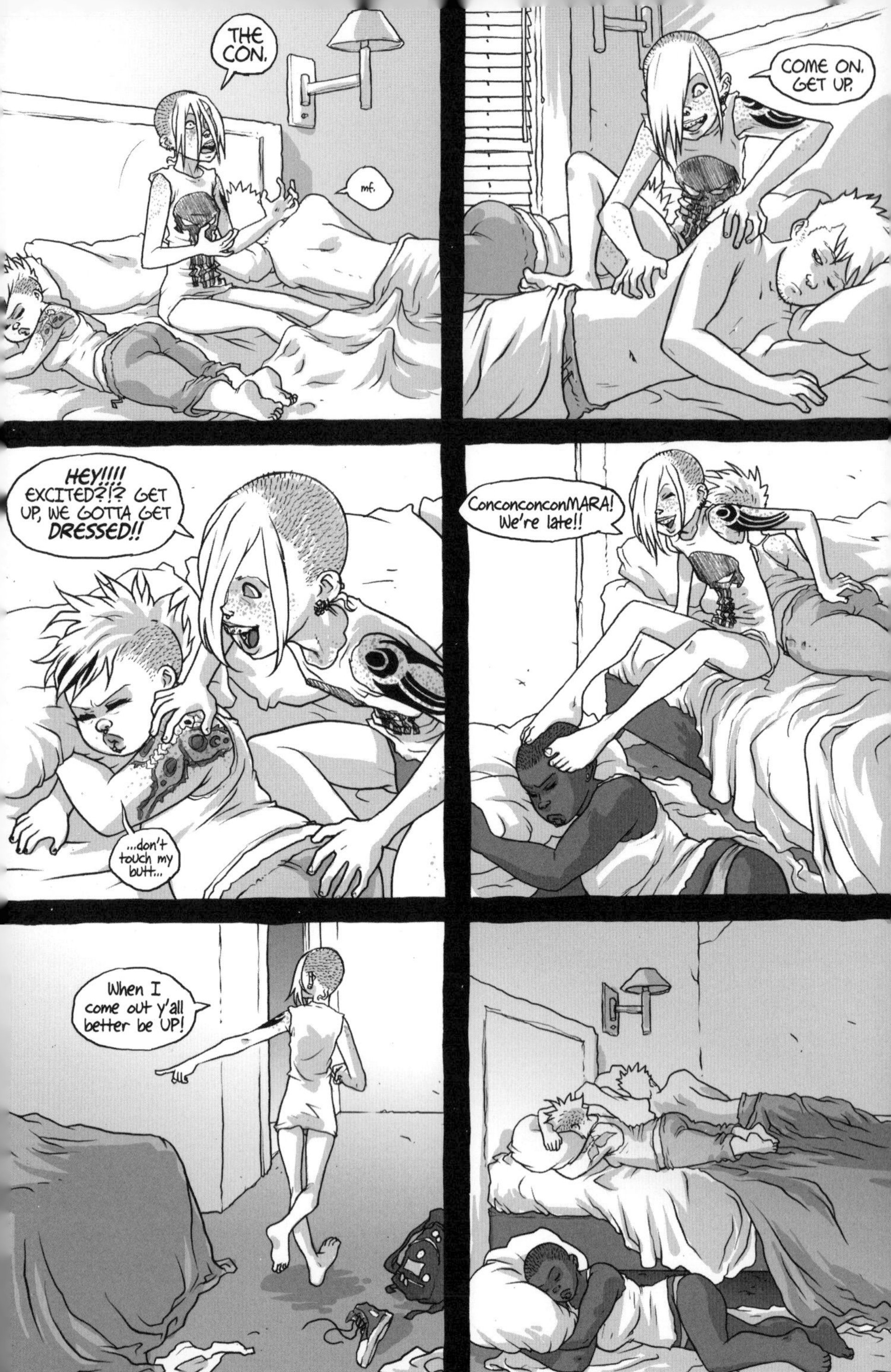
THE CON.
mf.
COME ON, GET UP.
HEY!!!! EXCITED?!? GET UP, WE GOTTA GET DRESSED!!
...don't touch my butt...
ConconconconMARA! We're late!!
When I come out y'all better be UP!

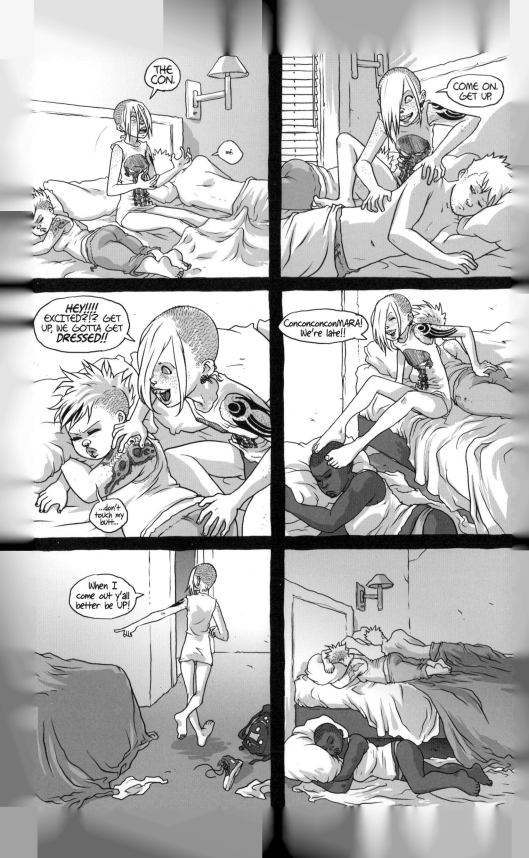

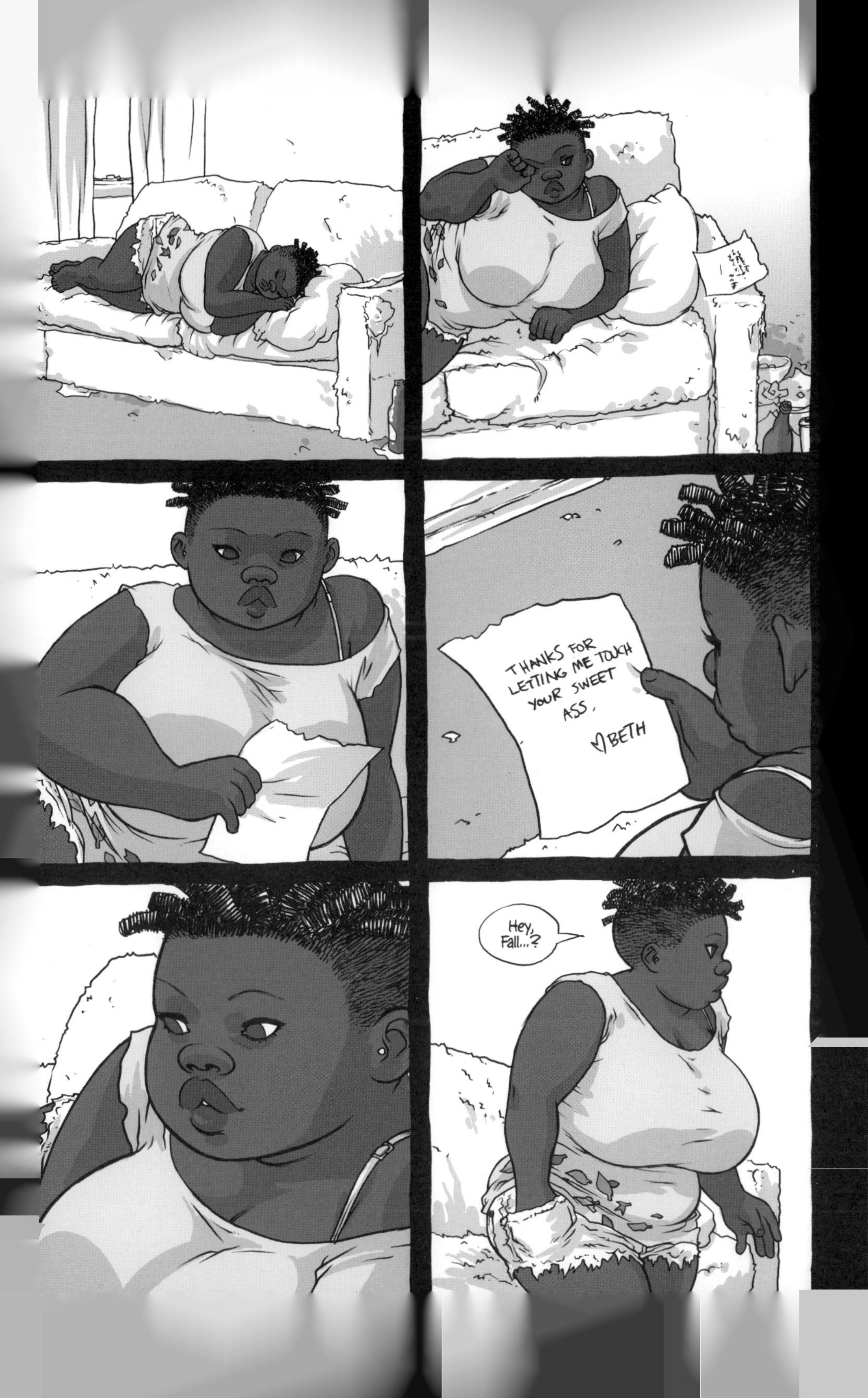
THANKS FOR LETTING ME TOUCH YOUR SWEET ASS.
♡BETH
Hey, Fall...?

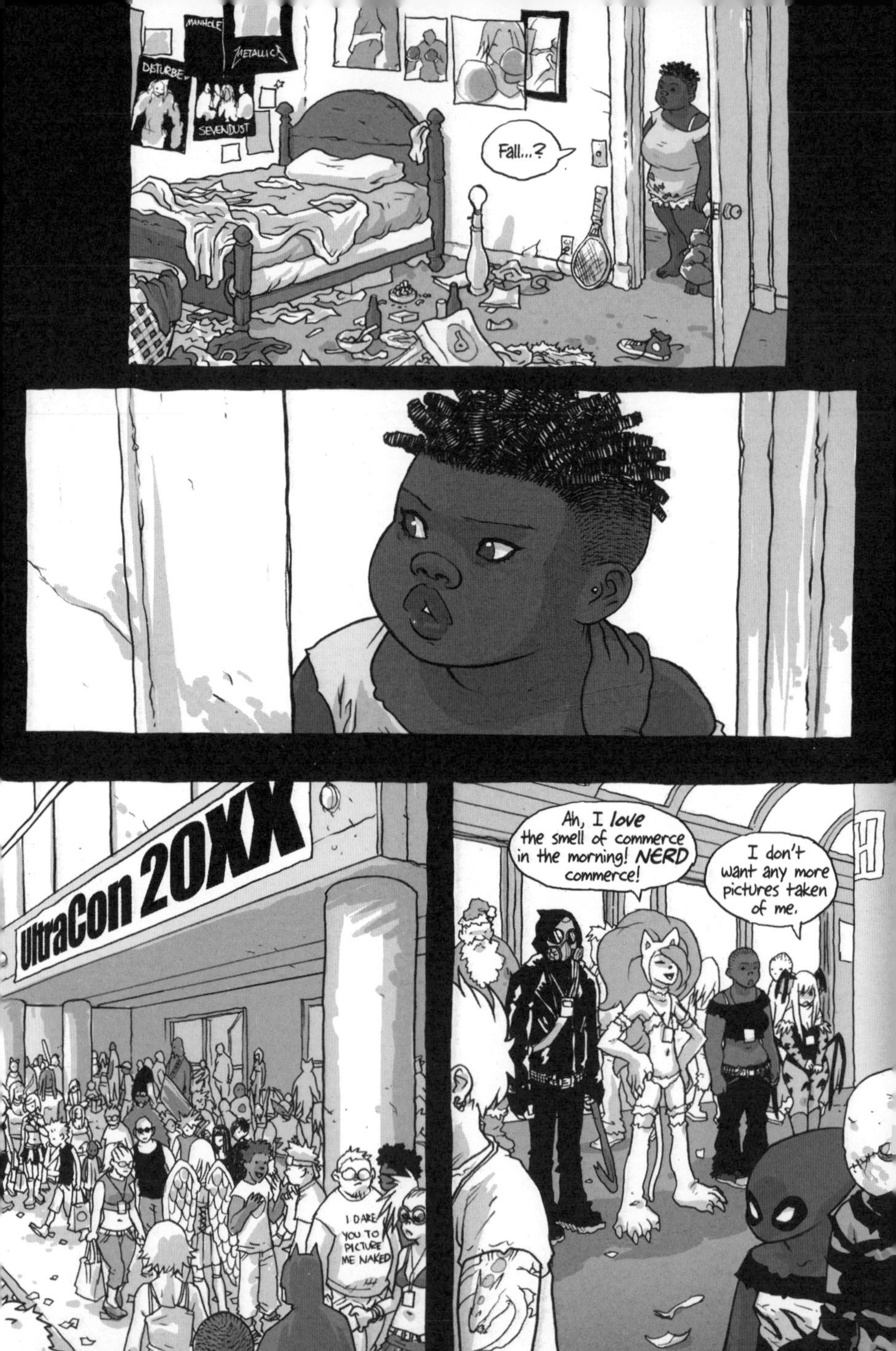
DETURBE
MANHOLE
METALLICA
SEVENDUST
Fall...?
UltraCon 20XX
I DARE YOU TO PICTURE ME NAKED
Ah, I love the smell of commerce in the morning! NERD commerce!
I don't want any more pictures taken of me.

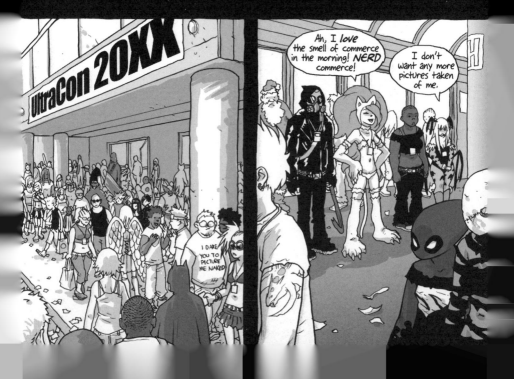

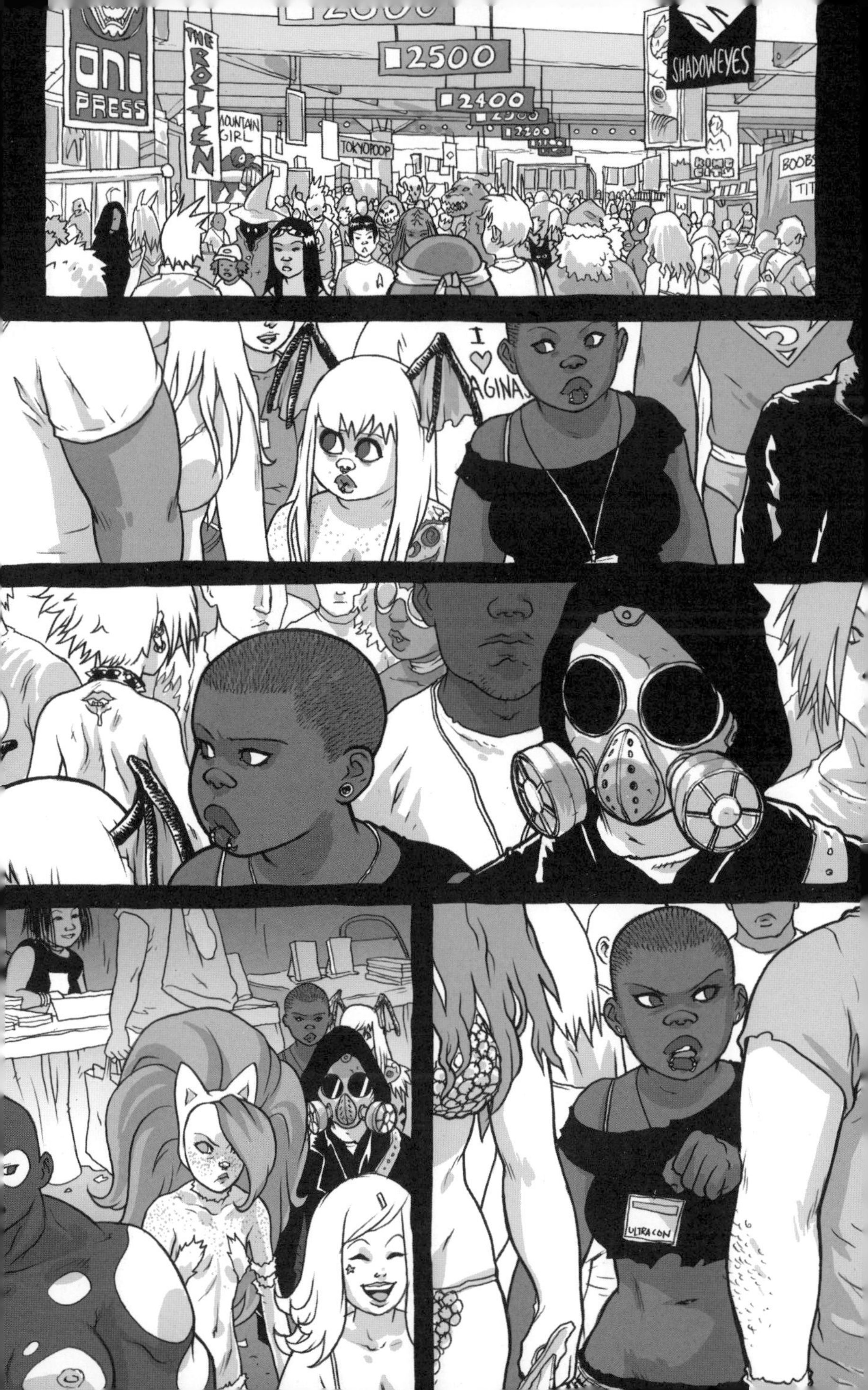
ONI PRESS
THE ROTTEN
2500
2400
MOUNTAIN GIRL
TOKYOPOP
SHADOWEYES
BOOBS
I ♥ AGINAS
ULTRACON

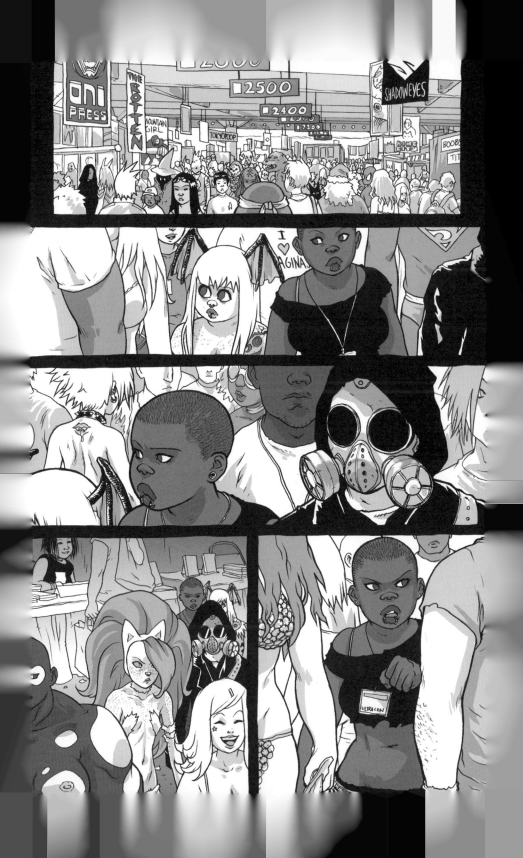

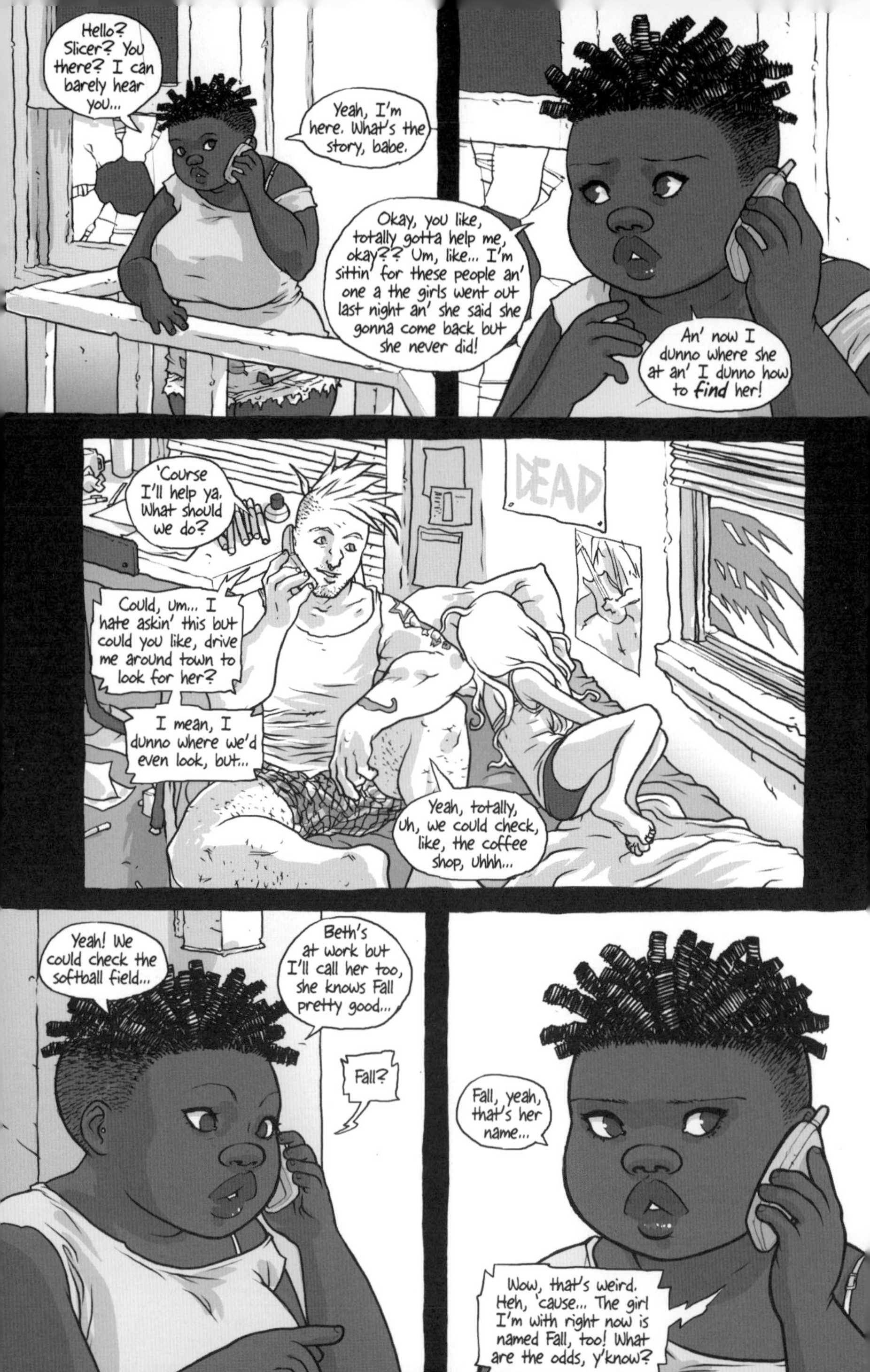
Hello? Slicer? You there? I can barely hear you...
Yeah, I'm here. What's the story, babe.
Okay, you like, totally gotta help me, okay?? Um, like... I'm sittin' for these people an' one a the girls went out last night an' she said she gonna come back but she never did!
An' now I dunno where she at an' I dunno how to *find* her!
DEAD
'Course I'll help ya. What should we do?
Could, um... I hate askin' this but could you like, drive me around town to look for her?
I mean, I dunno where we'd even look, but...
Yeah, totally, uh, we could check, like, the coffee shop, uhhh...
Yeah! We could check the softball field...
Beth's at work but I'll call her too, she knows Fall pretty good...
Fall?
Fall, yeah, that's her name...
Wow, that's weird. Heh, 'cause... The girl I'm with right now is named Fall, too! What are the odds, y'know?

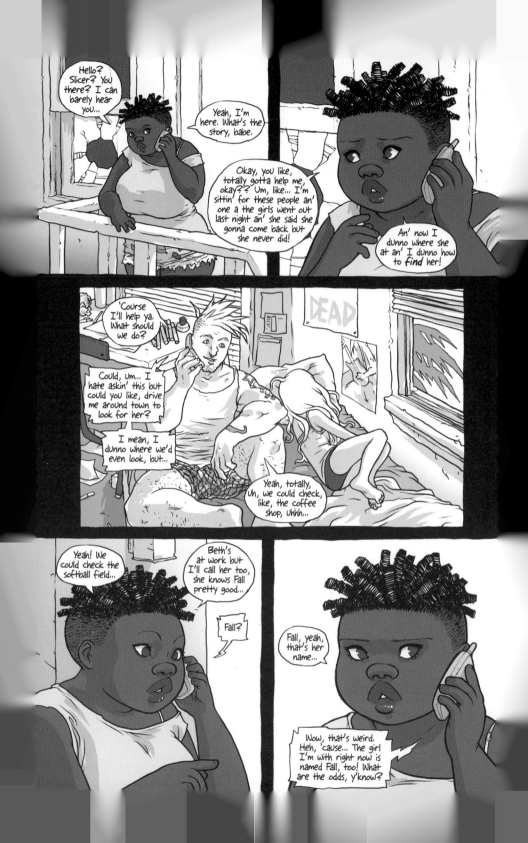

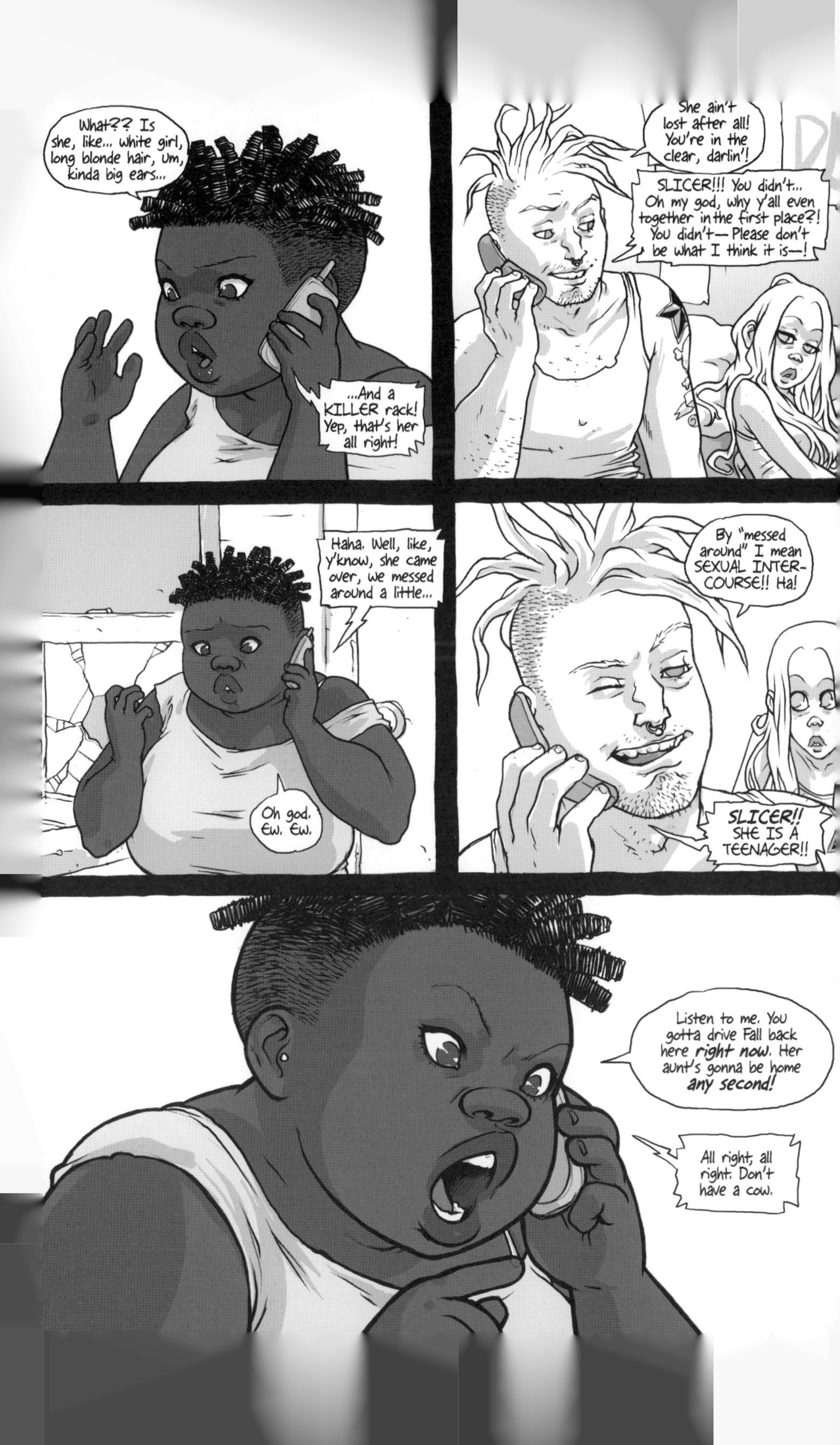

What?? Is she, like... white girl, long blonde hair, um, kinda big ears...
...And a KILLER rack! Yep, that's her all right!
She ain't lost after all! You're in the clear, darlin'!
SLICER!!! You didn't... Oh my god, why y'all even together in the first place?! You didn't— Please don't be what I think it is—!
Haha. Well, like, y'know, she came over, we messed around a little...
Oh god. Ew. Ew.
By "messed around" I mean SEXUAL INTER-COURSE!! Ha!
SLICER!! SHE IS A TEENAGER!!
Listen to me. You gotta drive Fall back here **right now**. Her aunt's gonna be home **any second!**
All right, all right. Don't have a cow.

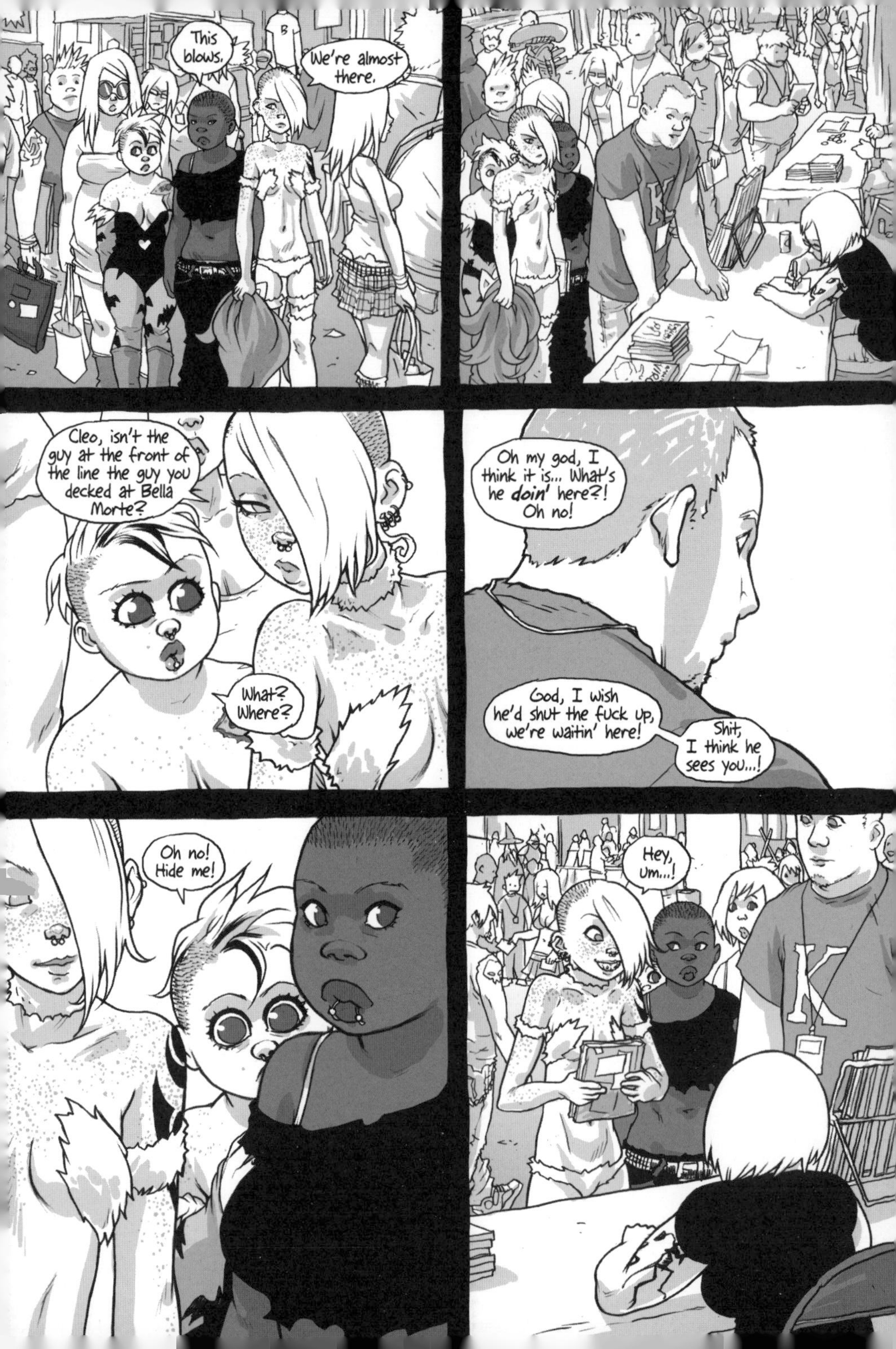
This blows.
We're almost there.
Cleo, isn't the guy at the front of the line the guy you decked at Bella Morte?
What? Where?
Oh my god, I think it is... What's he doin' here?! Oh no!
God, I wish he'd shut the fuck up, we're waitin' here!
Shit, I think he sees you...!
Oh no! Hide me!
Hey, um...!

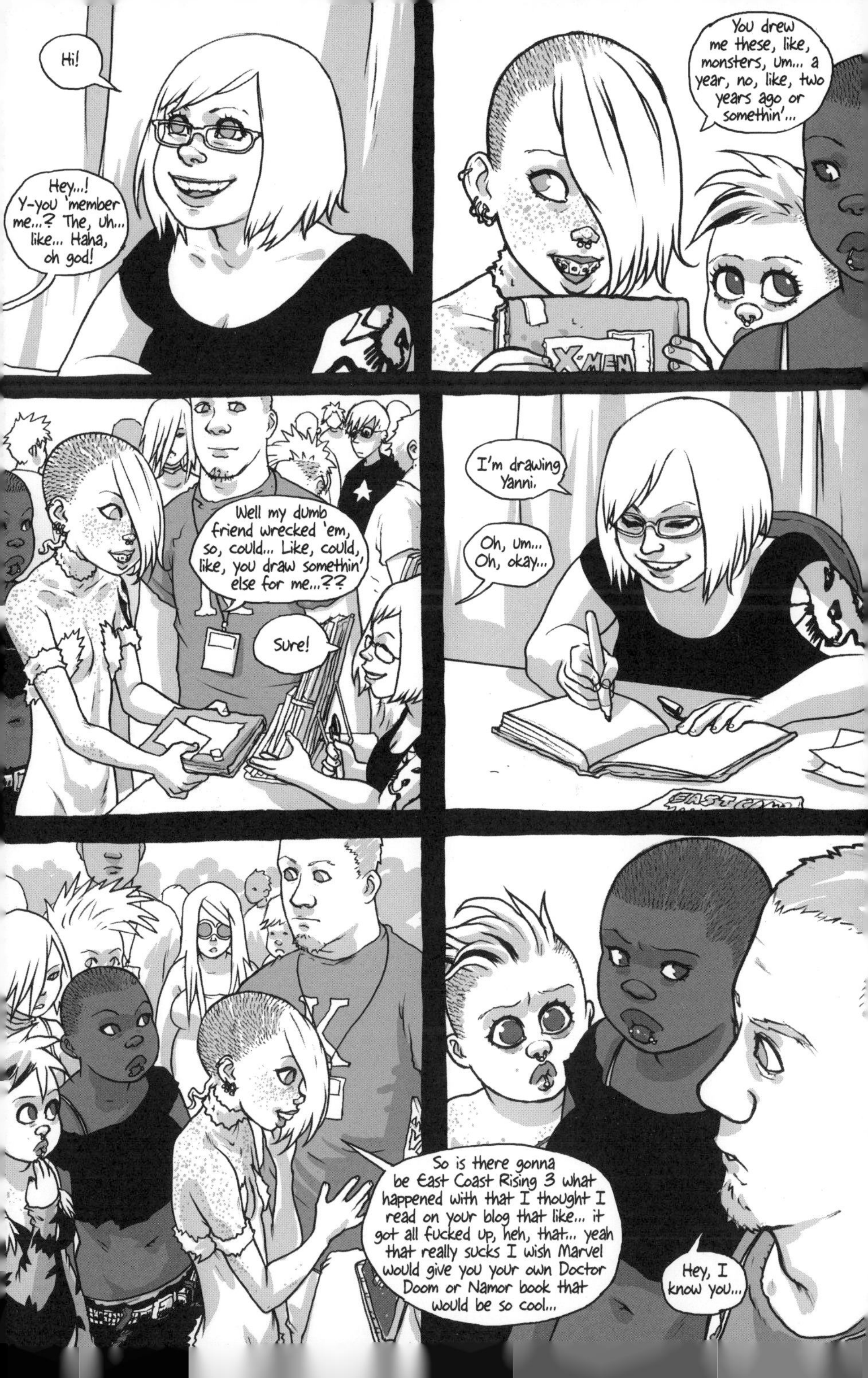
Hi!
Hey...! Y-you 'member me...? The, uh... like... Haha, oh god!
You drew me these, like, monsters, um... a year, no, like, two years ago or somethin'...
X-MEN
Well my dumb friend wrecked 'em, so, could... Like, could, like, you draw somethin' else for me...??
Sure!
I'm drawing Yanni.
Oh, um... Oh, okay...
So is there gonna be East Coast Rising 3 what happened with that I thought I read on your blog that like... it got all fucked up, heh, that... yeah that really sucks I wish Marvel would give you your own Doctor Doom or Namor book that would be so cool...
Hey, I know you...

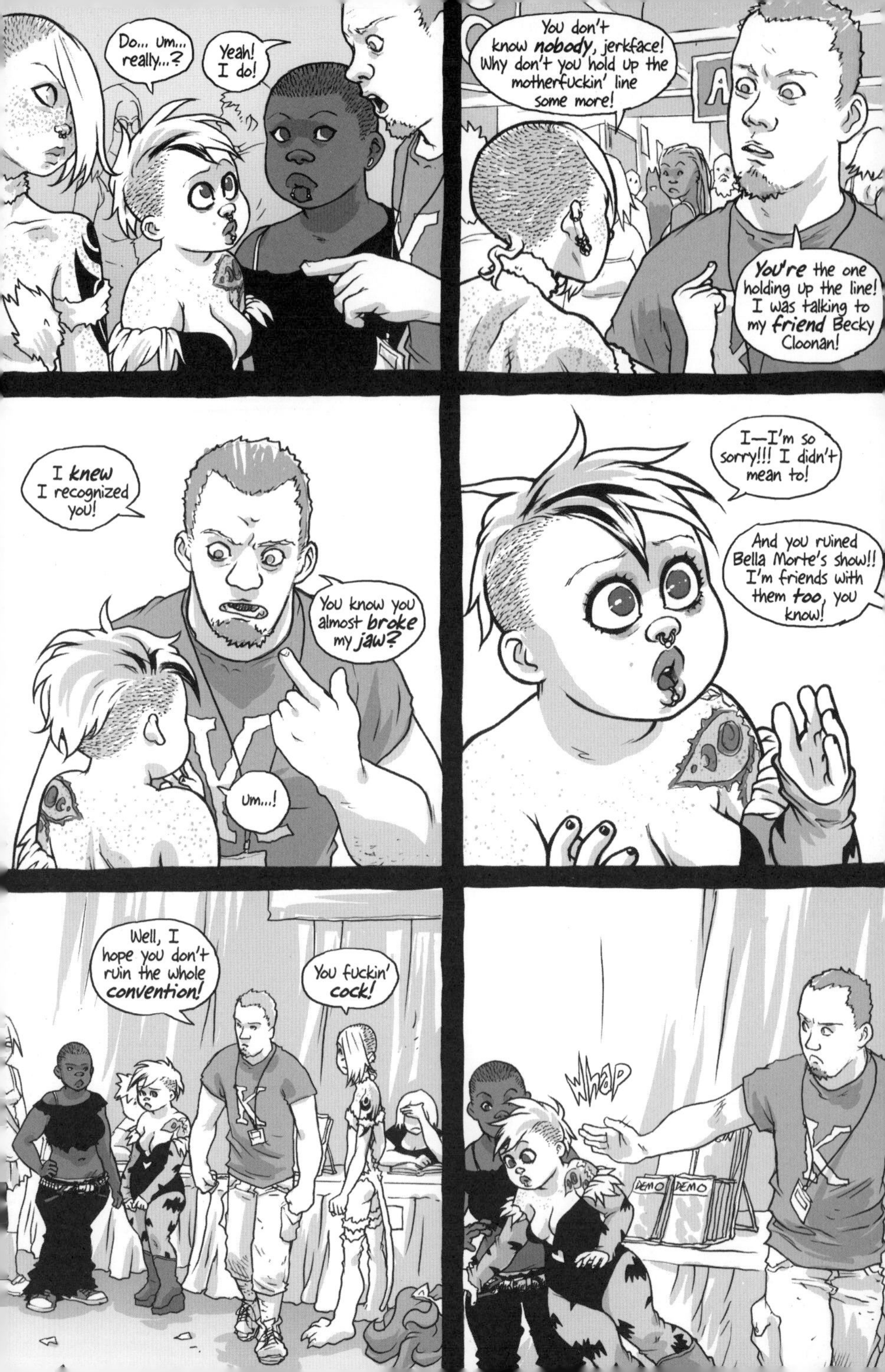
Do... um... really...?
Yeah! I do!
You don't know nobody, jerkface! Why don't you hold up the motherfuckin' line some more!
You're the one holding up the line! I was talking to my friend Becky Cloonan!
I knew I recognized you!
You know you almost broke my jaw?
Um...!
I—I'm so sorry!!! I didn't mean to!
And you ruined Bella Morte's show!! I'm friends with them too, you know!
Well, I hope you don't ruin the whole convention!
You fuckin' cock!
WHAP
DEMO
DEMO

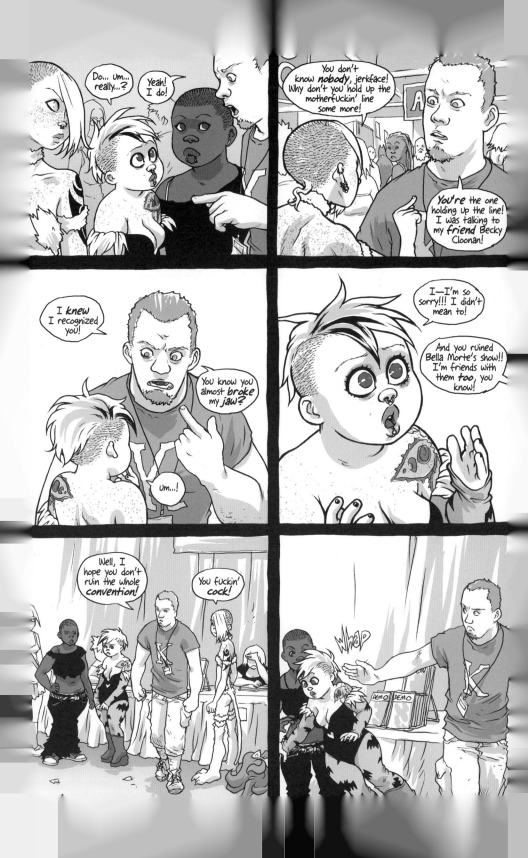

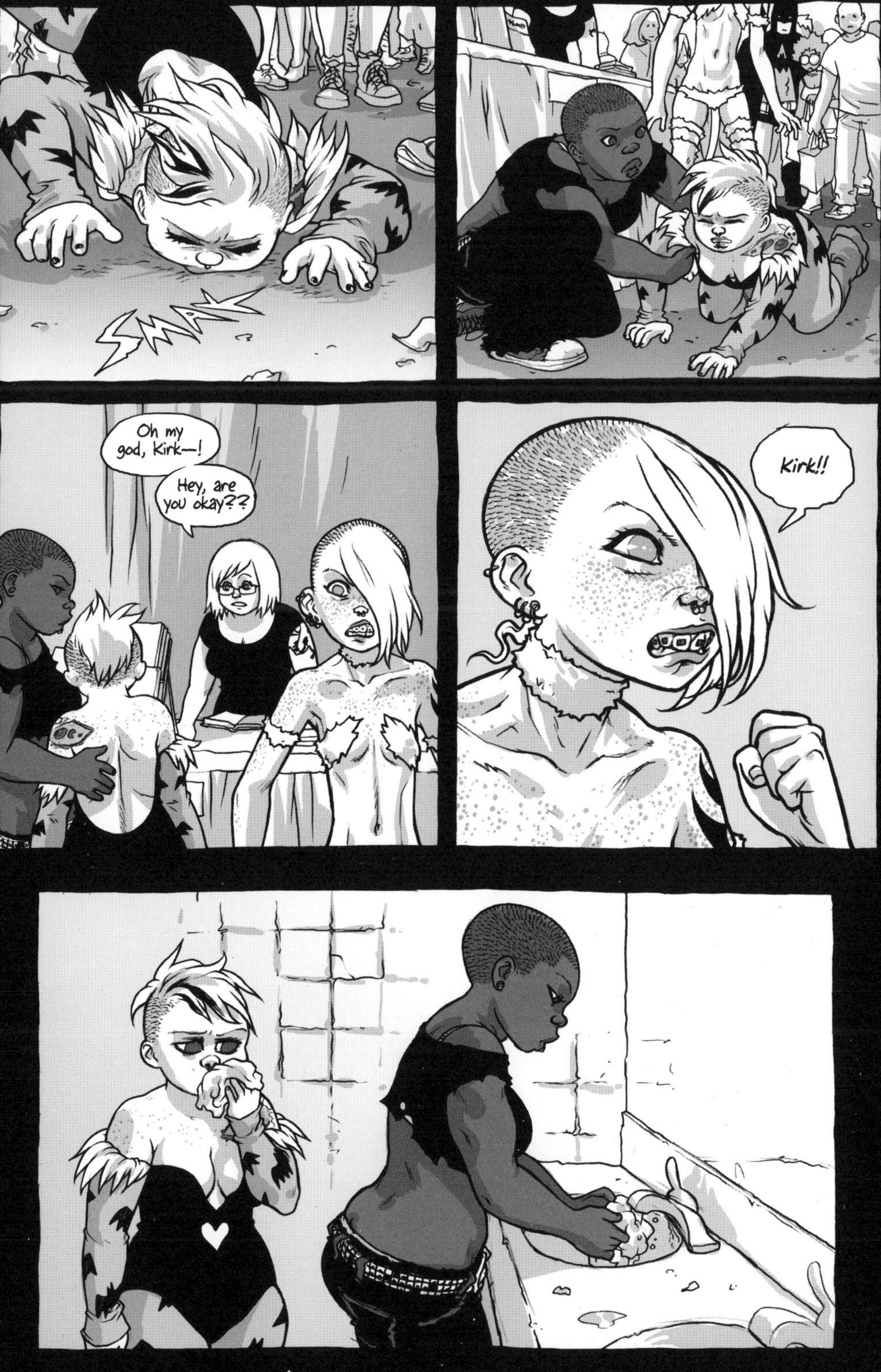
SMAK
Oh my god, Kirk—!
Hey, are you okay??
Kirk!!

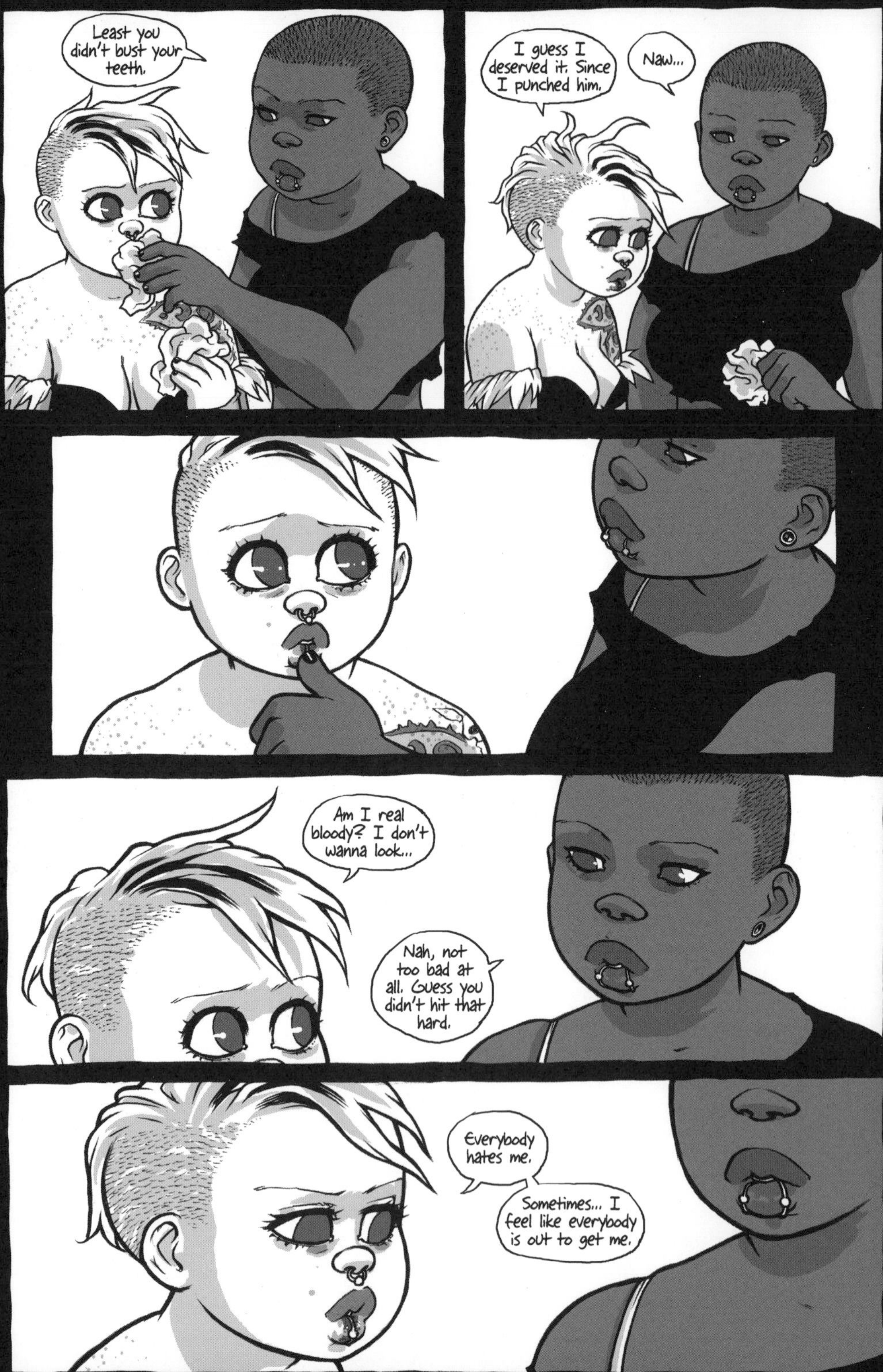
Least you didn't bust your teeth.
I guess I deserved it. Since I punched him.
Naw...
Am I real bloody? I don't wanna look...
Nah, not too bad at all. Guess you didn't hit that hard.
Everybody hates me.
Sometimes... I feel like everybody is out to get me.

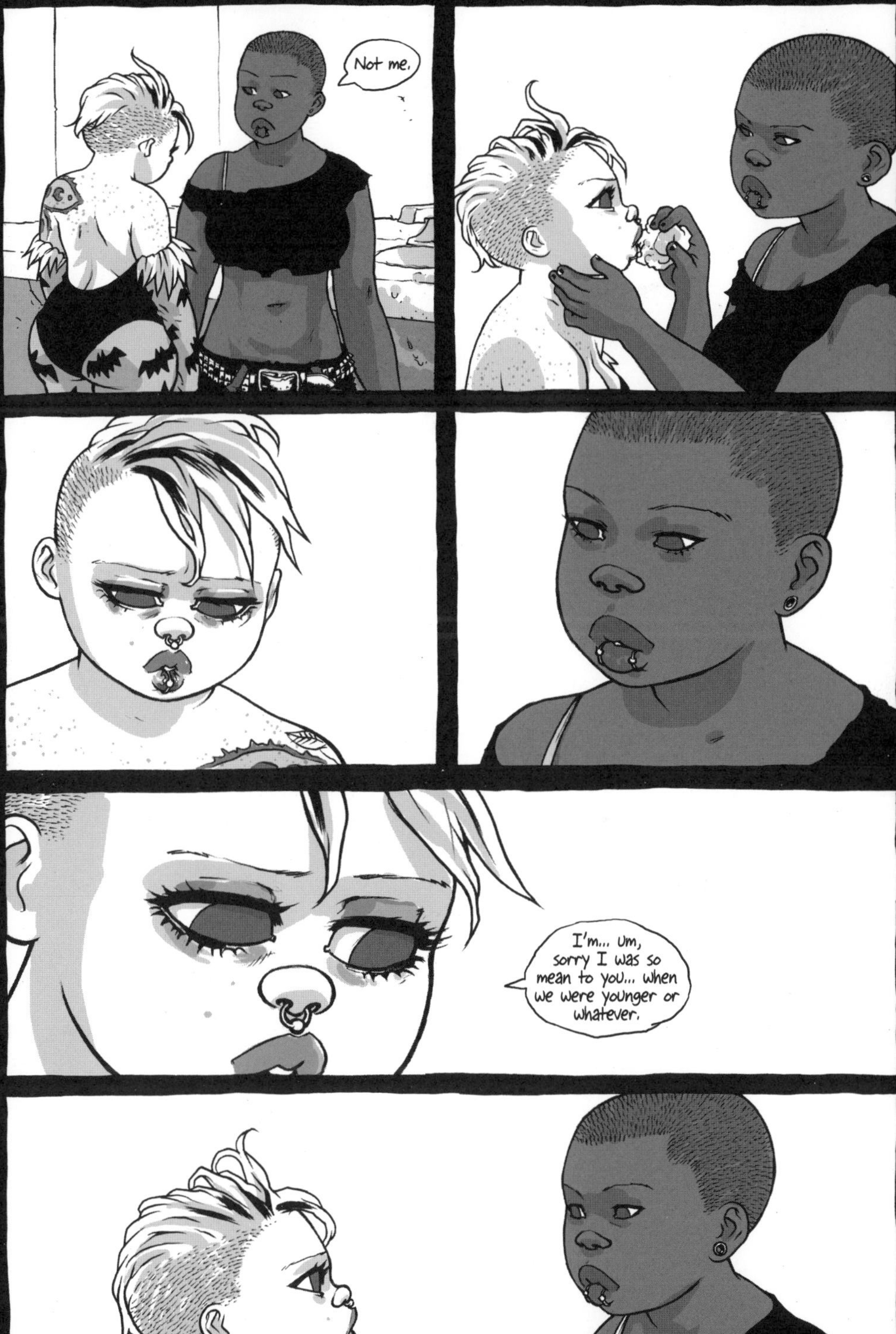
Not me.
I'm... Um, sorry I was so mean to you... when we were younger or whatever.

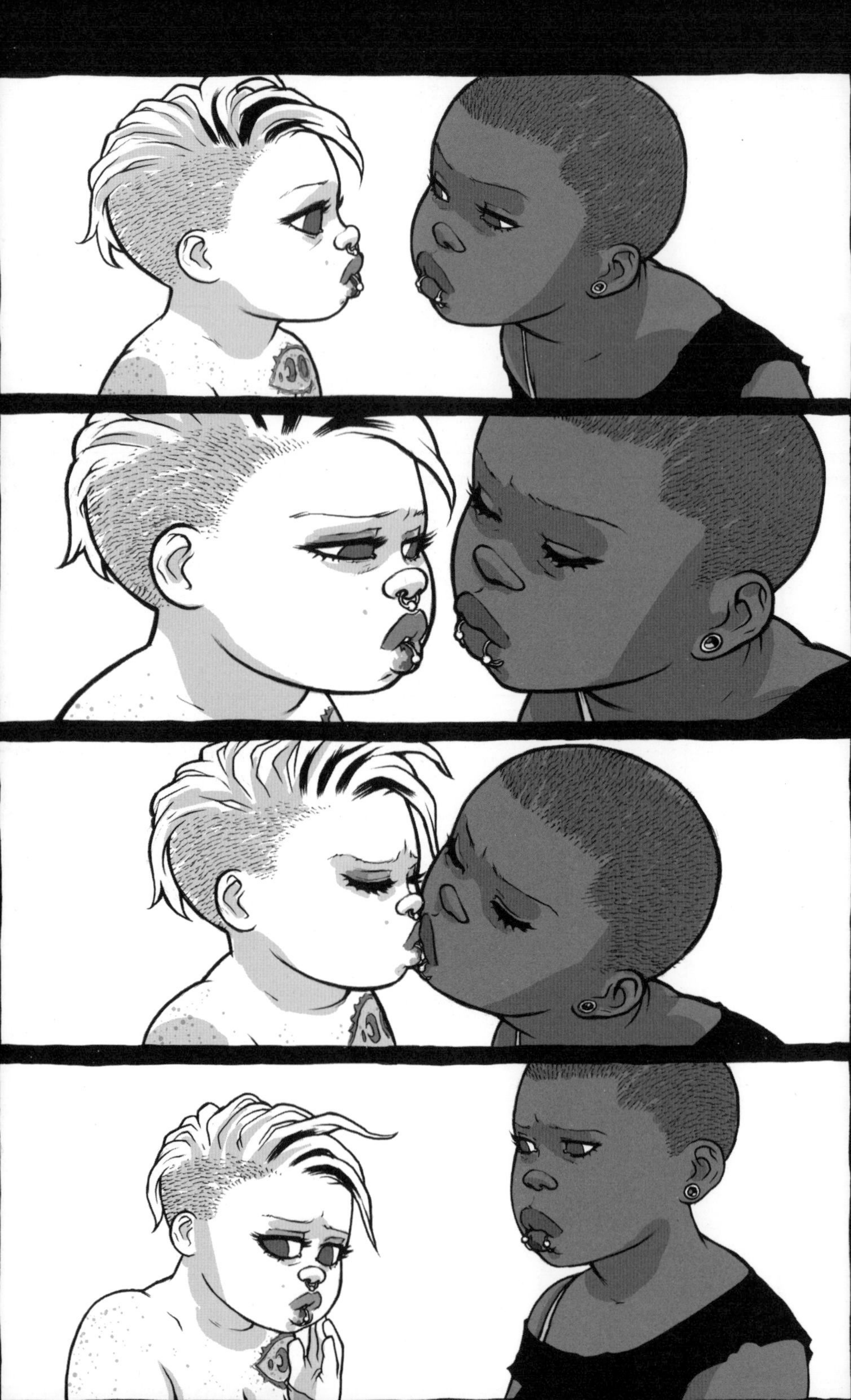

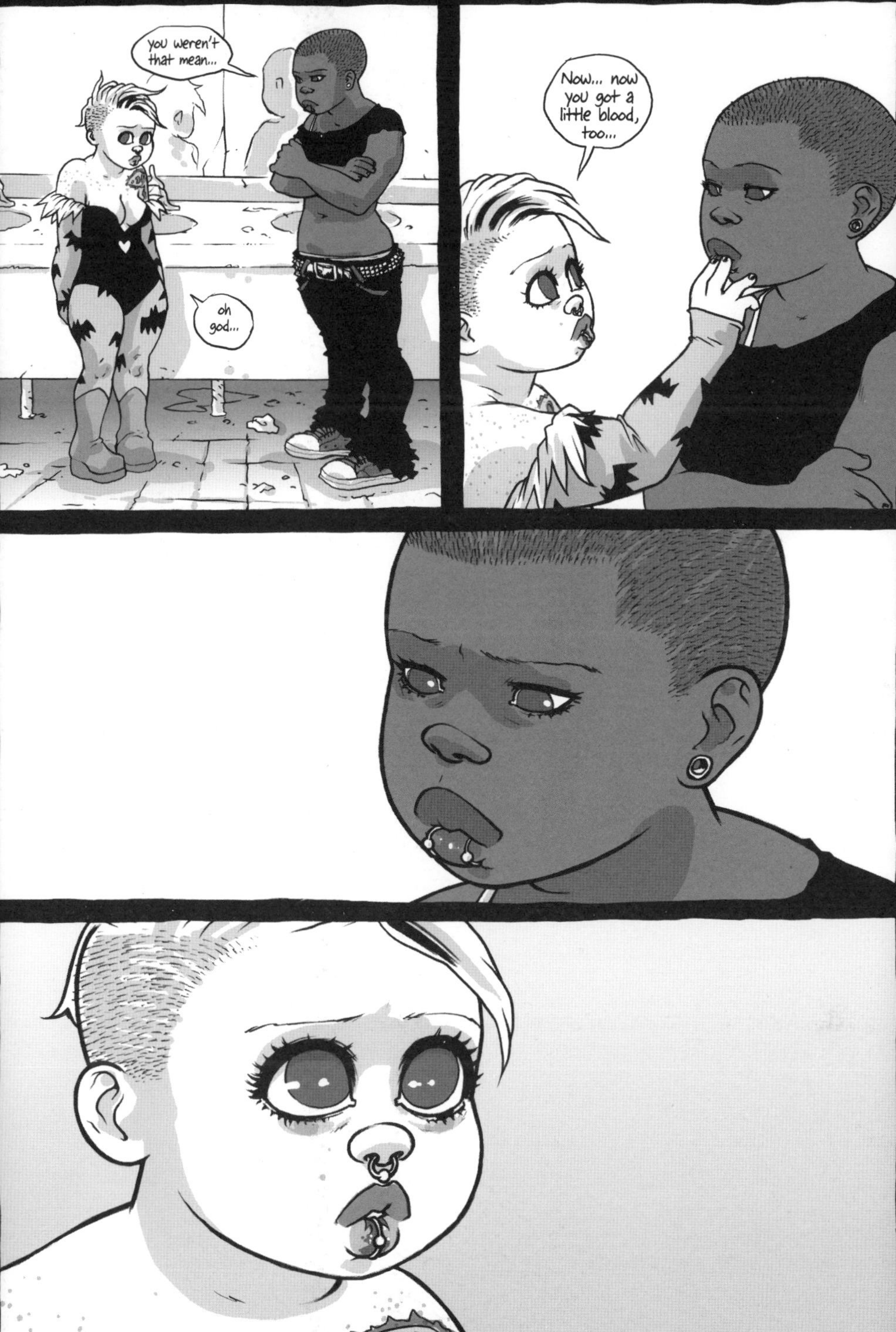
you weren't that mean...
oh god...
Now... now you got a little blood, too...

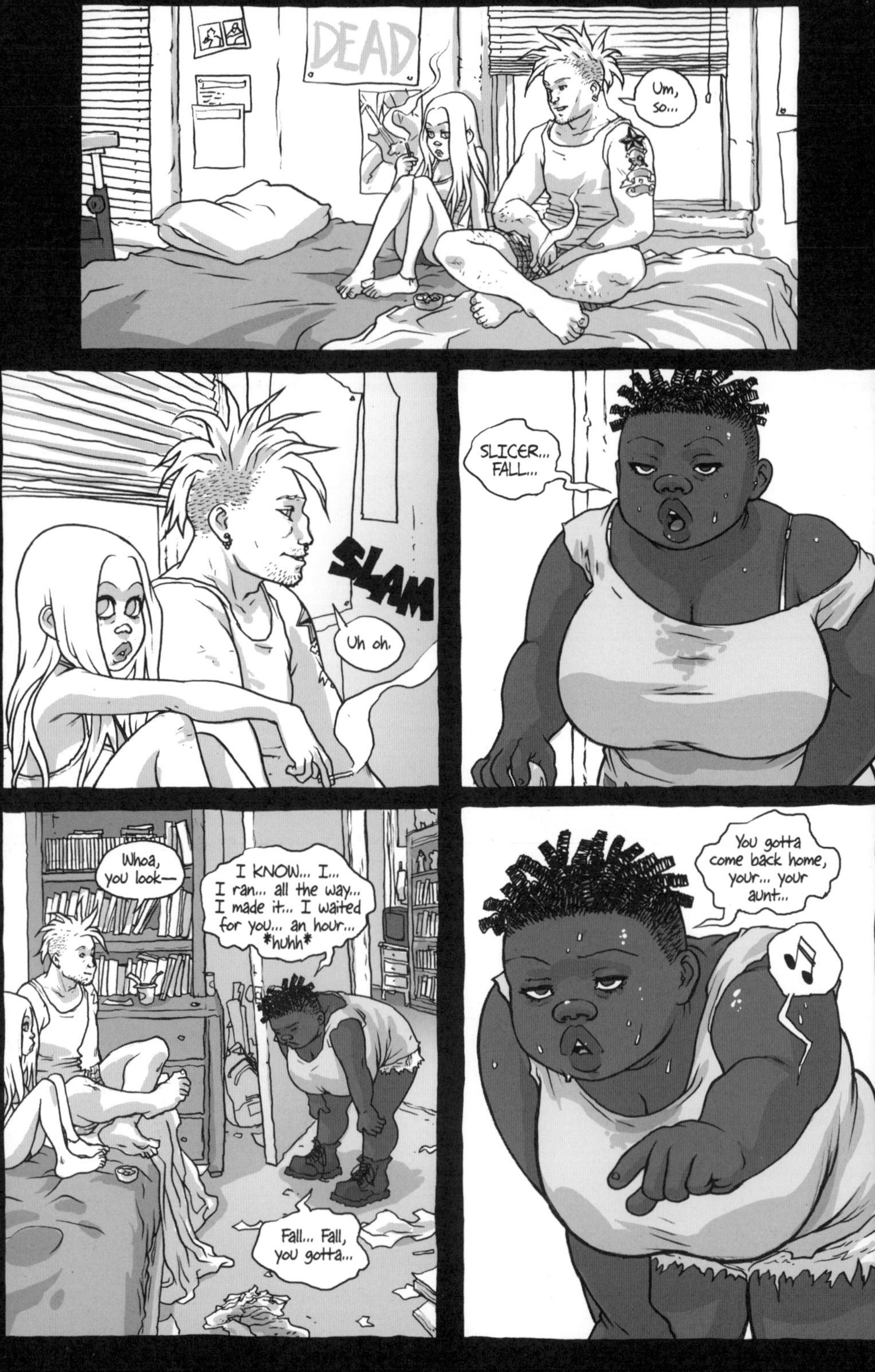
DEAD
Um, so...
SLAM
Uh oh.
SLICER... FALL...
Whoa, you look—
I KNOW... I... I ran... all the way... I made it... I waited for you... an hour... *huhh*
Fall... Fall, you gotta...
You gotta come back home, your... your aunt...

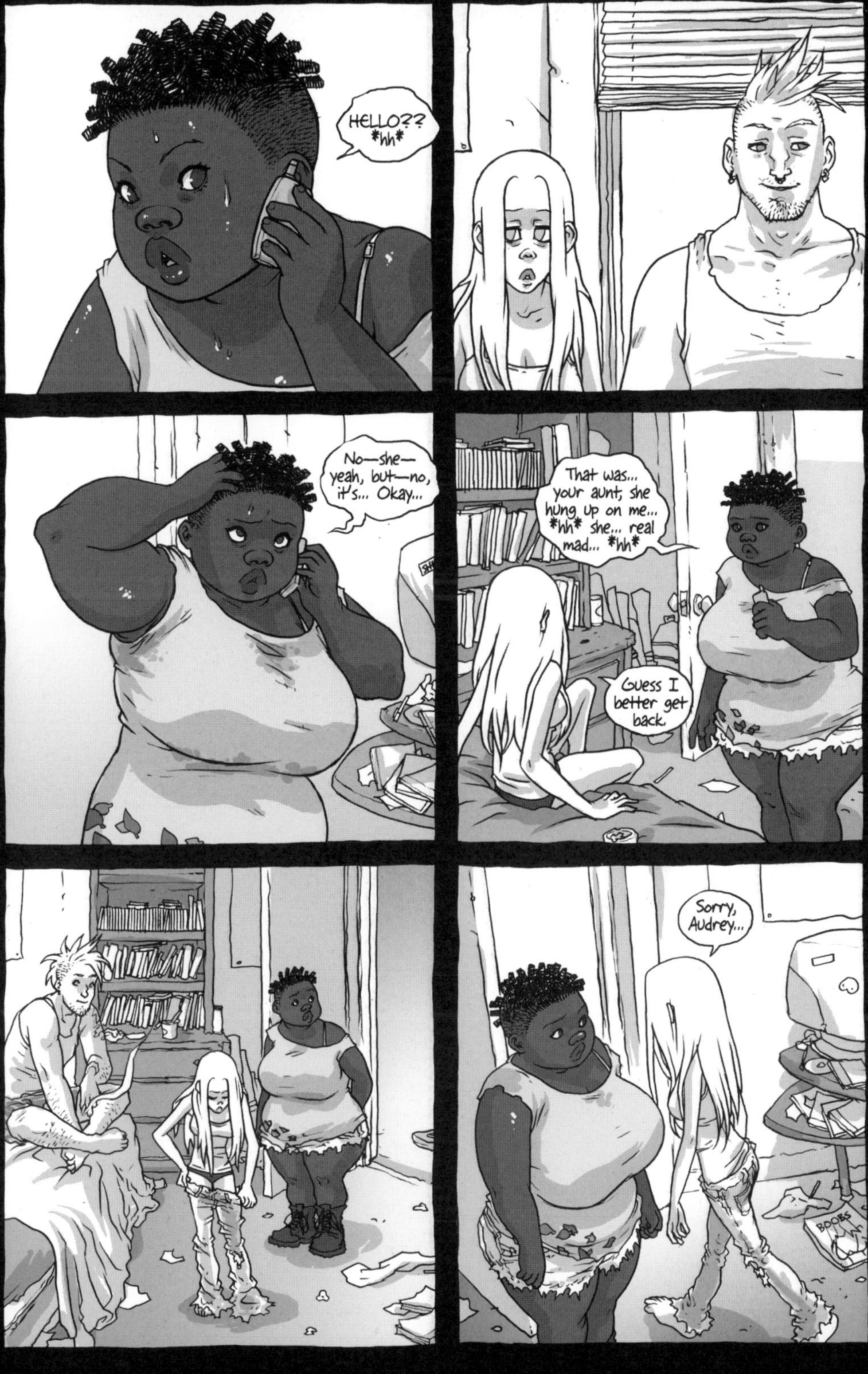
HELLO?? *hh*
No—she— yeah, but—no, it's... Okay...
That was... your aunt, she hung up on me... *hh* she... real mad... *hh*
Guess I better get back.
Sorry, Audrey...
BOOBS

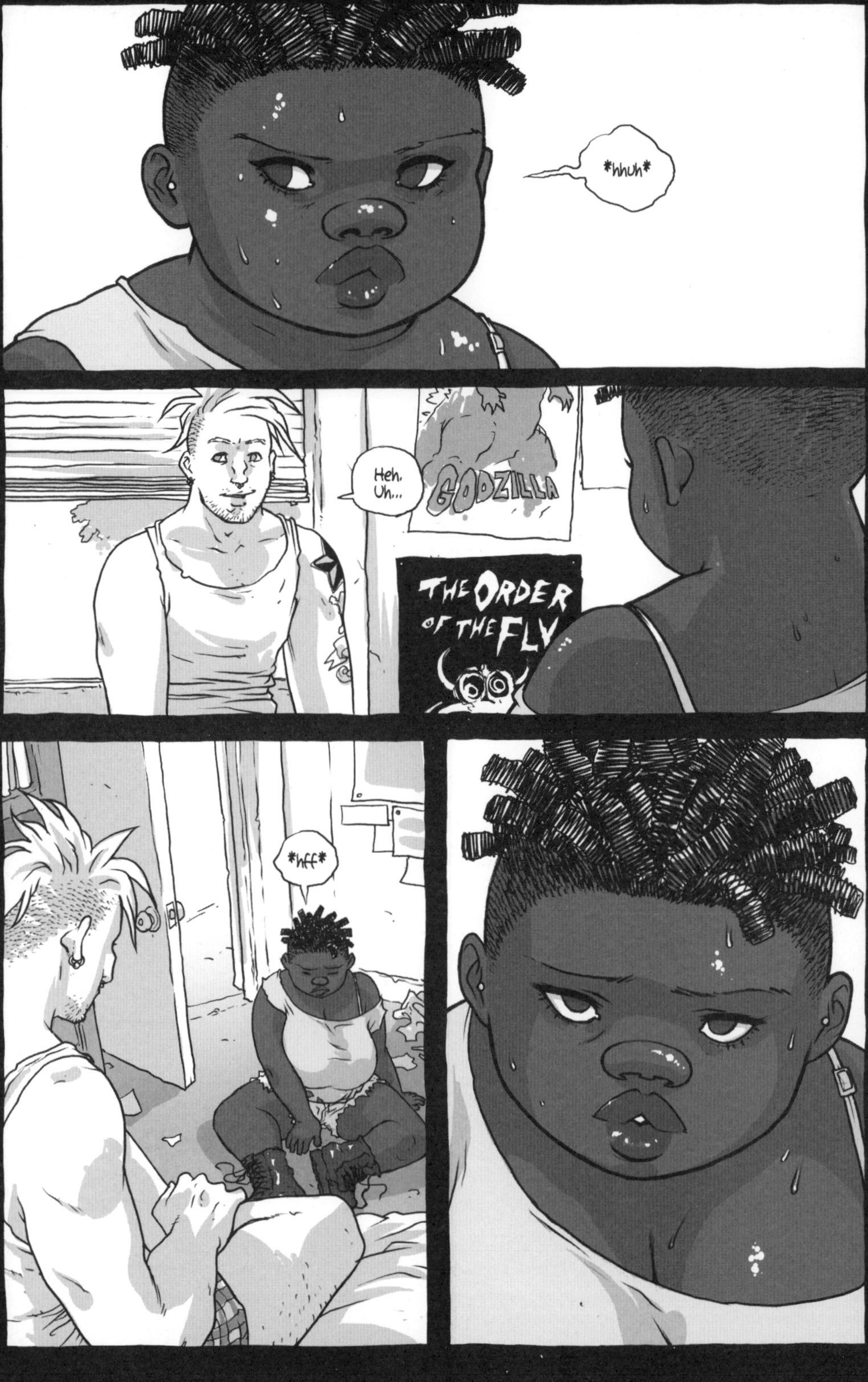
hhuh
Heh. Uh...
GODZILLA
THE ORDER OF THE FLY
hff

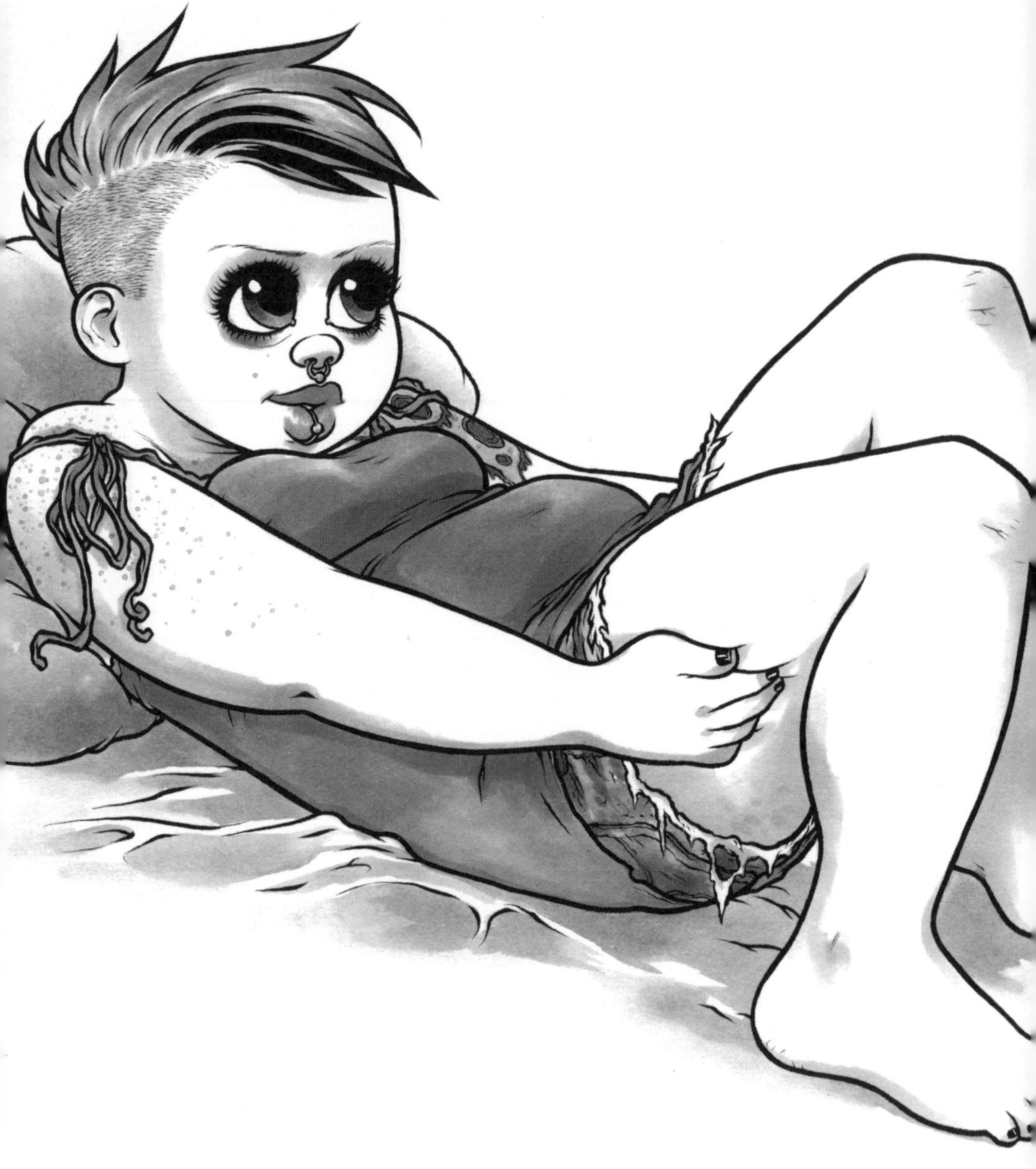

20

The Wonders At Your Feet

[friendtoroaches@gmail.com]

Recent Entries Archive Friends User Info

mara's journal

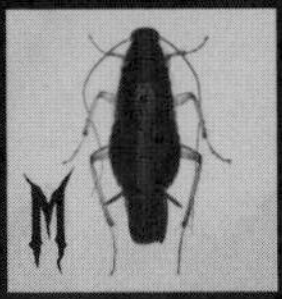

profile

October 31st, 10:38pm

SPEAR MY HEART.

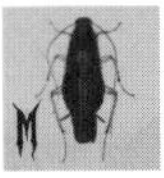

the con is over with. thank god we're only here for one day. this whole thing was Trilby's idea but she doesn't seem like she had that good of a time. she bought a lot of stuff though. Cleo got hurt by this guy she punched a week or so ago, he showed up at the con here. something big happened, also, but i don't think i want to write about it now. i might do a custom post later about it. i don't know. but it's big and i don't know what's going to happen with it. people say that everyone has something to hide but i feel like i have more than most people. but then i think about how some people hide shit like murder or incest or child pornography or conspiracies and how my stuff is totally stupid meaningless stuff compared to that. instead of revealing my one big secret from the con trip, i'll reveal some other smaller stuff that is probably more embarrassing but won't get me in trouble.

- i used to have lots of piercings because i thought they would make me pretty. didn't work.

- i masturbate a lot but i can't orgasm.

- i lie about what i've done with boys (which is pretty much nothing) to sound experienced.

- i bite myself when shit gets too stressful.

- i write stories besides my screenplay stuff but none of my friends know i do.

- i think this one probably goes for everyone, but sometimes i get real freaked out that nobody likes being around me but won't tell me.

- i have a secret tattoo on my left buttcheek that i've never shown anyone except obviously the tattooist who did it. i never wear thongs or change in front of people because of it. it's kind of a stupid tattoo and i won't say what it is here. i guess that'll be for another "secrets" post. i don't know why i keep it so secret, but it's really private to me. maybe Natalie will have to see it for the photoshoot. oh no.

mood: honest
current music: none

[0 comments | leave a comment]

October 31st, 2:22am

OFFERING OF RED RAGE.

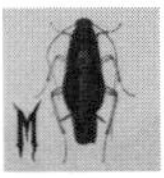

it's officially Halloween, and i have no costume. i'm very pleased about that, i think Halloween is overrated and i hate how people don't dress up in spooky or scary costumes anymore. i thought Halloween was supposed to be about monsters and ghosts and zombies, not nurses or video game characters or pirates. i guess nurses can be scary. but i'm rebelling against that and not dressing up at all. i'm scarier as my regular self than anything i could dress up as.

we finally made it to the hotel which is okay. it's kind of small and a little smelly and there's only one bed, but they actually have wireless internet. the drive down was okay. not too bad. we drove past a big car accident, though, and i saw a bloody guy laying on the road all twisted up like a red, wet pretzel. that's the first time i've ever seen a corpse and i have to say it wasn't that bad. maybe it would be worse if we werent driving by at 50 miles an hour. Cleo seems really upset by it though. she's very sensitive. right now Trilby is watching some alien show on the sci-fi channel, and Martin is taking a shower for some reason.

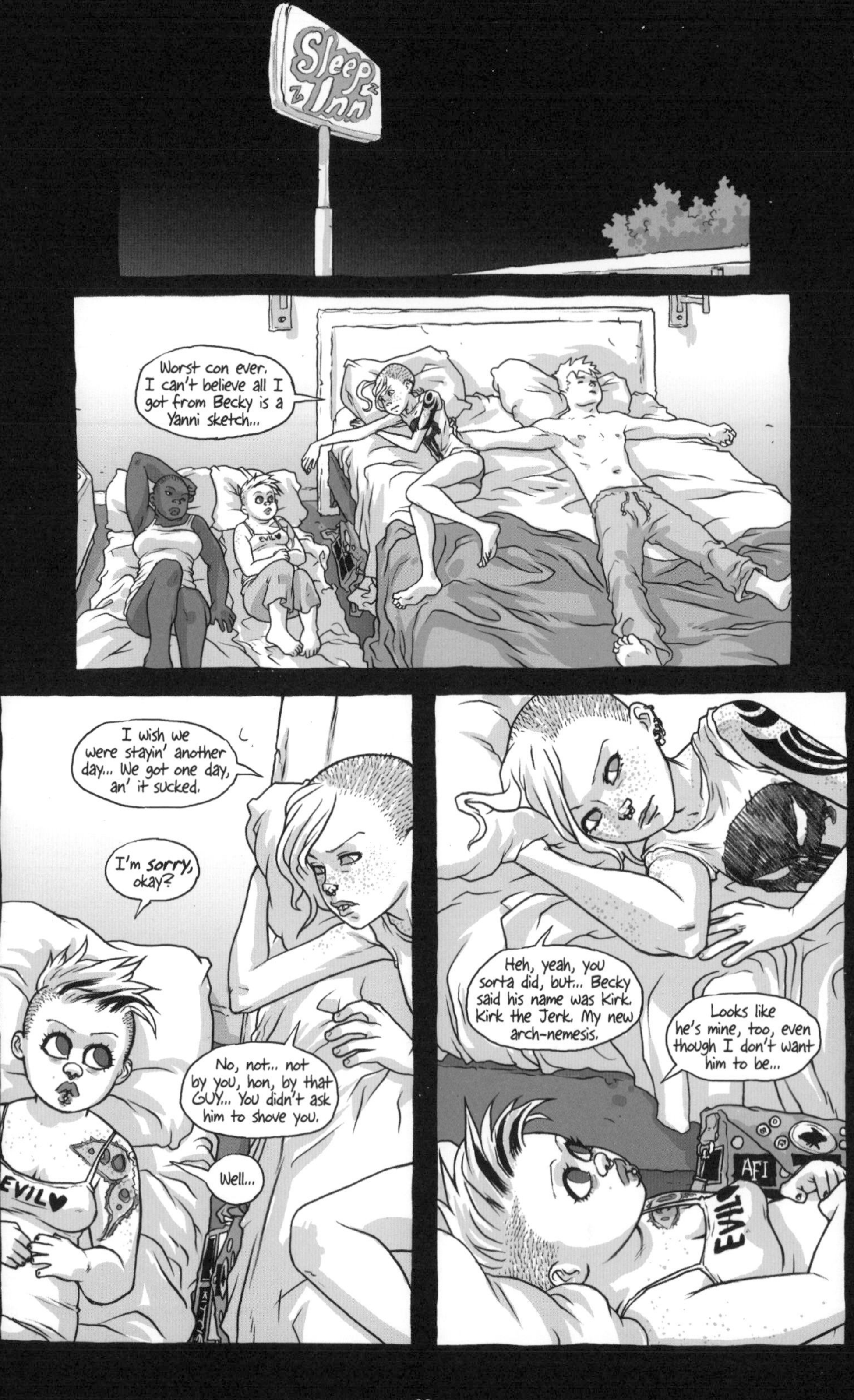
Sleep Inn
Worst con ever. I can't believe all I got from Becky is a Yanni sketch...
I wish we were stayin' another day... We got one day, an' it sucked.
I'm sorry, okay?
No, not... not by you, hon, by that GUY... You didn't ask him to shove you.
Well...
Heh, yeah, you sorta did, but... Becky said his name was Kirk. Kirk the Jerk. My new arch-nemesis.
Looks like he's mine, too, even though I don't want him to be...

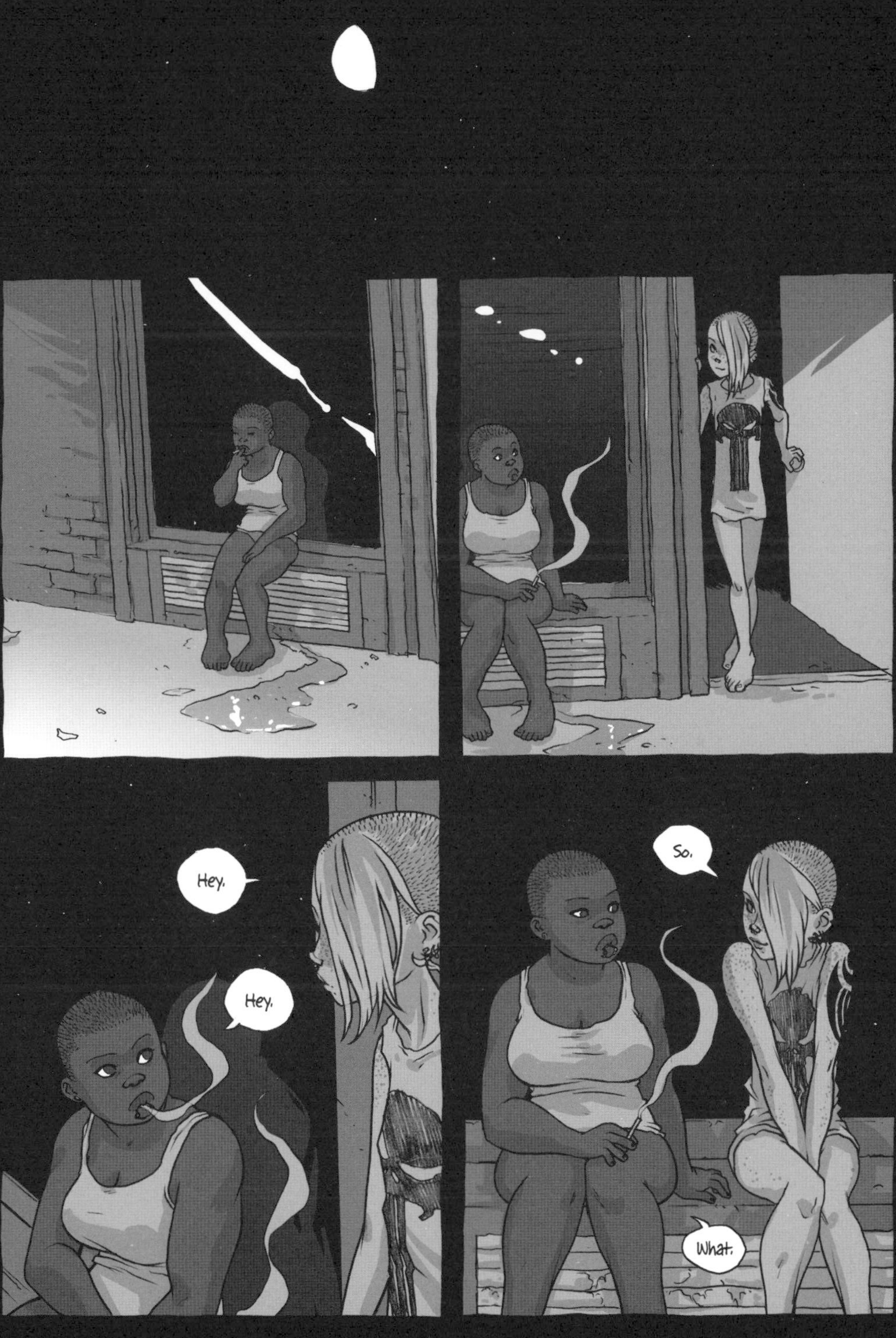
Hey.
Hey.
So.
What.

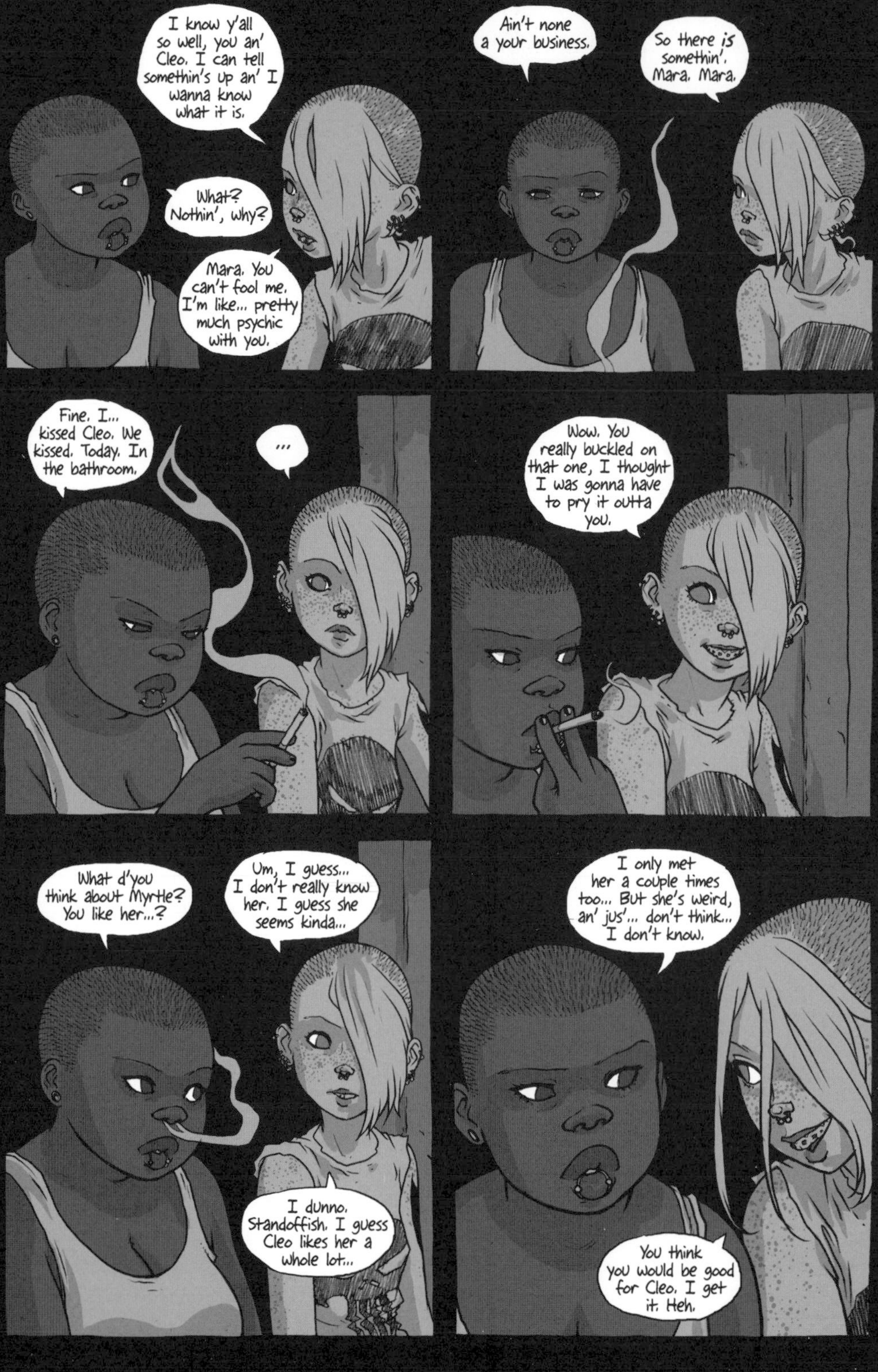
I know y'all so well, you an' Cleo. I can tell somethin's up an' I wanna know what it is.
What? Nothin', why?
Mara. You can't fool me. I'm like... pretty much psychic with you.
Ain't none a your business.
So there *is* somethin'. Mara. Mara.
Fine. I... kissed Cleo. We kissed. Today. In the bathroom.
...
Wow. You really buckled on that one, I thought I was gonna have to pry it outta you.
What d'you think about Myrtle? You like her...?
Um, I guess... I don't really know her. I guess she seems kinda...
I dunno. Standoffish. I guess Cleo likes her a whole lot...
I only met her a couple times too... But she's weird, an' jus'... don't think... I don't know.
You think you would be good for Cleo. I get it. Heh.

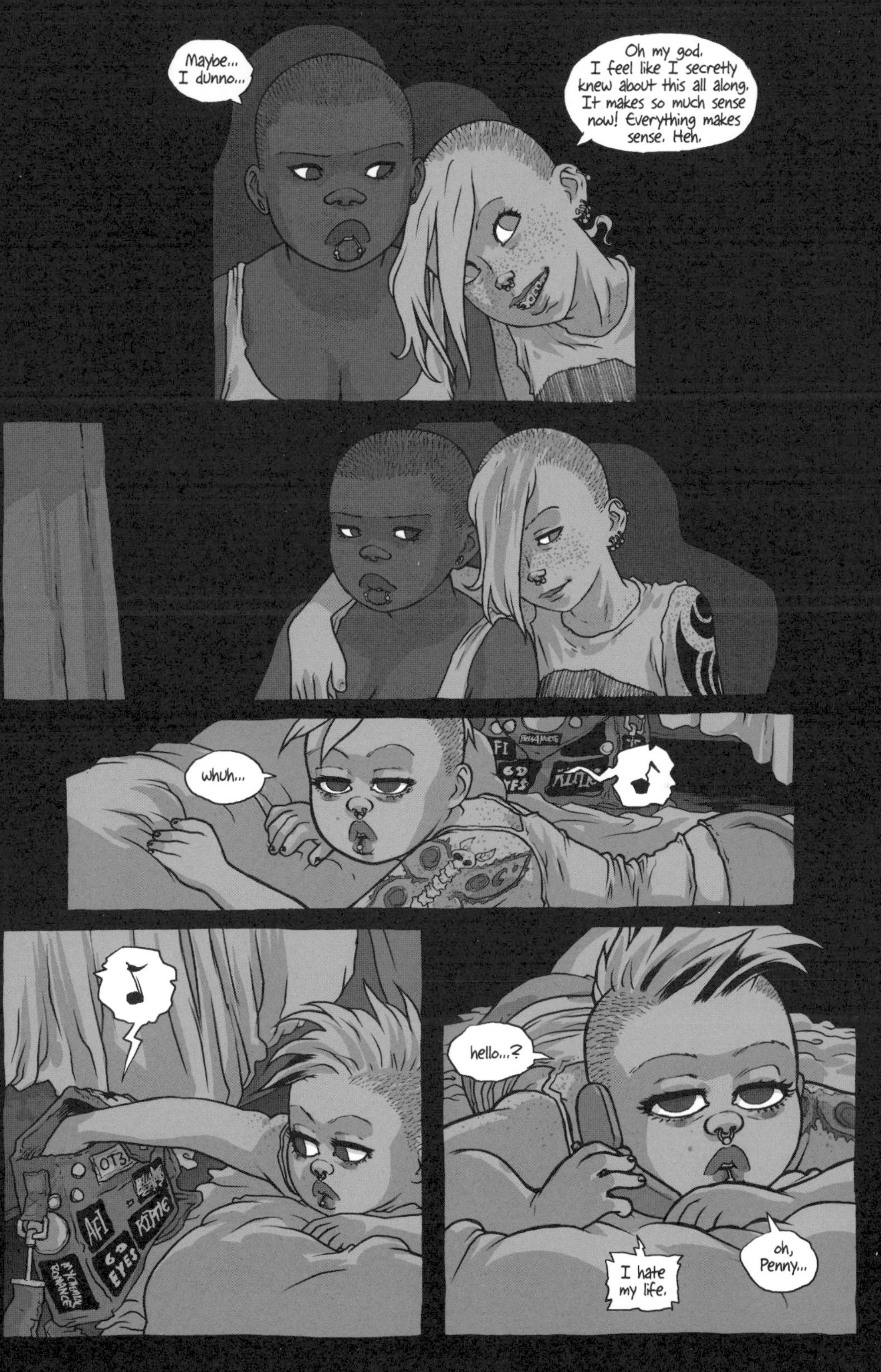
Maybe... I dunno...
Oh my god. I feel like I secretly knew about this all along. It makes so much sense now! Everything makes sense. Heh.
whuh...
hello...?
I hate my life.
oh, Penny...

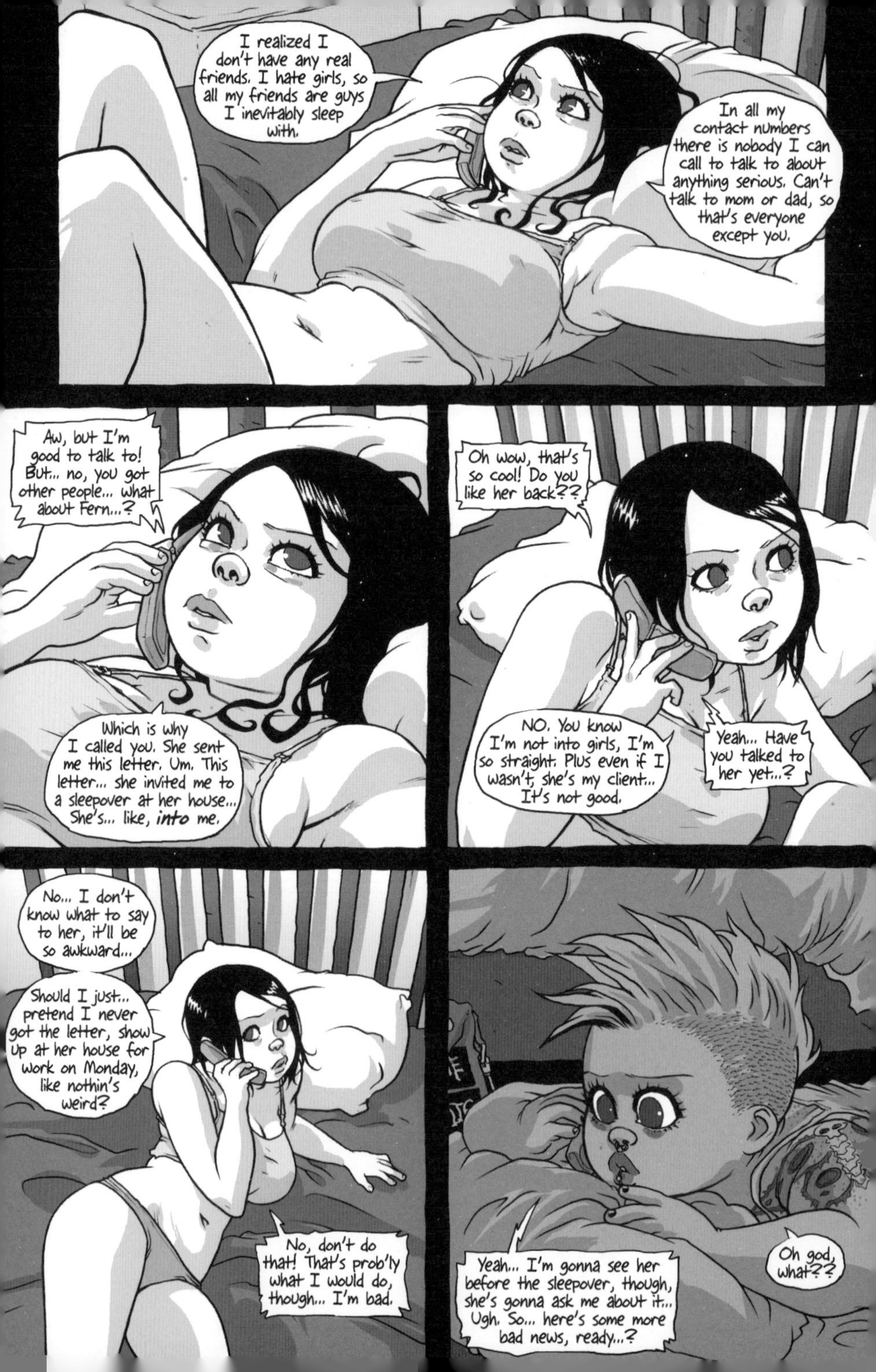

I realized I don't have any real friends. I hate girls, so all my friends are guys I inevitably sleep with.
In all my contact numbers there is nobody I can call to talk to about anything serious. Can't talk to mom or dad, so that's everyone except you.
Aw, but I'm good to talk to! But... no, you got other people... what about Fern...?
Which is why I called you. She sent me this letter. Um. This letter... she invited me to a sleepover at her house... She's... like, *into* me.
Oh wow, that's so cool! Do you like her back??
NO. You know I'm not into girls, I'm so straight. Plus even if I wasn't, she's my client... It's not good.
Yeah... Have you talked to her yet...?
No... I don't know what to say to her, it'll be so awkward...
Should I just... pretend I never got the letter, show up at her house for work on Monday, like nothin's weird?
No, don't do that! That's prob'ly what I would do, though... I'm bad.
Yeah... I'm gonna see her before the sleepover, though, she's gonna ask me about it... Ugh. So... here's some more bad news, ready...?
Oh god, what??

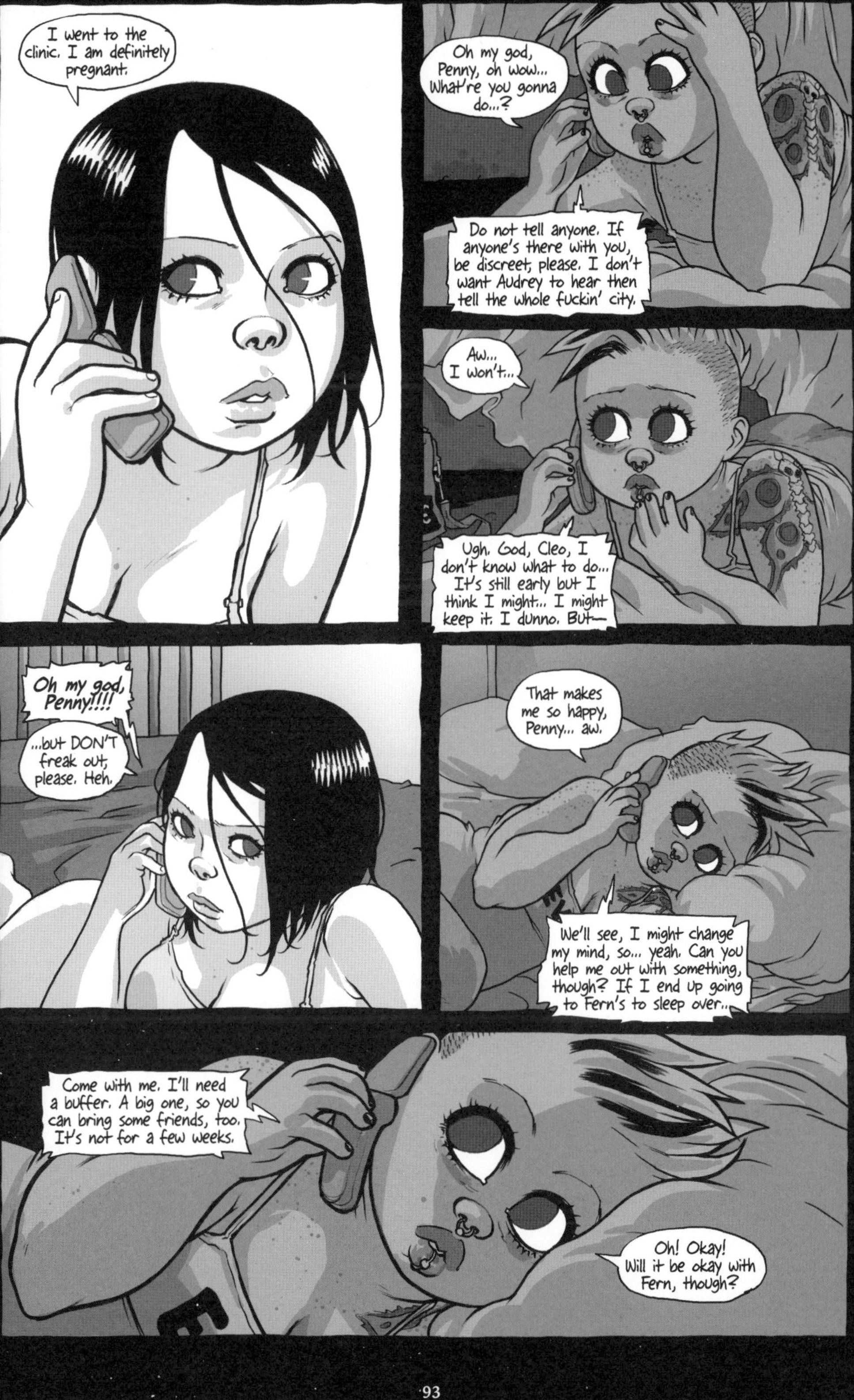
I went to the clinic. I am definitely pregnant.
Oh my god, Penny, oh wow... What're you gonna do...?
Do not tell anyone. If anyone's there with you, be discreet, please. I don't want Audrey to hear then tell the whole fuckin' city.
Aw... I won't...
Ugh. God, Cleo, I don't know what to do... It's still early but I think I might... I might keep it. I dunno. But—
Oh my god, Penny!!!!
...but DON'T freak out, please. Heh.
That makes me so happy, Penny... aw.
We'll see, I might change my mind, so... yeah. Can you help me out with something, though? If I end up going to Fern's to sleep over...
Come with me. I'll need a buffer. A big one, so you can bring some friends, too. It's not for a few weeks.
Oh! Okay! Will it be okay with Fern, though?

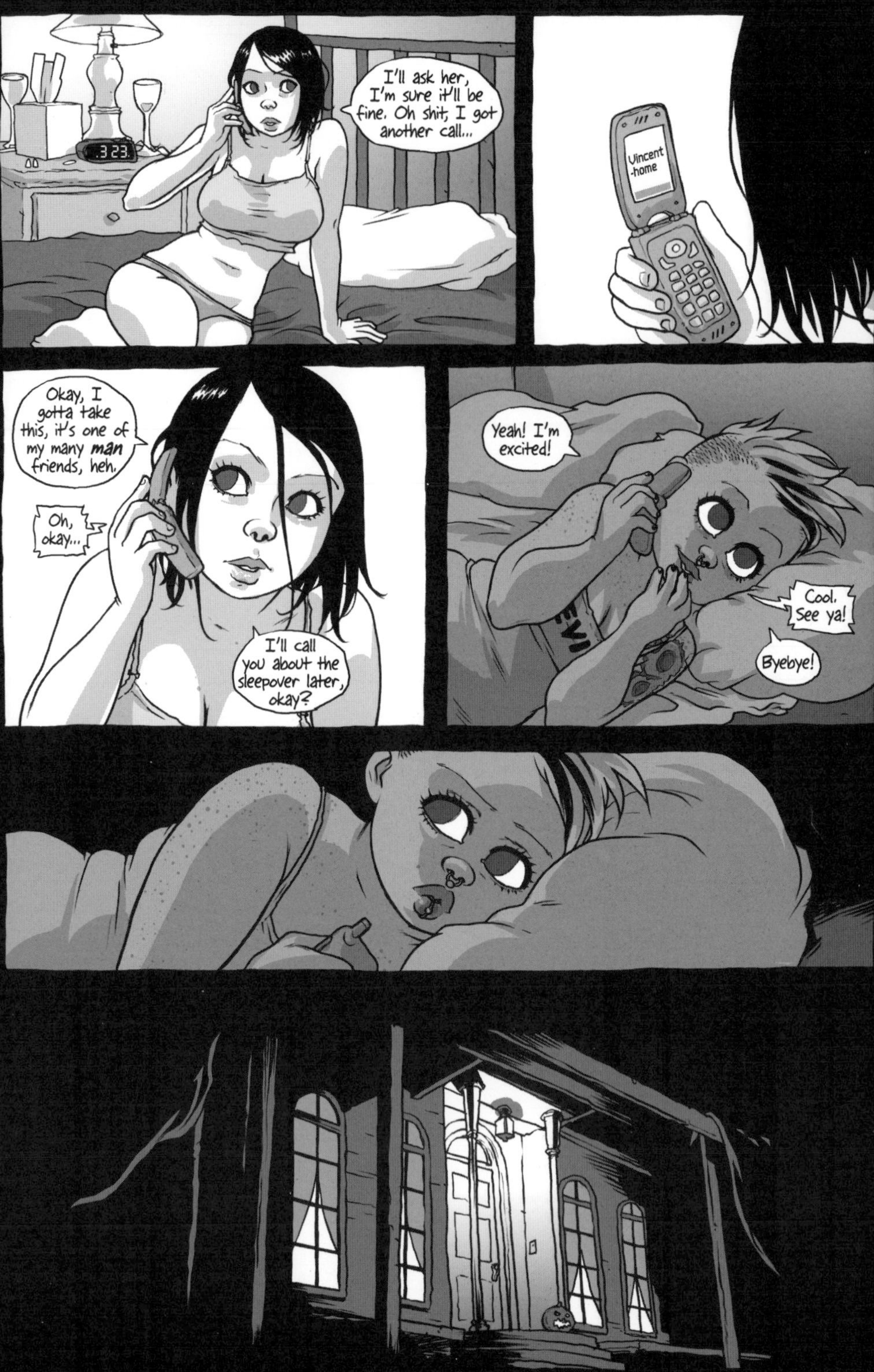
3:23
I'll ask her, I'm sure it'll be fine. Oh shit, I got another call...
Vincent -home
Okay, I gotta take this, it's one of my many **man** friends, heh.
Oh, okay...
I'll call you about the sleepover later, okay?
Yeah! I'm excited!
Cool. See ya!
Byebye!

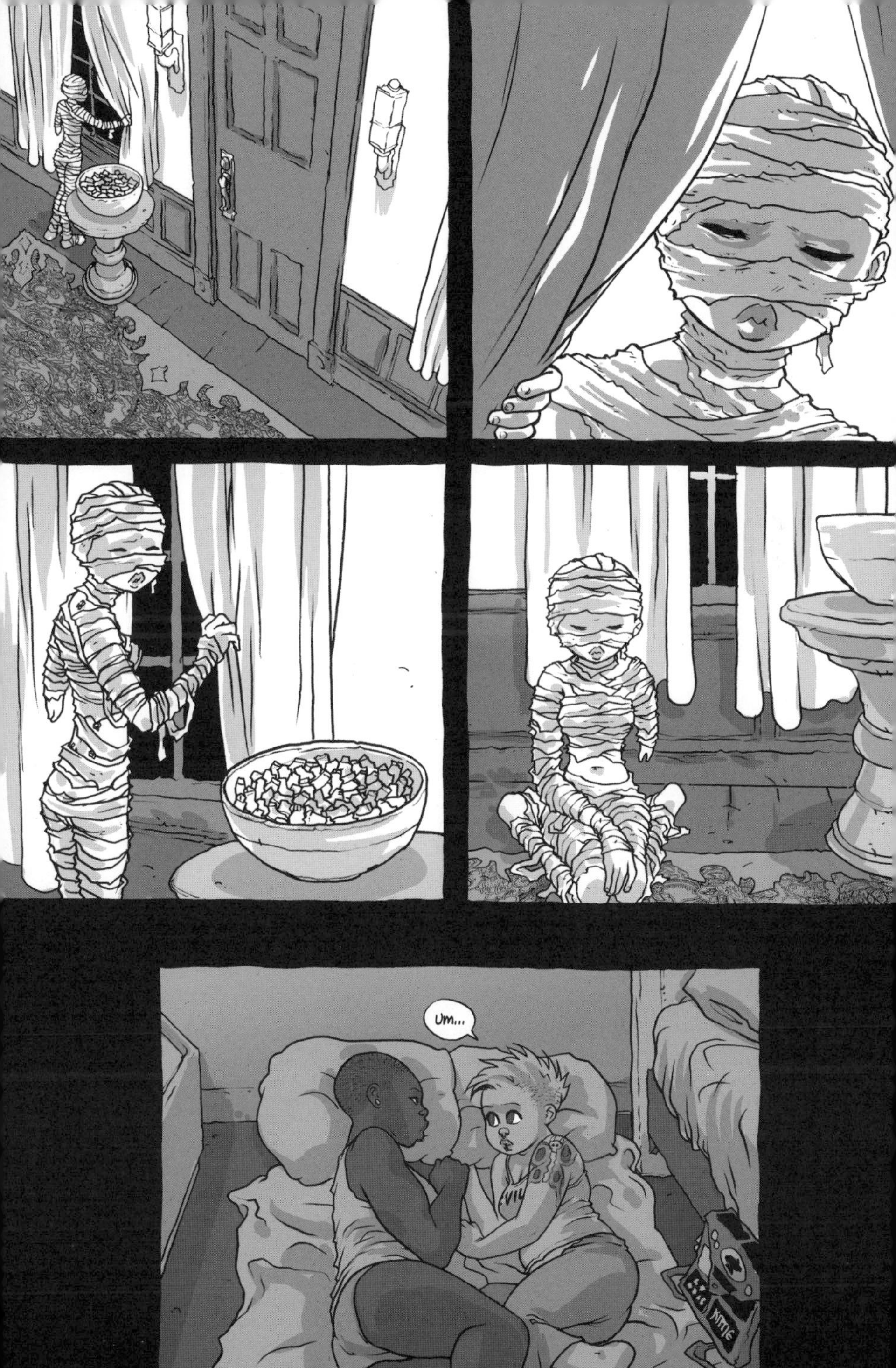
Um...
Kittie

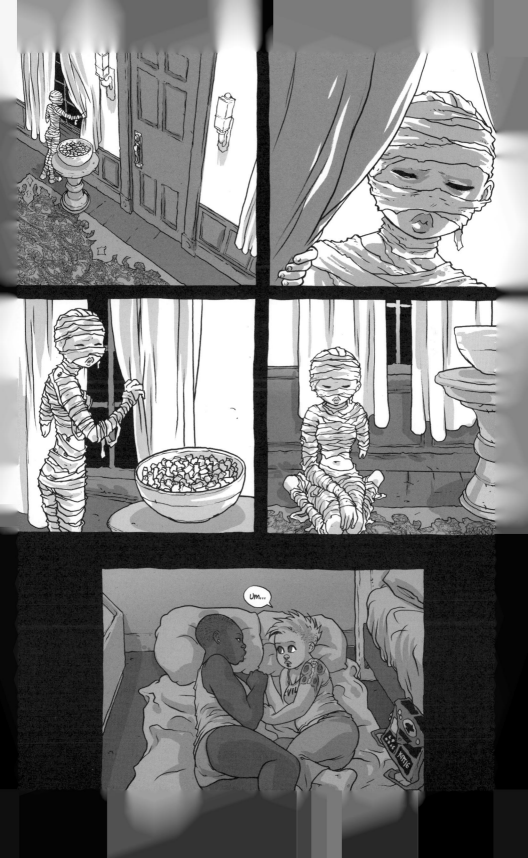

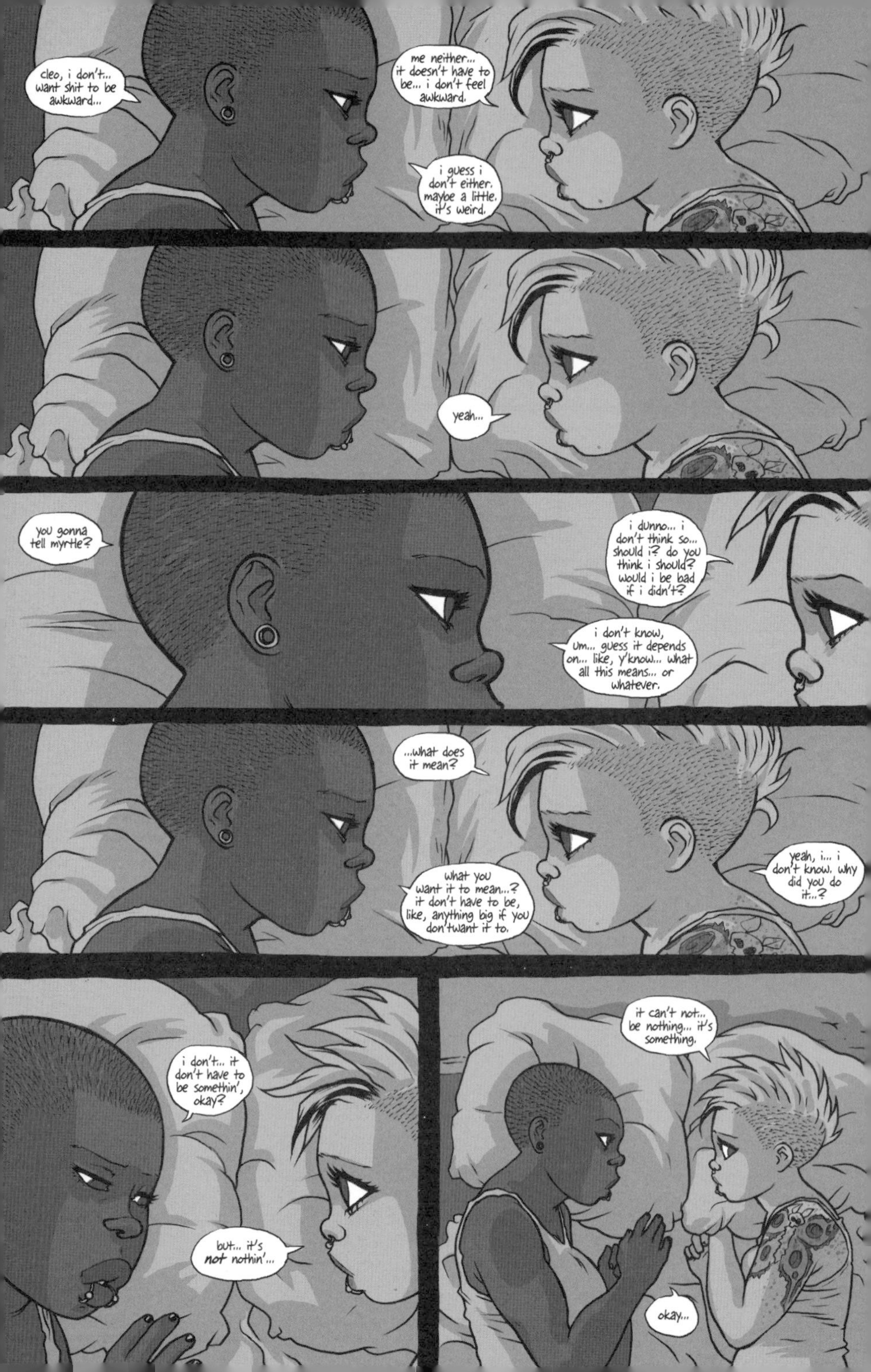
cleo, i don't... want shit to be awkward...
me neither... it doesn't have to be... i don't feel awkward.
i guess i don't either. maybe a little. it's weird.
yeah...
you gonna tell myrtle?
i dunno... i don't think so... should i? do you think i should? would i be bad if i didn't?
i don't know, um... guess it depends on... like, y'know... what all this means... or whatever.
...what does it mean?
what you want it to mean...? it don't have to be, like, anything big if you don't want it to.
yeah, i... i don't know. why did you do it...?
i don't... it don't have to be somethin', okay?
but... it's **not** nothin'...
it can't not... be nothing... it's something.
okay...

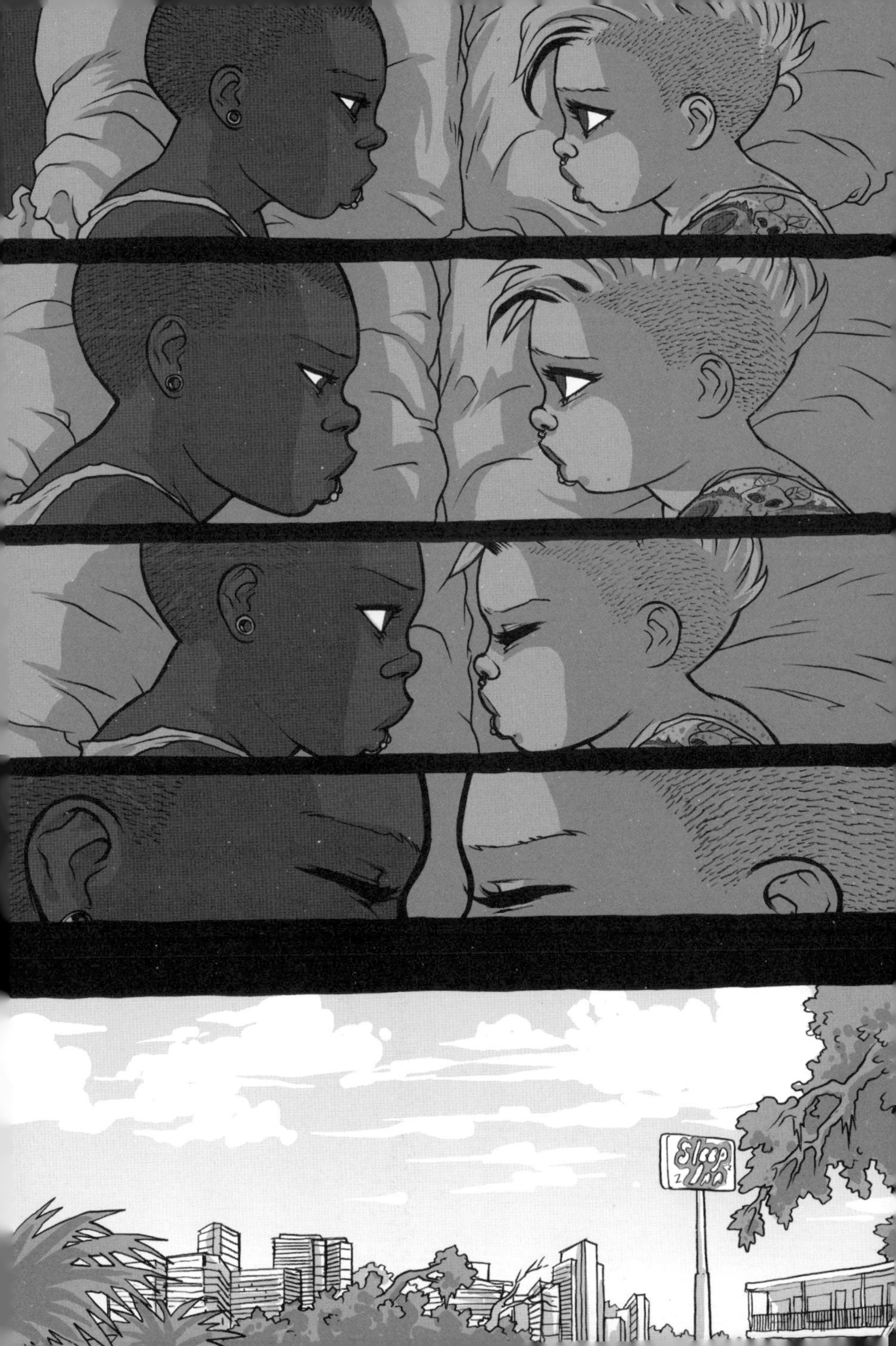
Sleep Inn

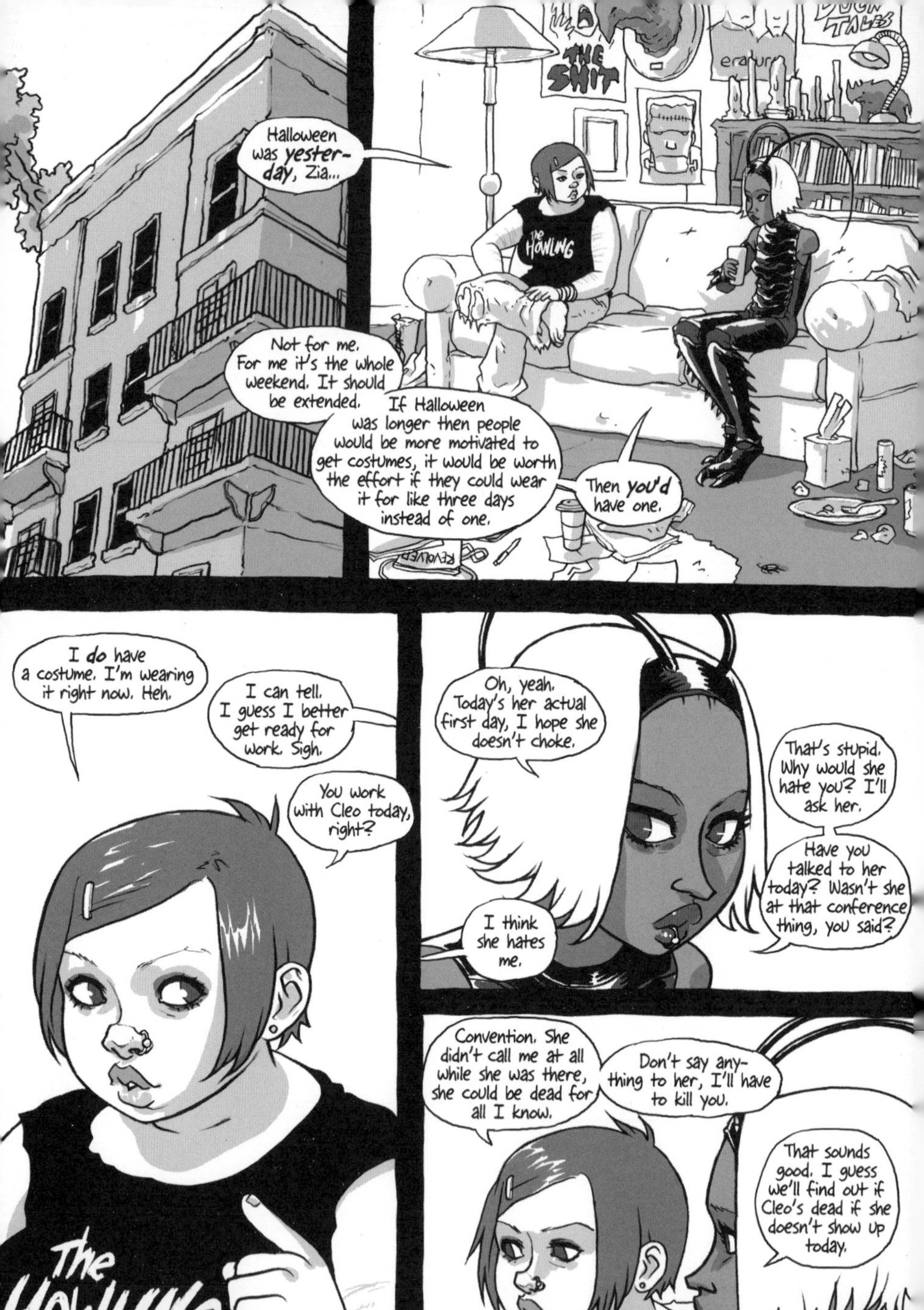
Halloween was yester-day, Zia...
THE SHIT
THE HOWLING
Not for me. For me it's the whole weekend. It should be extended.
If Halloween was longer then people would be more motivated to get costumes, it would be worth the effort if they could wear it for like three days instead of one.
Then you'd have one.
REVOLVER
I do have a costume. I'm wearing it right now. Heh.
I can tell. I guess I better get ready for work. Sigh.
You work with Cleo today, right?
The HOWLING
Oh, yeah. Today's her actual first day, I hope she doesn't choke.
I think she hates me.
That's stupid. Why would she hate you? I'll ask her.
Have you talked to her today? Wasn't she at that conference thing, you said?
Convention. She didn't call me at all while she was there, she could be dead for all I know.
Don't say any-thing to her, I'll have to kill you.
That sounds good. I guess we'll find out if Cleo's dead if she doesn't show up today.

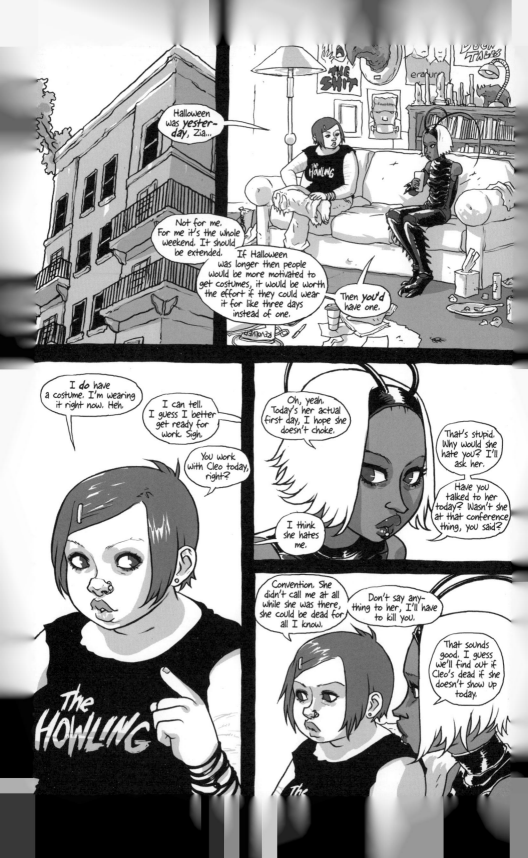

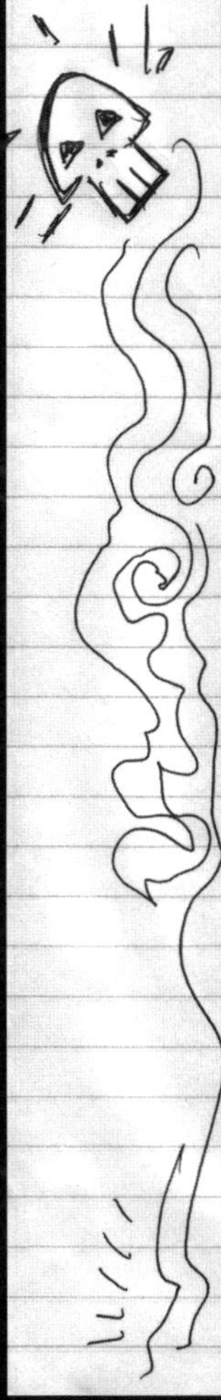

November 1

i'm writing this before my first day at work! Oh my god, I am actually going to work, a real job, I'm so nervous! I don't even know what to wear, they don't have a uniform or any dress code really, so anything goes! I'd almost rather them have a uniform, then I wouldn't have to think so much about it! thank god my lip isn't bad or swollen. its a little yucky on the inside where i bit it but that's okay.

the Slutty Angels are performing in a couple of weeks, I'm so excited. i wish they had more gigs but they're such a small band (so far!). it's also going to be weird because they're going to play the song Myrtle's writing for me! i know its a really sweet and amazing gesture but i still feel kind of pressured by it...
i think i was saying before how much of an undertaking creating a song is, since it requires writing so many different parts and takes the whole band to perform... all for me. i don't know. i feel

so great about it but at the same time it's still scary in some ways. and... something happened with mara that makes it even scarier. i ran afoul of that guy from the Bella Morte show who I punched, there was violence, mara took me into the bathroom to clean up and...

we kissed. i feel like... totally alien writing that, but it happened and can't be denied. it just came out of nowhere. and I think normally i'd be freaking out or grossed out because she's my friend and i've known her for so long but on the other hand i don't feel that weird about it, at least not the kiss itself or what it might mean. but i do feel confused about it. does it **HAVE** to mean anything? can two friends do something like this and just be normal about it? i know some girls can can do that. but mara also is like sort of into me in some extrafriend way, so does she want this to mean something more? we haven't really talked about it much yet, but i hope it isn't grossed over even though i'd feel weird bringing it up now. and what if it does turn out to mean something? do i have to choose, will it come down to me having to choose one girl over the other? Myrtle's writing me a song, but Mara... she's my best friend pretty much, what would a romance be like with that sort of foundation? but then a romance would WRECK a best friendship, too... and what if it did happen, i can't even bear thinking about us telling our families... at least we know each other's families so that wouldn't be weird. i can't believe i'm even on this train of thought, i can't believe any of this is happening. it's so crazy.

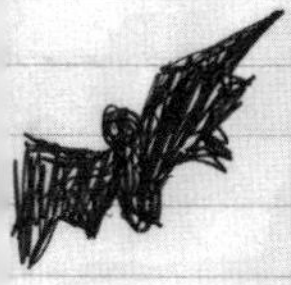

it's really scary liking girls now. I find myself noticing things about random girls that i didn't before and then i start questioning it and myself. I keep thinking about telling everyone, that maybe that's the best and easiest thing to do, but then i think i have to keep everything inside because it might not be okay if everyone knew, i don't know

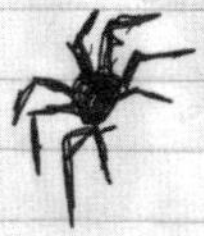

how they would react, and i don't think i'm even comfortable yet coming out, am i even IN?? i don't know!! and like even if all ~~omg~~ my friends and family knew, is it okay to go out to like a restaurant or something and hold Myrtle's hand? what would people do? i think ~~about~~ a lot about Audrey, how, besides in our friend group she's still in the closet, and how terrifying being in there is AND how terrifying being out could be. i don't know how she lives everyday with this gigantic secret plus the knowledge that if it wasn't a secret anymore, things might be ~~even~~ WORSE for her. her parents could disown her, everyone ~~could~~ could shun her and throw things at her even, or be all prejudiced all the time. or i read about in the news how gay people get attacked and stuff like that. what if Audrey committed suicide because things got so bad? could i get to that point if i came out of the closet? i just said i was in the closet. am i? i don't know. i don't know where I am.
   time ~~for~~ my first day at BURIAL GRANDS!!! i'm excited about working with that girl Zia, she is super cool.

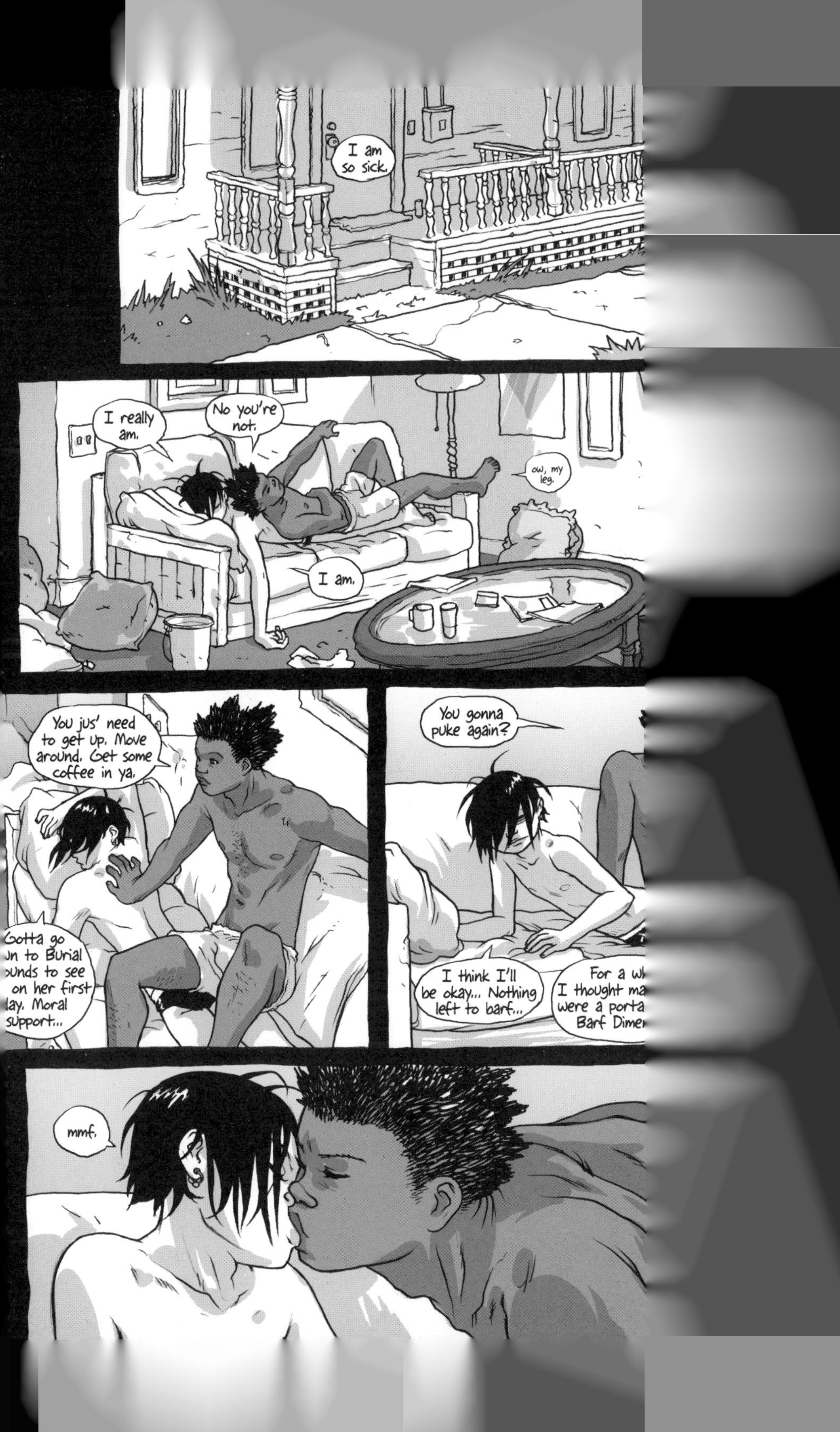

I am so sick.
I really am.
No you're not.
ow, my leg.
I am.
You jus' need to get up. Move around. Get some coffee in ya.
Gotta go
un to Burial
ounds to see
on her first
day. Moral
support...
You gonna puke again?
I think I'll be okay... Nothing left to barf...
For a wh
I thought ma
were a porta
Barf Dime
mmf.

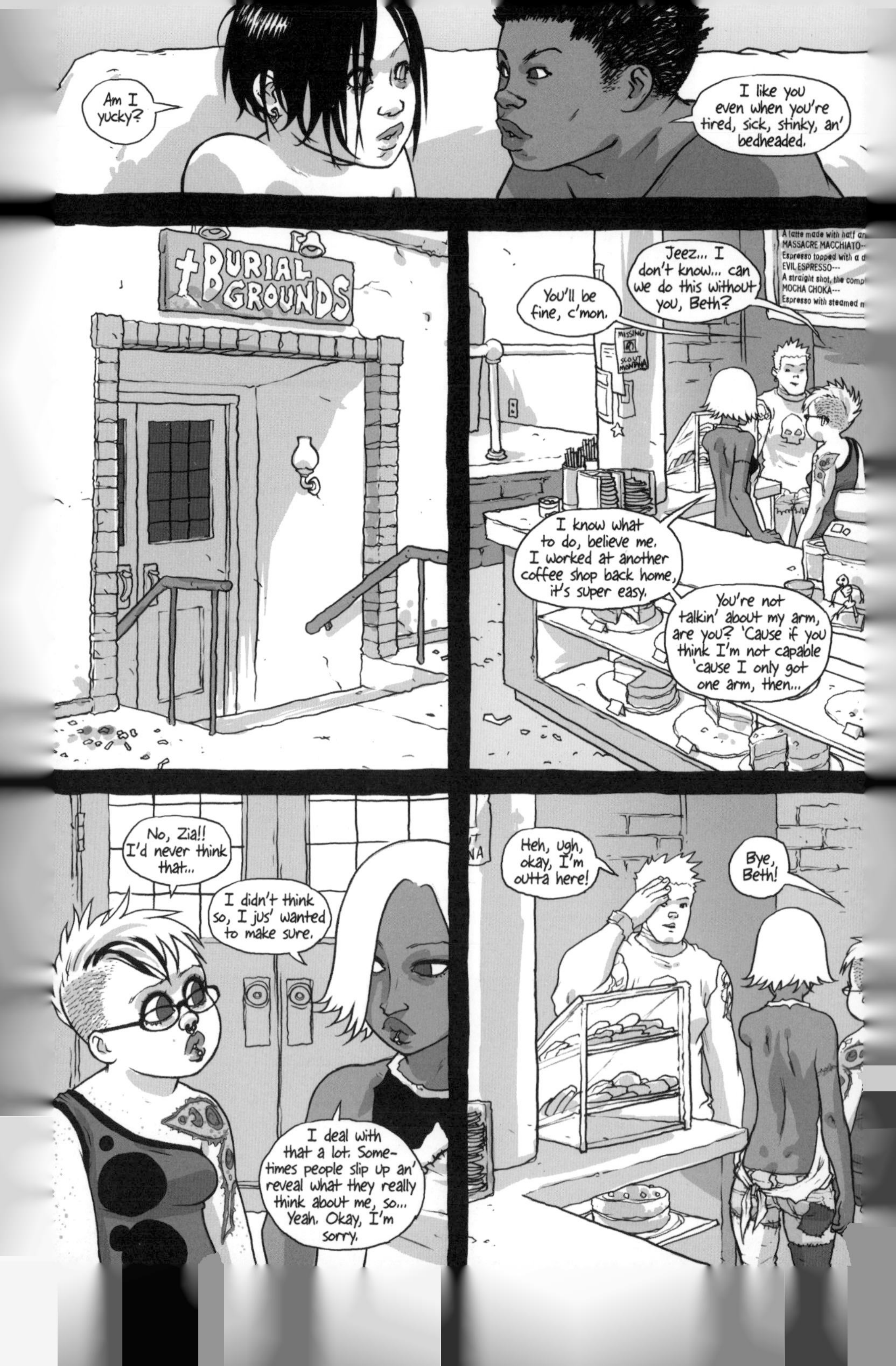
Am I yucky?
I like you even when you're tired, sick, stinky, an' bedheaded.
BURIAL GROUNDS
MASSACRE MACCHIATO---
EVIL ESPRESSO---
MOCHA CHOKA---
MISSING SCOUT MONTANA
Jeez... I don't know... can we do this without you, Beth?
You'll be fine, c'mon.
I know what to do, believe me. I worked at another coffee shop back home, it's super easy.
You're not talkin' about my arm, are you? 'Cause if you think I'm not capable 'cause I only got one arm, then...
No, Zia!! I'd never think that...
I didn't think so, I jus' wanted to make sure.
I deal with that a lot. Sometimes people slip up an' reveal what they really think about me, so... Yeah. Okay, I'm sorry.
Heh, ugh, okay, I'm outta here!
Bye, Beth!

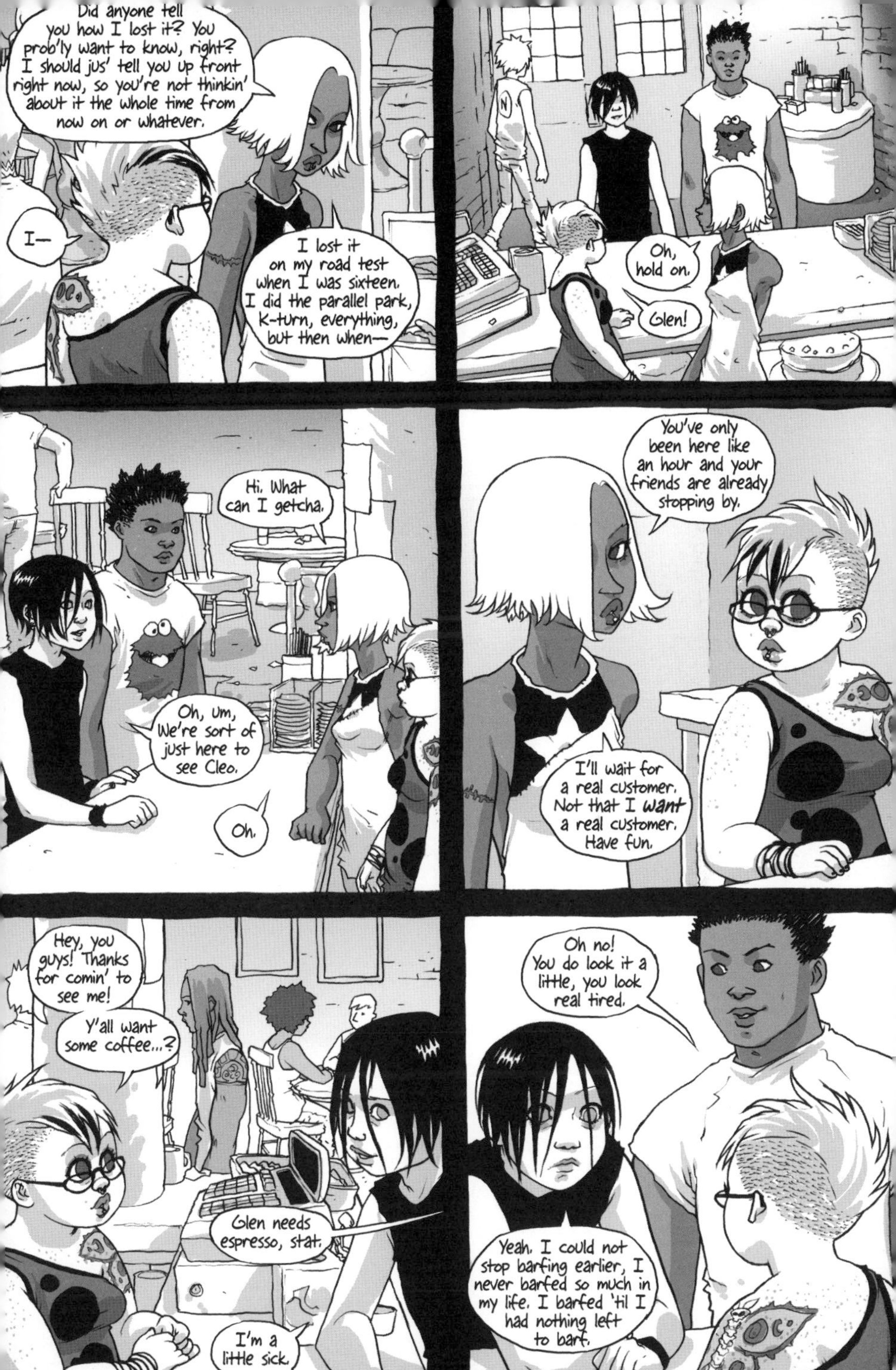

Did anyone tell you how I lost it? You prob'ly want to know, right? I should jus' tell you up front right now, so you're not thinkin' about it the whole time from now on or whatever.
I—
I lost it on my road test when I was sixteen. I did the parallel park, K-turn, everything, but then when—
Oh, hold on.
Glen!
Hi. What can I getcha.
Oh, um, We're sort of just here to see Cleo.
Oh.
You've only been here like an hour and your friends are already stopping by.
I'll wait for a real customer. Not that I *want* a real customer. Have fun.
Hey, you guys! Thanks for comin' to see me!
Y'all want some coffee...?
Glen needs espresso, stat.
I'm a little sick.
Oh no! You do look it a little, you look real tired.
Yeah. I could not stop barfing earlier, I never barfed so much in my life. I barfed 'til I had nothing left to barf.

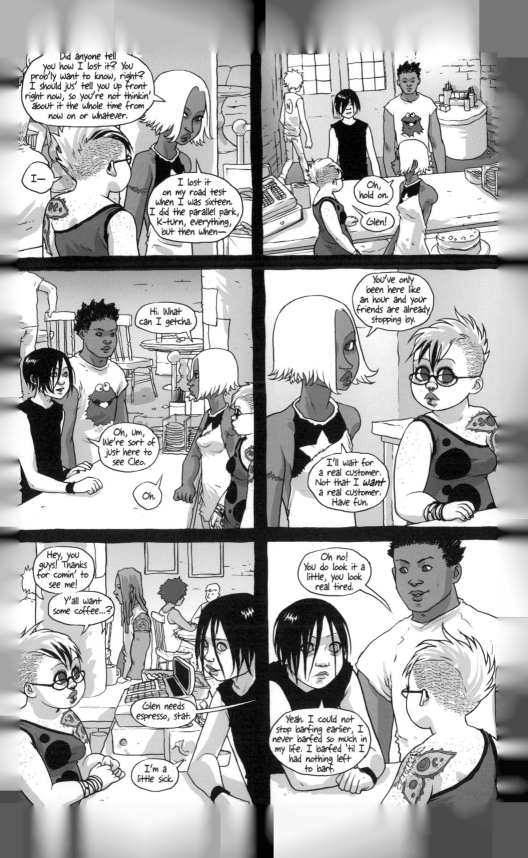

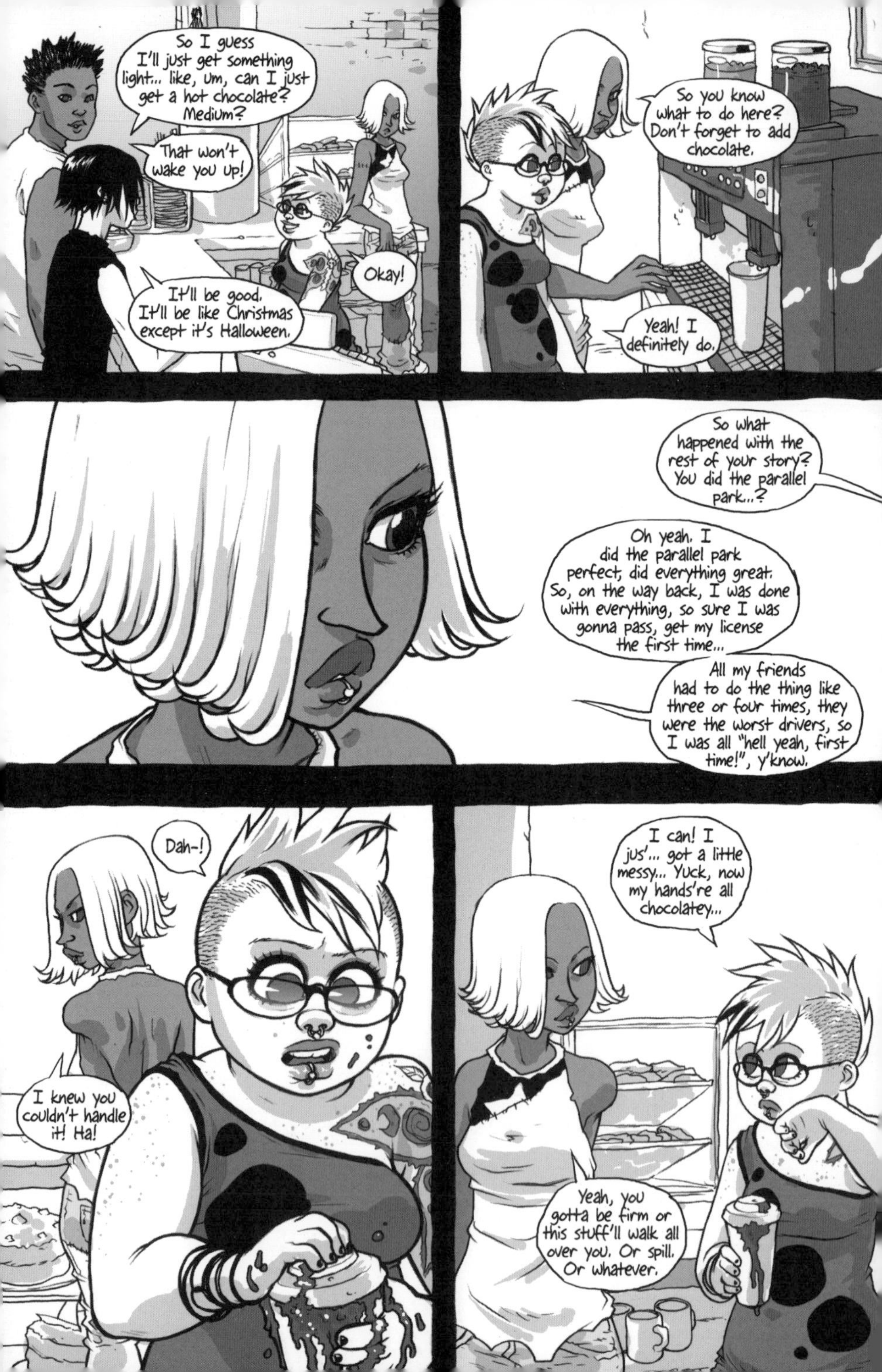
So I guess I'll just get something light... like, um, can I just get a hot chocolate? Medium?
That won't wake you up!
It'll be good. It'll be like Christmas except it's Halloween.
Okay!
So you know what to do here? Don't forget to add chocolate.
Yeah! I definitely do.
So what happened with the rest of your story? You did the parallel park...?
Oh yeah. I did the parallel park perfect, did everything great. So, on the way back, I was done with everything, so sure I was gonna pass, get my license the first time...
All my friends had to do the thing like three or four times, they were the worst drivers, so I was all "hell yeah, first time!", y'know.
Dah-!
I knew you couldn't handle it! Ha!
I can! I jus'... got a little messy... Yuck, now my hands're all chocolatey...
Yeah, you gotta be firm or this stuff'll walk all over you. Or spill. Or whatever.

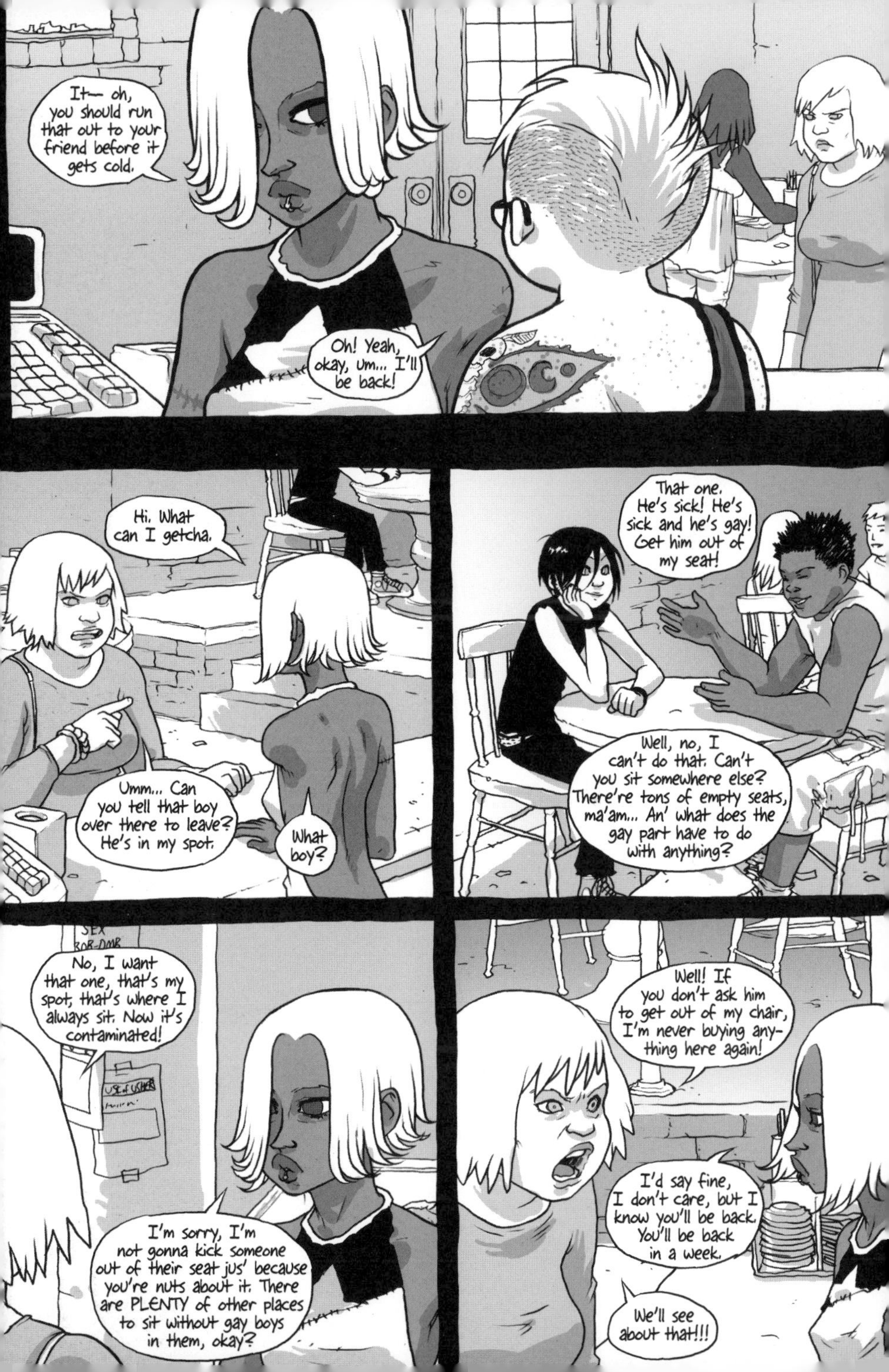
It— oh, you should run that out to your friend before it gets cold.
Oh! Yeah, okay, um... I'll be back!
Hi. What can I getcha.
Umm... Can you tell that boy over there to leave? He's in my spot.
What boy?
That one. He's sick! He's sick and he's gay! Get him out of my seat!
Well, no, I can't do that. Can't you sit somewhere else? There're tons of empty seats, ma'am... An' what does the gay part have to do with anything?
No, I want that one, that's my spot, that's where I always sit. Now it's contaminated!
I'm sorry, I'm not gonna kick someone out of their seat jus' because you're nuts about it. There are PLENTY of other places to sit without gay boys in them, okay?
Well! If you don't ask him to get out of my chair, I'm never buying anything here again!
I'd say fine, I don't care, but I know you'll be back. You'll be back in a week.
We'll see about that!!!

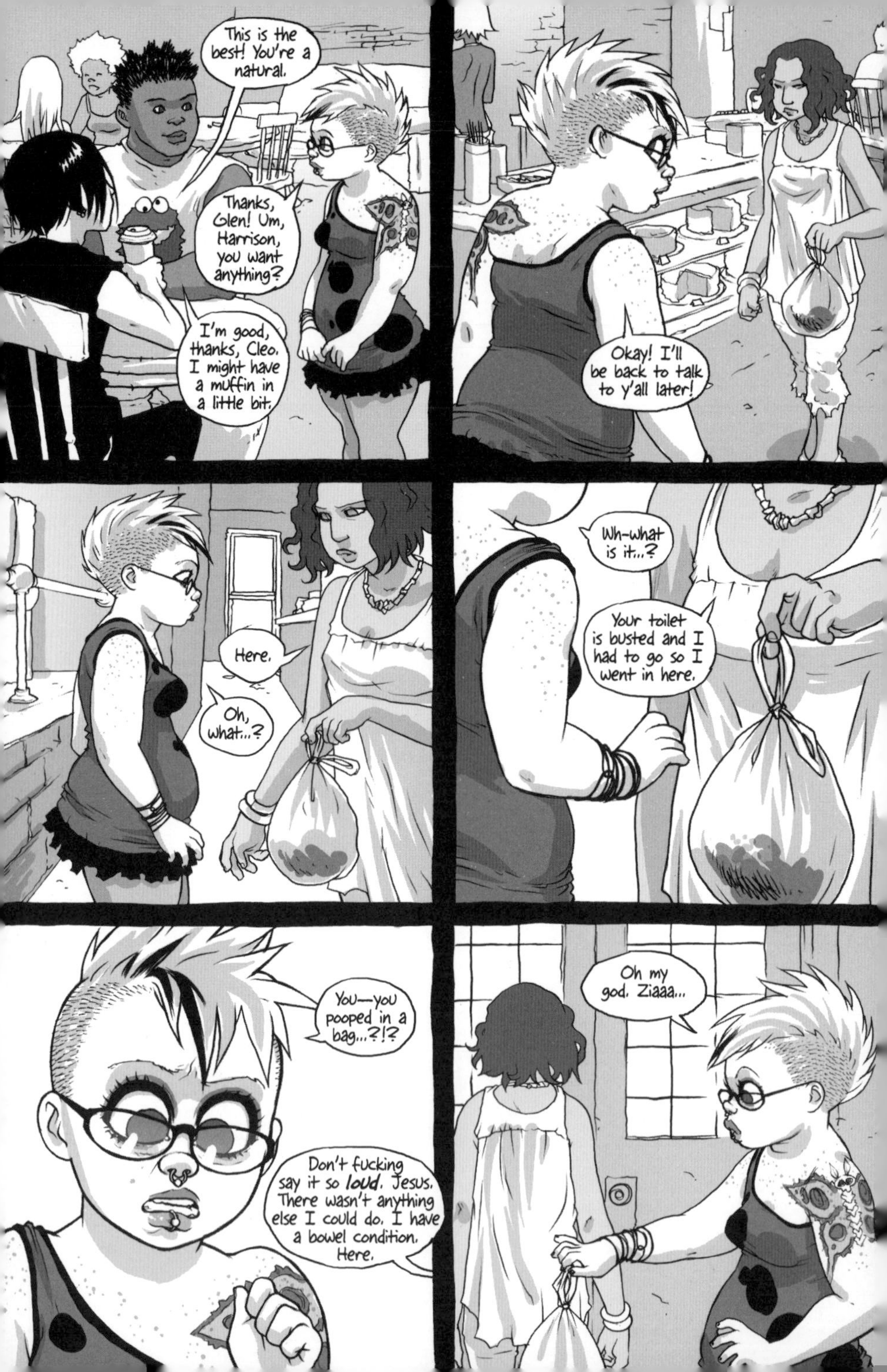
This is the best! You're a natural.
Thanks, Glen! Um, Harrison, you want anything?
I'm good, thanks, Cleo. I might have a muffin in a little bit.
Okay! I'll be back to talk to y'all later!
Here.
Oh, what...?
Wh-what is it...?
Your toilet is busted and I had to go so I went in here.
You—you pooped in a bag...?!?
Don't fucking say it so loud. Jesus. There wasn't anything else I could do. I have a bowel condition. Here.
Oh my god. Ziaaa...

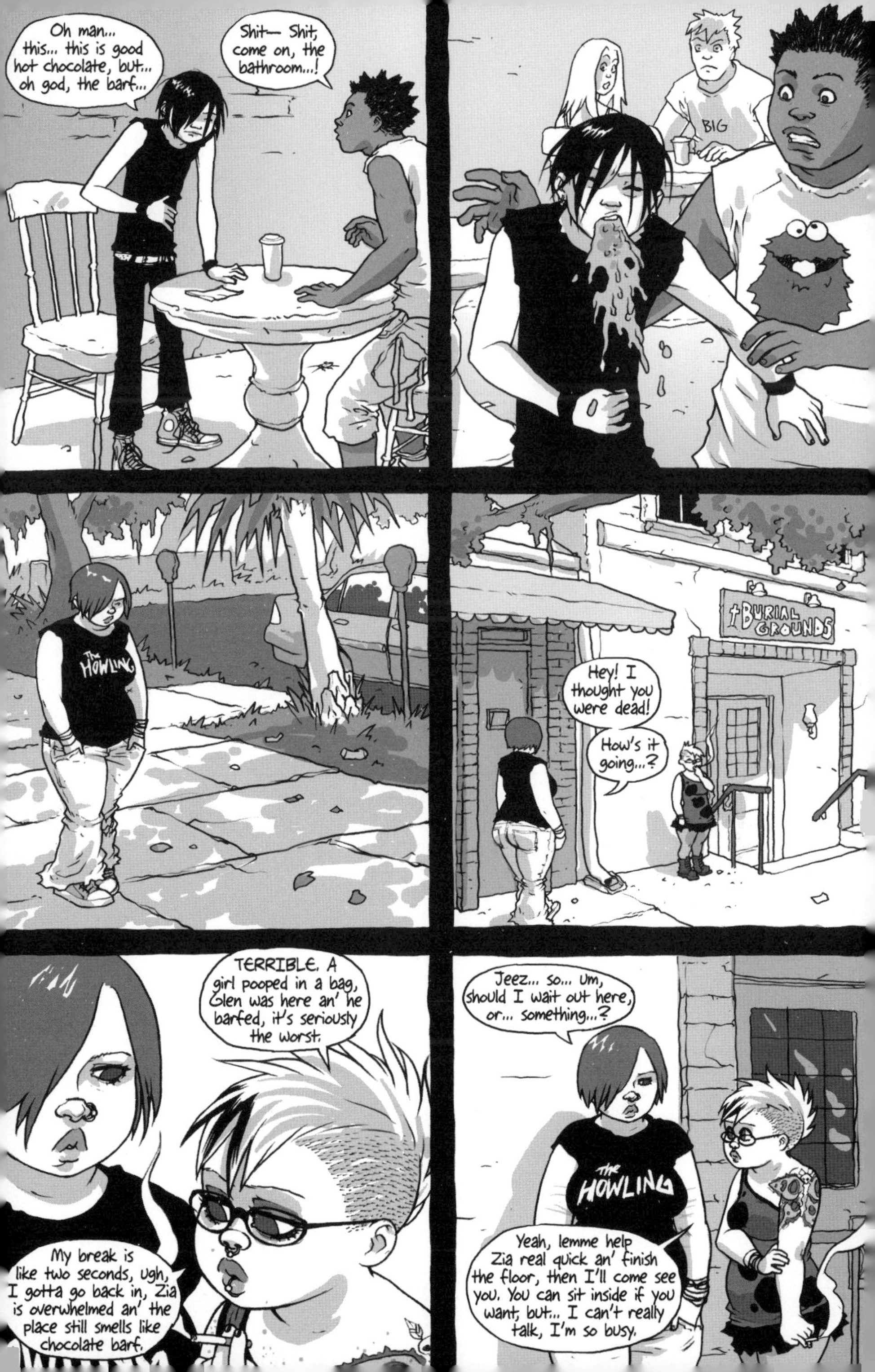
Oh man... this... this is good hot chocolate, but... oh god, the barf...
Shit— Shit, come on, the bathroom...!
BIG
THE HOWLING
BURIAL GROUNDS
Hey! I thought you were dead!
How's it going...?
TERRIBLE. A girl pooped in a bag, Glen was here an' he barfed, it's seriously the worst.
My break is like two seconds, ugh, I gotta go back in, Zia is overwhelmed an' the place still smells like chocolate barf.
Jeez... so... um, should I wait out here, or... something...?
THE HOWLING
Yeah, lemme help Zia real quick an' finish the floor, then I'll come see you. You can sit inside if you want, but... I can't really talk, I'm so busy.

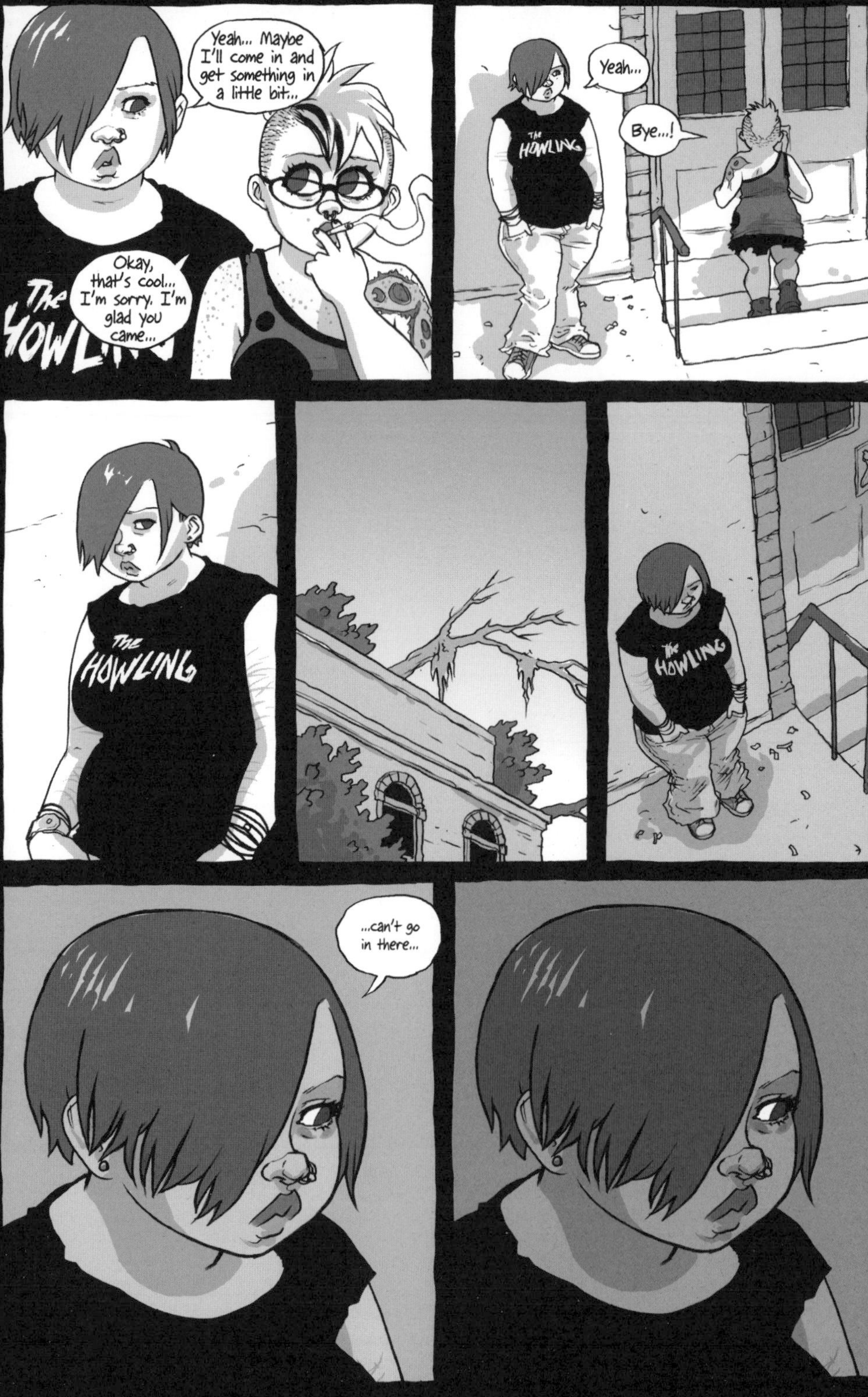
Yeah... Maybe I'll come in and get something in a little bit...
Okay, that's cool... I'm sorry. I'm glad you came...
Yeah...
Bye...!
...can't go in there...

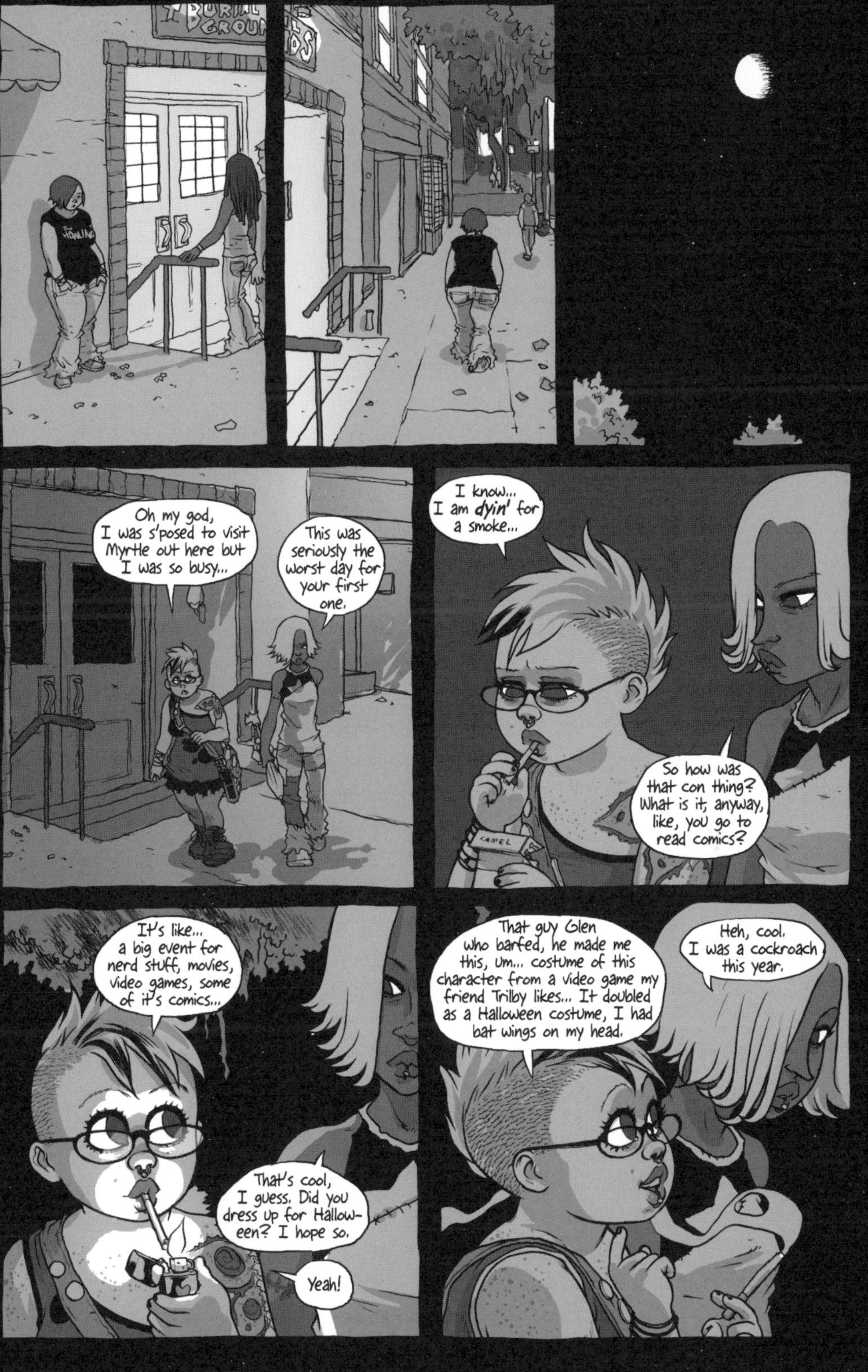
Oh my god, I was s'posed to visit Myrtle out here but I was so busy...
This was seriously the worst day for your first one.
I know... I am **dyin'** for a smoke...
So how was that con thing? What is it, anyway, like, you go to read comics?
CAMEL
It's like... a big event for nerd stuff, movies, video games, some of it's comics...
That's cool, I guess. Did you dress up for Hallow-een? I hope so.
Yeah!
That guy Glen who barfed, he made me this, um... costume of this character from a video game my friend Trilby likes... It doubled as a Halloween costume, I had bat wings on my head.
Heh, cool. I was a cockroach this year.

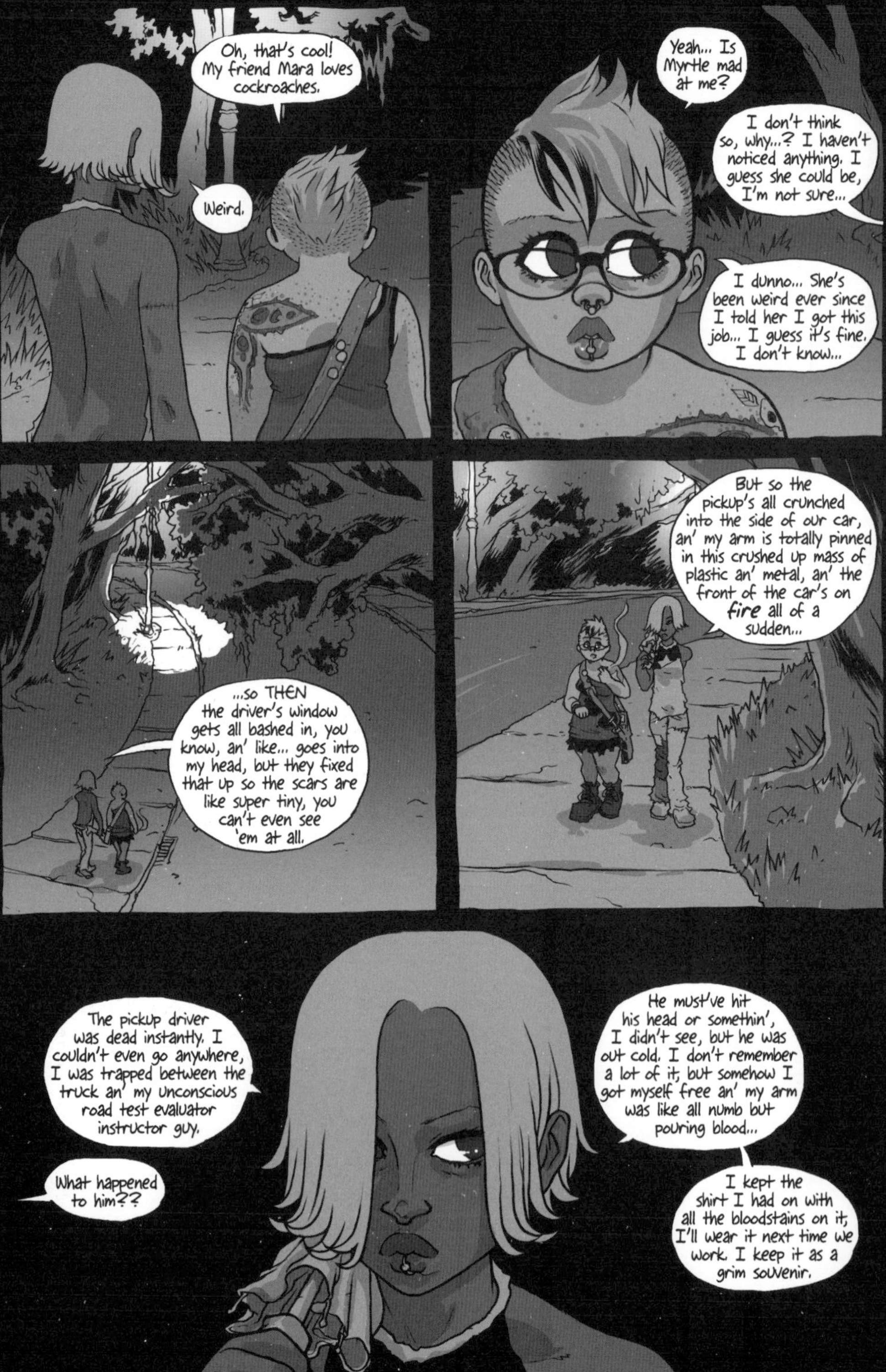
Oh, that's cool! My friend Mara loves cockroaches.
Weird.
Yeah... Is Myrtle mad at me?
I don't think so, why...? I haven't noticed anything. I guess she could be, I'm not sure...
I dunno... She's been weird ever since I told her I got this job... I guess it's fine. I don't know...
...so THEN the driver's window gets all bashed in, you know, an' like... goes into my head, but they fixed that up so the scars are like super tiny, you can't even see 'em at all.
But so the pickup's all crunched into the side of our car, an' my arm is totally pinned in this crushed up mass of plastic an' metal, an' the front of the car's on fire all of a sudden...
The pickup driver was dead instantly. I couldn't even go anywhere, I was trapped between the truck an' my unconscious road test evaluator instructor guy.
What happened to him??
He must've hit his head or somethin', I didn't see, but he was out cold. I don't remember a lot of it, but somehow I got myself free an' my arm was like all numb but pouring blood...
I kept the shirt I had on with all the bloodstains on it, I'll wear it next time we work. I keep it as a grim souvenir.

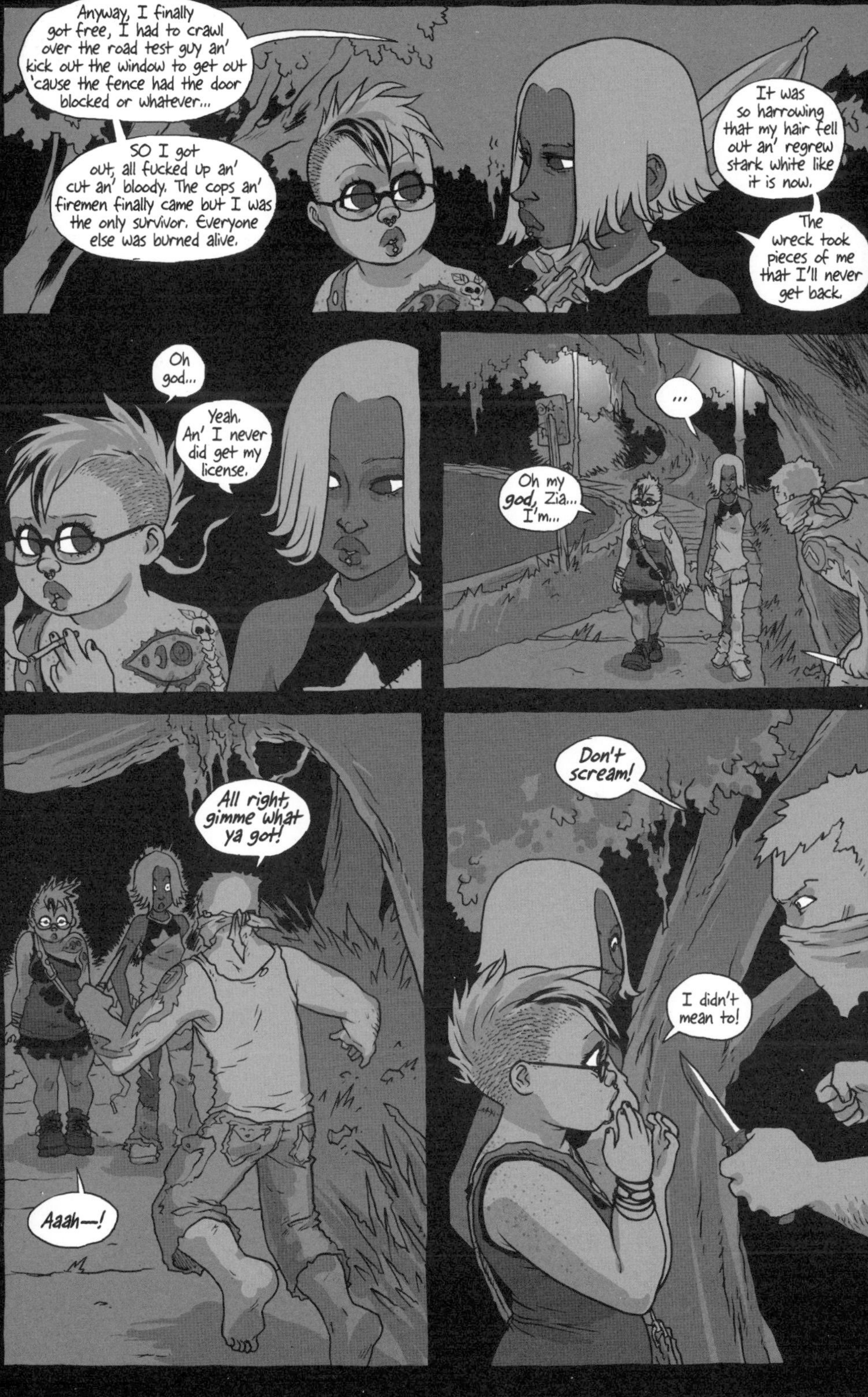
Anyway, I finally got free, I had to crawl over the road test guy an' kick out the window to get out 'cause the fence had the door blocked or whatever...
SO I got out, all fucked up an' cut an' bloody. The cops an' firemen finally came but I was the only survivor. Everyone else was burned alive.
It was so harrowing that my hair fell out an' regrew stark white like it is now.
The wreck took pieces of me that I'll never get back.
Oh god...
Yeah. An' I never did get my license.
...
Oh my god, Zia... I'm...
All right, gimme what ya got!
Aaah—!
Don't scream!
I didn't mean to!

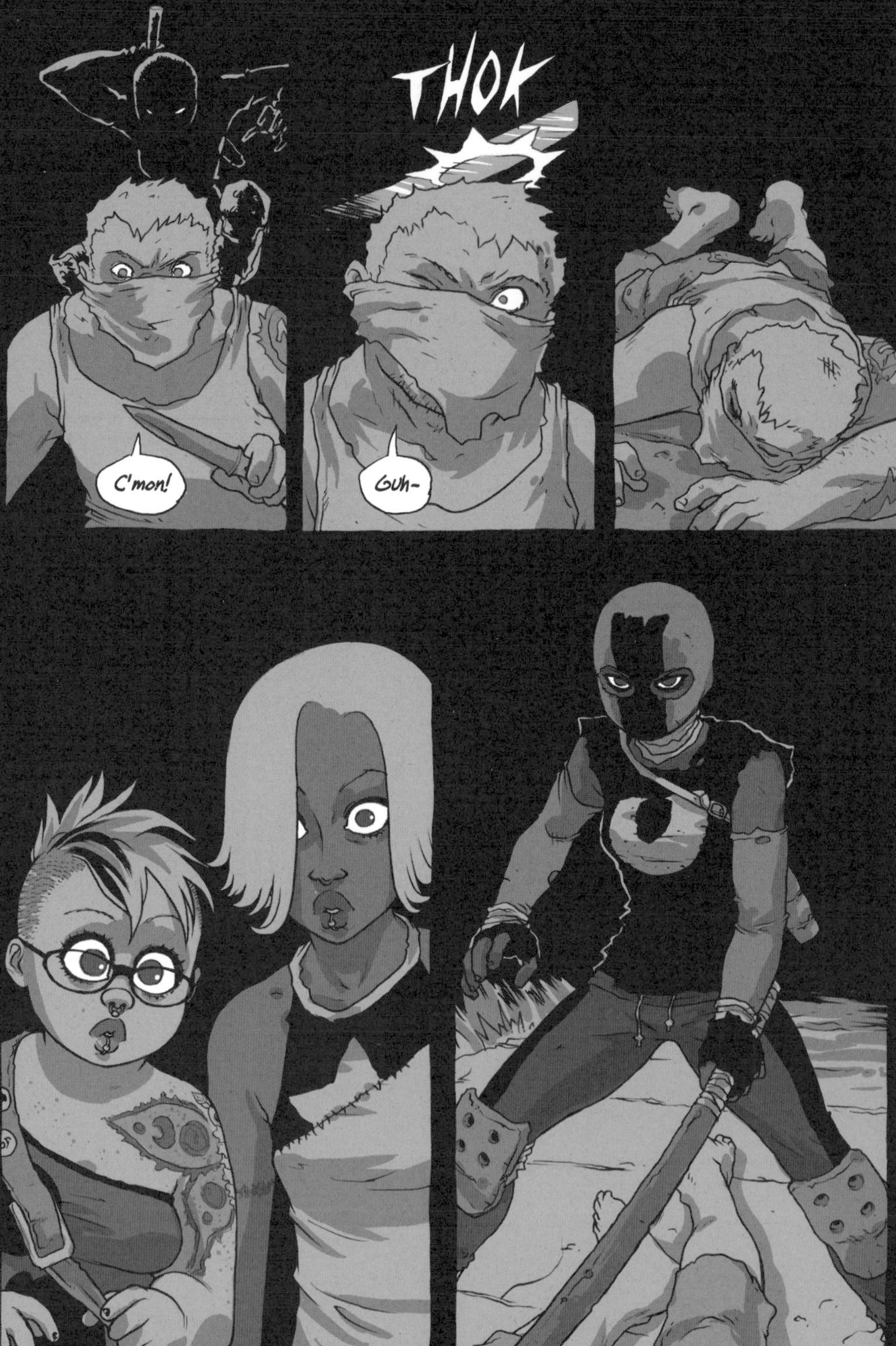
C'mon!
THOK
Guh-

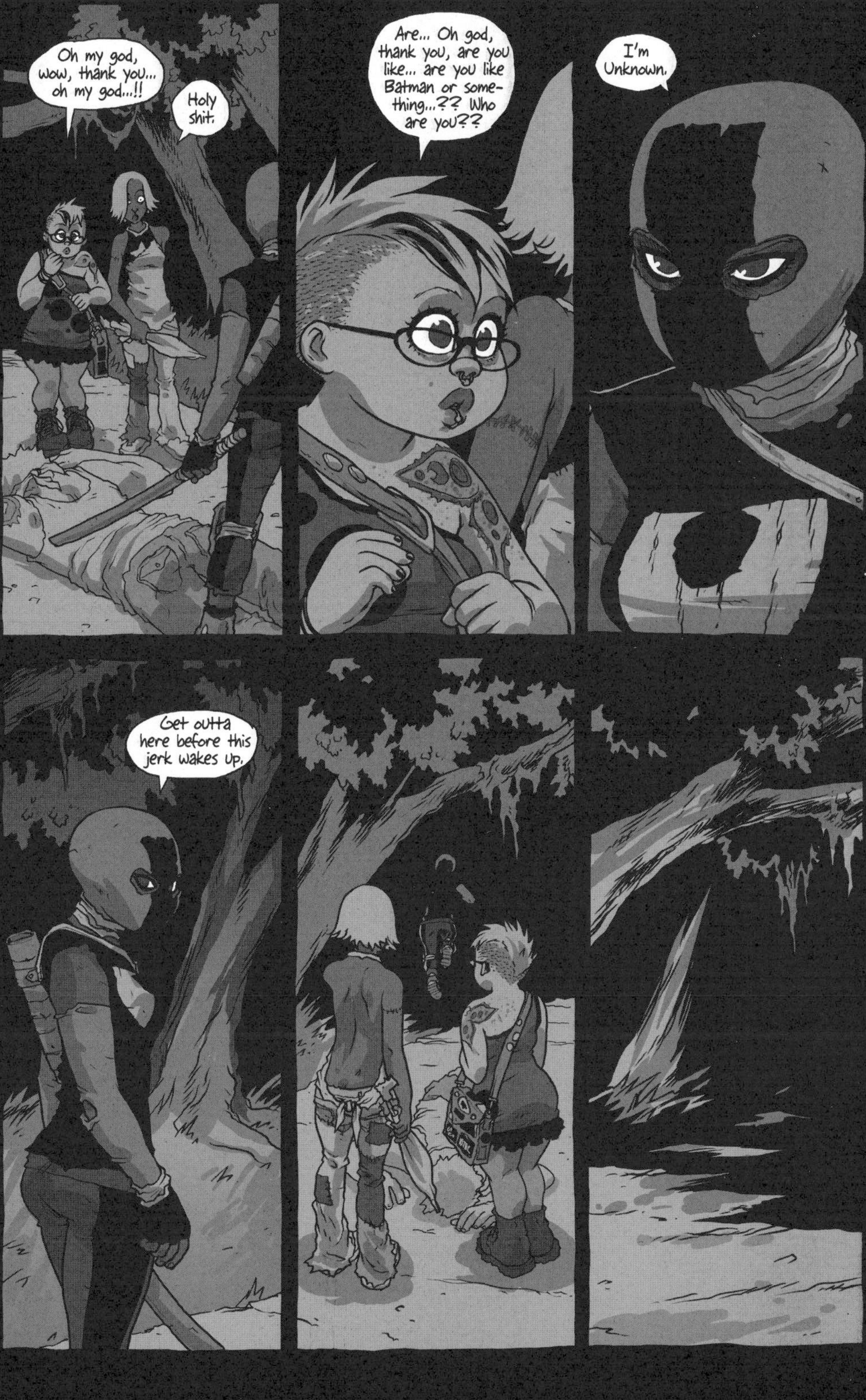
Oh my god, wow, thank you... oh my god...!!
Holy shit.
Are... Oh god, thank you, are you like... are you like Batman or something...?? Who are you??
I'm Unknown.
Get outta here before this jerk wakes up.

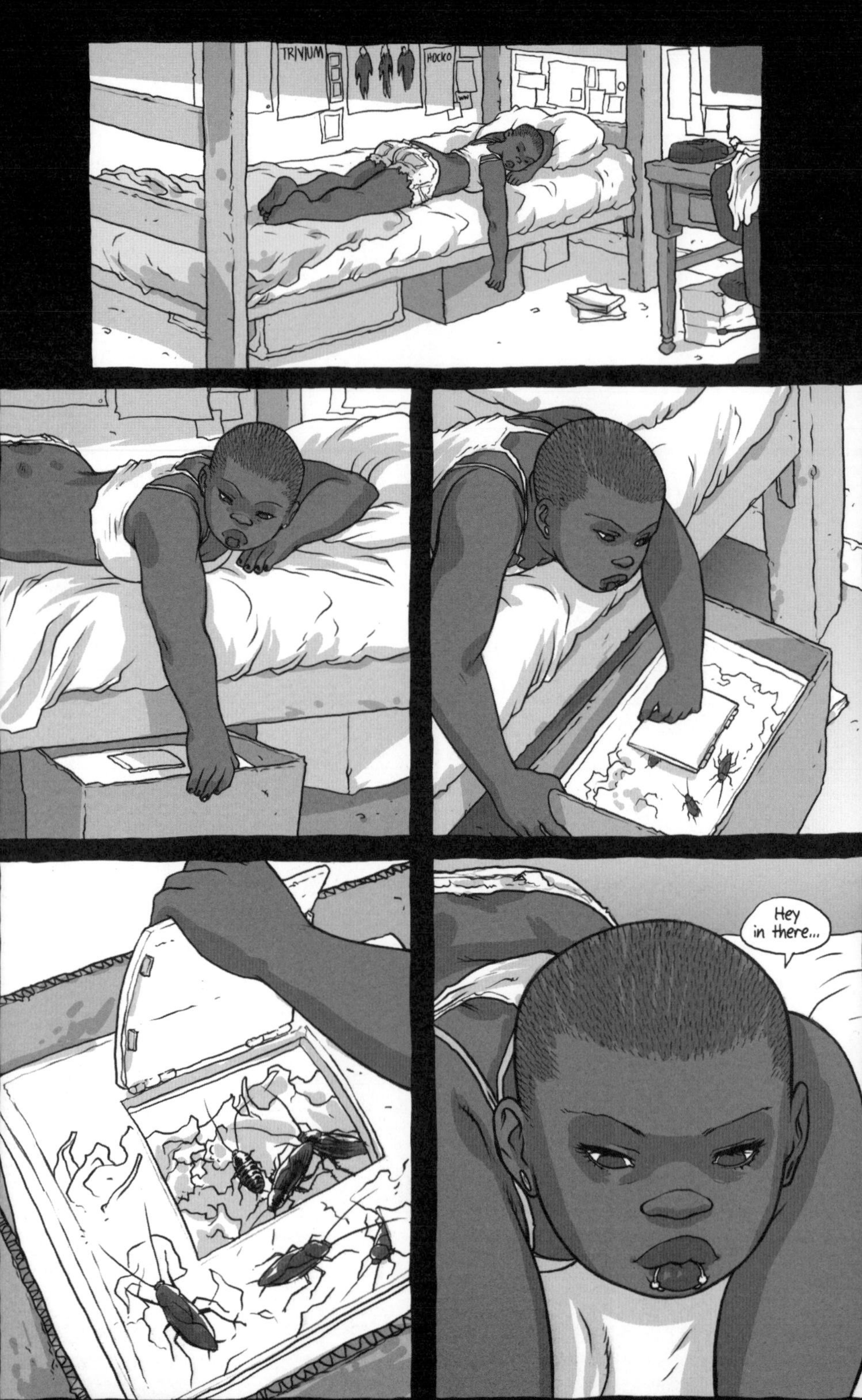
TRIVIUM
HOCKO
Hey in there...

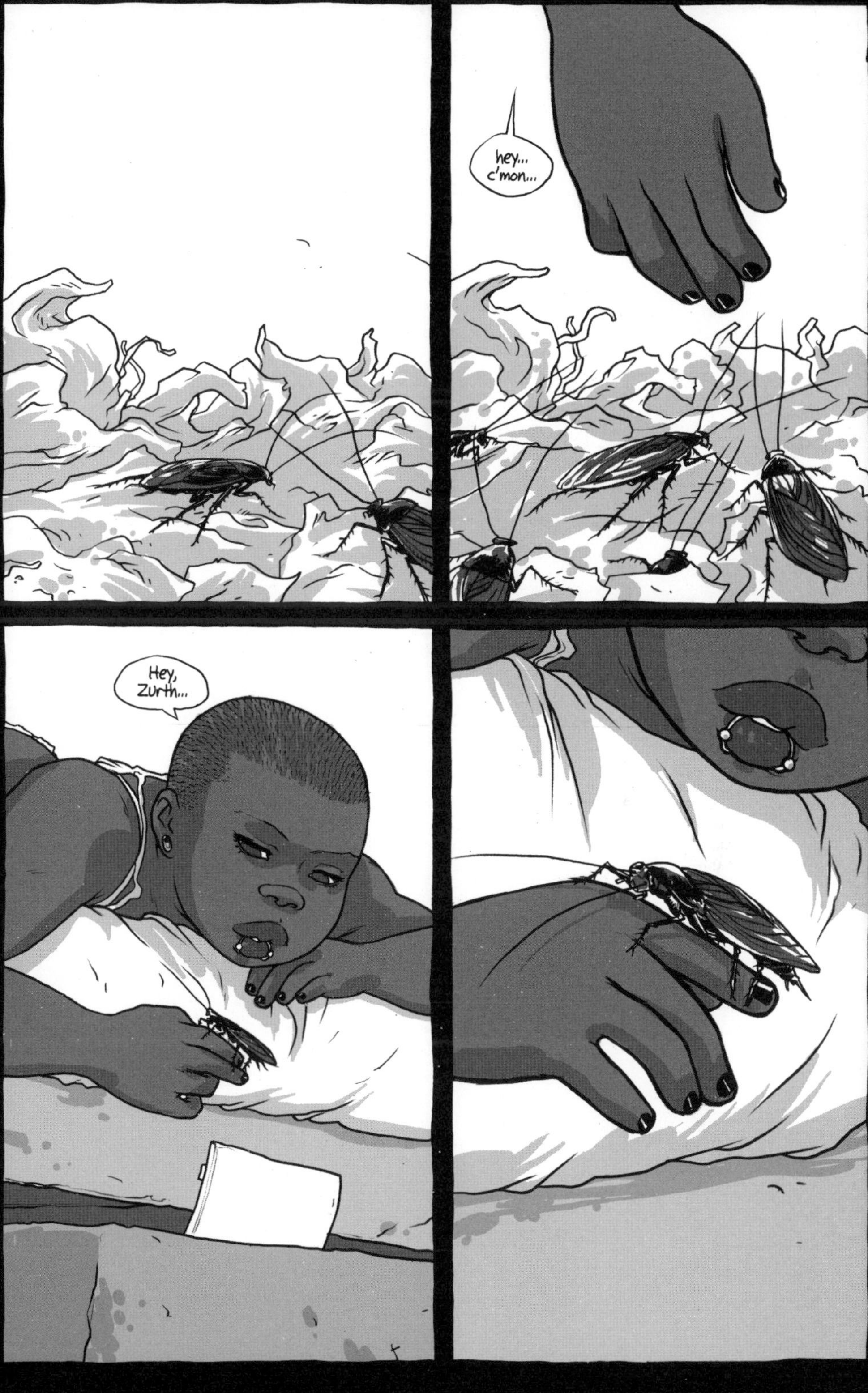
hey...
c'mon...
Hey,
Zurth...

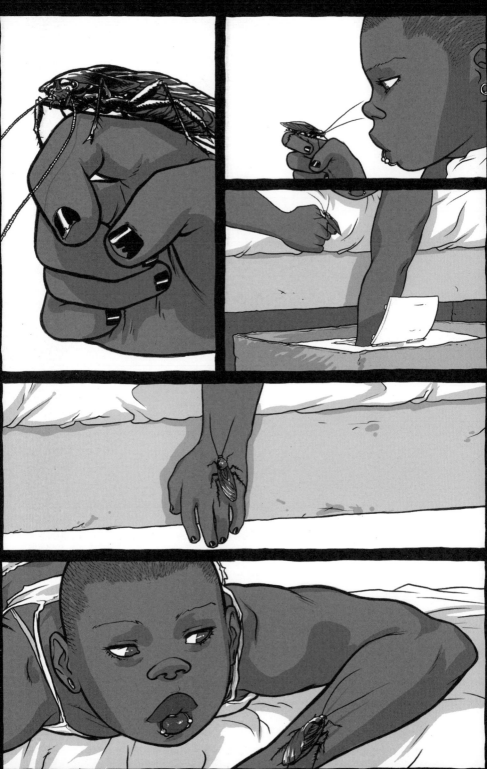

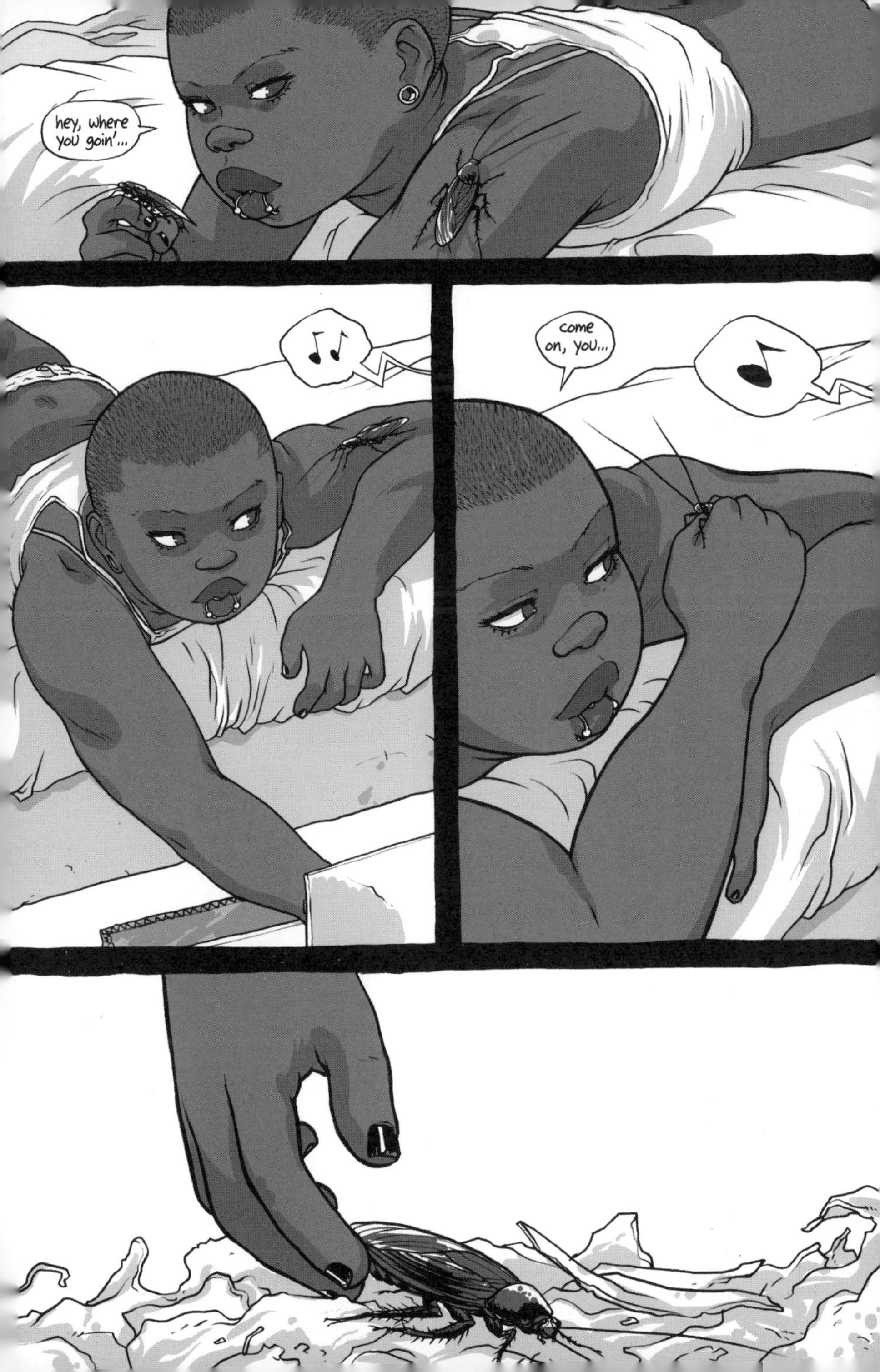
hey, where you goin'...
come on, you...

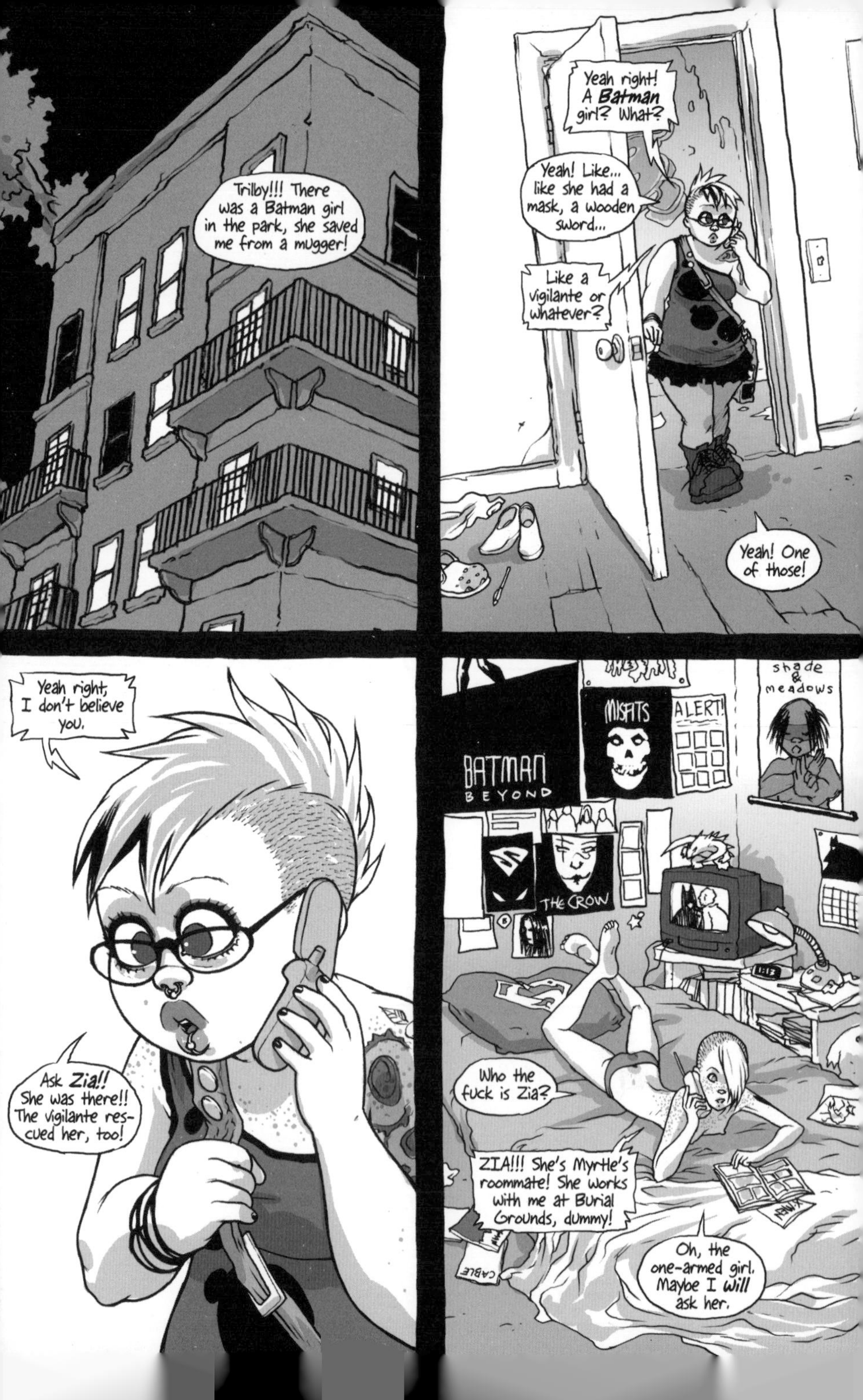
Trilby!!! There was a Batman girl in the park, she saved me from a mugger!
Yeah right! A **Batman** girl? What?
Yeah! Like... like she had a mask, a wooden sword...
Like a vigilante or whatever?
Yeah! One of those!
Yeah right, I don't believe you.
Ask **Zia!!** She was there!! The vigilante rescued her, too!
BATMAN BEYOND
MISFITS
ALERT!
shade & meadows
THE CROW
CABLE
Who the fuck is Zia?
ZIA!!! She's Myrtle's roommate! She works with me at Burial Grounds, dummy!
Oh, the one-armed girl. Maybe I **will** ask her.

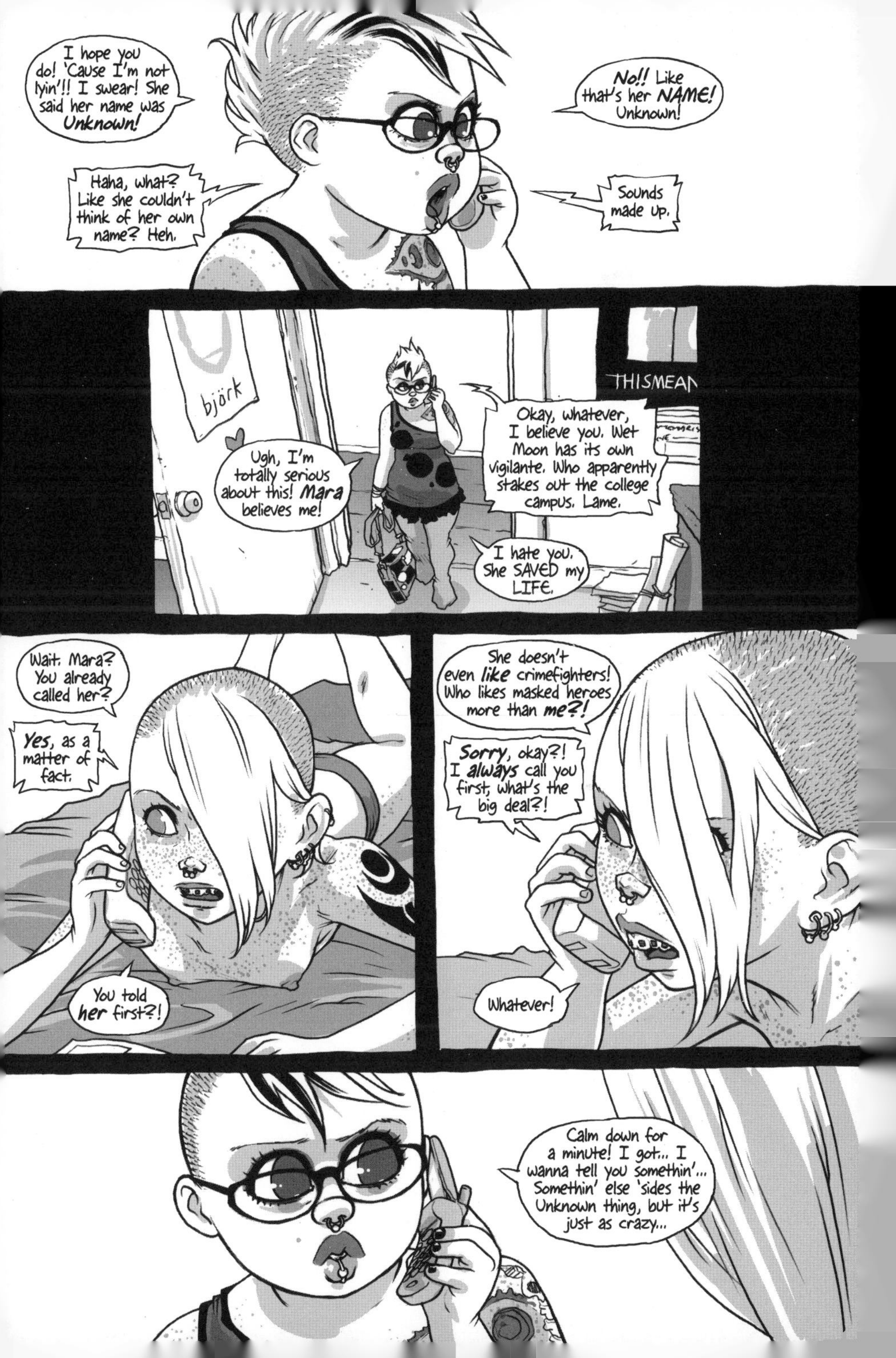
I hope you do! 'Cause I'm not lyin'!! I swear! She said her name was Unknown!
Haha, what? Like she couldn't think of her own name? Heh.
No!! Like that's her NAME! Unknown!
Sounds made up.
björk
THISMEAN
Ugh, I'm totally serious about this! Mara believes me!
Okay, whatever, I believe you. Wet Moon has its own vigilante. Who apparently stakes out the college campus. Lame.
I hate you. She SAVED my LIFE.
Wait. Mara? You already called her?
Yes, as a matter of fact.
You told her first?!
She doesn't even like crimefighters! Who likes masked heroes more than me?!
Sorry, okay?! I always call you first, what's the big deal?!
Whatever!
Calm down for a minute! I got... I wanna tell you somethin'... Somethin' else 'sides the Unknown thing, but it's just as crazy...

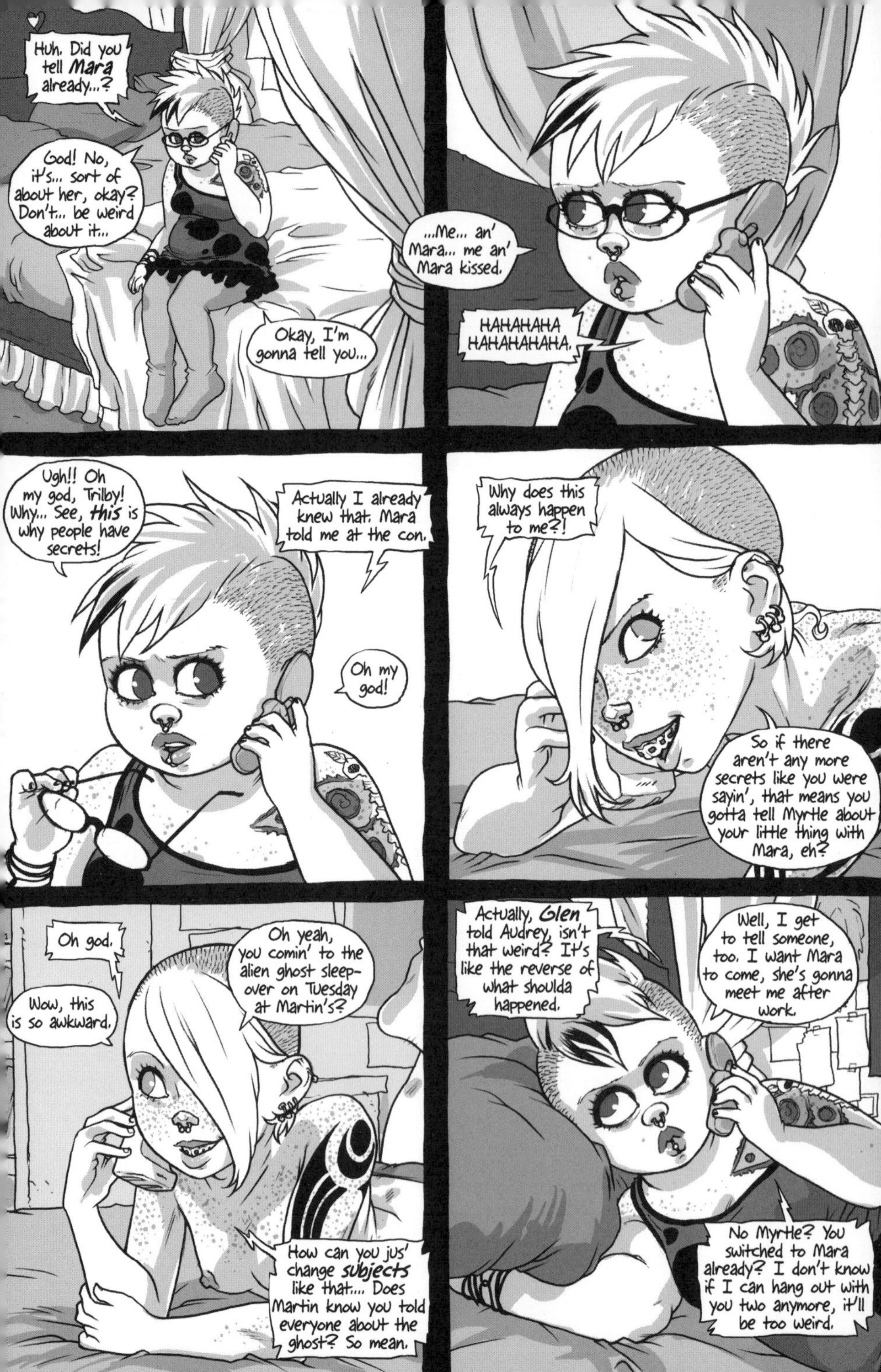
Huh. Did you tell Mara already...?
God! No, it's... sort of about her, okay? Don't... be weird about it...
Okay, I'm gonna tell you...
...Me... an' Mara... me an' Mara kissed.
HAHAHAHA HAHAHAHAHA.
Ugh!! Oh my god, Trilby! Why... See, this is why people have secrets!
Actually I already knew that. Mara told me at the con.
Oh my god!
Why does this always happen to me?!
So if there aren't any more secrets like you were sayin', that means you gotta tell Myrtle about your little thing with Mara, eh?
Oh god.
Wow, this is so awkward.
Oh yeah, you comin' to the alien ghost sleep-over on Tuesday at Martin's?
How can you jus' change subjects like that.... Does Martin know you told everyone about the ghost? So mean.
Actually, Glen told Audrey, isn't that weird? It's like the reverse of what shoulda happened.
Well, I get to tell someone, too. I want Mara to come, she's gonna meet me after work.
No Myrtle? You switched to Mara already? I don't know if I can hang out with you two anymore, it'll be too weird.

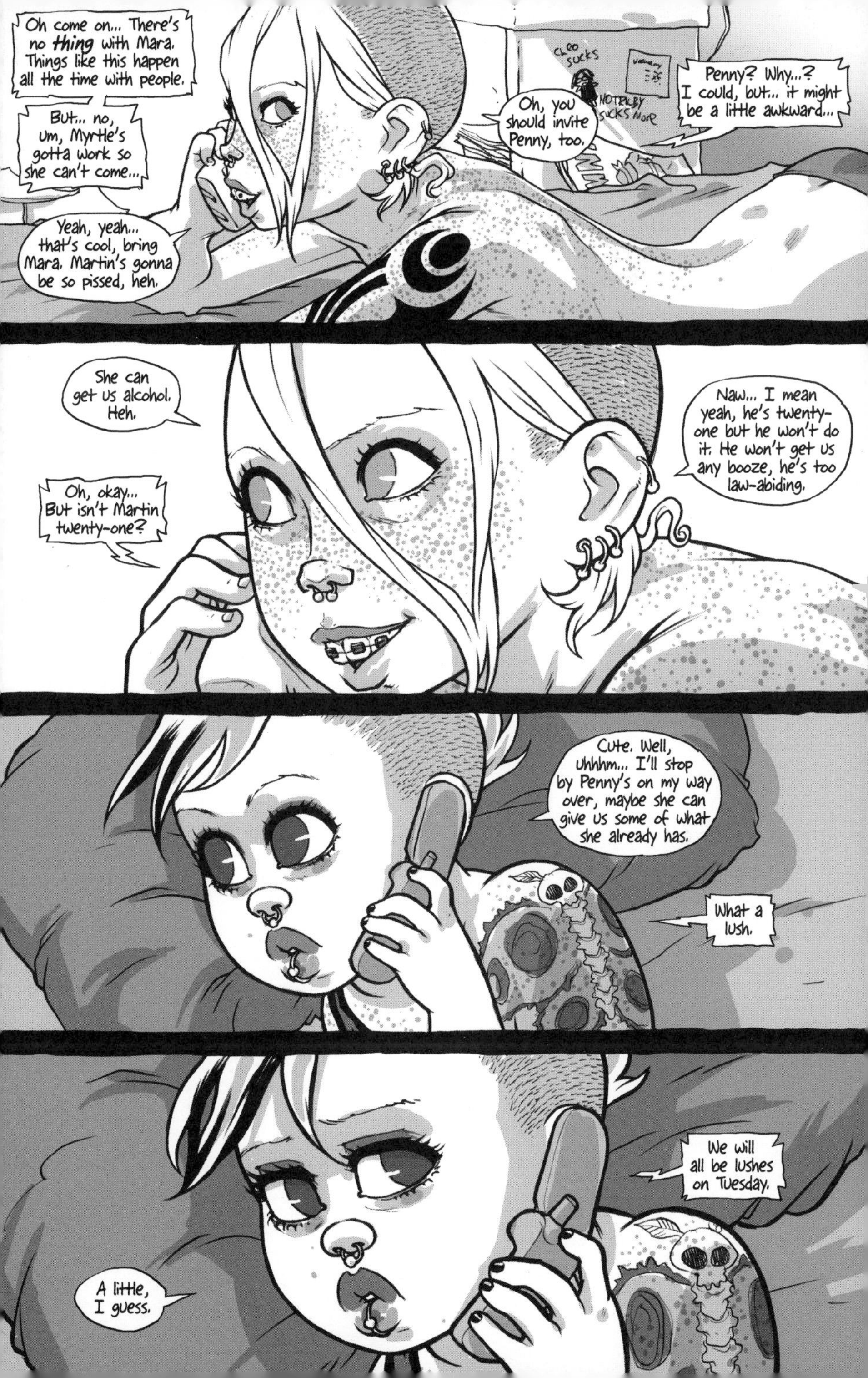
Oh come on... There's no *thing* with Mara. Things like this happen all the time with people.
But... no, um, Myrtle's gotta work so she can't come...
Yeah, yeah... that's cool, bring Mara. Martin's gonna be so pissed, heh.
Oh, you should invite Penny, too.
Penny? Why...? I could, but... it might be a little awkward...
She can get us alcohol. Heh.
Oh, okay... But isn't Martin twenty-one?
Naw... I mean yeah, he's twenty-one but he won't do it. He won't get us any booze, he's too law-abiding.
Cute. Well, uhhhm... I'll stop by Penny's on my way over, maybe she can give us some of what she already has.
What a lush.
We will all be lushes on Tuesday.
A little, I guess.

21

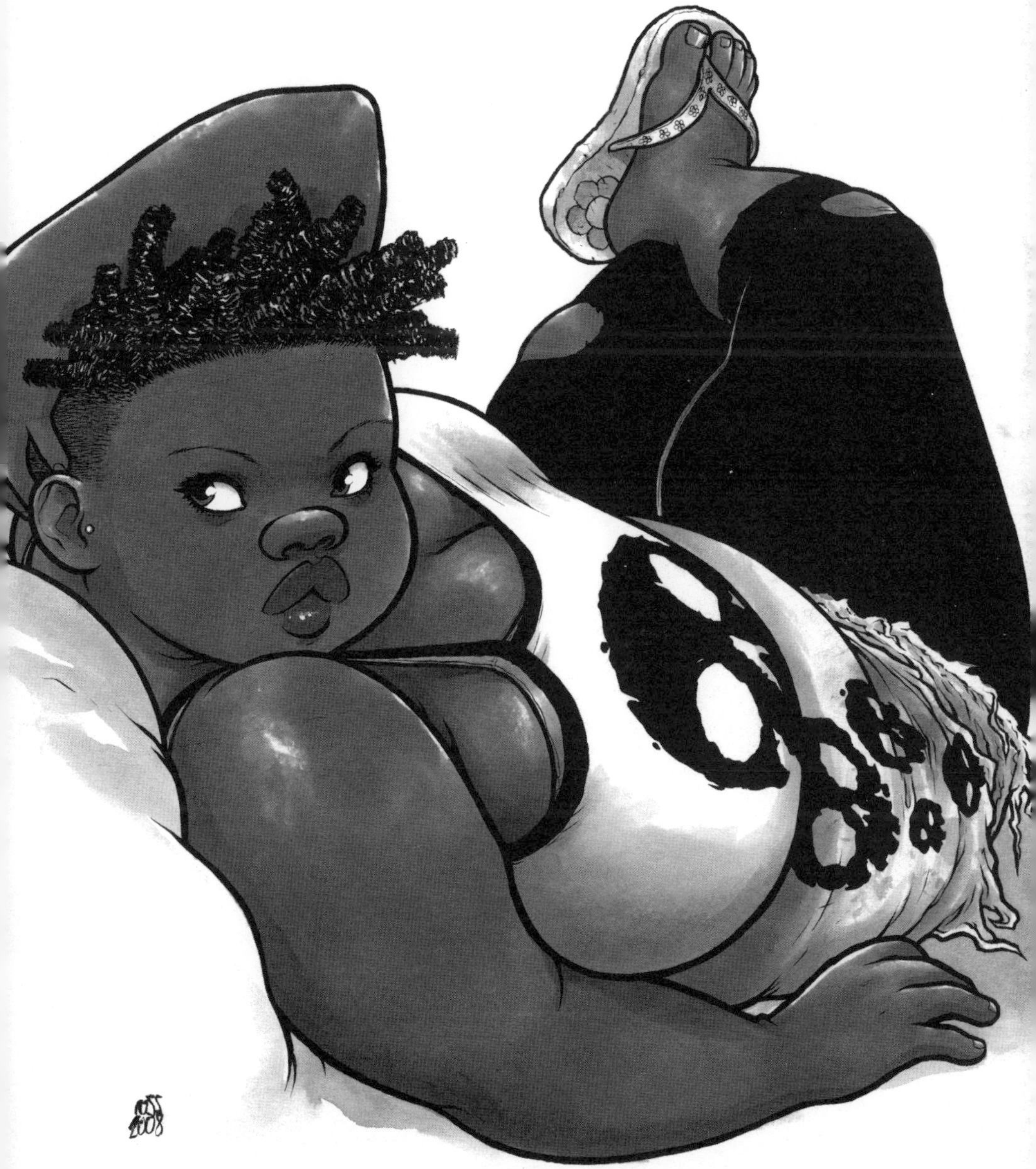

November 2

Burial Grounds kind of sucks.
it's so hectic and crazy and the
most fucked up people come in there,
and i only get three smoke
breaks for like seven hours of
work, i was freaking out. i just
can't make it that long but i guess
i'm going to have to learn how.
i'm up to about two packs a day,
i need a cigarette like every 20
minutes, it's so awful, i have got
to cut down. i guess this job will
help regulate it. i like smoking
most of the time but i still wish
i could quit. a girl actually gave
me a bag of her own shit at
work because the toilet was
broken. oh my god. and Glen
threw up, i feel so bad for him.
he didn't even ask how the con
went with the costume he
made for me.
    but the biggest thing that

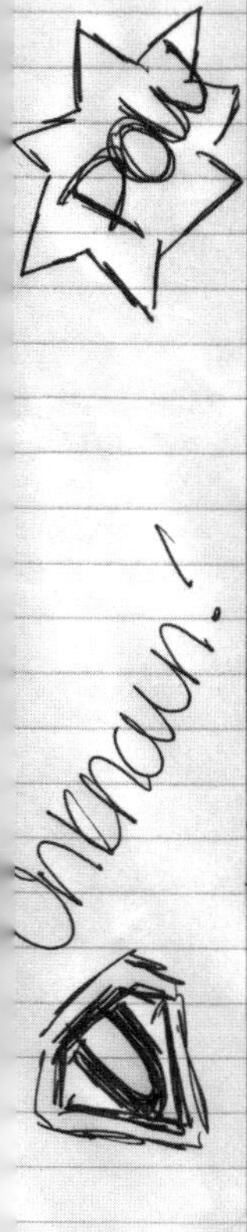
POW!
Unknown!

makes that other stuff seem so stupid is that there's this superhero vigilante girl called Unknown on campus. it is CRAZY!! me and Zia (who is the best!) were walking back from work and there's that part of campus leading into the city where it's just swampy, wooded kind of road without anything nearby really, and this mugger guy jumped out from behind a tree with a KNIFE and I nearly had a heart attack and almost barfed all over the place and he goes GIVE ME YOUR MONEY or something! then before we could even do anything, this Unknown girl drops out of a TREE and knocks the guy out!!! it was amazing!! for a second i thought i was ~~totally~~ in love at first sight, but now that i'm writing it down and thinking more about it, i think it would be a bad idea. plus there's Myrtle AND Mara and... fuck, what is even going on in my life??! Unknown?! am i crazy?? besides that i do feel a lot better about walking at night,

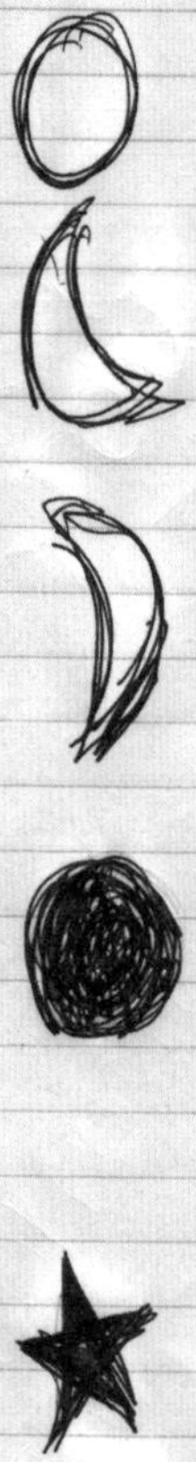

though, knowing that Unknown is out there keeping people safe!! i know she can't be everywhere at once (could she have a partner or sidekick??) but just knowing she's out there makes me feel better about muggers and rapists. somebody told me there were a caple girls who got raped in the Forest of Doom near the campus park, i wonder if that was before Unknown showed up. i wonder how long she's been out there, i can't imagine it could be that long without me hearing about it, without rumors going bonkers all over school!! sometimes i hear people talking about how Wet Moon sucks, how it's such a stupid, lame, boring city with nothing to do and how they're moving out the first chance they get, and i used to be like that, i think, but as i got older the more i see how great it is in a lot of ways. except for the weather being so hot all the time and i wish it would snow just once. can you believe i've never <u>seen</u> real snow besides in a movie!?

also, i told Trilby about me and Mara, and she totally knew already, ugh! she tried to act like she didn't care about myrtle, but i know she cares about this thing with mara. tiny changes in her tone of voice and i know next time i see her she'll have equally tiny changes in her body language. she can't fool me. i wish she was okay with all this, but i know she's kind of... i don't know, i don't want to say homophobic, but she's definitely weirded out by all the girl/girl stuff even though there's Audrey and now me... sigh. and Mara being our friend, not a stranger like myrtle was, i know Trilby is uneasy with it. maybe i am too.

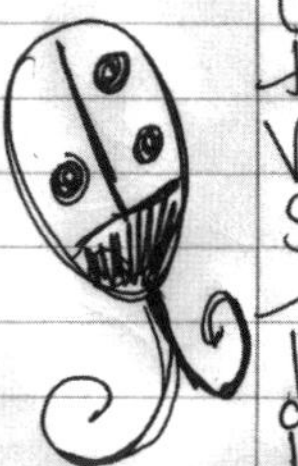

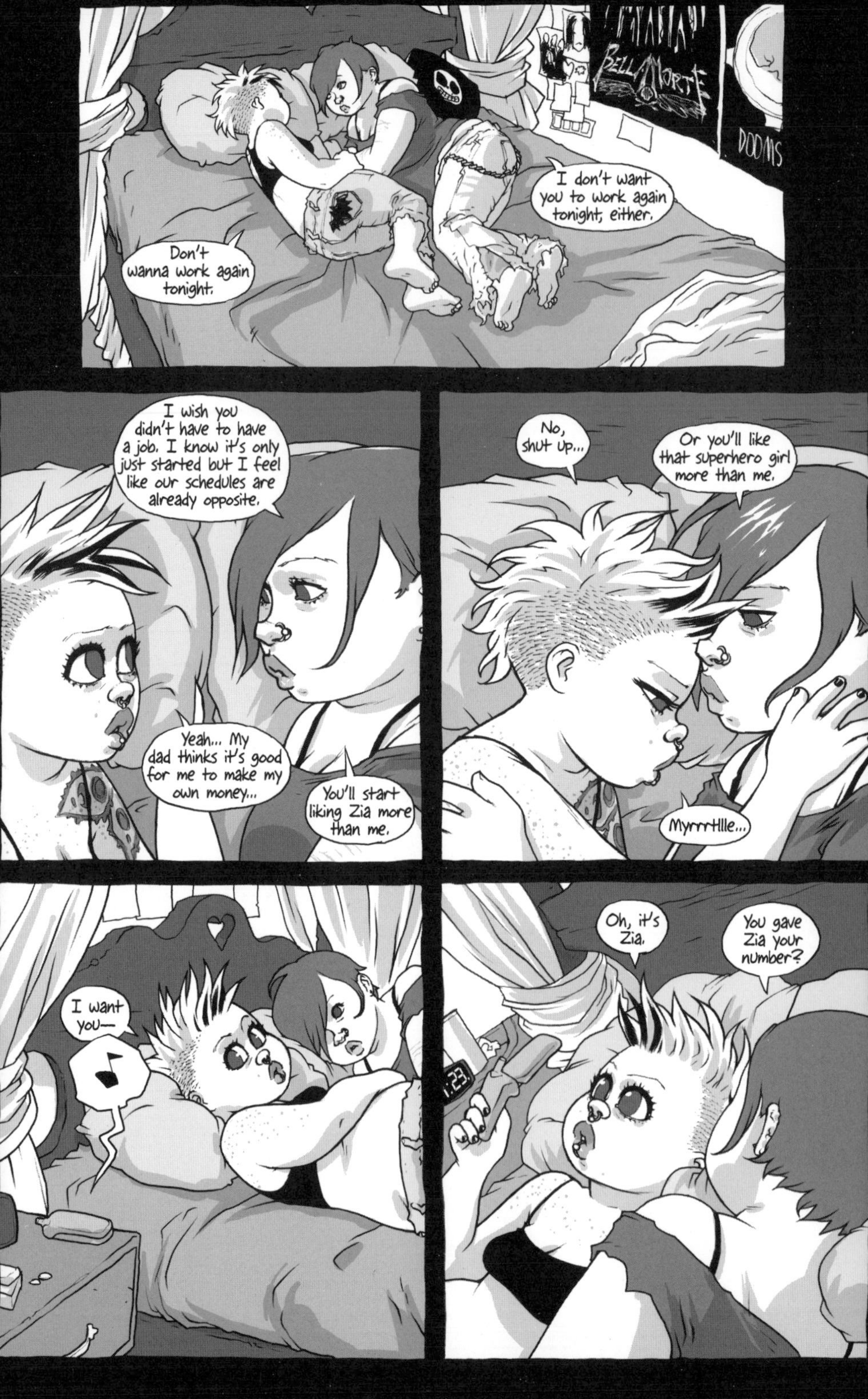
BELLA MORTE
DOOMS
I don't want you to work again tonight, either.
Don't wanna work again tonight.
I wish you didn't have to have a job. I know it's only just started but I feel like our schedules are already opposite.
Yeah... My dad thinks it's good for me to make my own money...
You'll start liking Zia more than me.
No, shut up...
Or you'll like that superhero girl more than me.
Myrrrtllle...
I want you—
Oh, it's Zia.
You gave Zia your number?

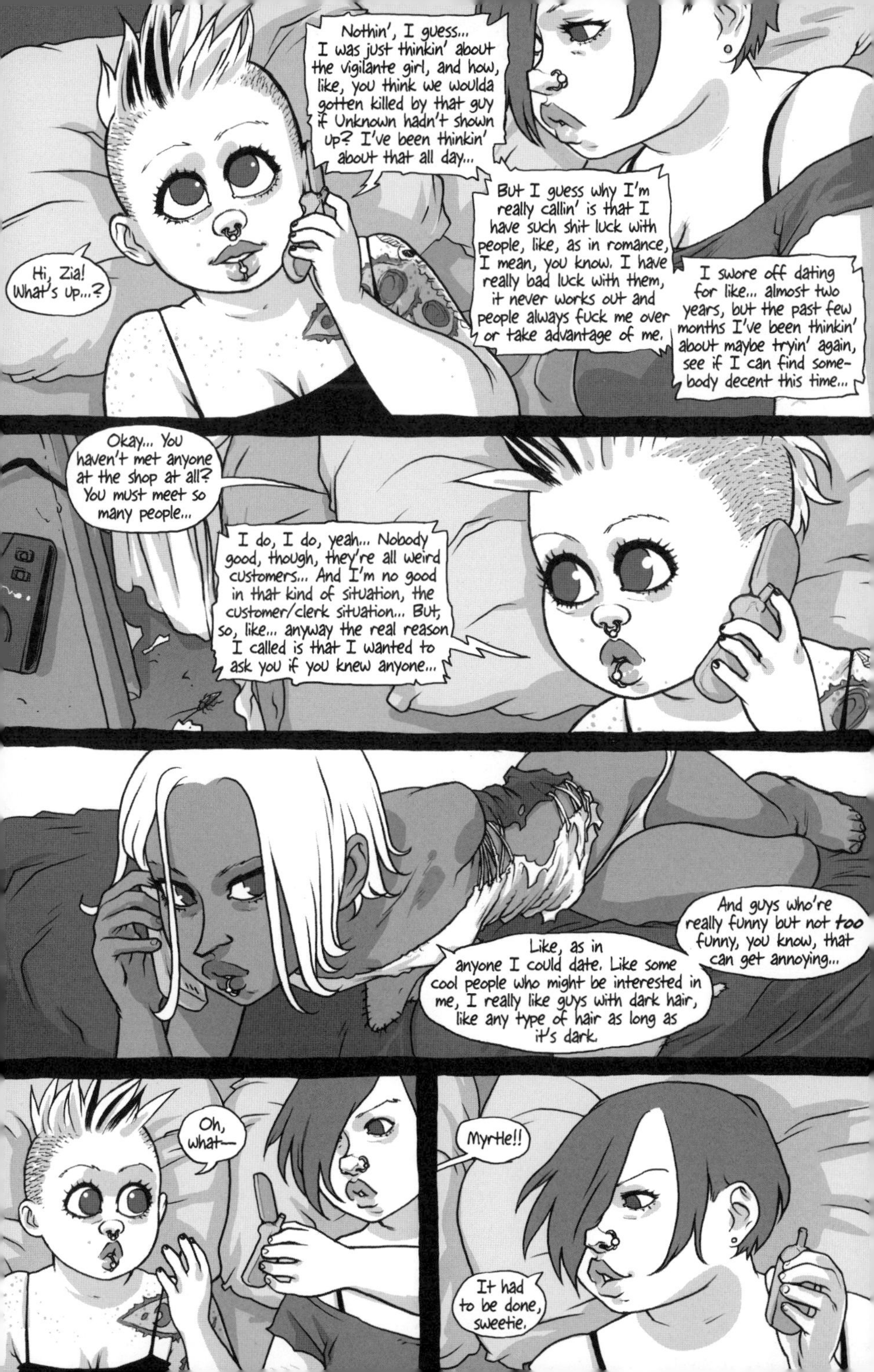
Hi, Zia! What's up...?
Nothin', I guess... I was just thinkin' about the vigilante girl, and how, like, you think we woulda gotten killed by that guy if Unknown hadn't shown up? I've been thinkin' about that all day...
But I guess why I'm really callin' is that I have such shit luck with people, like, as in romance, I mean, you know. I have really bad luck with them, it never works out and people always fuck me over or take advantage of me.
I swore off dating for like... almost two years, but the past few months I've been thinkin' about maybe tryin' again, see if I can find somebody decent this time...
Okay... You haven't met anyone at the shop at all? You must meet so many people...
I do, I do, yeah... Nobody good, though, they're all weird customers... And I'm no good in that kind of situation, the customer/clerk situation... But, so, like... anyway the real reason I called is that I wanted to ask you if you knew anyone...
Like, as in anyone I could date. Like some cool people who might be interested in me, I really like guys with dark hair, like any type of hair as long as it's dark.
And guys who're really funny but not *too* funny, you know, that can get annoying...
Oh, what—
Myrtle!!
It had to be done, sweetie.

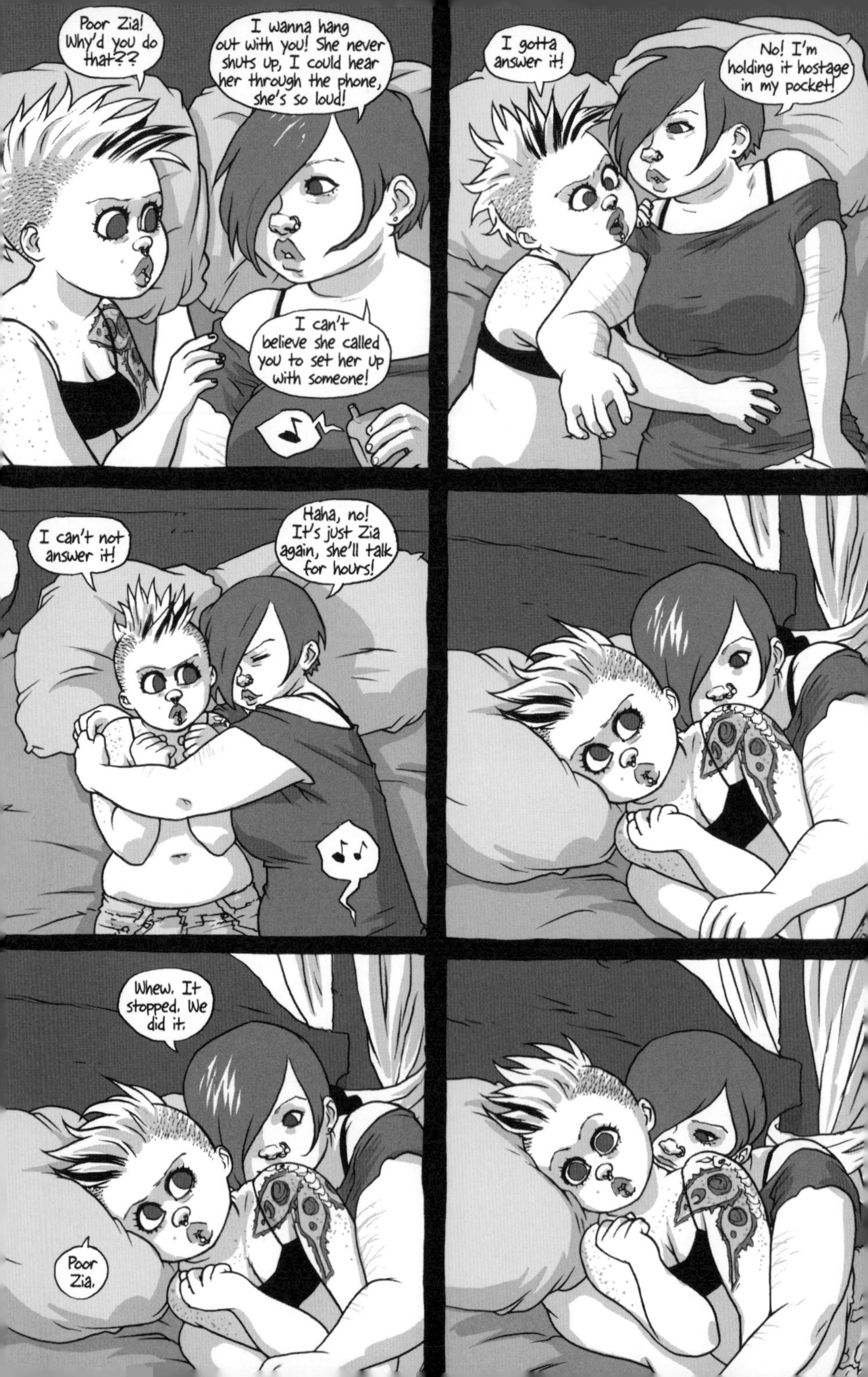
Poor Zia! Why'd you do that??
I wanna hang out with you! She never shuts up, I could hear her through the phone, she's so loud!
I can't believe she called you to set her up with someone!
I gotta answer it!
No! I'm holding it hostage in my pocket!
I can't not answer it!
Haha, no! It's just Zia again, she'll talk for hours!
Whew. It stopped. We did it.
Poor Zia.

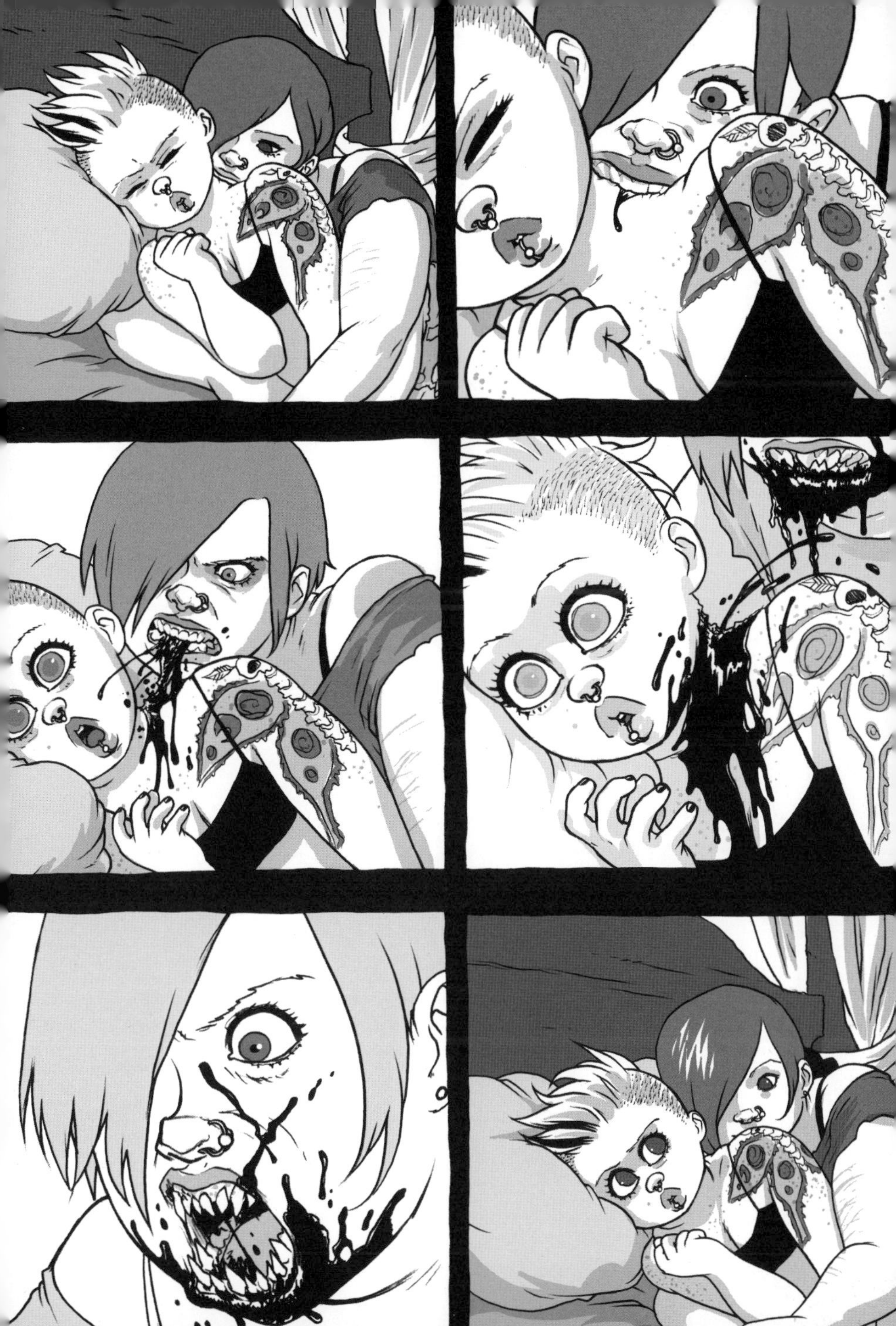

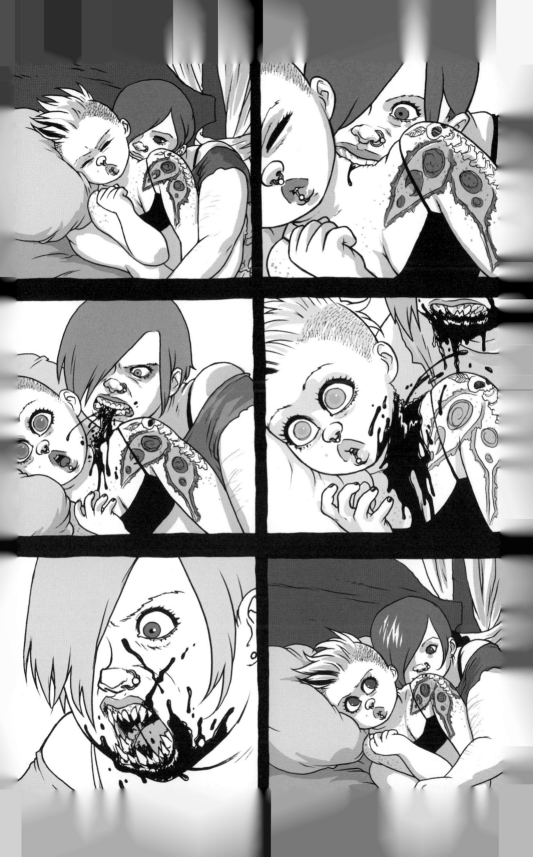

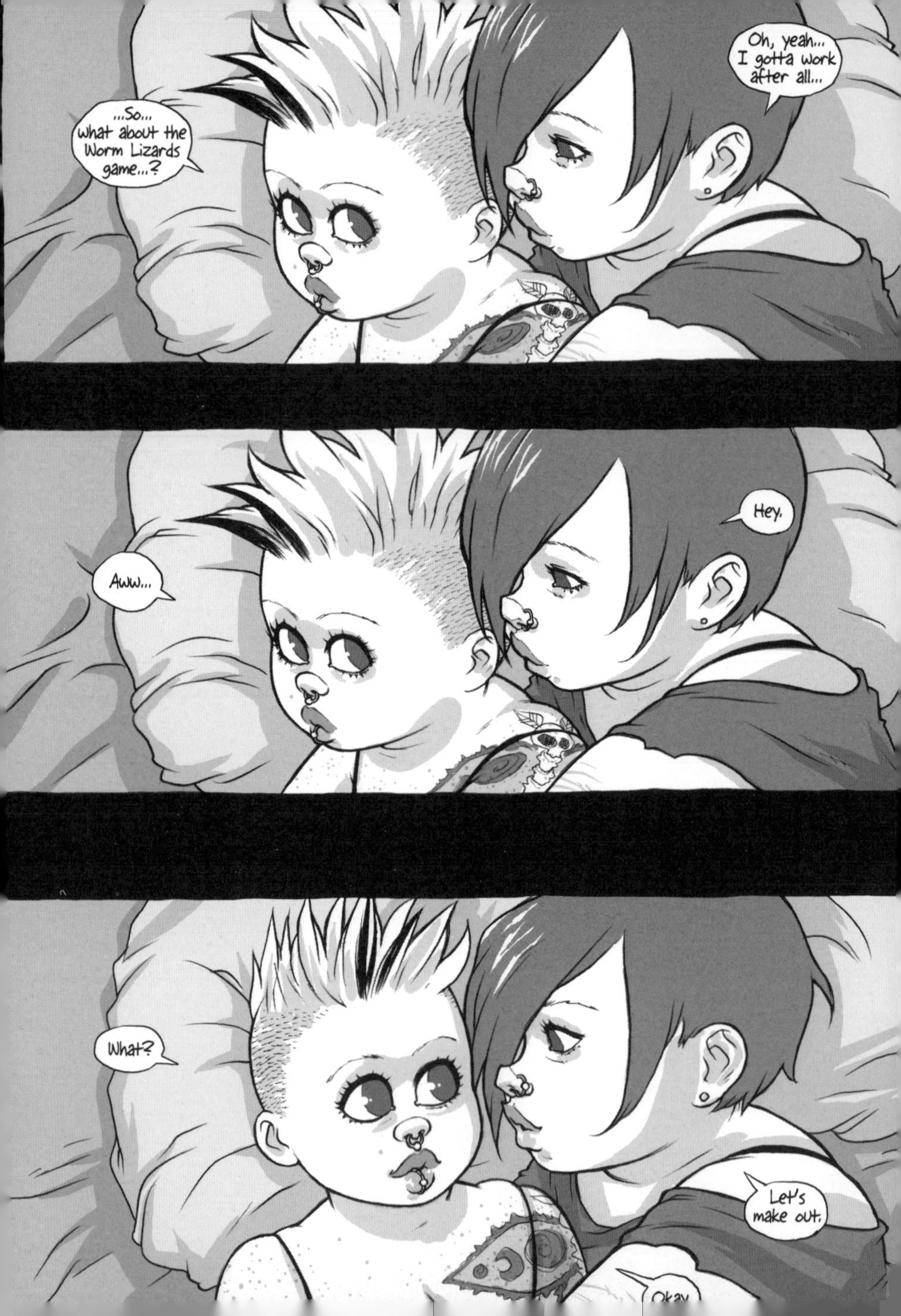
...So... what about the Worm Lizards game...?
Oh, yeah... I gotta work after all...
Aww...
Hey.
What?
Let's make out.

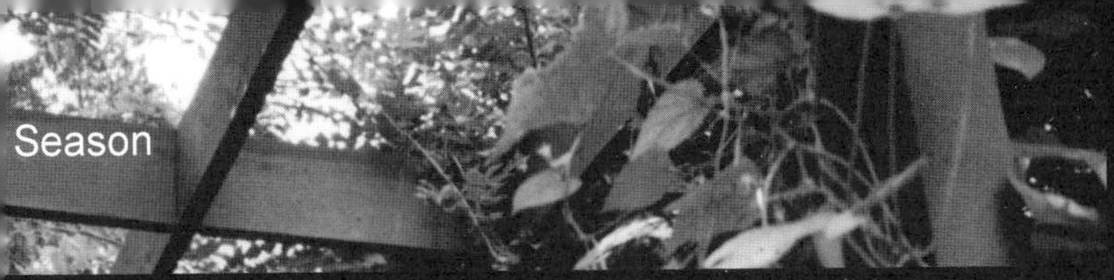
Season

Previous 20

Who knows.

November 3rd, 7:26pm

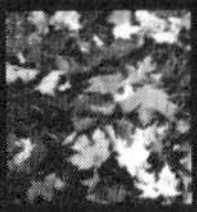

What the heck. That babysitting gig... where do I start? It is definitely the worst one I've ever had, the kids were absolute terrors. The oldest one is 15, she turned out all right except... well, I don't want to write what happened with her. It's got nothing to do with me, it wasn't a malicious thing, but boy... yeah, I can't say it, it doesn't seem right. Everyone's always on me about spilling the beans when i shouldn't, so this is me going against that.

The other two kids were young, and they both insulted me, threw things (including an entire CAKE) at me, locked me out of the apartment, poured beer on me... yes, they actually managed to get beer and got drunk. I know, I'm the worst babysitter. I finally got them in bed, at least, but not before being covered in frosting and beer and being thoroughly humiliated. I won't get into the rest.

I like to think that I have a generally strong self-esteem, at least compared to most girls I know. I try not to obsess over my body and I don't beat myself up over not being "good enough" at something or worry too much about if somebody likes me or anything like that. At least not usually, but everyone does once in a while. One of the kids called me the ugliest girl he's ever seen (his actual words were a bit nastier), and on one hand it's like, okay, he's 8, he probably doesn't even LIKE girls in "that" way yet, and he's already a big jerk, who cares. But it really struck me in a bad way and I still feel down about it. I know, it's so dumb... a jerky 8-year-old boy. sigh. I guess part of it, I hate to drag this aspect into it, but often I feel like nobody, as in the masses or "society" or whatever, will ever think I'm pretty. Because I'm a Woman of Color, and everything is steered away from presenting us as attractive... Sometimes I look in the mirror and I think I'm "too much," my face, my hair, my butt, everything... I've been really fighting it, though. I used to straighten my hair and I only stopped recently, and I'm much happier with it now. But I feel bombarded by everyone trying to get me to buy straightening stuff and "tame" my hair or whatever, and all these magazine ads where they lighten Black women... It's really sad. I know I've written a little about this before in Social Abattoir, but I want to tackle more about it, it's such a big, sprawling issue that's really important to me. I actually sort of don't like writing about it because I'm so upset by it, thinking about all those little girls who never see positive images of girls who look like them (well, there are SOME but not nearly enough). I don't want to write about it but I have to, I think it's important to get stuff like that out there. So stay tuned on that.

I'm also putting together some stuff on crime in Wet Moon since there's so much; not really street-level stuff, but forensics and crime investigation. I've always been really interested in the topic but I've thought more about inserting it into the zine because of this FBI guy that's around town recently, and an actual masked vigilante my friend told me about! I was sort of skeptical at first but I believe it, I'm going to try to set up an interview with her somehow, wouldn't that be amazing? Anyway, I want to talk to some forensic science people and maybe have some articles about historic crime in

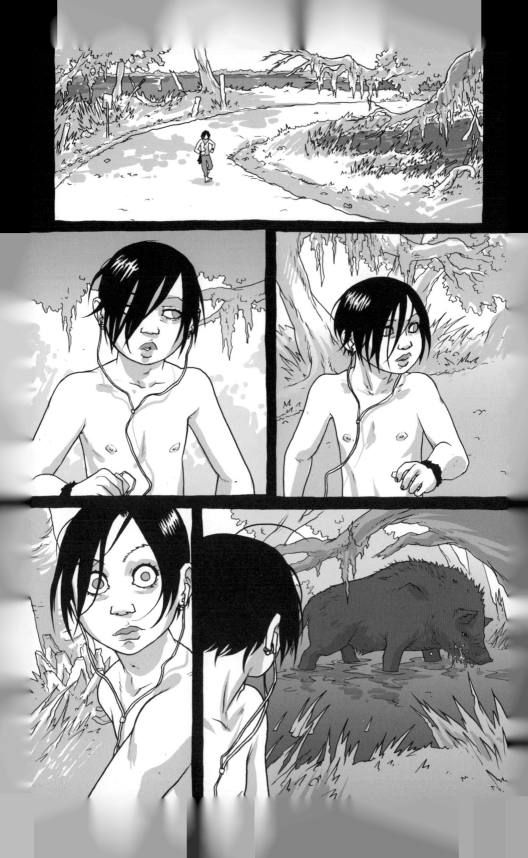

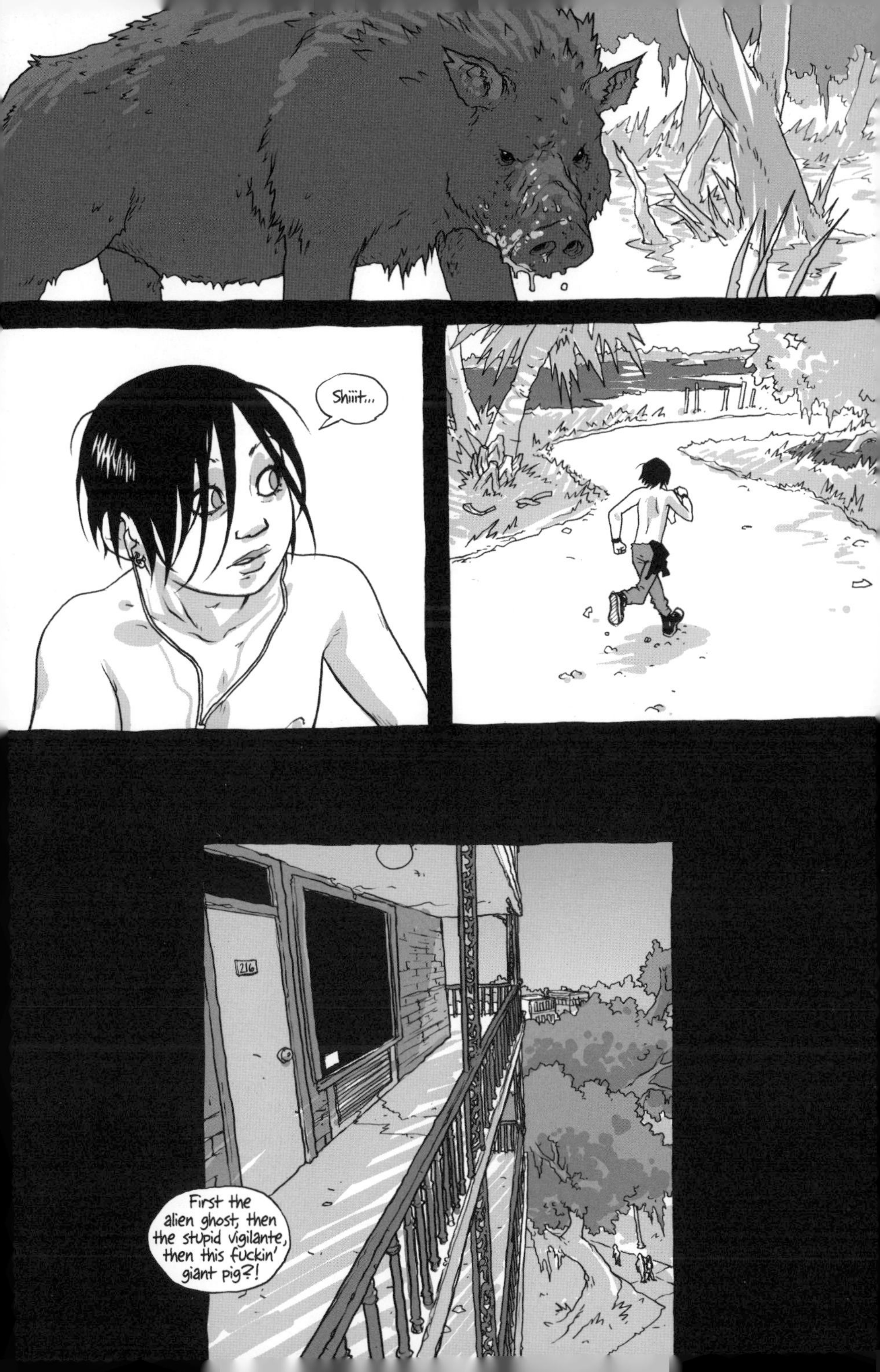
Shiiit...
First the alien ghost; then the stupid vigilante, then this fuckin' giant pig?!

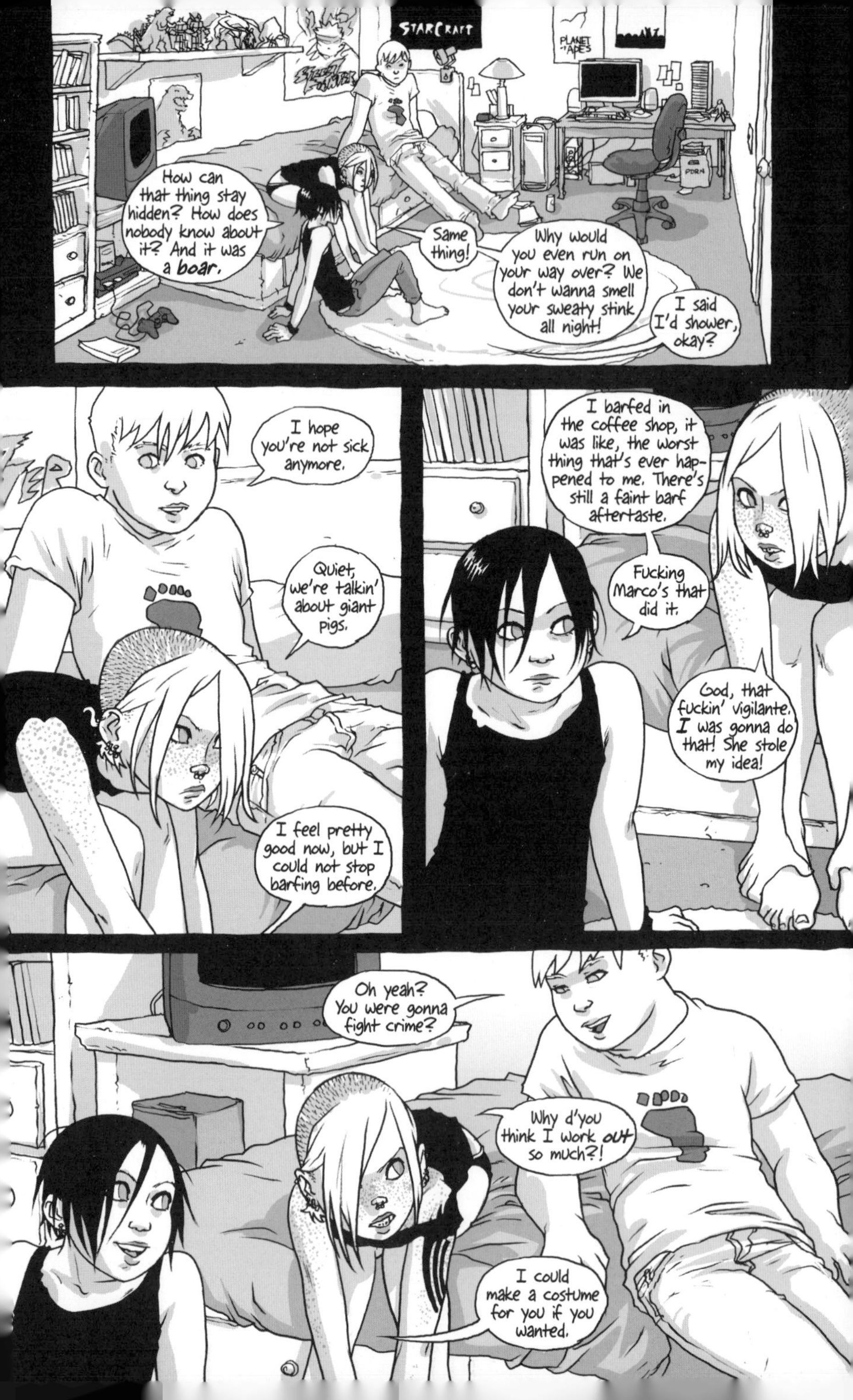
STARCRAFT
How can that thing stay hidden? How does nobody know about it? And it was a **boar**.
Same thing!
Why would you even run on your way over? We don't wanna smell your sweaty stink all night!
I said I'd shower, okay?
I hope you're not sick anymore.
Quiet, we're talkin' about giant pigs.
I feel pretty good now, but I could not stop barfing before.
I barfed in the coffee shop, it was like, the worst thing that's ever happened to me. There's still a faint barf aftertaste.
Fucking Marco's that did it.
God, that fuckin' vigilante. *I* was gonna do that! She stole my idea!
Oh yeah? You were gonna fight crime?
Why d'you think I work *out* so much?!
I could make a costume for you if you wanted.

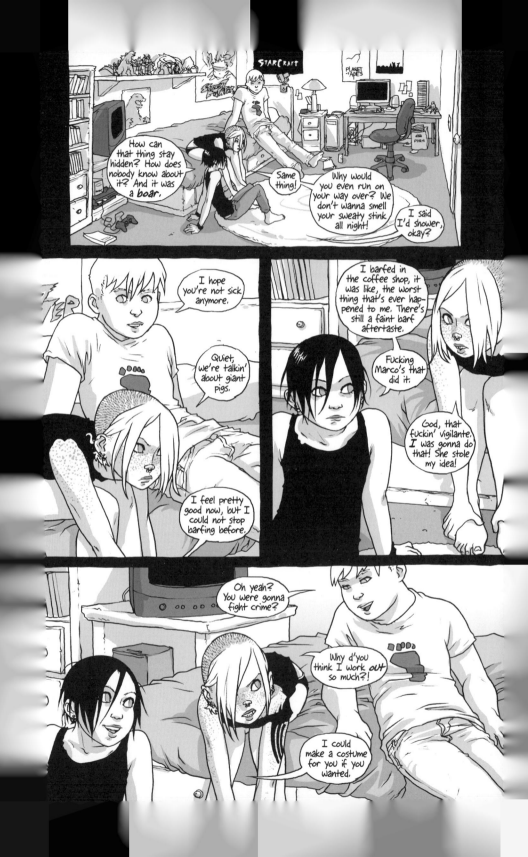

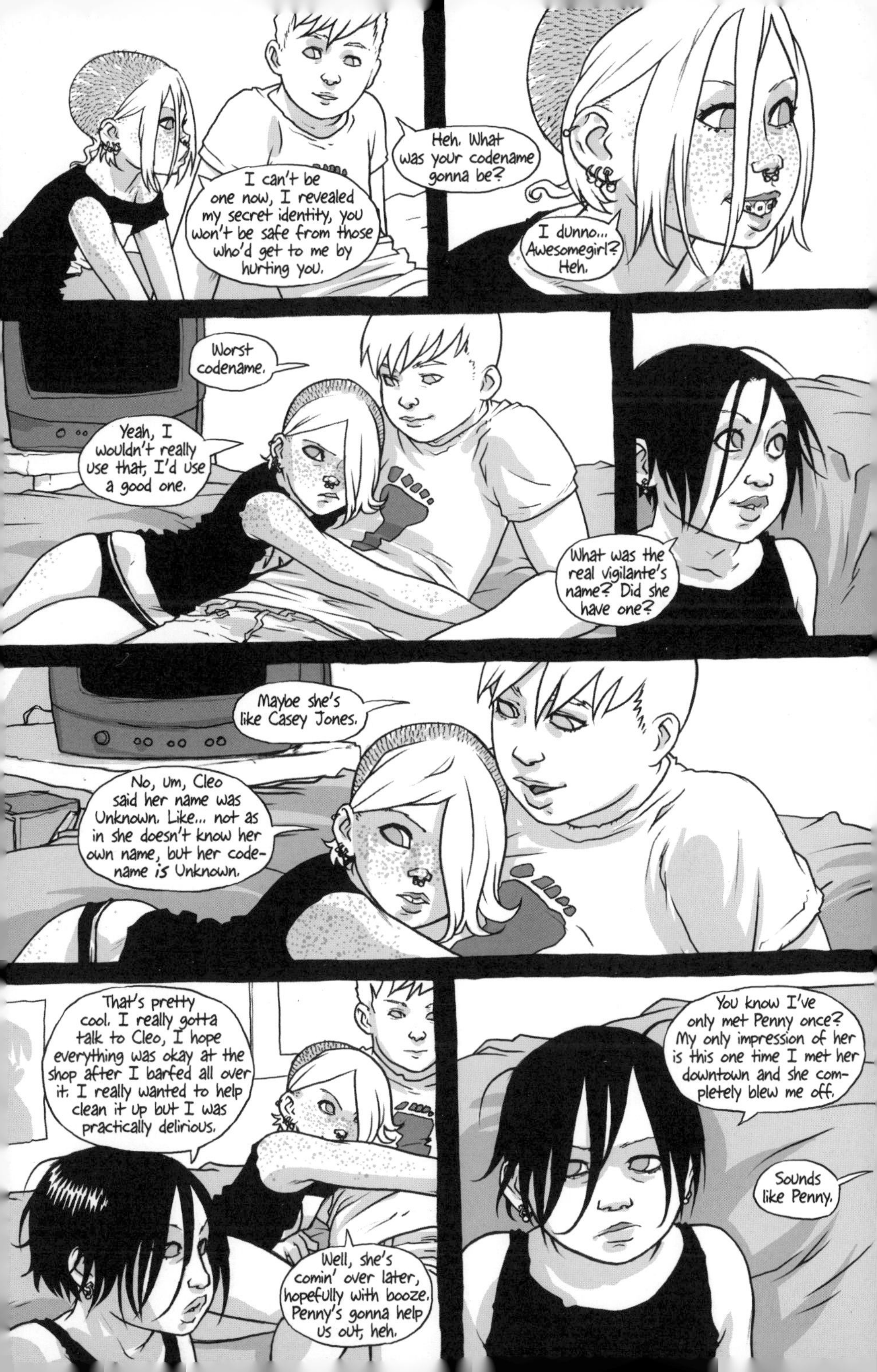
I can't be one now, I revealed my secret identity, you won't be safe from those who'd get to me by hurting you.
Heh. What was your codename gonna be?
I dunno... Awesomegirl? Heh.
Worst codename.
Yeah, I wouldn't really use that, I'd use a good one.
What was the real vigilante's name? Did she have one?
Maybe she's like Casey Jones.
No, um, Cleo said her name was Unknown. Like... not as in she doesn't know her own name, but her code-name *is* Unknown.
That's pretty cool. I really gotta talk to Cleo, I hope everything was okay at the shop after I barfed all over it. I really wanted to help clean it up but I was practically delirious.
Well, she's comin' over later, hopefully with booze. Penny's gonna help us out, heh.
You know I've only met Penny once? My only impression of her is this one time I met her downtown and she completely blew me off.
Sounds like Penny.

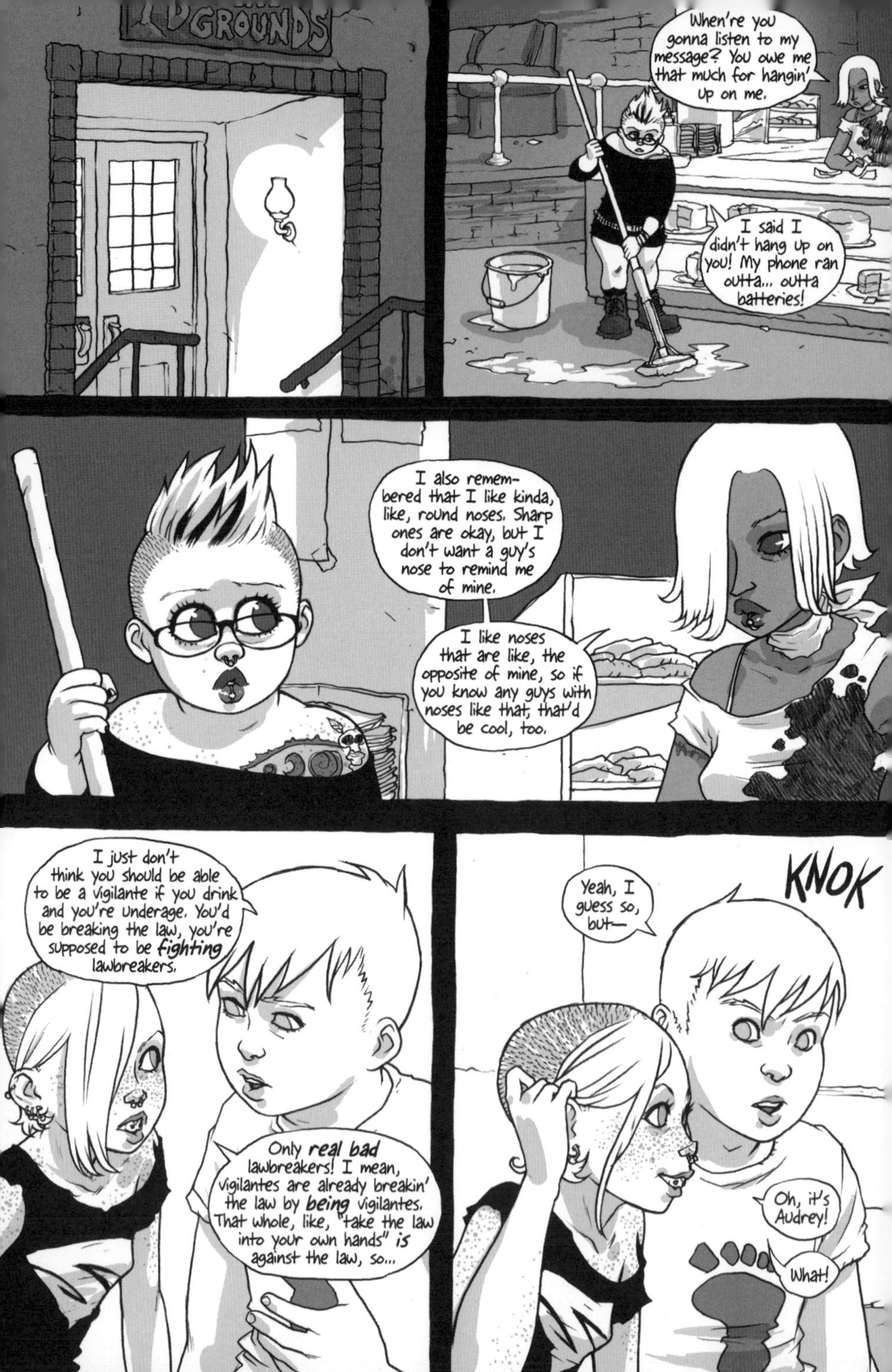
GROUNDS
When're you gonna listen to my message? You owe me that much for hangin' up on me.
I said I didn't hang up on you! My phone ran outta... outta batteries!
I also remembered that I like kinda, like, round noses. Sharp ones are okay, but I don't want a guy's nose to remind me of mine.
I like noses that are like, the opposite of mine, so if you know any guys with noses like that, that'd be cool, too.
I just don't think you should be able to be a vigilante if you drink and you're underage. You'd be breaking the law, you're supposed to be *fighting* lawbreakers.
Only ***real bad*** lawbreakers! I mean, vigilantes are already breakin' the law by ***being*** vigilantes. That whole, like, "take the law into your own hands" ***is*** against the law, so...
Yeah, I guess so, but—
KNOK
Oh, it's Audrey!
What!

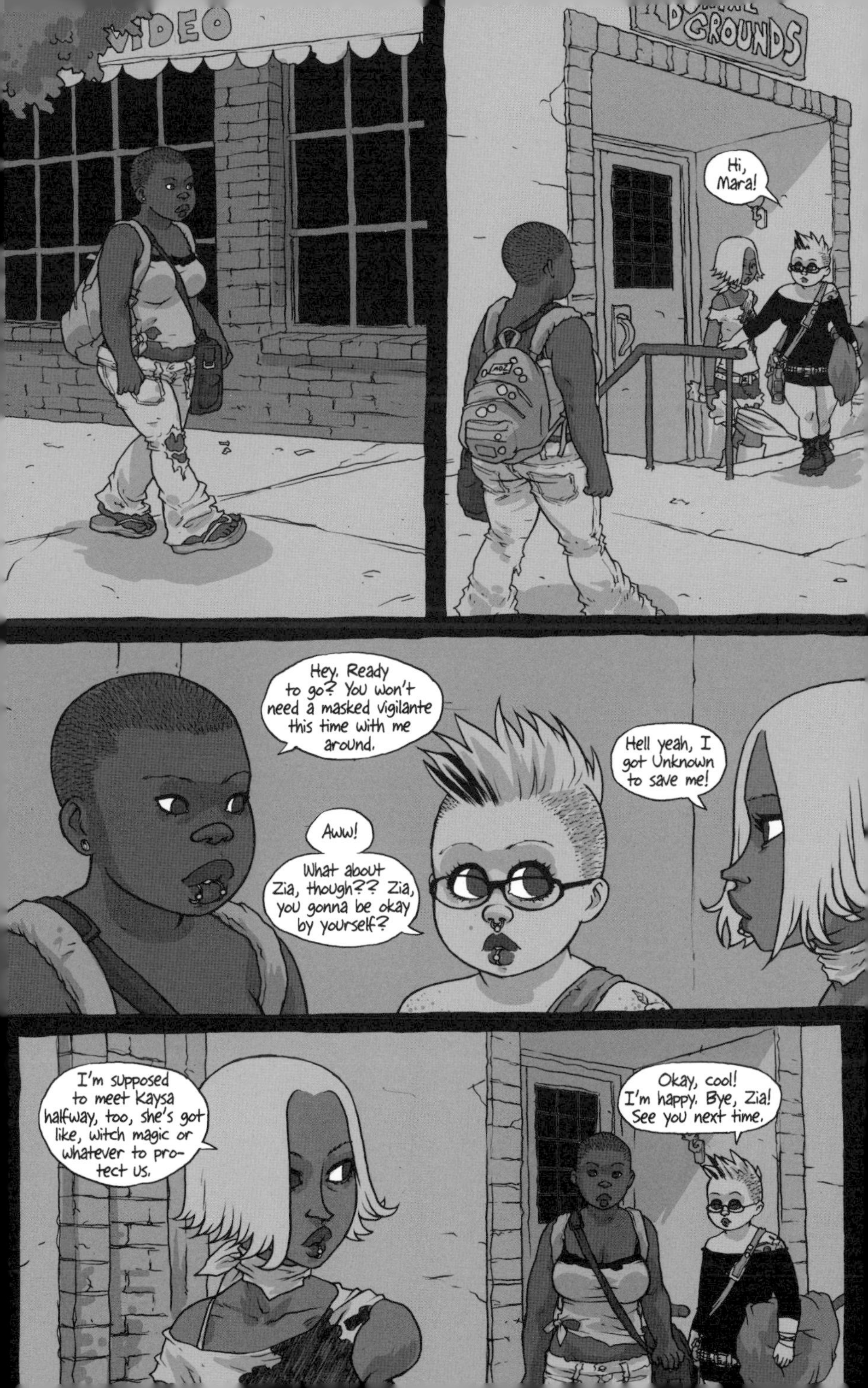
VIDEO
GROUNDS
Hi, Mara!
Hey. Ready to go? You won't need a masked vigilante this time with me around.
Hell yeah, I got Unknown to save me!
Aww!
What about Zia, though?? Zia, you gonna be okay by yourself?
I'm supposed to meet Kaysa halfway, too, she's got like, witch magic or whatever to protect us.
Okay, cool! I'm happy. Bye, Zia! See you next time.

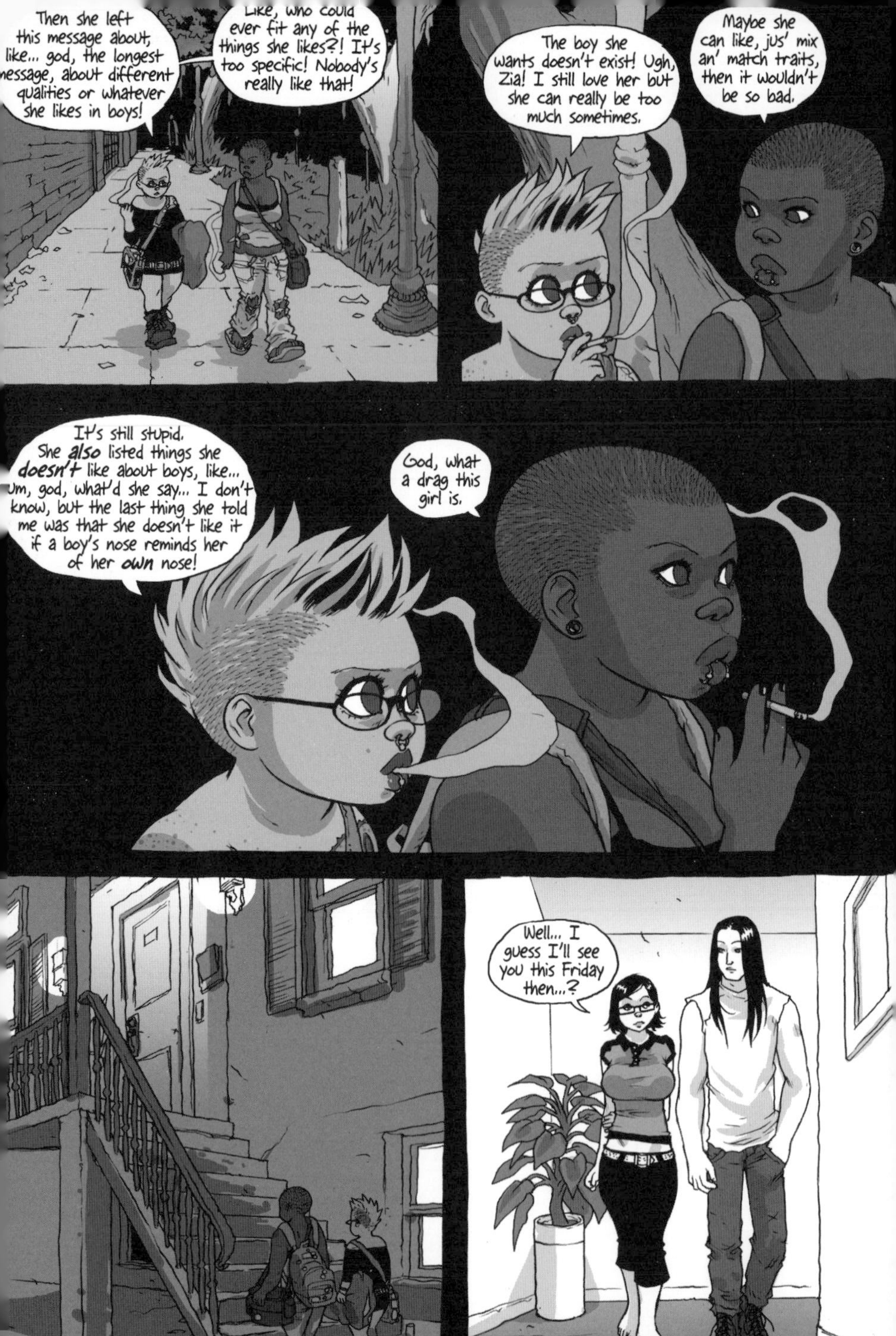
Then she left this message about, like... god, the longest message, about different qualities or whatever she likes in boys!
Like, who could ever fit any of the things she likes?! It's too specific! Nobody's really like that!
The boy she wants doesn't exist! Ugh, Zia! I still love her but she can really be too much sometimes.
Maybe she can like, jus' mix an' match traits, then it wouldn't be so bad.
It's still stupid. She also listed things she doesn't like about boys, like... um, god, what'd she say... I don't know, but the last thing she told me was that she doesn't like it if a boy's nose reminds her of her own nose!
God, what a drag this girl is.
Well... I guess I'll see you this Friday then...?

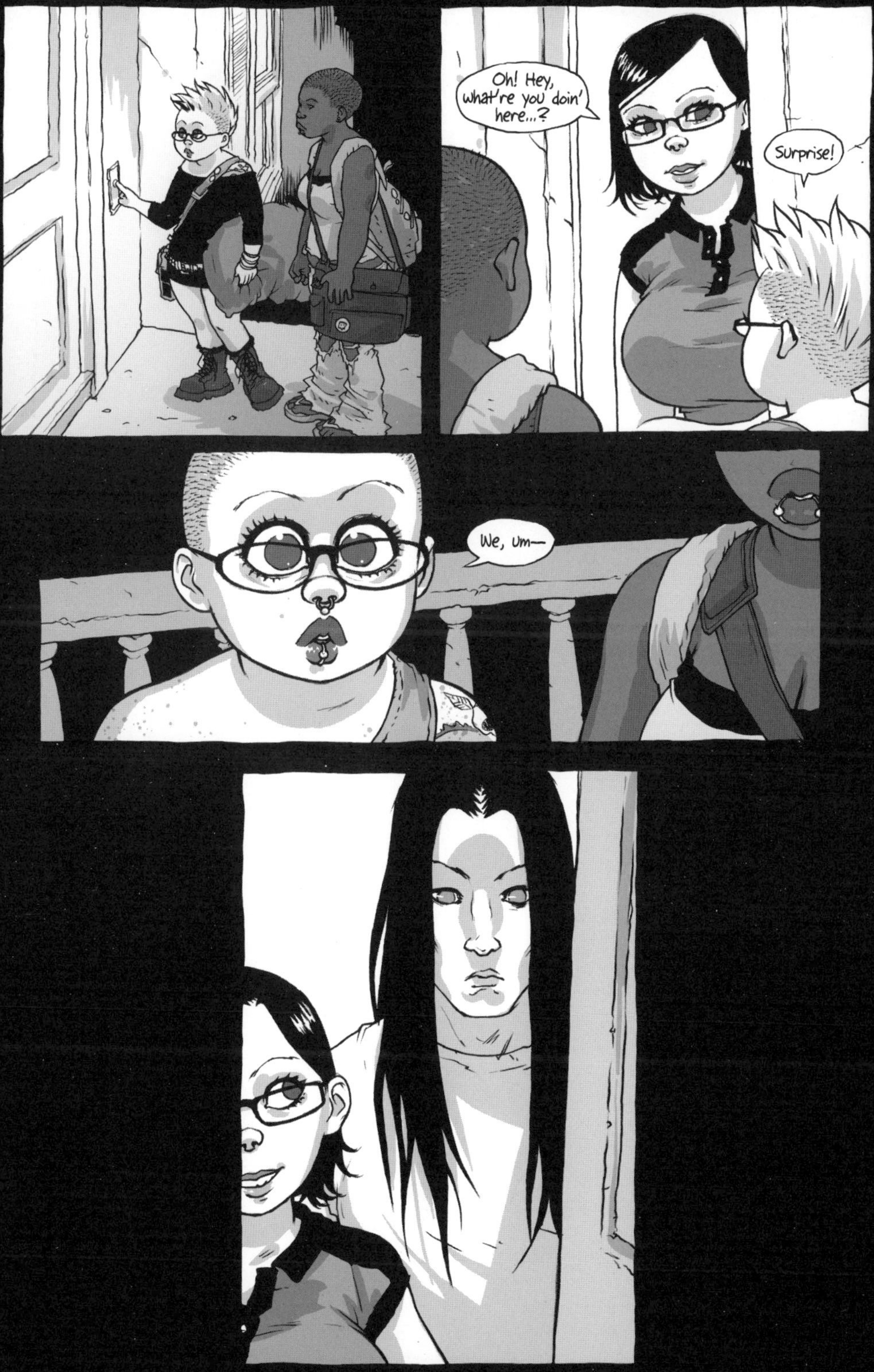
Oh! Hey, what're you doin' here...?
Surprise!
We, um—

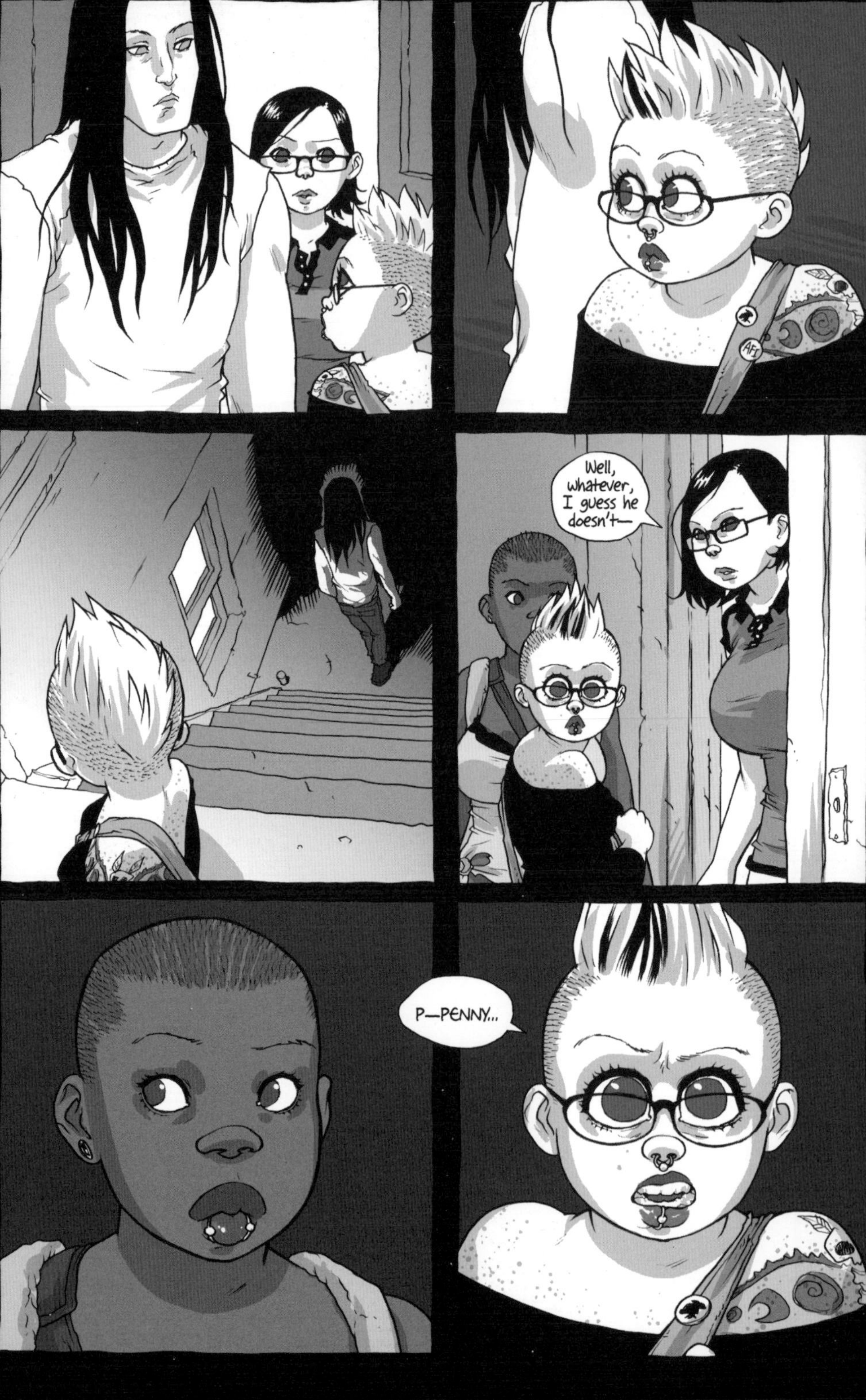
Well, whatever, I guess he doesn't—
P—PENNY...

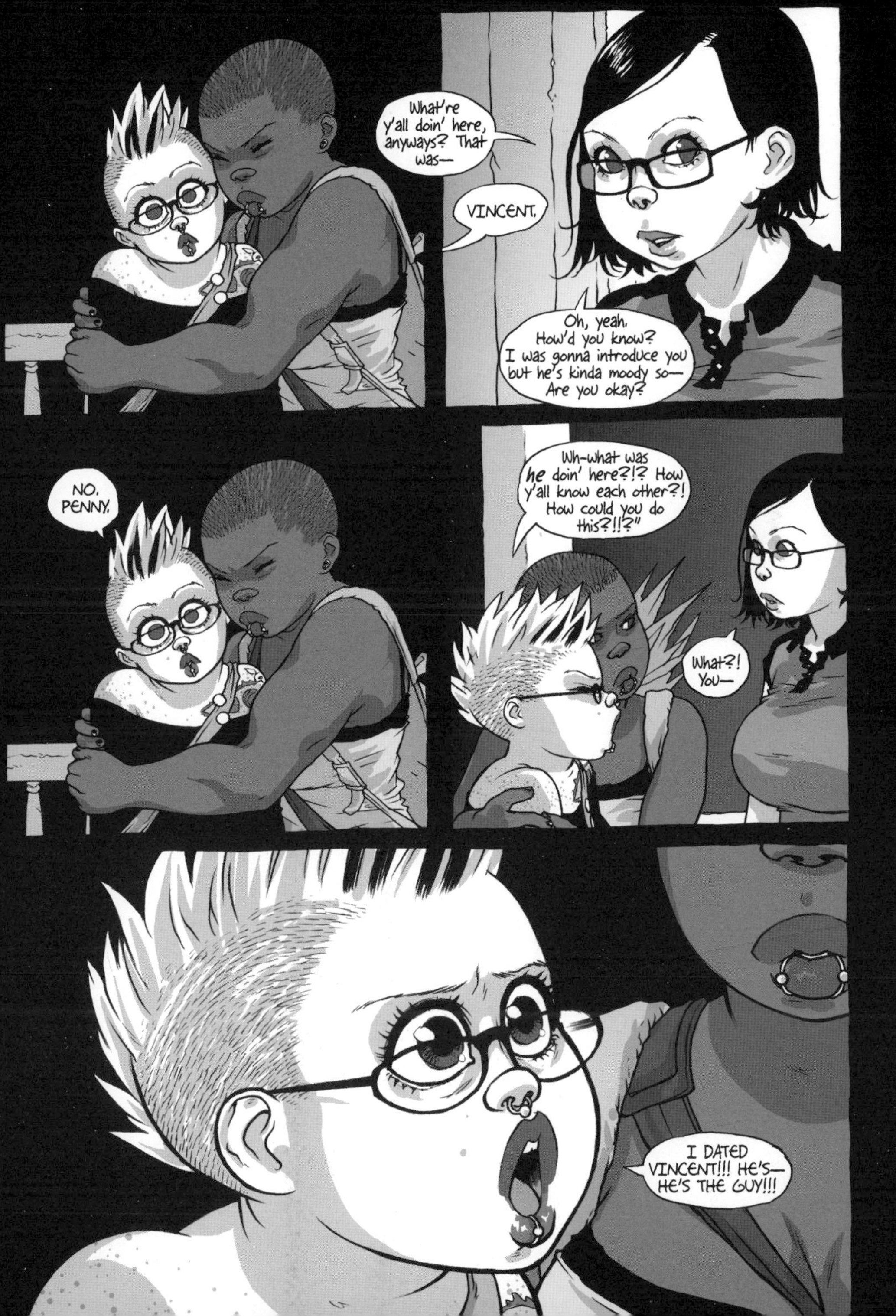

What're y'all doin' here, anyways? That was—
VINCENT.
Oh, yeah. How'd you know? I was gonna introduce you but he's kinda moody so— Are you okay?
NO, PENNY.
Wh-what was he doin' here?!? How y'all know each other?! How could you do this?!!?"
What?! You—
I DATED VINCENT!!! HE'S— HE'S THE GUY!!!

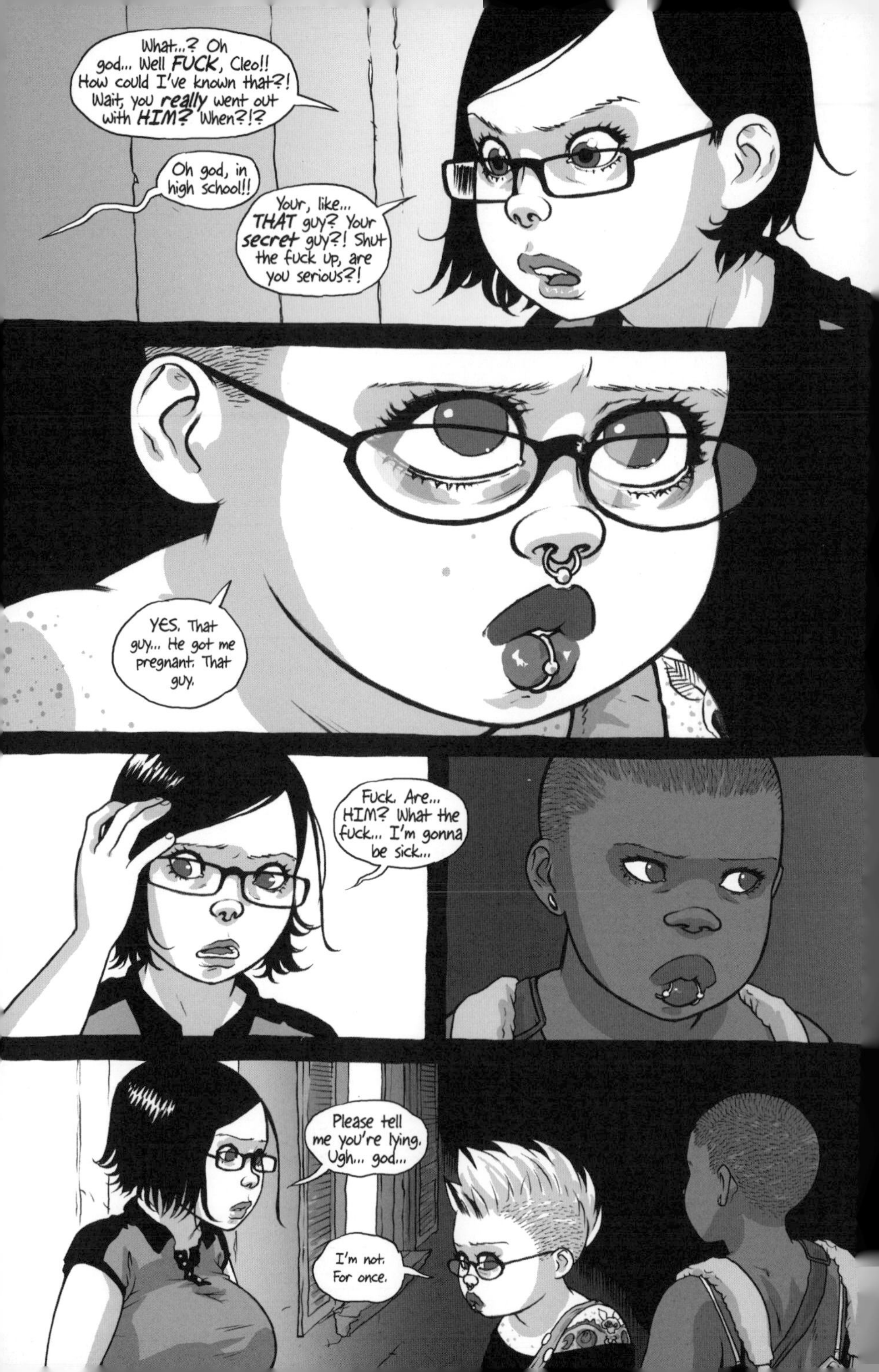
What...? Oh god... Well FUCK, Cleo!! How could I've known that?! Wait, you really went out with HIM? When?!?
Oh god, in high school!!
Your, like... THAT guy? Your secret guy?! Shut the fuck up, are you serious?!
YES. That guy... He got me pregnant. That guy.
Fuck. Are... HIM? What the fuck... I'm gonna be sick...
Please tell me you're lying. Ugh... god...
I'm not. For once.

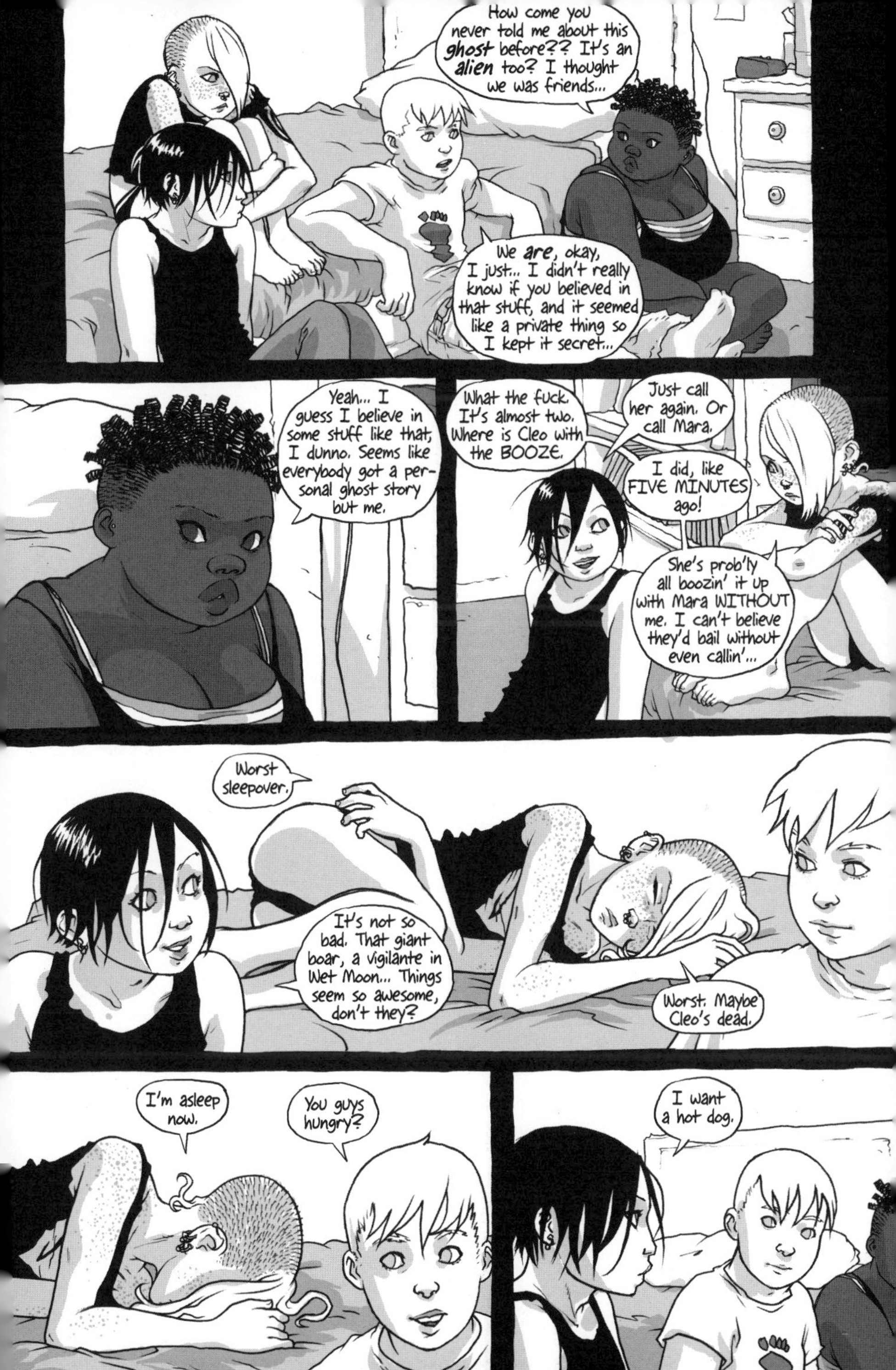
How come you never told me about this **ghost** before?? It's an **alien** too? I thought we was friends...
We **are**, okay, I just... I didn't really know if you believed in that stuff, and it seemed like a private thing so I kept it secret...
Yeah... I guess I believe in some stuff like that, I dunno. Seems like everybody got a personal ghost story but me.
What the fuck. It's almost two. Where is Cleo with the BOOZE.
Just call her again. Or call Mara.
I did, like FIVE MINUTES ago!
She's prob'ly all boozin' it up with Mara WITHOUT me. I can't believe they'd bail without even callin'...
Worst sleepover.
It's not so bad. That giant boar, a vigilante in Wet Moon... Things seem so awesome, don't they?
Worst. Maybe Cleo's dead.
I'm asleep now.
You guys hungry?
I want a hot dog.

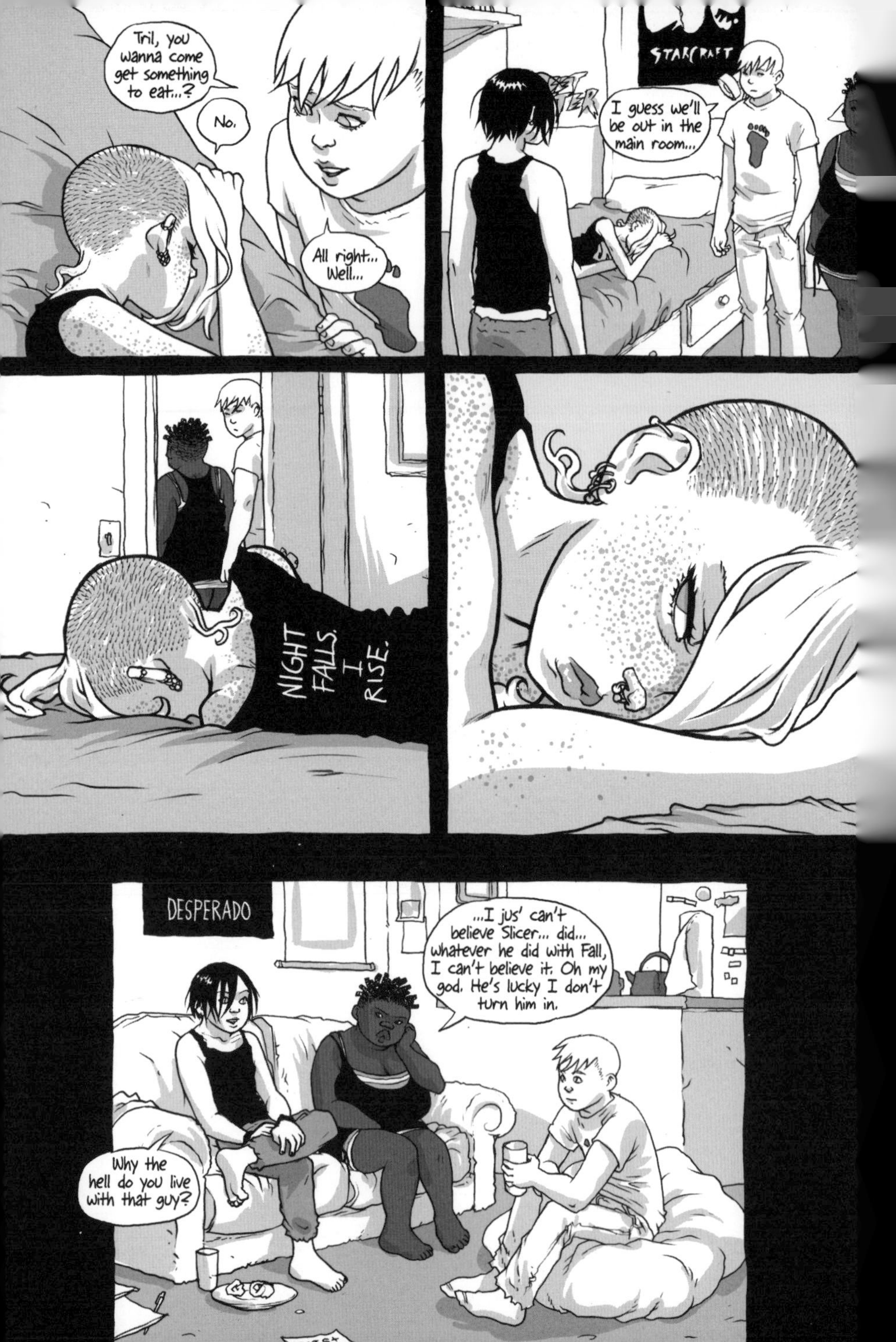

Tril, you wanna come get something to eat...?
No.
All right... Well...
STARCRAFT
I guess we'll be out in the main room...
NIGHT FALLS. I RISE.
DESPERADO
...I jus' can't believe Slicer... did... whatever he did with Fall, I can't believe it. Oh my god. He's lucky I don't turn him in.
Why the hell do you live with that guy?

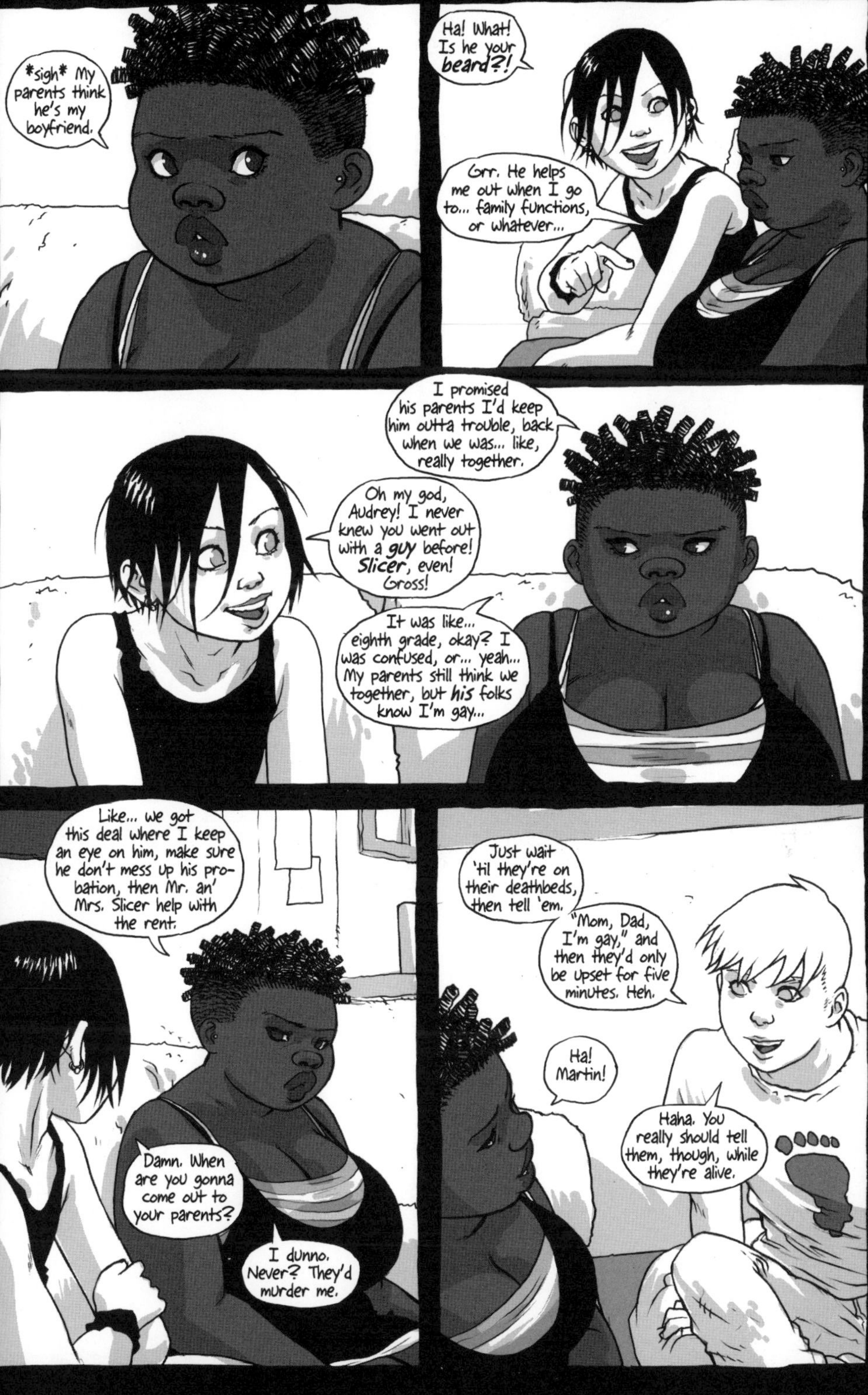
sigh My parents think he's my boyfriend.
Ha! What! Is he your **beard?!**
Grr. He helps me out when I go to... family functions, or whatever...
I promised his parents I'd keep him outta trouble, back when we was... like, really together.
Oh my god, Audrey! I never knew you went out with a ***guy*** before! ***Slicer***, even! Gross!
It was like... eighth grade, okay? I was confused, or... yeah... My parents still think we together, but ***his*** folks know I'm gay...
Like... we got this deal where I keep an eye on him, make sure he don't mess up his probation, then Mr. an' Mrs. Slicer help with the rent.
Damn. When are you gonna come out to your parents?
I dunno. Never? They'd murder me.
Just wait 'til they're on their deathbeds, then tell 'em.
"Mom, Dad, I'm gay," and then they'd only be upset for five minutes. Heh.
Ha! Martin!
Haha. You really should tell them, though, while they're alive.

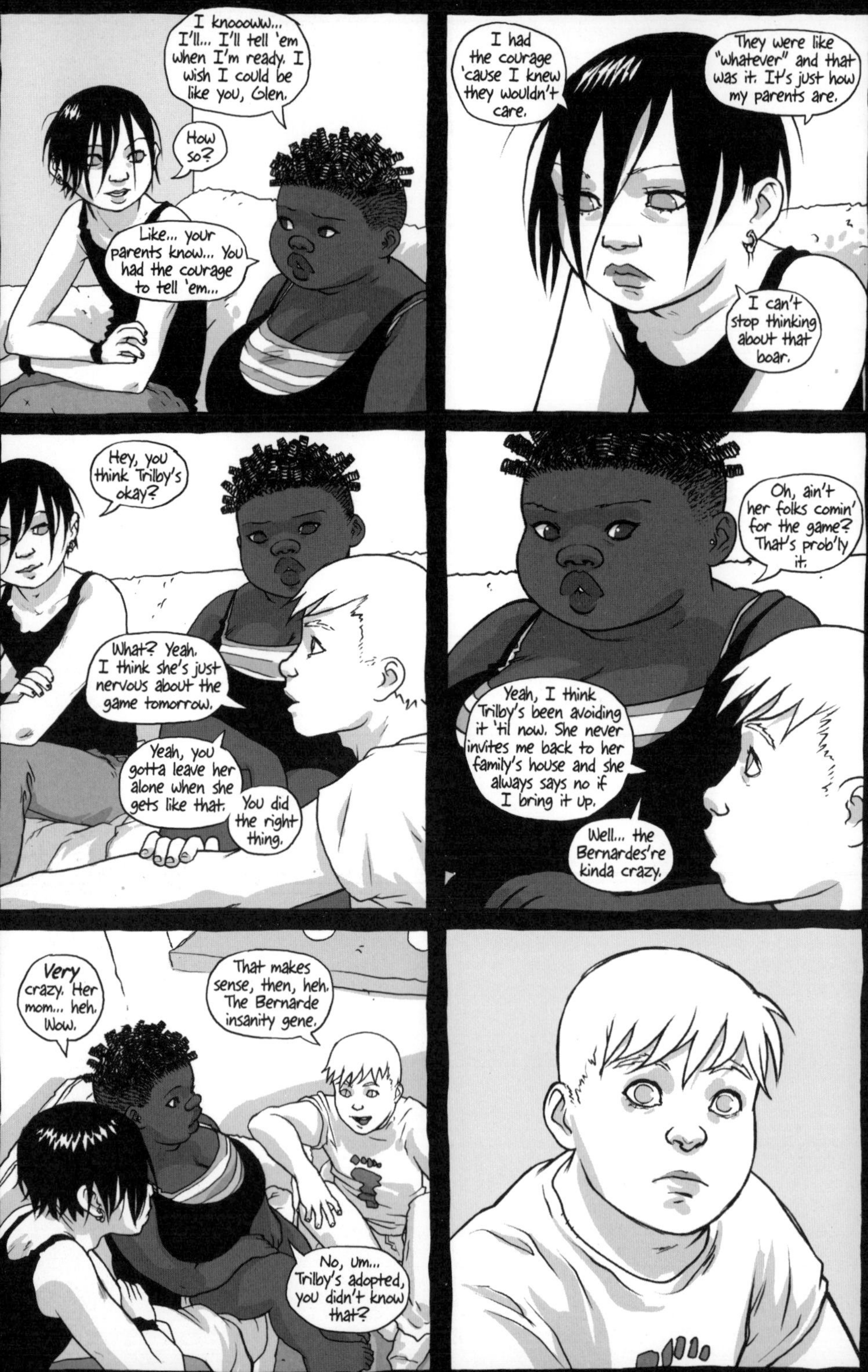
I knooowww... I'll... I'll tell 'em when I'm ready. I wish I could be like you, Glen.
How so?
Like... your parents know... You had the courage to tell 'em...
I had the courage 'cause I knew they wouldn't care.
They were like "whatever" and that was it. It's just how my parents are.
I can't stop thinking about that boar.
Hey, you think Trilby's okay?
What? Yeah. I think she's just nervous about the game tomorrow.
Yeah, you gotta leave her alone when she gets like that.
You did the right thing.
Oh, ain't her folks comin' for the game? That's prob'ly it.
Yeah, I think Trilby's been avoiding it 'til now. She never invites me back to her family's house and she always says no if I bring it up.
Well... the Bernardes're kinda crazy.
Very crazy. Her mom... heh. Wow.
That makes sense, then, heh. The Bernarde insanity gene.
No, um... Trilby's adopted, you didn't know that?

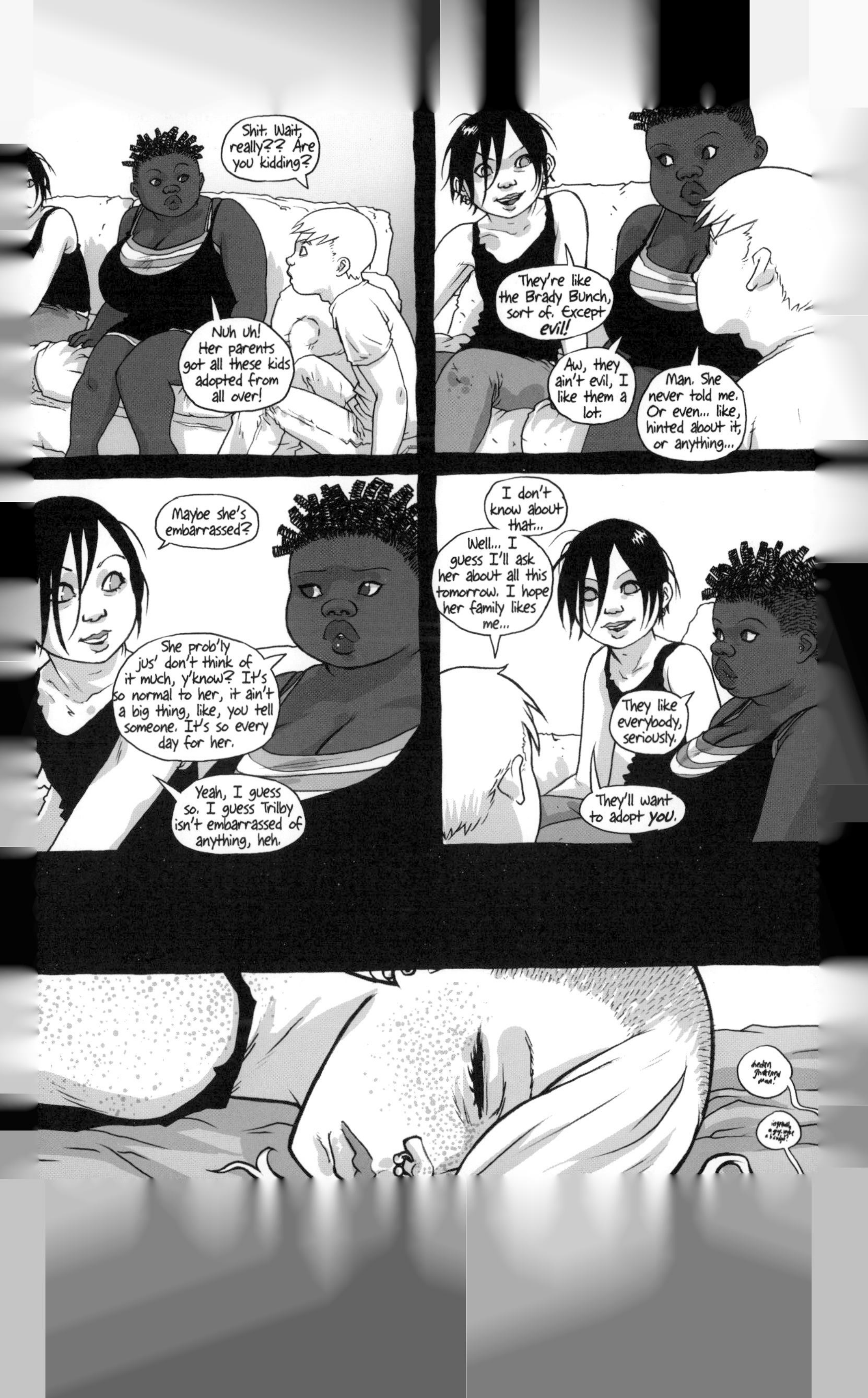
Shit. Wait, really?? Are you kidding?
Nuh uh! Her parents got all these kids adopted from all over!
They're like the Brady Bunch, sort of. Except **evil!**
Aw, they ain't evil, I like them a lot.
Man. She never told me. Or even... like, hinted about it, or anything...
Maybe she's embarrassed?
She prob'ly jus' don't think of it much, y'know? It's so normal to her, it ain't a big thing, like, you tell someone. It's so every day for her.
Yeah, I guess so. I guess Trilby isn't embarrassed of anything, heh.
I don't know about that...
Well... I guess I'll ask her about all this tomorrow. I hope her family likes me...
They like everybody, seriously.
They'll want to adopt **YOU.**

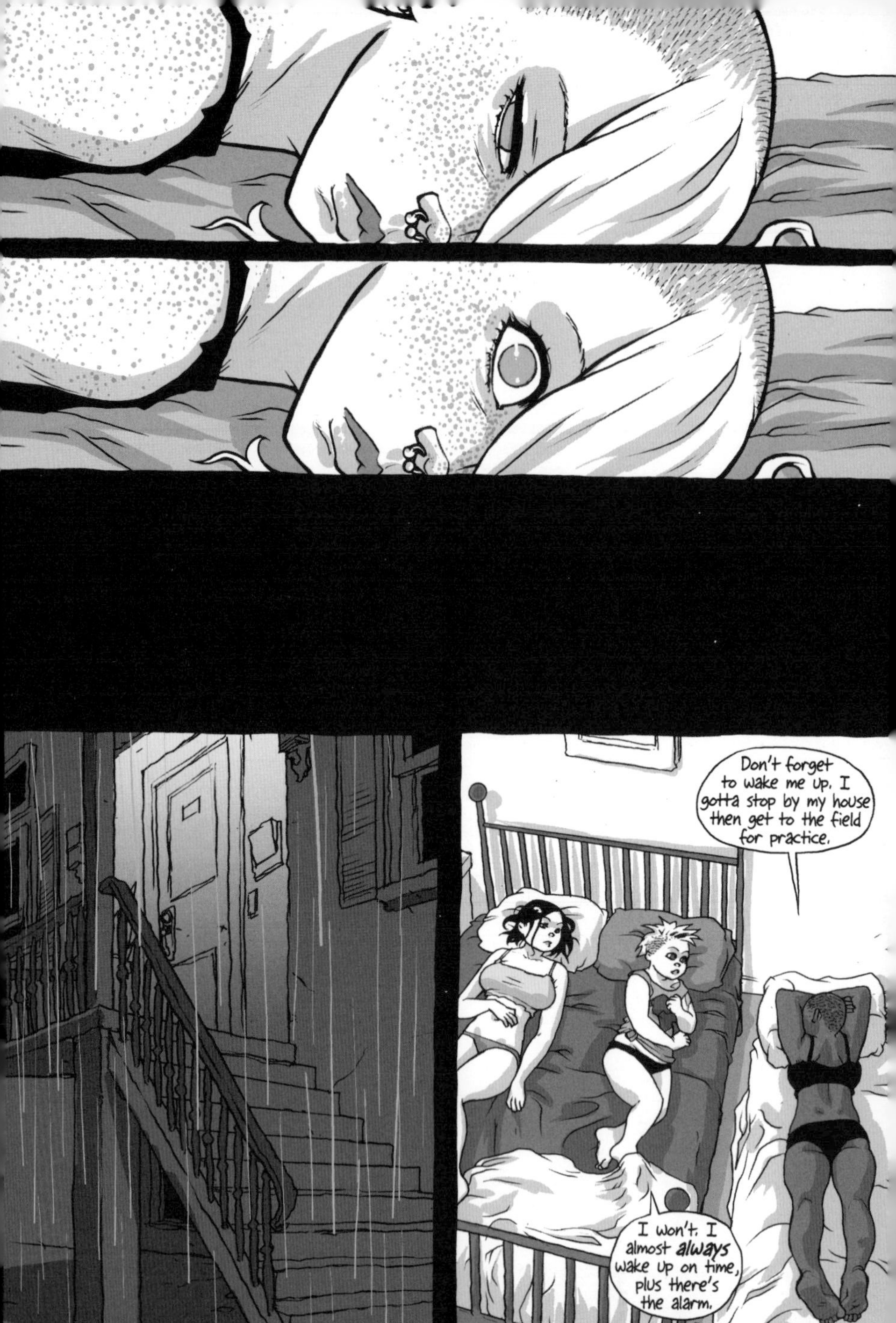
Don't forget to wake me up. I gotta stop by my house then get to the field for practice.
I won't. I almost **always** wake up on time, plus there's the alarm.

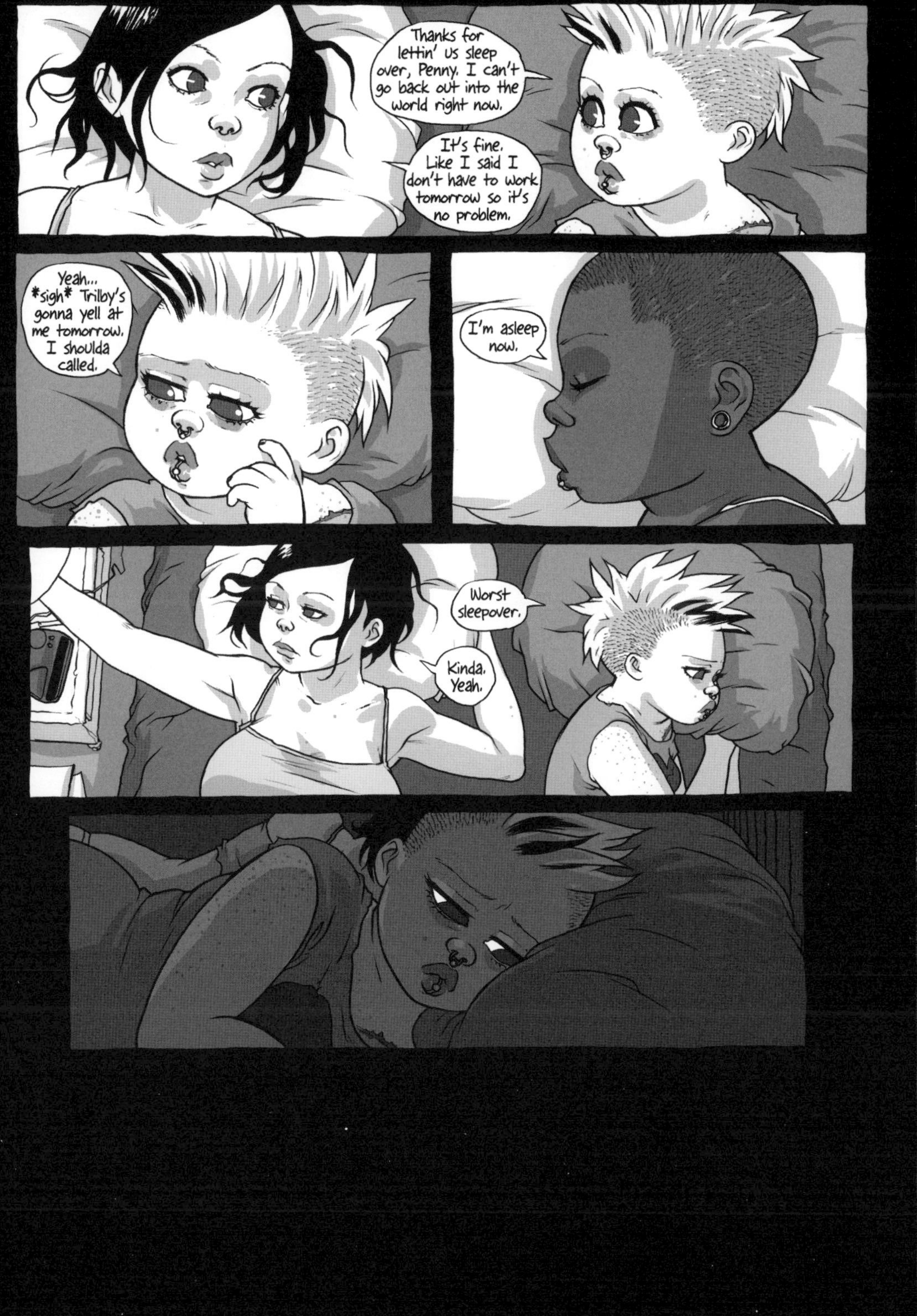
Thanks for lettin' us sleep over, Penny. I can't go back out into the world right now.
It's fine. Like I said I don't have to work tomorrow so it's no problem.
Yeah... *sigh* Trilby's gonna yell at me tomorrow. I shoulda called.
I'm asleep now.
Worst sleepover.
Kinda. Yeah.

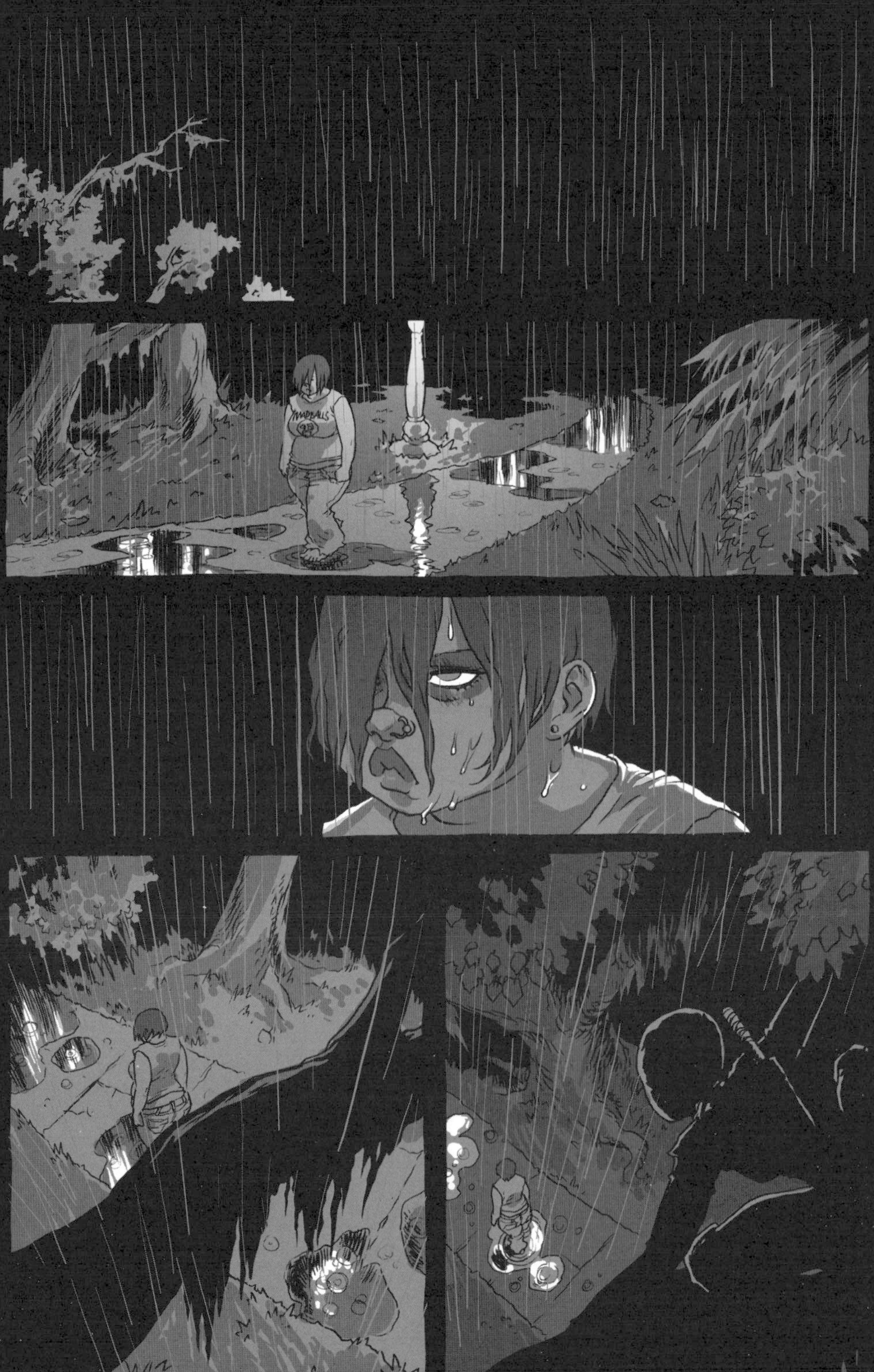
MADBALLS

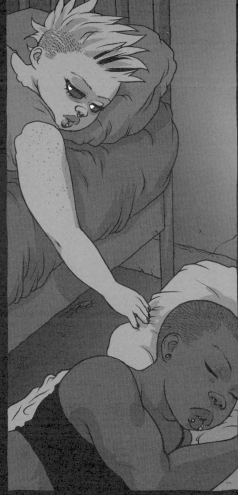

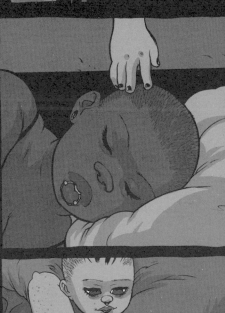

hey.

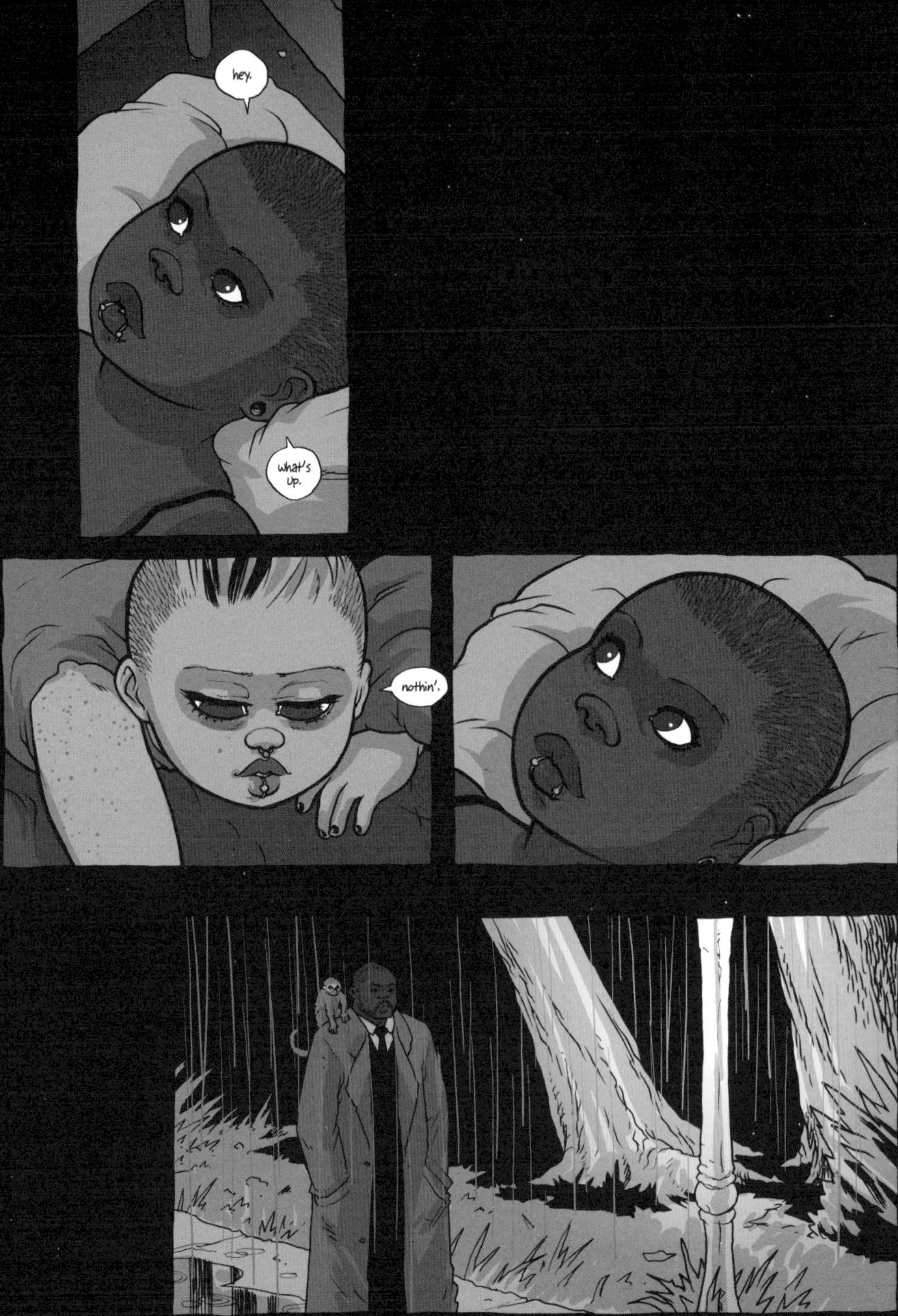
hey.
what's up.
nothin'.

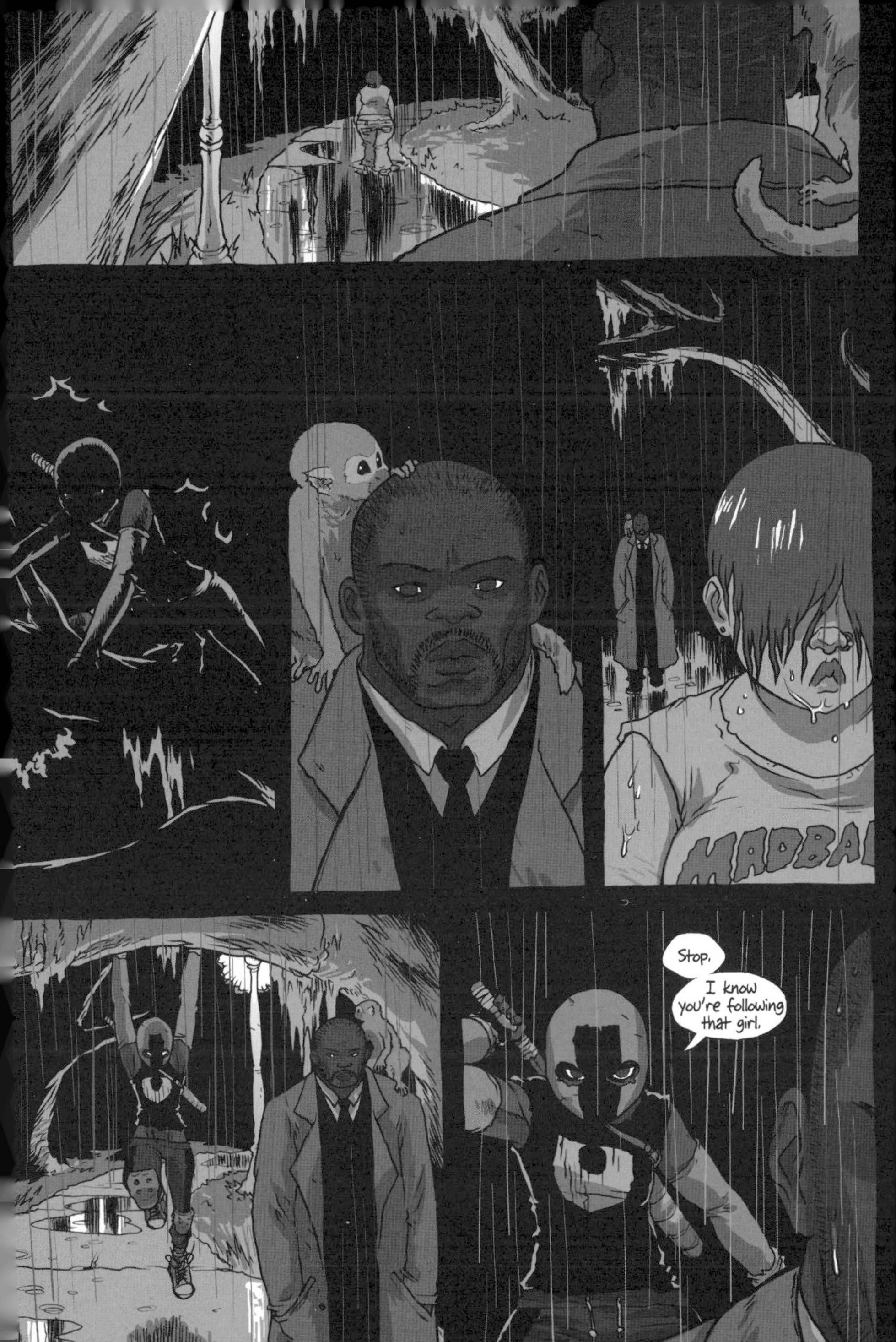
Stop.
I know you're following that girl.

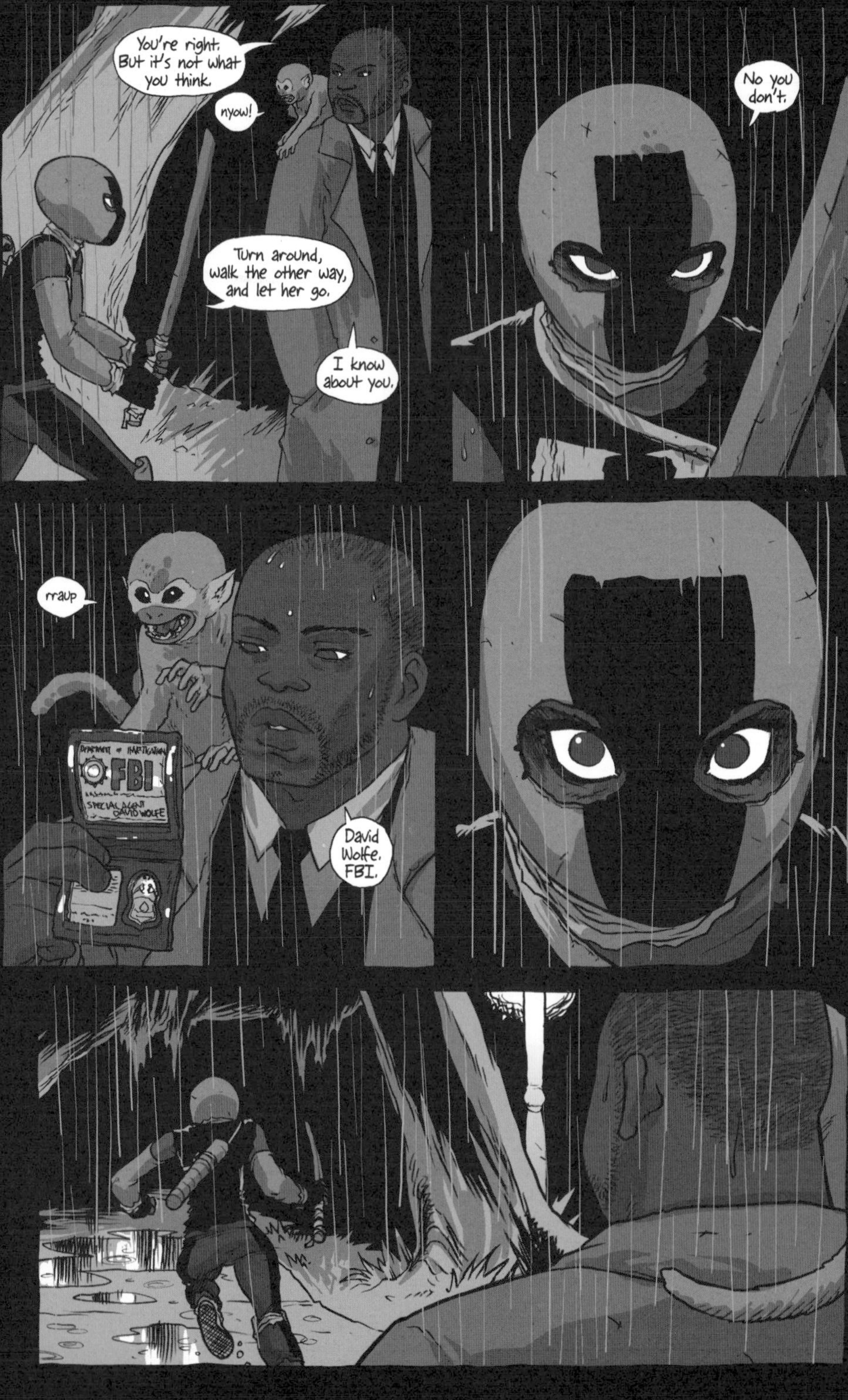
You're right. But it's not what you think.
nyow!
Turn around, walk the other way, and let her go.
I know about you.
No you don't.
rraup
FBI
SPECIAL AGENT DAVID WOLFE
David Wolfe. FBI.

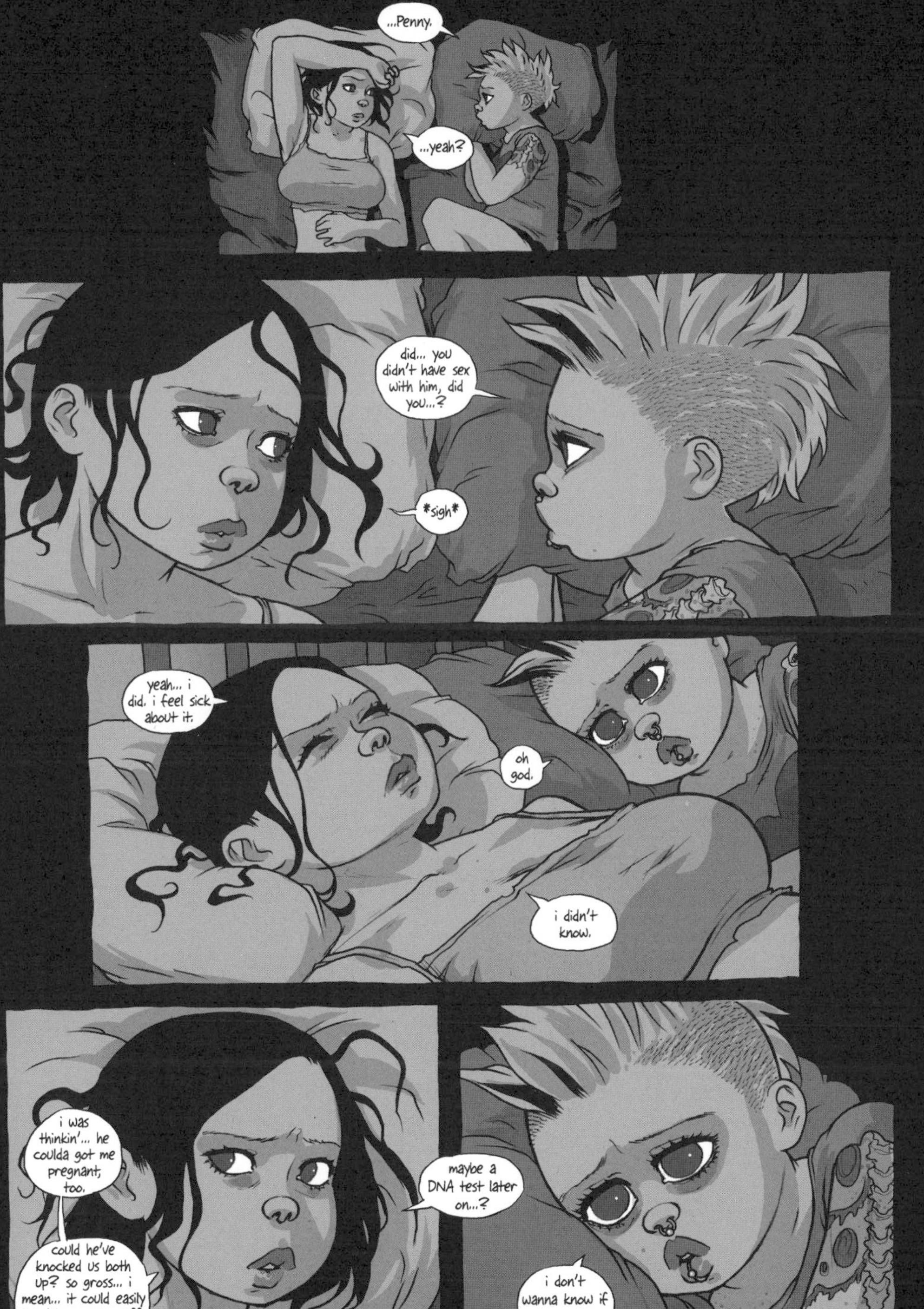
...Penny.
...yeah?
did... you didn't have sex with him, did you...?
sigh
yeah... i did. i feel sick about it.
oh god.
i didn't know.
i was thinkin'... he coulda got me pregnant, too.
could he've knocked us both up? so gross... i mean... it could easily be dale or even jeff, but... the timing is so weird.
maybe a DNA test later on...?
i don't wanna know if it was him or not.

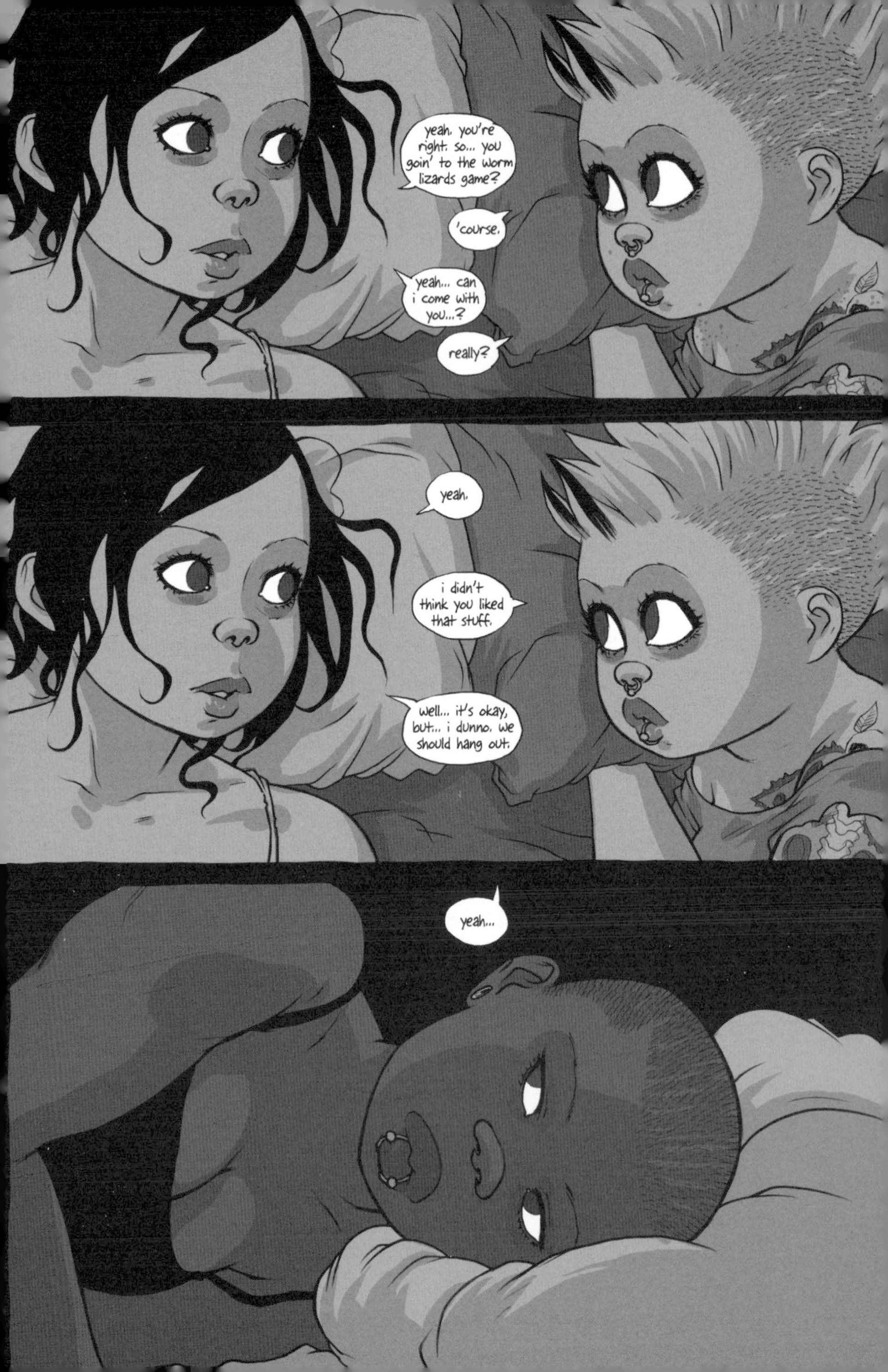
yeah. you're right. so... you goin' to the worm lizards game?
'course.
yeah... can i come with you...?
really?
yeah.
i didn't think you liked that stuff.
well... it's okay, but... i dunno. we should hang out.
yeah...

November 3
i'm writing at Penny's in secret
while she and Mara are asleep.
the worst thing. so many great
(but confusing) things and now a
terrible and also confusing thing
has happened. i found out that

Penny was seeing Vincent. he
was one of her guys. he was at
her apartment and i totally
froze like i was a zombie or
encased in ice, i completely didn't
know what to do or how to
do anything. i'm not mad at
Penny. she never met Vincent
when i was with him, she had
no way of knowing who he was.
but it is still agony. i feel like
even though we're not together
that i don't want anyone to have
him or know him except me. i
say to myself that i would never
go back to him, that i don't
even want him at all, that i
even want to hurt him like
how he hurt me, but i'm afraid
because i think if he did
want me back i'd be powerless
to say no. my heart feels like
its on fire, burning inside my
chest with sticky bonfire, and
it hurts more than anything.
writing this now is almost
unbearable. my heart can't
take it. literally. tonight when
i saw Vincent... usually what
happens is that i either paint or
throw up; I throw up when i'm

on my medicine and faint the other times if i forget to take it... but tonight neither of them happened. i was immobile. i don't know what that means.

everything reminds me of him. even though i had a bunch of flings with guys over the years, i always believed in indomitable love, but after Vincent i don't anymore. it's simply not how things are. but i'm still consumed by all this emotion swirling around the idea, like i can't escape it. like Vincent is a walking manifestation of an ideal that i don't want to believe in but from which i can never escape, like it's part of my beliefs whether i want it to be or not and i flip-flop between the idealist that i used to be and who i am now while also being both simultaneously.

i'm writing about something else.

i'm not surprised Vincent went for Penny. they're both gorgeous. i don't know why he ever got with me in the first place, he's perfect and i'm... me. how much

did Penny and Vincent do? how
far did they go... i don't know...
i don't know. was penny better
than me? did he enjoy her
more? probably. how could
he not. i don't blame him.
   i think after vincent i'm a
little afraid of sex even though
i really want to have it all
the time, and i'm especially
afraid of getting to the sex
level with myrne. it seems
nice thinking about it, but i know
actually doing it will be a
totally different thing. i'm not
sure i could go through with it,
i wonder if i could even feel
satisfied sexually with a girl,
but i know things will have to
arrive at that point sooner
or later. i remember having
sex for the first time, still
vivid. i was 13 and he was 18.
it was disappointing like pretty
much everything in my life
after that. and now possibly
having sex with a girl is
like doing it all over again
for the first time. the first
time with a guy i was eager
and curious, but this second

first time seems frightening
and insurmantable. the first
time with that boy, it wasn't
anything like i imagined, i guess
nothing is or ever will 'be', like
i never imagined that what
happened tonight could've
happened, or anything in the
past we could have happened
but it did.

Penny told me she is definitely
pregnant for sure. i didn't
want to write about it at first
but i have to, at least a little.
i don't know. i don't know how to
feel about that. i know it was
vincent. he did the same thing
to Penny as he did to me,
and i feel like even though this
is happening to Penny, it's happening
to me all over again, at the
same time. except i don't think
Penny ever really cared about
him like how i did. he's just
another guy to her, no, that's
mean. i know she cares ~~about~~
about the guys she gets with,
but... i still know it was
different for me. i guess in
some ways he was also just
another guy for me too.

i really really hope Penny keeps the baby. i know how possessive that sounds and i know its totally up to her and it would really change her life and she's still so young, i guess, but....? wouldn't it also be great....? i'm even sadder thinking about her baby possibly being snuffed out. but i know that sometimes that's how it has to be.

i'm crying as i write this. i feel like my life is over. i feel like when i put down this pen and go to sleep, that i'll never wake up because my life is plainly over and simply doesn't have the momentum required to continue. i will slip into a coma because that will become my natural state. i don't think i would mind that. except i would feel sad for my dad, Trilby, Aubrey, Penny, Meiko, Myrtle, Zia, Glen... and Mara. she might be the saddest. sad everything.

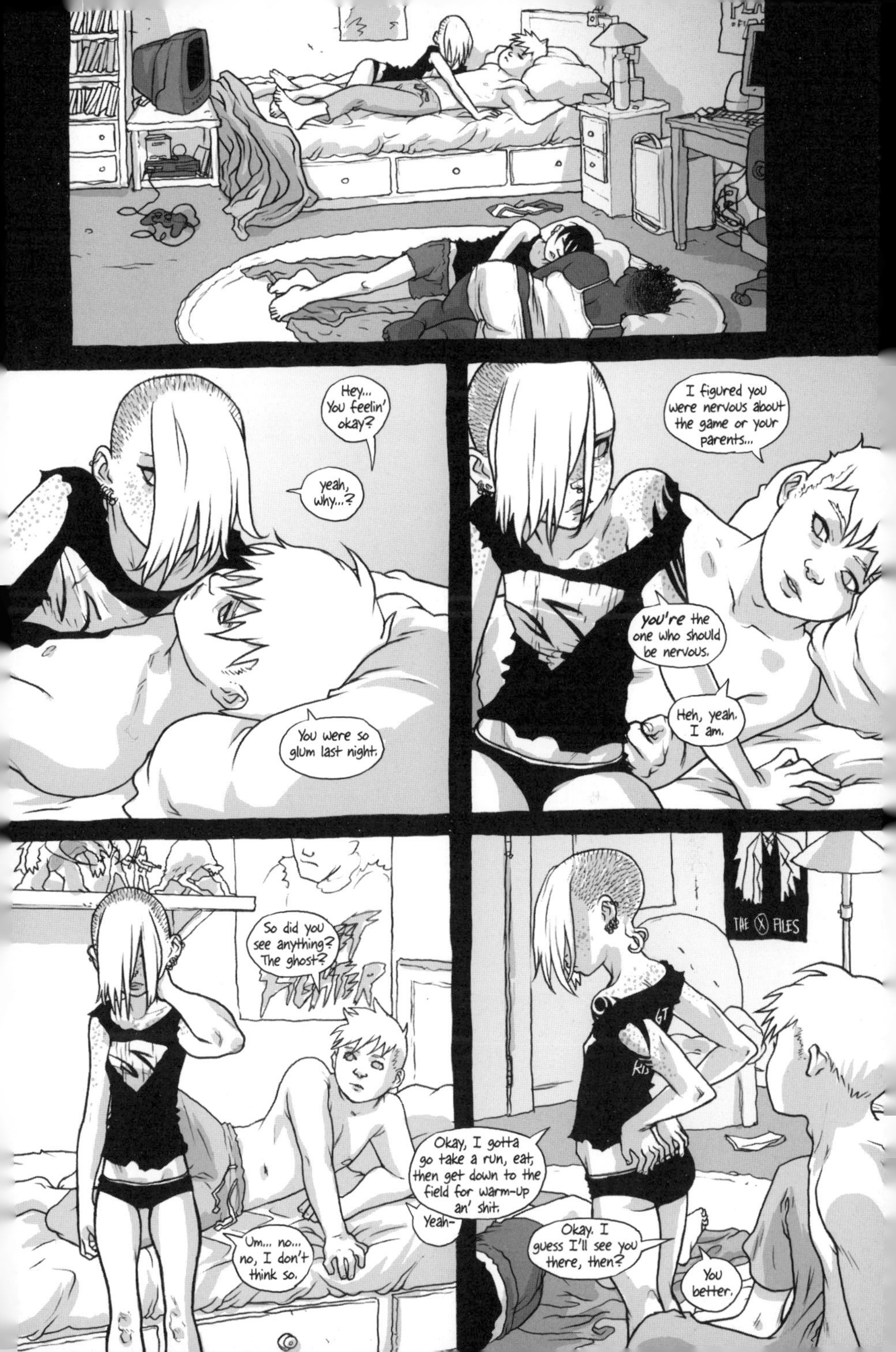
Hey... You feelin' okay?
yeah, why...?
You were so glum last night.
I figured you were nervous about the game or your parents...
you're the one who should be nervous.
Heh, yeah. I am.
So did you see anything? The ghost?
Um... no... no, I don't think so.
Yeah-
Okay, I gotta go take a run, eat, then get down to the field for warm-up an' shit.
Okay. I guess I'll see you there, then?
You better.
THE X FILES

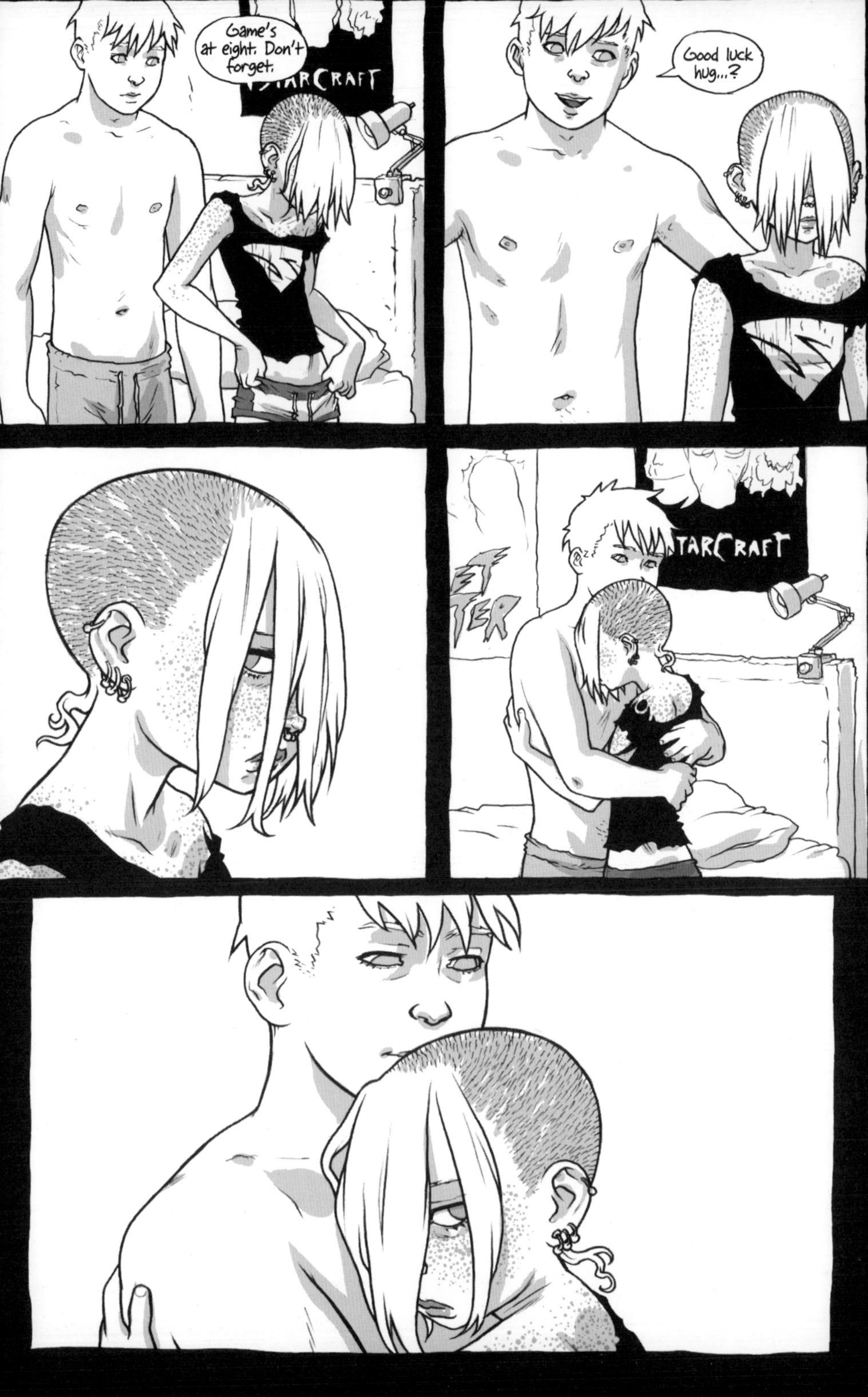
Game's at eight. Don't forget.
STARCRAFT
Good luck hug...?
STARCRAFT

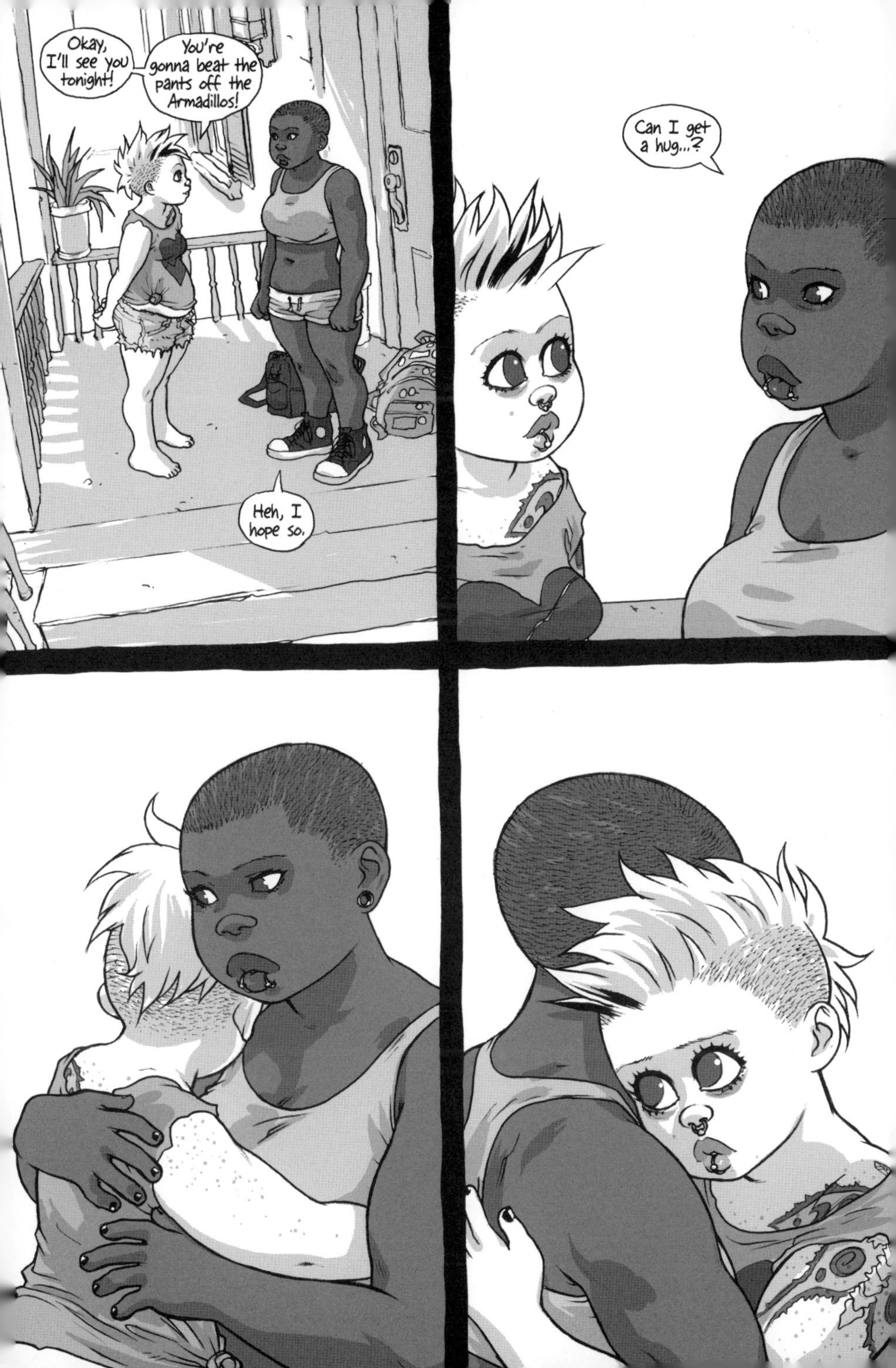

Okay, I'll see you tonight!
You're gonna beat the pants off the Armadillos!
Heh, I hope so.
Can I get a hug...?

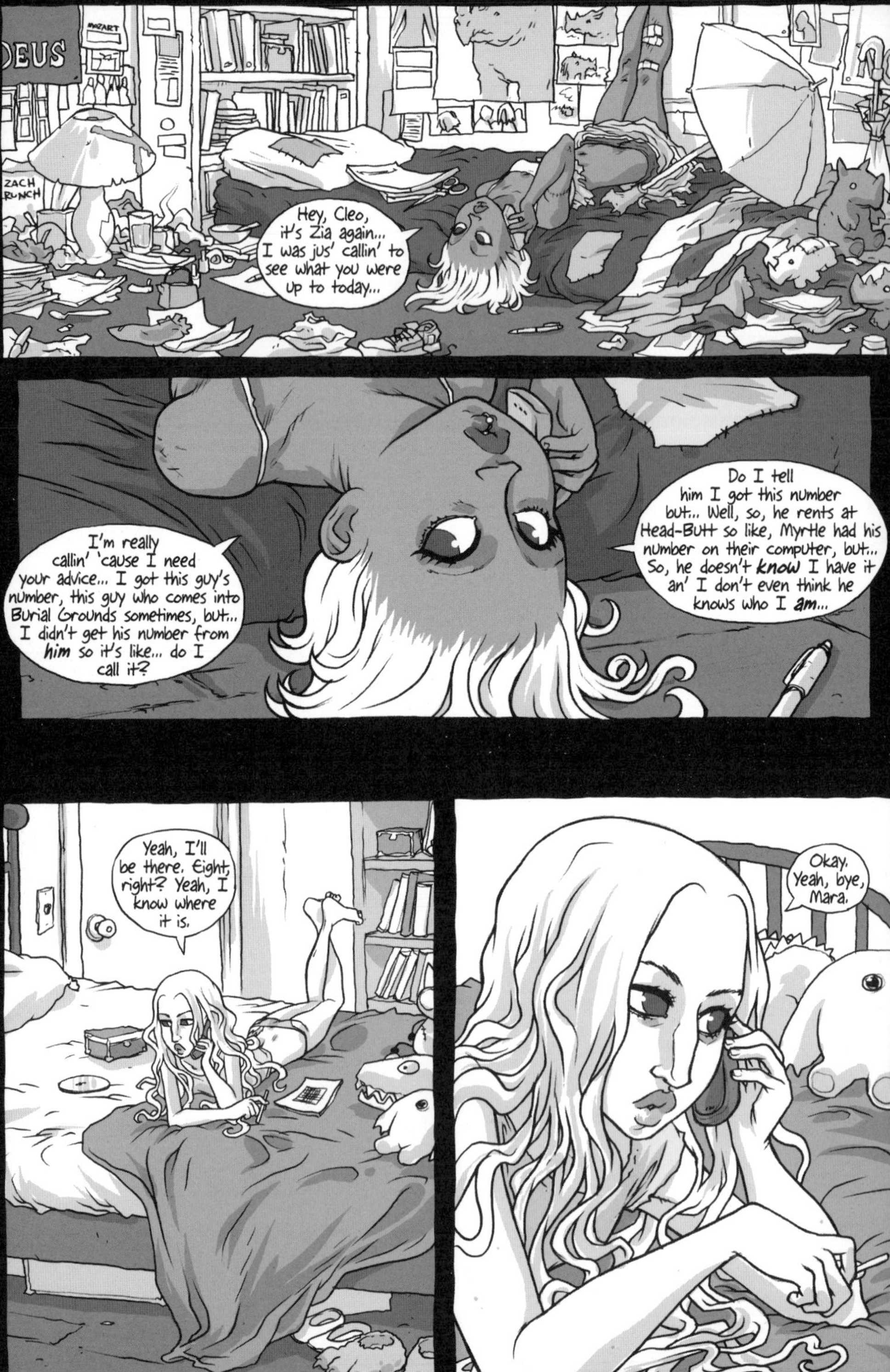
DEUS
MOZART
ZACH
RUNCH
Hey, Cleo, it's Zia again... I was jus' callin' to see what you were up to today...
I'm really callin' 'cause I need your advice... I got this guy's number, this guy who comes into Burial Grounds sometimes, but... I didn't get his number from **him** so it's like... do I call it?
Do I tell him I got this number but... Well, so, he rents at Head-Butt so like, Myrtle had his number on their computer, but... So, he doesn't **know** I have it an' I don't even think he knows who I **am**...
Yeah, I'll be there. Eight, right? Yeah, I know where it is.
Okay. Yeah, bye, Mara.

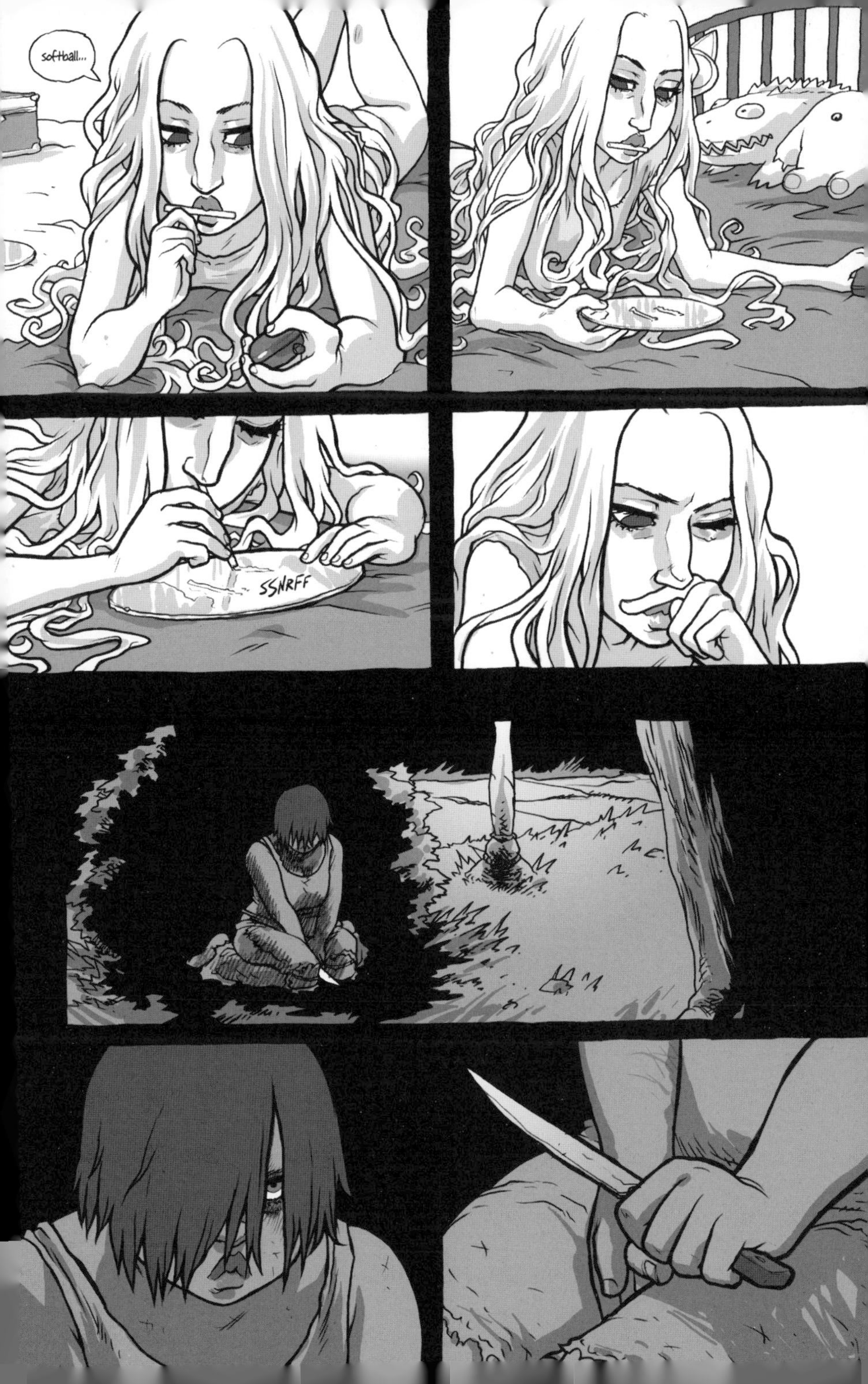
softball...
SSNRFF

The Wonders At Your Feet

[friendtoroaches@gmail.com]

Recent Entries Archive Friends User Info

mara's journal

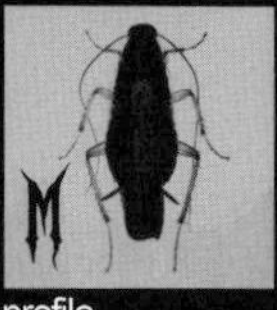

profile

November 4th, 11:35am

PRINCESS OF SLAUGHTER.

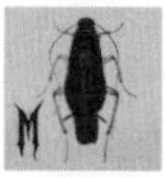

i'm at home real quick before i go to the field for practice. we're doing one last serious long practice before the game at 8. i think i wrote before about how Shoshana quit, and now we have this new girl Galaxy (crazy name) who is cool but i feel really uncertain about her. whether she can perform out there. Nisha is pretty flakey recently, i don't know what the hell is up with her. Paquita is good, we can count on her. and Fall, she is an awesome player but she's the biggest flake of all, you can never count on her to do anything and i always expect she won't even show up. she's really into boxing, i guess, i think she spends more of her time focusing on that. whatever.

yestrday i dumped a ton of my old clothes off at goodwill. all the goth shit i was into for those three or four years or whatever. i kept some of it, i still like some of the cool pants i had that aren't so gothy. i thought about giving some of it to Cleo since she's still kind of into that shit, but i decided to get rid of it without telling her. i thought about how she might show up wearing some old outfit i used to wear and that would just be weird. our sizes are so different anyway. my tits are huge. it feels liberating to get rid of that stuff, i don't even want to look at it anymore. good thing most of my old clothes still fit. i'm a little bigger now, mostly muscle i guess (i hope), but at least my ass seems to be pretty much the same size.

i wrote a big chunk on my serial killer screenplay yesterday, too. i still haven't come up with a title, that's seriously the hardest part for me. i can make up dumb story after story but the title always stumps me. i kind of hate how the real reason things have titles is to separate them from other things, or to describe the material to somebody who hasn't experienced it like Gremlins, or Escape From New York, while others don't even have anything to do with the movie. and titles are also good so you can remember a movie or find it or talk about it. okay i guess titles are pretty useful. but i wonder if movies could be numbered somehow instead of named, i don't know. something more technical. then my screenplay could just be 17334876X or something. actually that's not a bad title.

i made this a custom post because now i'm going to talk about what happened at the con. i decided i should. a while ago Cleo was talking about getting a livejournal, i'm sort of dreading it because then i'll have to have her on my f-list and then she'll get to read all my posts unless i make them totally private. but i also like your guys input. i don't know. okay, so Cleo and me kissed at the con. it was totally weird and spontanoeous. that guy pushed her and she fell on her face and got a bloody lip, so we were in the bathroom and then i don't know what i was thinking but there was a weird pause between exchanges and i bent down and fucking kissed her. not a long sloppy kiss but a little more than a peck. it lasted for less than two seconds. right then i was afraid i ruined everything between us but things actually seem fine. we even kissed again after that, a little longer. i don't know if it means anything, i know some girls who've done shit like that with their friends all the time and it's not a romantic thing or awkward. i think i want this to be a romantic thing though. except Myrtle is in the way. i really don't give a shit about Trilby or whoever giving us shit about a possible relationship. i say fuck off. i don't even care what my parents would say. the other big thing is that i know Cleo, even though she's with Myrtle, is still seriously hung up on this guy Vincent she dated. turns out Penny was also dating him recently but she didn't know Cleo had dated him or something, it's all kinda fucked up. we ran into him at Penny's last night and Cleo flipped out, i thought she was going to melt or go into a coma or something. she actually didn't cry that much at all, she was more like... i guess shocked or like beyond tears or something. she really seems okay, though, i'm glad. oh someone is at the door i think its Louisa to pick me up. wish me luck at the game tonight.

mood: hungry
current music: his name is alive - your cheating heart

[3 comments | leave a comment]

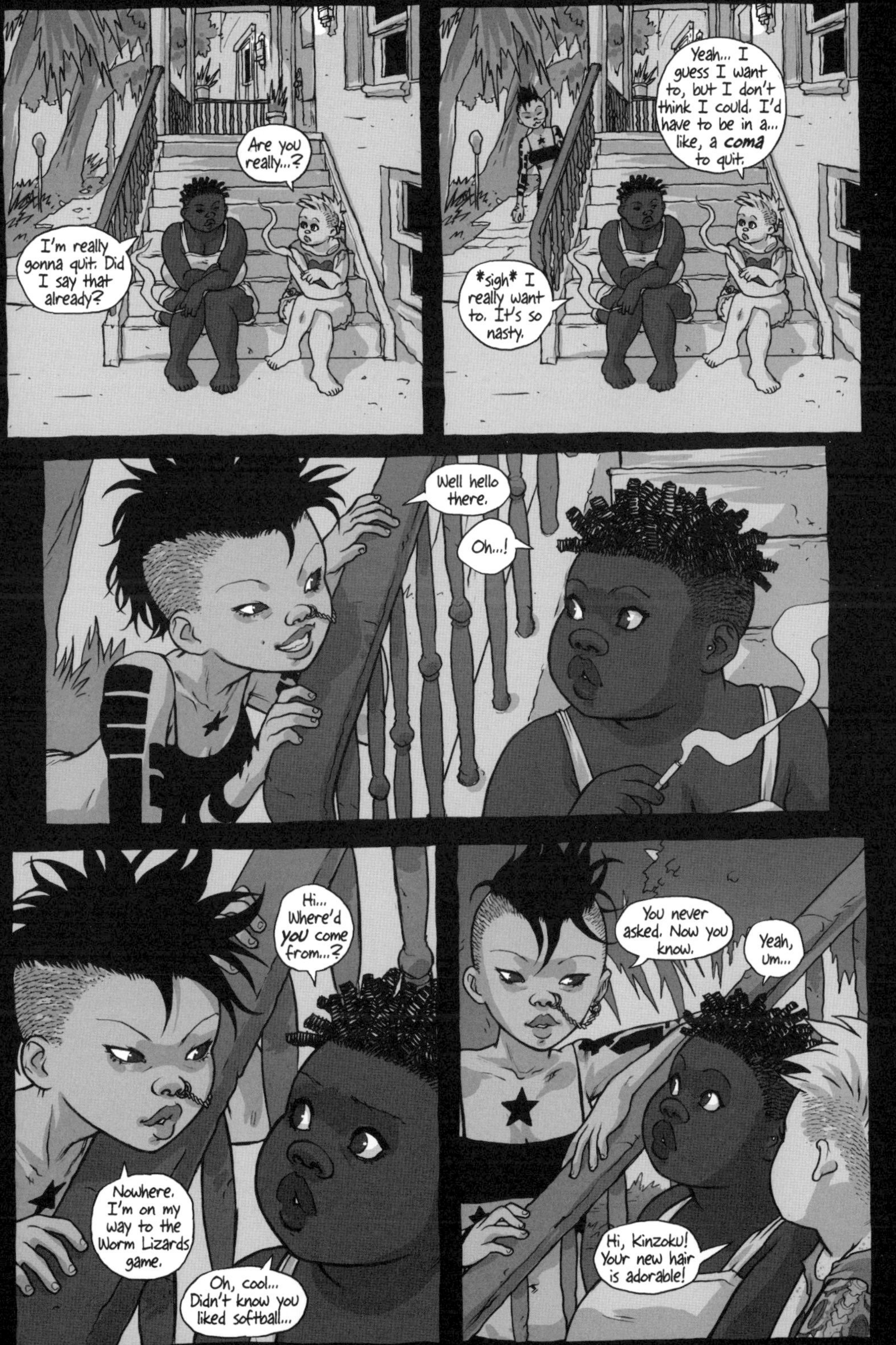
I'm really gonna quit. Did I say that already?
Are you really...?
sigh I really want to. It's so nasty.
Yeah... I guess I want to, but I don't think I could. I'd have to be in a... like, a **coma** to quit.
Well hello there.
Oh...!
Hi... Where'd **you** come from...?
Nowhere. I'm on my way to the Worm Lizards game.
Oh, cool... Didn't know you liked softball...
You never asked. Now you know.
Yeah, um...
Hi, Kinzoku! Your new hair is adorable!

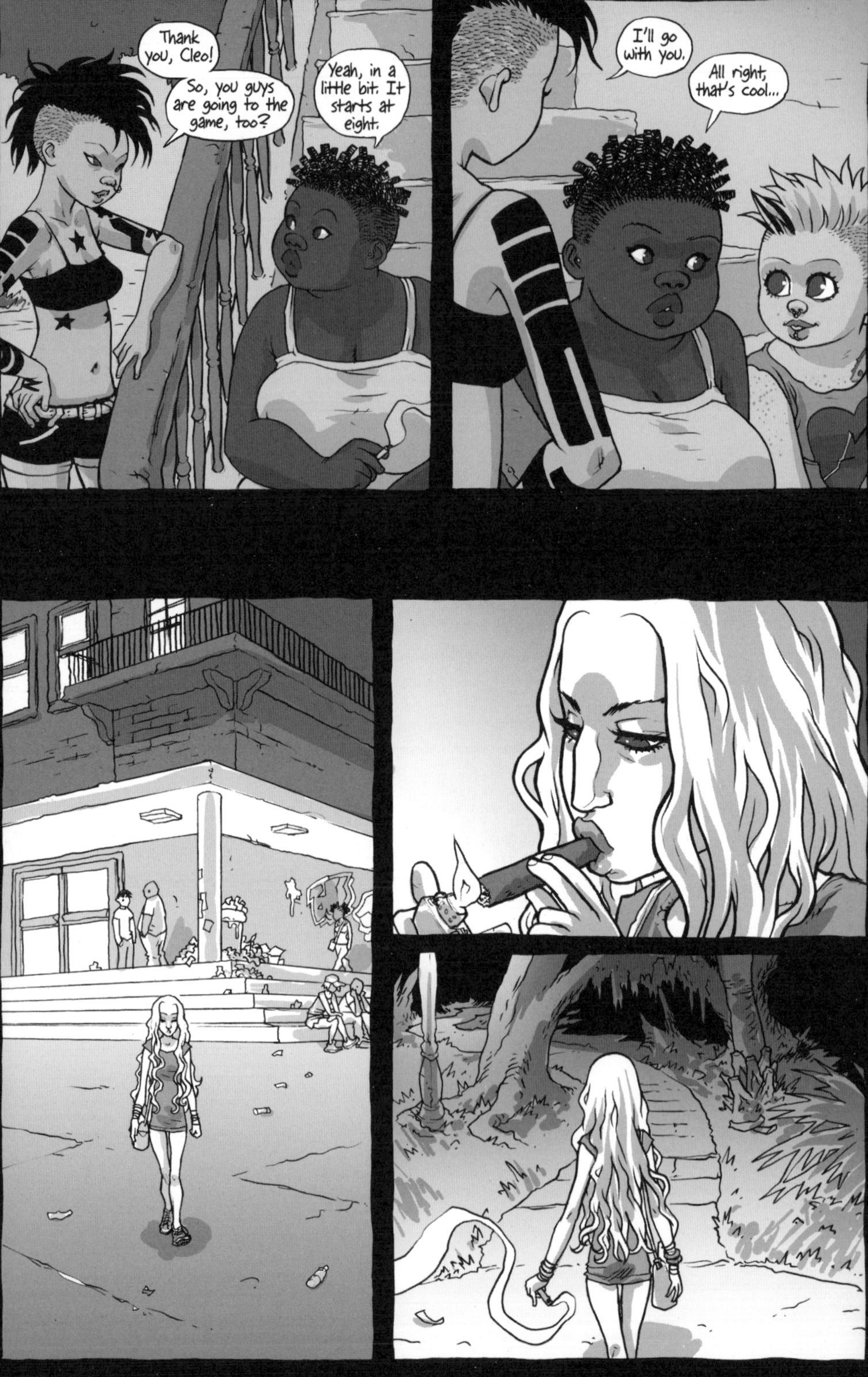
Thank you, Cleo!
So, you guys are going to the game, too?
Yeah, in a little bit. It starts at eight.
I'll go with you.
All right, that's cool...

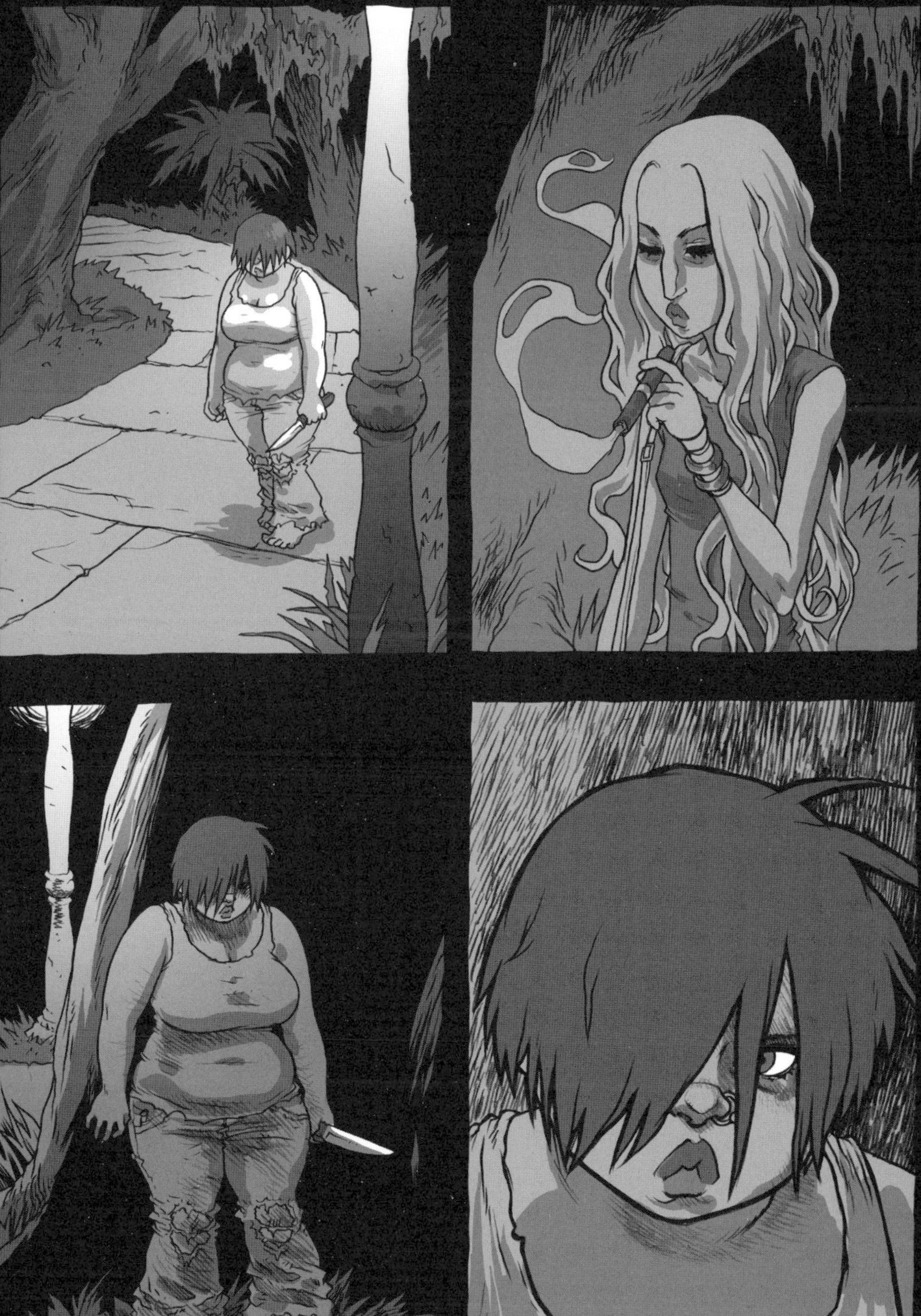

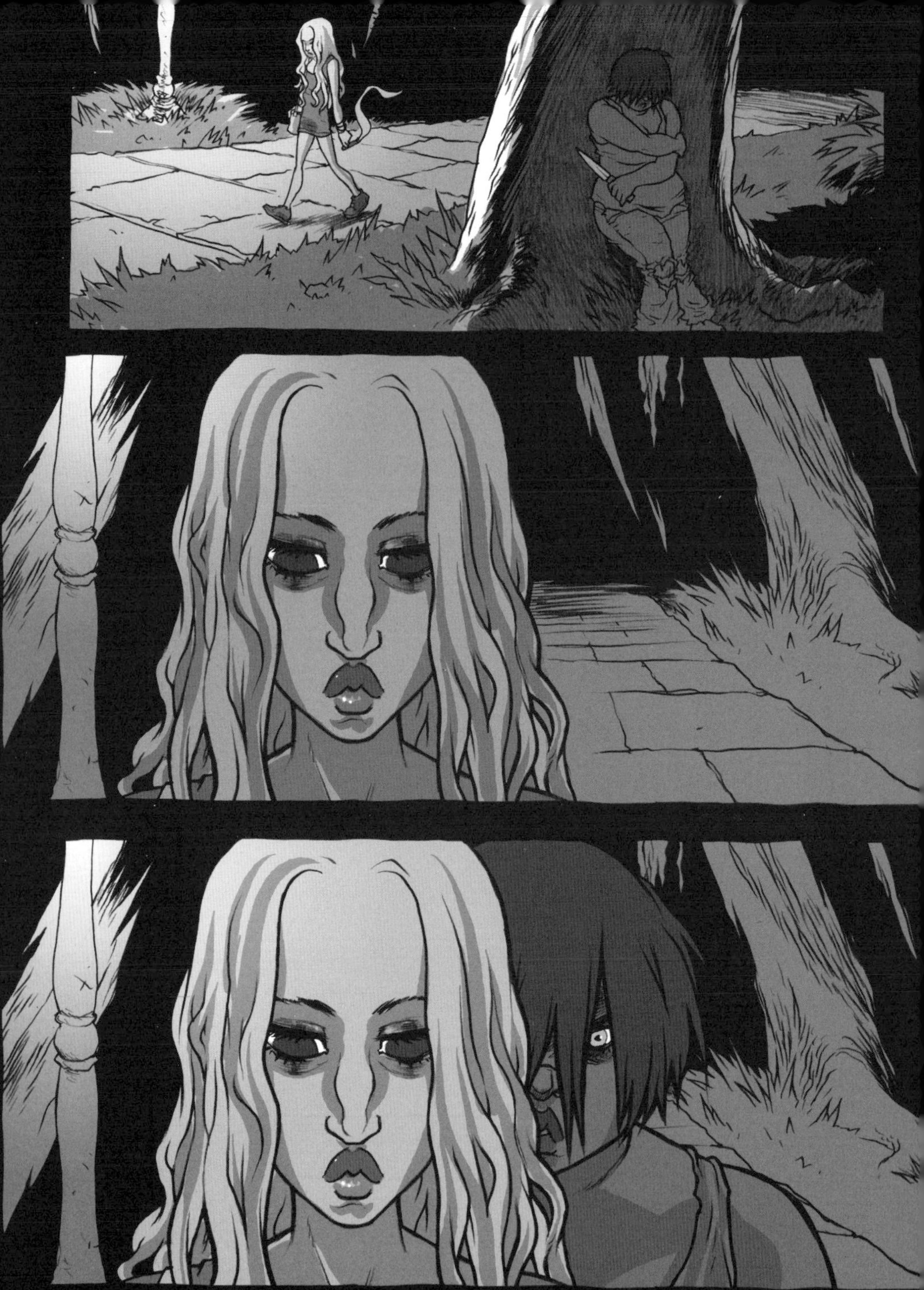

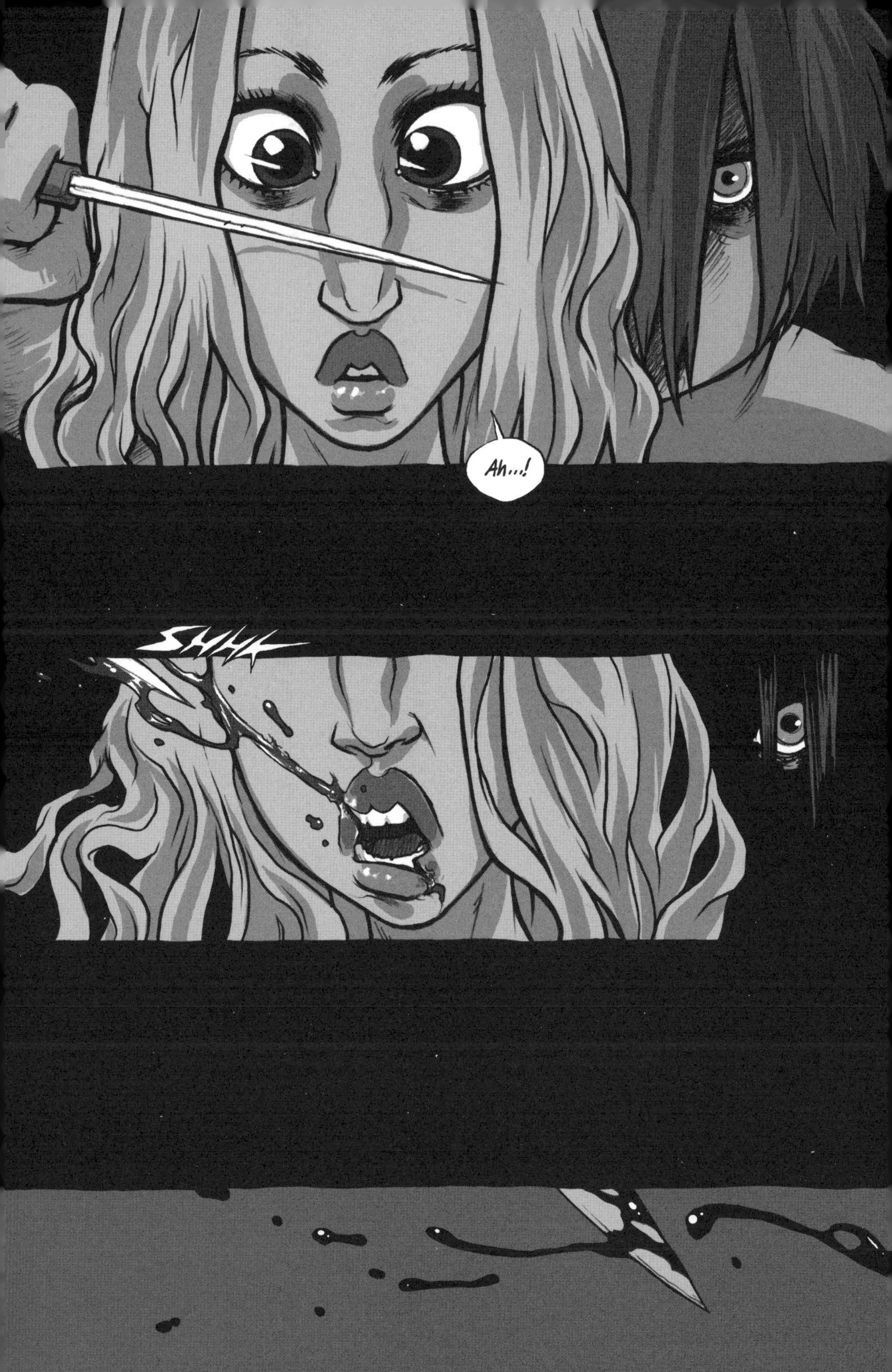
Ah...!
SHHK

to be continued...

WHO'S WHO IN WET MOON

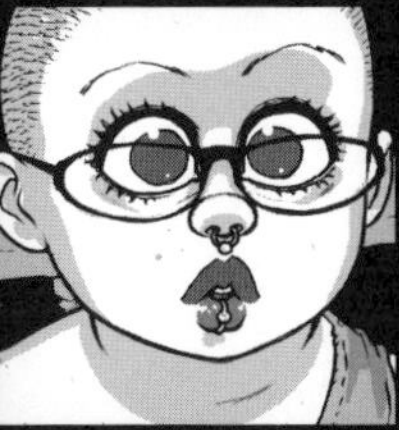
cleo lovedrop
(18)

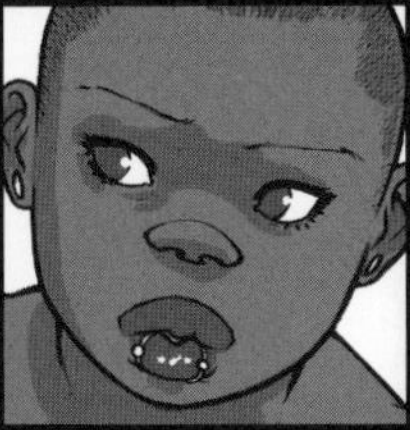
mara zuzanny
(18)

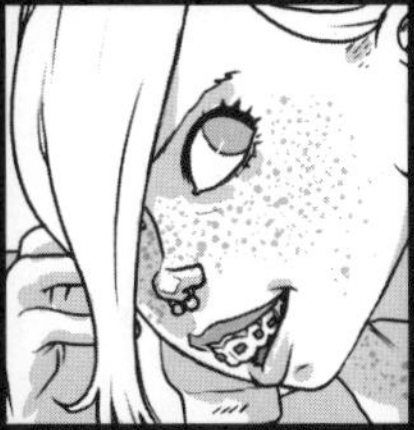
trilby bernarde
(18)

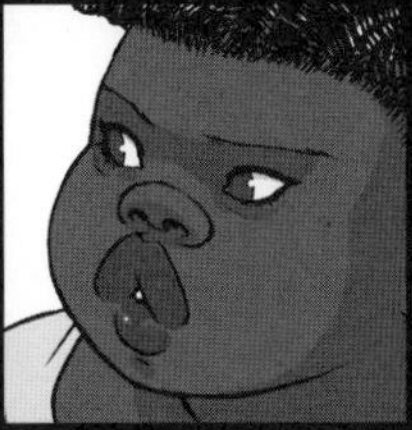
audrey richter
(19)

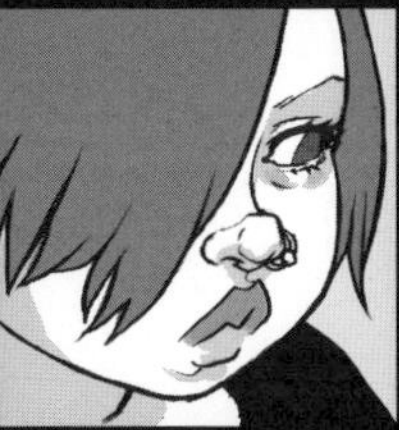
myrtle turenne
(19)

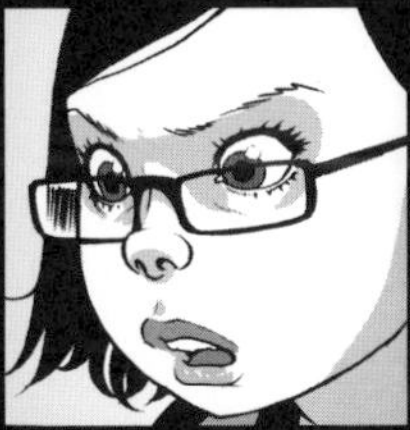
penny lovedrop
(23)

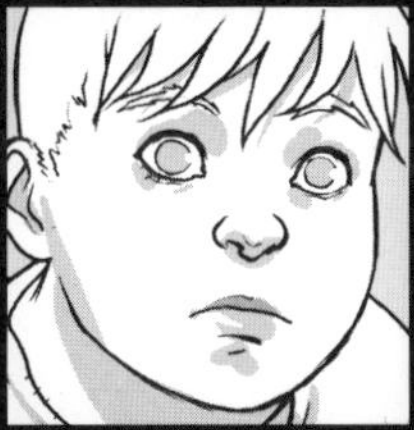
martin samson
(21)

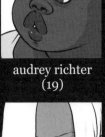

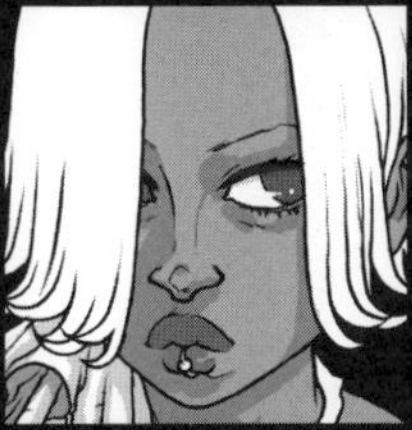
zia morlón
(19)

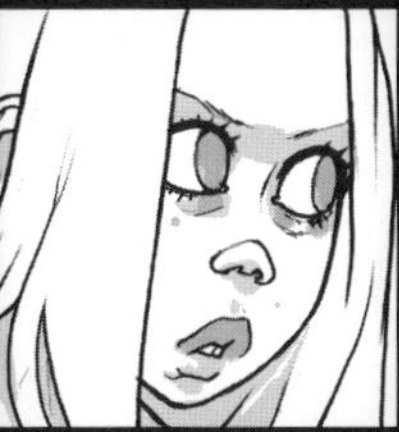
fall swanhilde
(15)

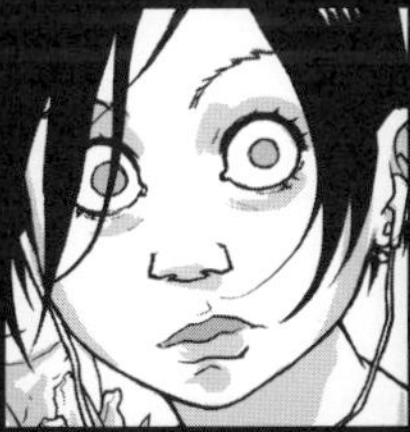
glen neuhoff
(20)

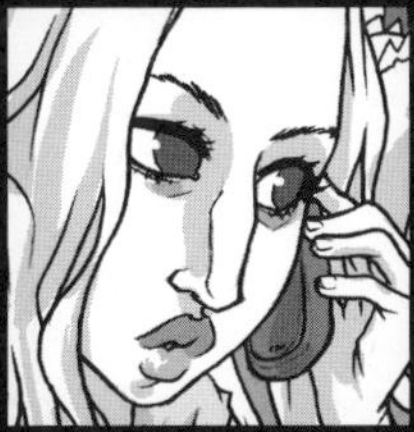
natalie ringtree
(21)

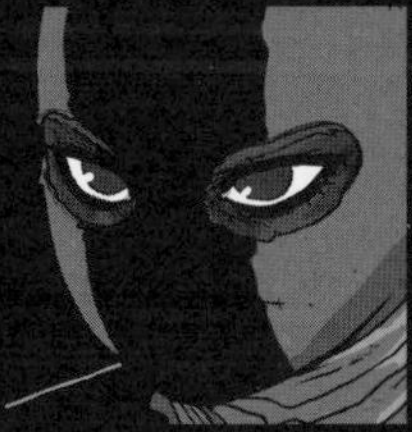
unknown
(?)

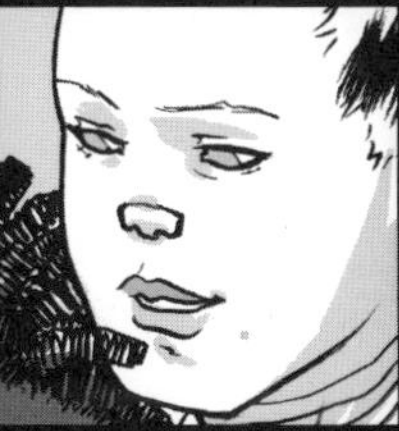
beth mckenzie
(17)

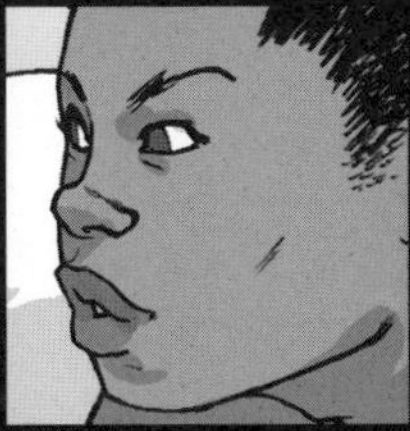
harrison pete
(21)

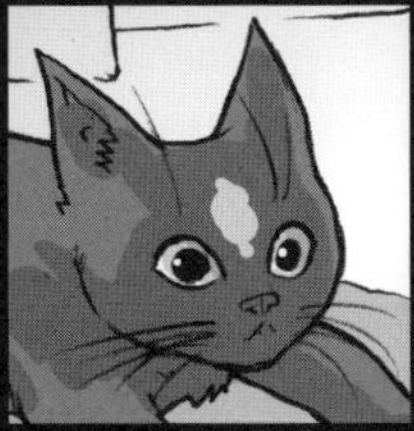
meiko
(5)

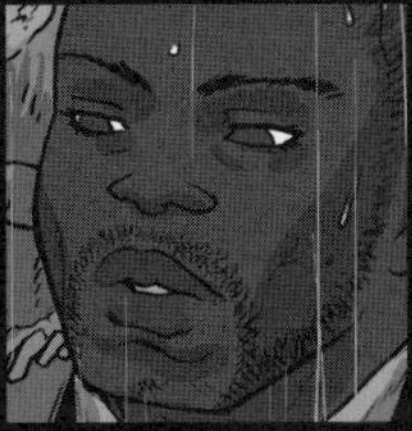
david wolfe
(37)

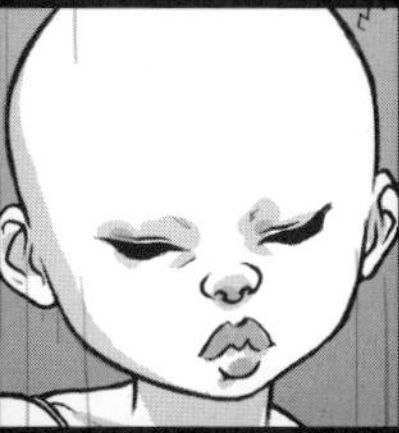
fern
(?)

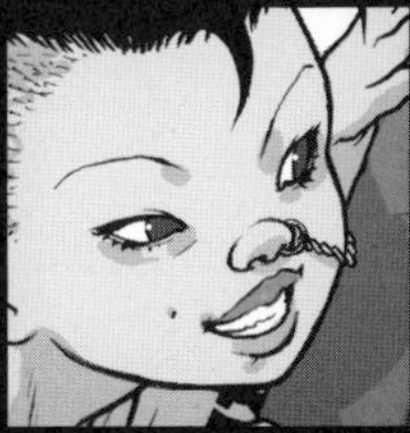
kinzoku
(19)

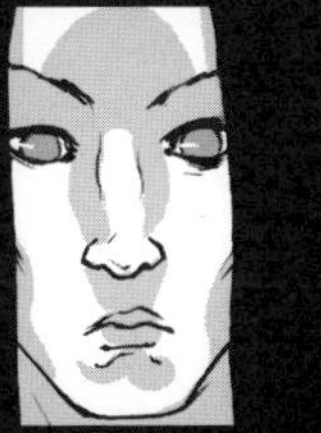
vincent verrier
(24)

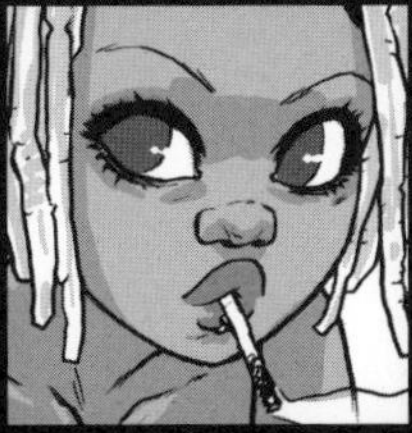
malady mayapple
(20)

GLEN SEUNG-WOO NEUHOFF

AGE: 20

SIGN: Pisces (March 4th)

HEIGHT: 5 ft. 9 in.

HAIR DYE: None

MAJOR: Film/Special Effects

HOMETOWN: Rochester, New York

MUSIC: Joy Division, Majority Rule, pg. 99, Ampere, IWRESTLEDABEARONCE, Bauhaus, Peter Murphy, Sisters of Mercy, Tori Amos, Red Sparowes, Corn on Macabre, Clan of Xymox

READING: Stephen King, Clive Barker, Henry Rollins, Brian Keene, Ursula K. Le Guin, Haruki Murakami

MOVIES/TV: Bride of Frankenstein, Let The Right One In, The Lost Boys, Near Dark, Night/Dawn/Day/Land of the Dead, Pan's Labyrinth, Mulholland Dr., Inland Empire, Dead Alive, Gremlins, Doom Generation, The Blob (1988 version)

LIKES: Pillows, pineapple pizza, potato bugs, researching diseases, animatronics, vampires, and soccer

DISLIKES: Birthday presents, fish, techno music, cauliflower, lawyer shows, and sleeping on a mattress

FUN FACTS:

— One of Glen's dream projects when he breaks into the film industry is to produce a remake of cult classic The Boogens.

— Glen is constantly getting sick despite being in top physical condition. Since childhood, he's had twelve mystery illnesses that doctors were unable to diagnose

ZIA PARMINDER MORLÓN

AGE: 19
SIGN: Virgo (September 4th)
HEIGHT: 5 ft. 4 in.
HAIR DYE: Unknown
MAJOR: Fashion (she is considering minoring in Photography)
HOMETOWN: Coffeeville, Alabama
MUSIC: Cocteau Twins, Mozart, Roger Eno, Rachel's, Cranes, Basque, Bach, Amethystium, Durutti Column, Explosions in the Sky, The Album Leaf, Miranda Sex Garden
READING: Nightwood by Djuna Barnes, Geek Love by Katherine Dunn, Dhalgren by Samuel Delany
MOVIES/TV: Dead Ringers, Amadeus, Visitor Q, Un Chien Andalou, Jodorowsky (Holy Mountain, El Topo), David Lynch, Cries & Whispers, Videodrome
LIKES: Rhinoceroses, leaves, sorrowful objects of unfulfilled affection, rust, gutter sludge, Margaret Keane, galoshes, and umbrellas
DISLIKES: Cold animal noses, sneezing, sudden loud noises, tuna, souls, animals following her, and her nose
FUN FACTS:
— She sews almost all of her clothes, which are pieced together from second-hand material, or cloth from non-clothing material like curtains or bedsheets.
— Zia used to be in a band called Nephele, which played ethereal industrial music inspired by classical composers. The group was short-lived and disbanded after one year.

MALADY MAYAPPLE

AGE: 20
SIGN: Leo (July 27th)
HEIGHT: 5 ft. 6 in.
HAIR DYE: Wasteland Orange
MAJOR: Painting
HOMETOWN: Kingsport, Tennessee
MUSIC: TSOL, The Banner, Scorpions, Television, From Ashes Rise, Misfits, Suicidal Tendencies, Heart, Murderdolls, 45 Grave, Aus-Rotten, Samhain
READING: Nuclear Engineering International magazine
MOVIES/TV: Mad Max, Warning Sign, Equinox, Nightmare City, Wallace & Gromit, the work of Brothers Quay, Princess Mononoke, Clash of the Titans, Rudolph and Frosty's Christmas in July, Ed Wood
LIKES: Radioactive things, 1950s nuclear fear, "atomic age" history, yelling, pie, breaking glass, masks, ninjas, mowing lawns, chains, crunchy gravel paths, reanimated skeletons, and jelly beans
DISLIKES: Pickles, fast food, plastic utensils, and jellyfish
FUN FACTS:
— The name "Malady" comes from her little sister, Roxanne, who as a baby was unable to pronounce Malady's real name, Mallory.
— She has a photographic memory.

DROWNED IN EVIL

──── PLAYLIST ────

BELLA MORTE — **NEVERLAND**

NEAERA — **SPEARHEADING THE SPAWN**

MIRANDA SEX GARDEN — **PEEP SHOW**

SWITCHBLADE SYMPHONY — **WALLFLOWER**

HIS NAME IS ALIVE — **YOUR CHEATING HEART**

FUGEES — **TEMPLE**

THE AGONIST — **MEMENTO MORI**

SONIC SYNDICATE — **ONLY INHUMAN**

THE CURE — **BURN**

COCOROSIE — **WEREWOLF**

THE BIRTHDAY MASSACRE — **TO DIE FOR**

ETERNIA — **LOVE**

ARCH ENEMY — **NEMESIS**

PETER MURPHY — **CUTS YOU UP**

PAGES 9-10: I had a hard time with ·he softball poses, I used a bunch of ·eference but I'm still not sure I got it quite right. Action has always been ·lifficult for me, especially throwing and ·unching, which in my opinion is similar ·o drawing softball action. Also baseball gloves are WAY too complicated!

All righty, it's rainin' an' I gotta get to work soon.
Next time we work on batting, ever since Shoshana quit we really don't got any good hitters.
Louisa's good but I mean like *real* good.

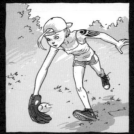

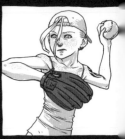

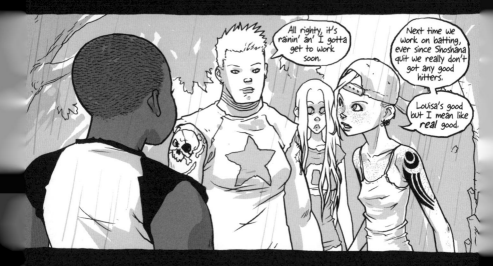

· don't know much about softball but I could do an entire spin-off series about the Wet Moor ·Vorm Lizards. I like how Mara, Trilby, Fall, and Beth have their softball world that's separate ·rom the rest of the characters, and when they leave the softball world to go back to the ·egular world, the dynamic between them totally changes. That would be a cool series.

Skeleton Season
audrey richter

Profile

kittyhawk1

97%!

October 24th, 5:25pm

Big babysitting gig this weekend! Actually it's not any different than any others, but I always feel more apprehensive when I get started with a new family who doesn't know me and I don't know how the kids will end up being. But the woman I'm working for, the kids' aunt, said they can be a handful, but I guess every parent/guardian says that.'

Anyway, it'll net me a good chunk of cash I can use to put together the next Social

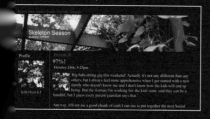

PAGE 14: Audrey gets a blog! I had a lot of fu· coming up with the Livejournal layouts, especially th· other blog names in the links sidebar. I really wan· to see Trilby's "trilbyhatescomics" blog. I should've given Audrey a journal earlier than volume 4, I thin· it reveals a lot of important aspects of who she is. · still want to do a mini-comic of Audrey birdwatching

PAGES 18-19: I love this scene. I love the idea that ·ern walks like a mile to get to the mailbox just ·o mail a single letter, rain or shine, and that she ·vants to do it herself rather than her butler doing ·t. And I really like her old-timey mailbox. It's an ·mportant scene for her.

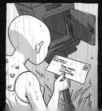

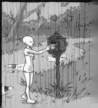

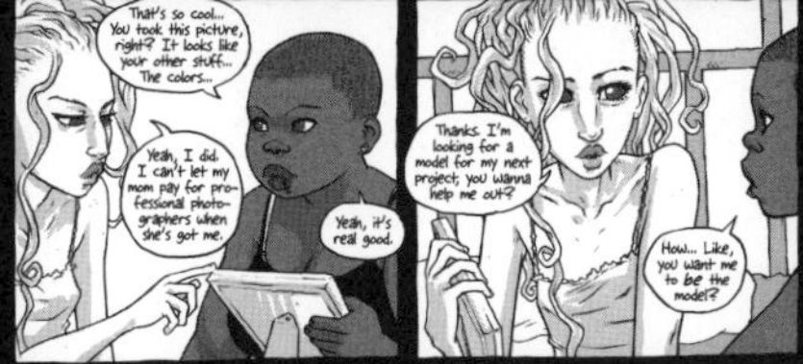
That's so cool... You took this picture, right? It looks like your other stuff... The colors...
Yeah, I did. I can't let my mom pay for professional photographers when she's got me.
Yeah, it's real good.
Thanks. I'm looking for a model for my next project, you wanna help me out?
How... Like, you want me to *be* the model?

PAGES 23-26: I love this scene too! Mara and Natalie hanging out is so much fun to do. This is another really important scene that says so much about both characters, looking back on it now it feels like such a pivotal moment for the series.

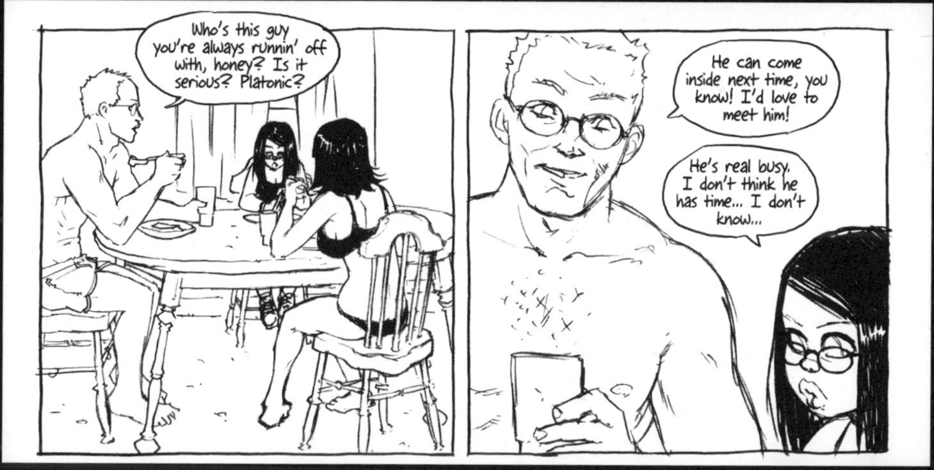
Who's this guy you're always runnin' off with, honey? Is it serious? Platonic?
He can come inside next time, you know! I'd love to meet him!
He's real busy. I don't think he has time... I don't know...

PAGE 28: Flashback! I have no idea why Larry and Penny are having breakfast in their underwear, I must have had a reason for this at the time but I can't remember what it was. I must have thought it was funny but now it's kind of weird, like wouldn't it be really uncomfortable to eat a meal with your daughter or father in their underwear? I'm regularly surprised and confused by the choices my past self made.

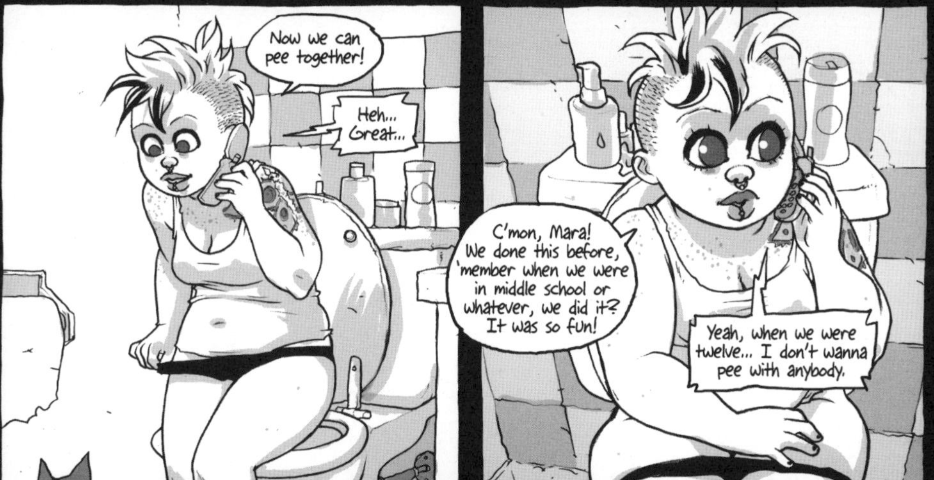
Now we can pee together!
Heh... Great...
C'mon, Mara! We done this before, 'member when we were in middle school or whatever, we did it? It was so fun!
Yeah, when we were twelve... I don't wanna pee with anybody.

PAGE 32: Yes, I also text my friends while I pee.

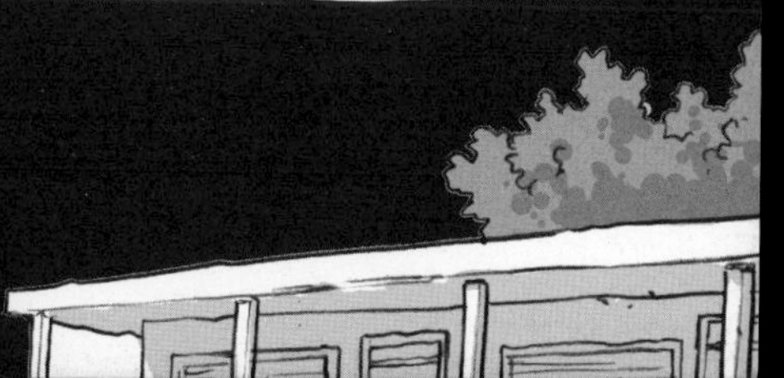

PAGE 51: Larry is a more muscular version of my own dad. My dad is really active and he's always running and hiking and doing marathons, and he has t-shirts from the events he goes to so that's what Larry's shirt is all about, and in the summer he used to wear little cut-off shorts. I can't remember what the "MCR" on Larry's shirt stood for.

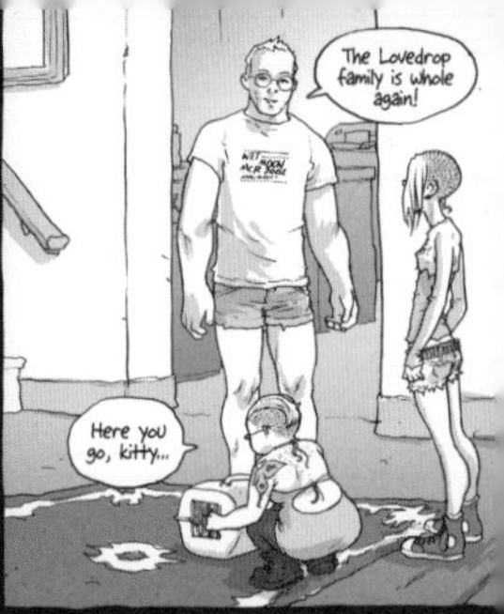
The Lovedrop family is whole again!
Here you go, kitty...

PAGE 52: I do not condone Cleo's use of the slur "g*psy." I always thought it would be cool to actually write Cleo's novel and make it available to people, but who has the time to write an entire novel. NOT ME.

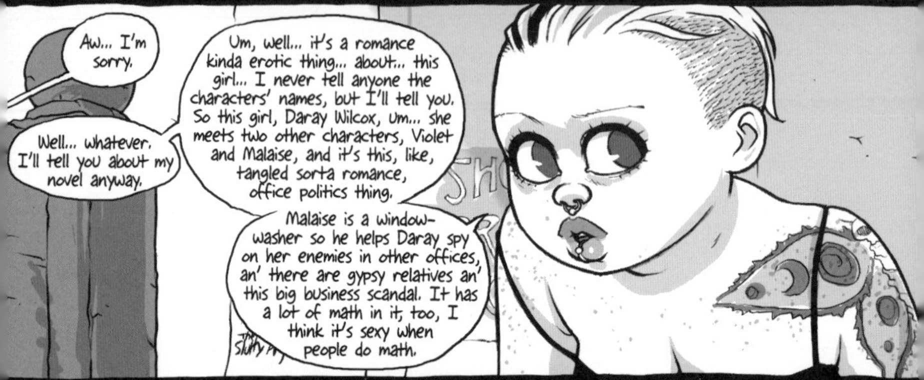
Aw... I'm sorry.
Well... whatever. I'll tell you about my novel anyway.
Um, well... it's a romance kinda erotic thing... about... this girl... I never tell anyone the characters' names, but I'll tell you. So this girl, Daray Wilcox, um... she meets two other characters, Violet and Malaise, and it's this, like, tangled sorta romance, office politics thing.
Malaise is a window-washer so he helps Daray spy on her enemies in other offices, an' there are gypsy relatives an' this big business scandal. It has a lot of math in it, too, I think it's sexy when people do math.

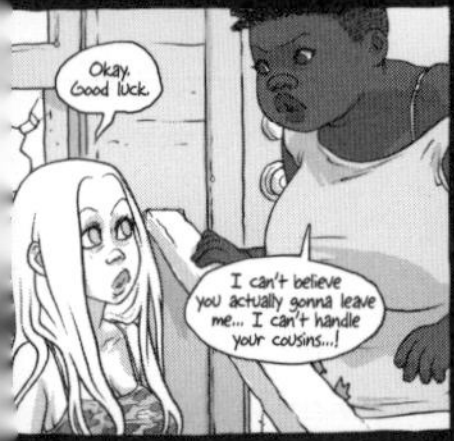
Okay. Good luck.
I can't believe you actually gonna leave me... I can't handle your cousins...!

PAGE 58: Fall was obviously looking for ANY excuse to throw a rock through a window. I kind of regret doing this scene with Audrey and putting her through all this humiliating shit, I thought it was funny at the time and I wanted it to be bad enough that she'd blow up at the little kids, but I think I went too far with it into possibly offensive territory, I can't decide if it comes off like I'm making fun of her. Poor Audrey!

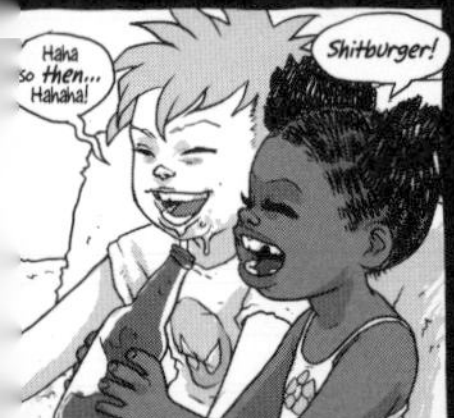
Haha so then... Hahaha!
Shitburger!

PAGE 62: I want to know what story the kids are laughing about: "So then... SHITBURGER."

PAGES 70-71: Drawing the convention scenes were time-consuming and horrible but soooo worth it. I was so in my element when drawing it, I knew exactly what to do. Martin is cosplaying as an unused design for Noah Mendoza from my other comic *Shadoweyes*, originally the character was going to wear a gas mask but I ditched it. Putting in all the cameos and in-jokes in these panels was so fun, can you spot them all?!

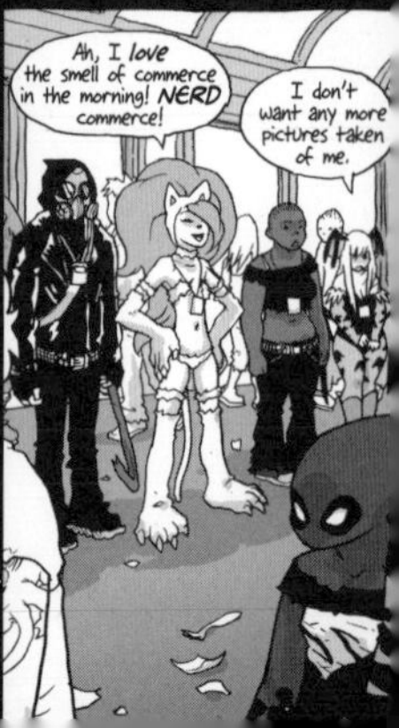
Ah, I love the smell of commerce in the morning! NERD commerce!
I don't want any more pictures taken of me.

PAGE 70, PANEL 3 AND PAGE 71, PANEL 2: The t-shirts "I dare you to picture me naked" and "I <3 Vaginas" are both actual shirts I saw a couple guys wearing at conventions. Gross!

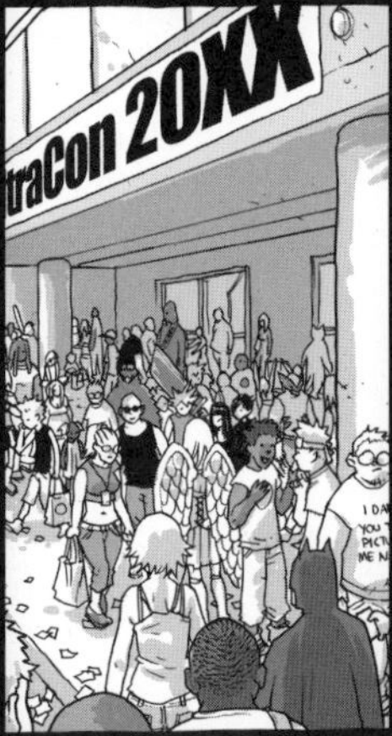
traCon 20XX

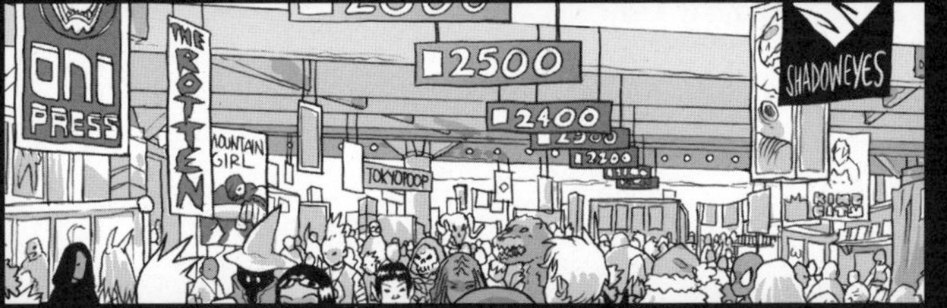
ONI PRESS
THE ROTTEN
MOUNTAIN GIRL
TOKYOPOP
2500
2400
SHADOWEYES

PAGE 71, PANEL 1: The banner on the left side that says "The Rotten" was the title of a zombie series I was pitching to Vertigo at the time, which was a sequel to my defunct Tokyopop book *The Abandoned*. I was so confident that *The Rotten* would get picked up that I put in a reference to it, but of course it ended up being rejected so now it's another cameo/reference that doesn't make sense.

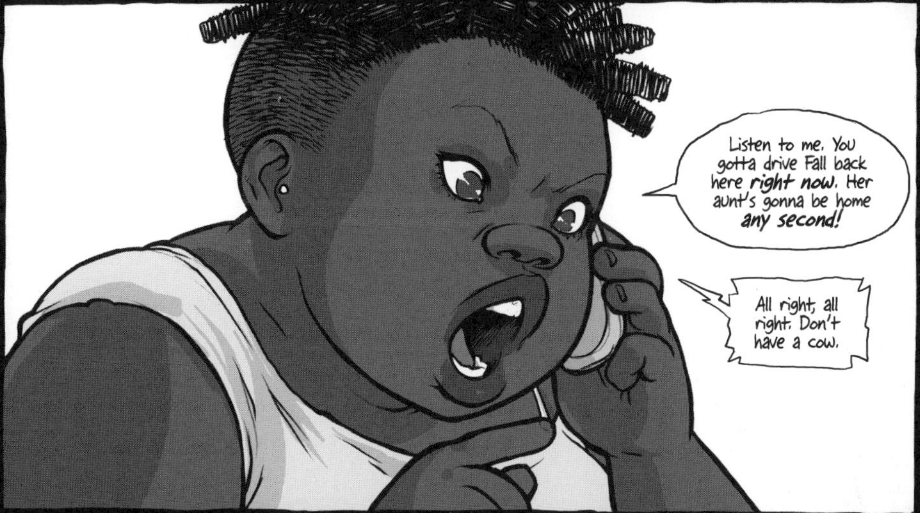
Listen to me. You gotta drive Fall back here **right now**. Her aunt's gonna be home **any second!**
All right, all right. Don't have a cow.

PAGE 73: This is another part I sometimes regret doing, Slicer and Fall together. I wanted it to be gross and horrible but maybe it's just too much the way I presented it. At least Slicer ends up in jail.

PAGE 75-76: Becky Cloonan! She and I go way back, she was one the first people who really encouraged me and one of the first comic professionals I knew personally, and we still talk to this day. I owe a large part of my career to Becky. Go check out her comics if you haven't, she is the best! This scene is also the return of Kirk!!! Look at Becky on **page 75, panel 5.**

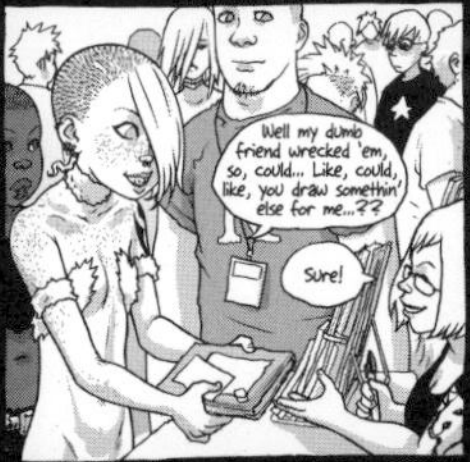
Well my dumb friend wrecked 'em, so, could... Like, could, like, you draw somethin' else for me...??
Sure!

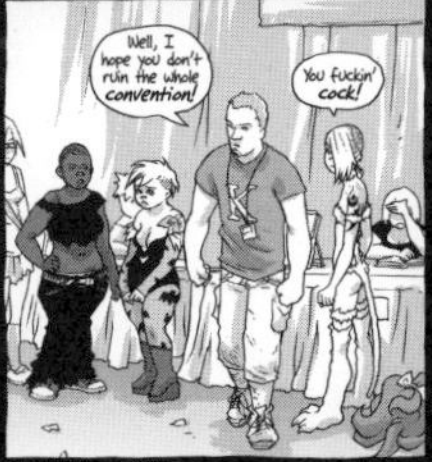
Well, I hope you don't ruin the whole convention!
You fuckin' cock!

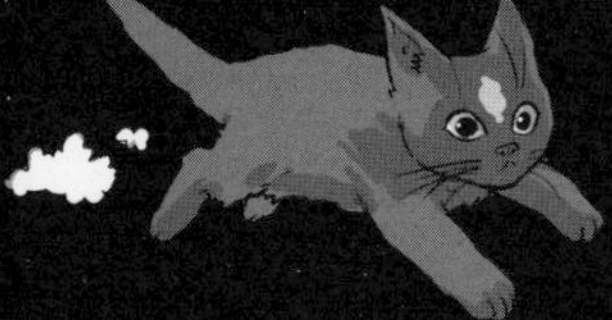

PAGE 104-109: Burial Grounds inspired an actual real-ife coffee shop of the same name, founded by a Wet Moon fan, located in Olympia, WA. I've never been there ınfortunately but they draw skulls in the coffee foam ınd have other goth stuff just like the shop in the comic! Check them out if you're ever in Olympia and online at ›urialgroundscoffee.com.

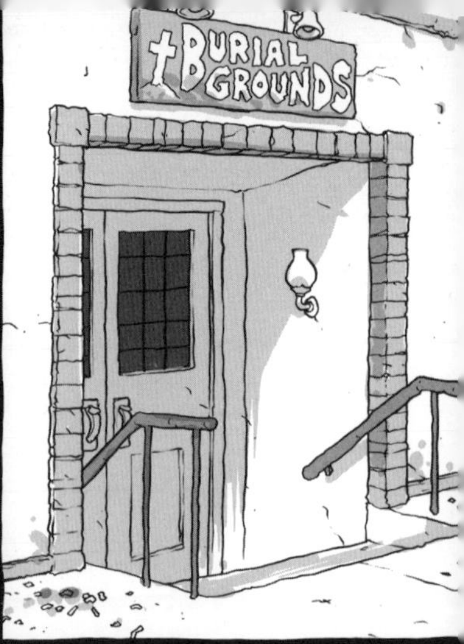
BURIAL GROUNDS

'd forgotten how much gross-out humor is in *Wet Moon* volume 4. Audrey getting beer and an entire cake thrown on her, the bag of poop (an actual thing that happened o a friend), the pee pals, Glen puking, Harrison's onsillitis, all following up the horrible semen disaster n volume 3. I don't know what it is with me and having characters dealing with bodily fluids and various types of slime and sludge.

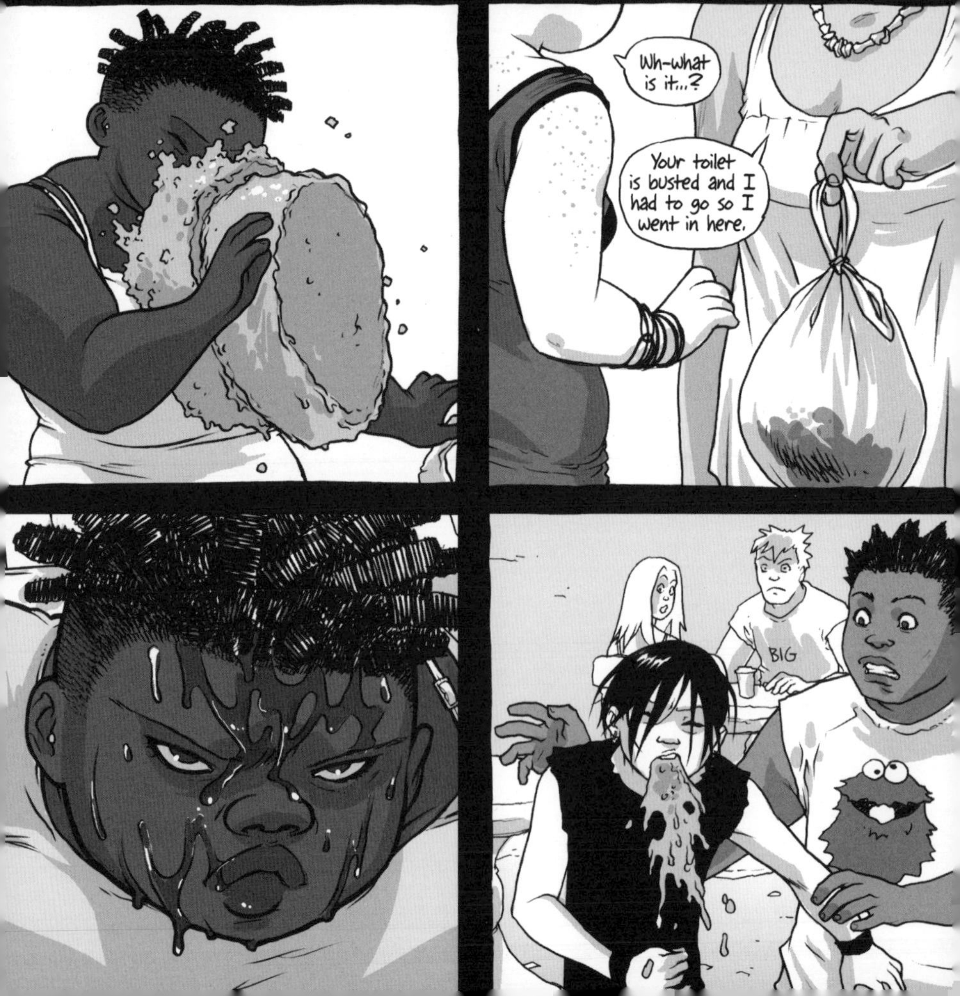
Wh-what is it...?
Your toilet is busted and I had to go so I went in here.
BIG

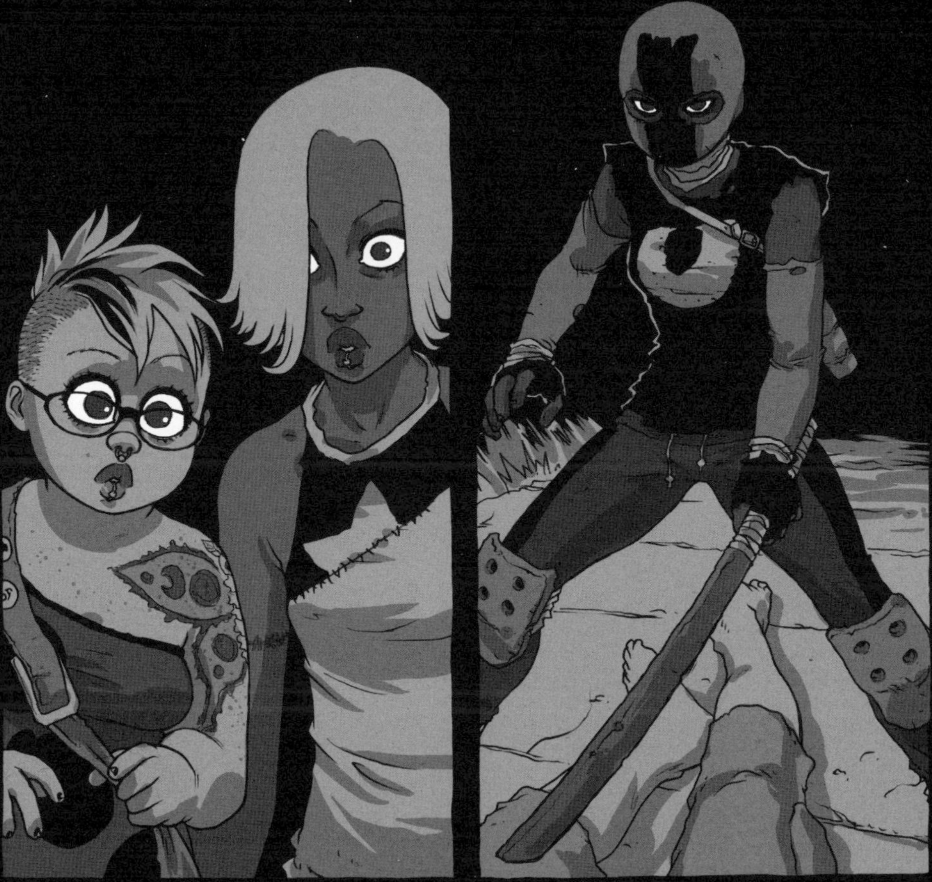

PAGE 114: Unknown's introduction! Readers went bananas trying to guess her secret identity, but my lips are sealed! She's another character I could do an entire spin-off about, her doing regular daily life stuff and then going out on the prowl as a college campus vigilante every so often.

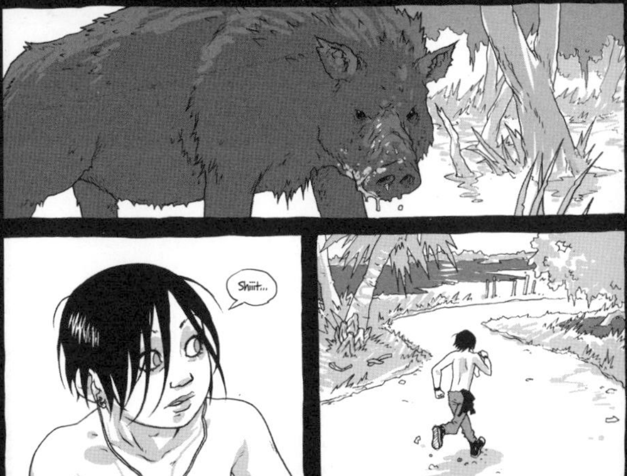
Shiiit...

PAGE 137: As you've probably noticed by now, *Wet Moon* is full of things that I was really into at the time I was creating each particular book, but after the fact I wonder why I put it in. Hogzilla is one of those things, and yeah a giant swamp pig is cool but I can't remember my reasoning as to why I made it an actual subplot. Maybe I just felt like drawing an evil feral pig that day.

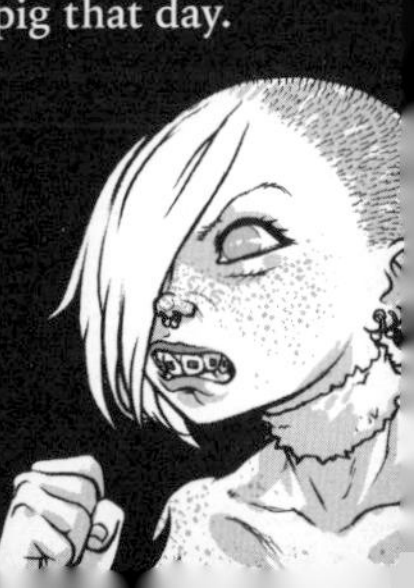

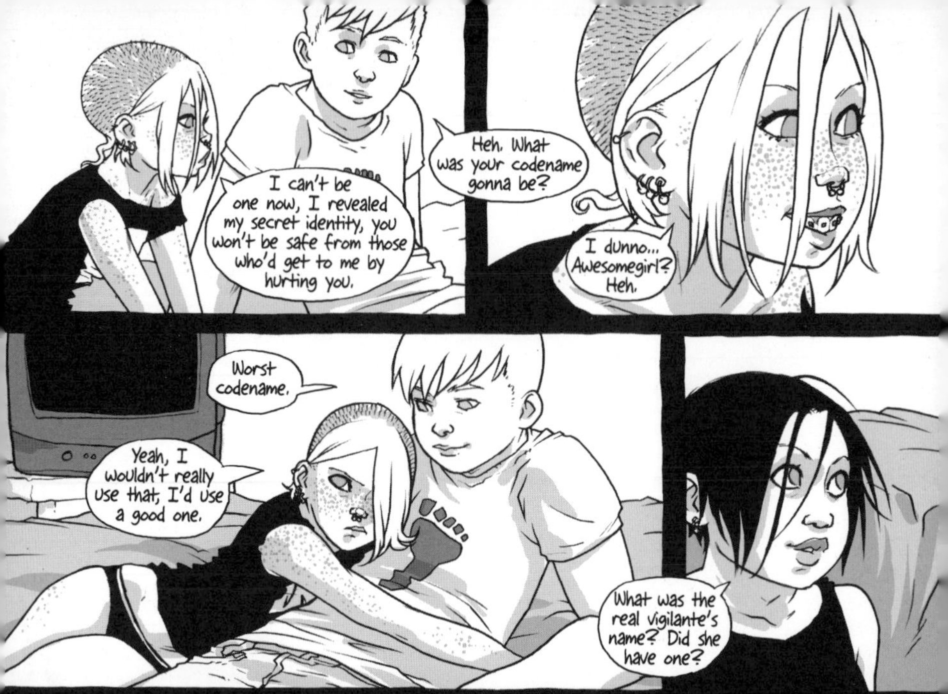
I can't be one now, I revealed my secret identity, you won't be safe from those who'd get to me by hurting you.
Heh. What was your codename gonna be?
I dunno... Awesomegirl? Heh.
Worst codename.
Yeah, I wouldn't really use that, I'd use a good one.
What was the real vigilante's name? Did she have one?

AGE 138: I love Trilby in this scene, she's all bristled about Unknown stealing her idea of being a asked crimefighter. Like Trilby would obviously never actually do that but she's still bitter abou meone else doing it, like it reflects badly on her as a person somehow.

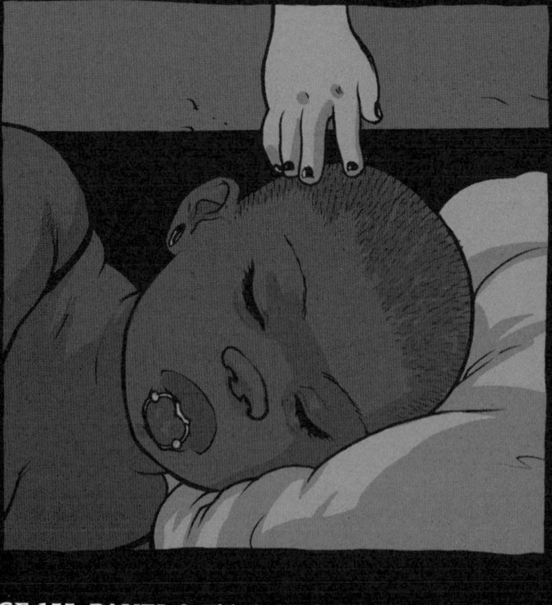

PAGE 155, PANEL 3: This is my favorite panel in the book